For Robin,
   for plenty of political mischief-making!

Seth Alexander Thévoz is an Associate Member of Nuffield College, Oxford, where he is a research assistant on the forthcoming official biography of Sir David Butler. He holds degrees from the universities of Cambridge, London and Warwick, and he completed his PhD in conjunction with the History of Parliament Trust. A former parliamentary researcher, his areas of expertise include the history of British politicians' outside financial interests, and the history of party political funding. He is Honorary Librarian of London's National Liberal Club. This is his first book.

'A fascinating forensic study of the period's networks of power.'
Ian Hislop, journalist and broadcaster

'Often mentioned in both literature and history books, and alluded to in journalistic accounts of British and Irish politics, gentlemen's clubs are supposed to have played a major role in policy making and in the shaping of leaders' choices. Yet, hitherto they lacked a proper, scholarly analysis. *Club Government* fills this gap. We are in Seth Thévoz's debt for this splendid book, at once a scholarly work and an insider's account.'
Eugenio Biagini, University of Cambridge

'This definitive study shows how smart London clubs played a crucial role in shaping mid-Victorian politics. Seth Alexander Thévoz takes us behind the scenes of the theatre of power at Westminster to reveal the fascinating backstage world of Pall Mall and St James's, where much of the real drama took place. Presenting a wealth of new evidence, he has produced a tour de force of scholarship.'
Piers Brendon, author of *The Decline and Fall of the British Empire, 1781–1997* and former Keeper of the Churchill Archives Centre

CLUB GOVERNMENT

How the Early Victorian World was Ruled from London Clubs

SETH ALEXANDER THÉVOZ

Published in 2018 by
I.B.Tauris & Co. Ltd
London • New York
www.ibtauris.com

Copyright © 2018 Seth Alexander Thévoz

The right of Seth Alexander Thévoz to be identified as the author of this work has been asserted by the author in accordance with the Copyright, Designs and Patents Act 1988.

All rights reserved. Except for brief quotations in a review, this book, or any part thereof, may not be reproduced, stored in or introduced into a retrieval system, or transmitted, in any form or by any means, electronic, mechanical, photocopying, recording or otherwise, without the prior written permission of the publisher.

Every attempt has been made to gain permission for the use of the images in this book. Any omissions will be rectified in future editions.

References to websites were correct at the time of writing.

International Library of Colonial History 25

ISBN: 978 1 78453 818 7
eISBN: 978 1 78672 372 7
ePDF: 978 1 78673 372 6

A full CIP record for this book is available from the British Library
A full CIP record is available from the Library of Congress

Library of Congress Catalog Card Number: available

Typeset in Garamond Three by OKS Prepress Services, Chennai, India
Printed and bound by CPI Group (UK) Ltd, Croydon, CR0 4YY

To Conrad Russell

CONTENTS

List of Illustrations ix
Acknowledgements xiii

Introduction 1

1. **The Development of Political Clubs** 21
   Introduction 21
   The Traditional Clubs 23
   The Carlton and Reform Clubs 31
   Political Clubs after the Carlton and Reform 40
   Politics in 'Apolitical' Clubs, 1832–68 45
   Conclusion 48

2. **Clubs and the MPs' World I: A Quantitative Analysis** 50
   Aims and Approach 50
   MPs and their Clubs 54
   Explaining MPs' Links to Clubs 70
   Membership of Multiple Clubs by MPs 77
   Trends in MPs' Elections to Clubs, Blackballing and Fast-Tracking 82
   MPs who were not Club Members 93
   Conclusion 97

3. **Clubs and the MPs' World II: Experiences in Clubland Space** 100
   Introduction 100
   Space: Its Politics and Dynamics 102
   Meetings: Use of Club Space and Purpose 115

	Clubs, Public Meetings and Protests	123
	Masculinity and Sociability: Clubs' Single-Sex Spaces and their Rival Social Spaces	124
	Gossip	131
	Conclusion	139
4.	**Clubs as an MP's Base: Accommodation, Dining, Information and Organisational Support**	141
	Introduction	141
	Accommodation	142
	Dining	143
	Information	147
	Organisational Support	150
	Conclusion	154
5.	**Clubs and Whips in the House of Commons**	156
	Introduction	156
	Whips in Clubs	158
	Subscriptions to the Whip	164
	Whips, Clubs and Party Identity	169
	Conclusion	173
6.	**Clubs and Electoral Interventions**	175
	Introduction	175
	Individuals: Agents and Central Organisation	177
	A Central Election Fund	186
	Petitioning	194
	Textual Influence	195
	Funds, Candidates and Registration	198
	Clubland in the Constituencies: Disraeli and the Gladstones	200
	Conclusion	206
Conclusion		209
Appendix	*Appendix to Chapter 2: List of sources used in the database of club memberships for MPs who sat in the House of Commons in 1832–68*	219
Notes		223
Bibliography		282
Index		301

LIST OF ILLUSTRATIONS

Figures

Figure 1.1 Map of London clubs in the St James's area 1832–68, including all the political clubs   23

Figure 1.2 James Gillray, *Promis'd Horrors of the French Invasion* (1796)   26

Figure 1.3 Thomas Shotter Boys, *The Club-Houses etc., Pall Mall. 1842*   30

Figure 2.1 Overlapping club memberships of MPs in key selected clubs, as a social network   81

Figure 3.1 Scale comparison of the ever-larger clubs, using a floor plan of their ground floors   107

Figure 3.2 Floor plan of the ground floor of the Athenaeum   108

Figure 3.3 Floor plan of the ground floor of the Carlton Club (second building, by Sidney Smirke, 1854)   109

Figure 3.4 Floor plan of the ground floor of the Carlton Club (first building, by Robert Smirke, 1836)   110

Figure 3.5 Posthumous print of Disraeli, portraying him addressing an unidentified meeting of Conservative MPs (c.1867) in the vestibule of the second Carlton Club building   111

Figure 3.6 'The Reform Club-House: Members awaiting intelligence of the formation of the new ministry'   133

Figure 3.7 Members talking in the main hall of the Carlton Club   134

Figure 3.8 Members talking in the gallery above the main lobby of the Carlton Club   135

Figure 4.1 The Reform Club banquet for Sir Charles Napier   148

Tables

Table 1.1 London clubs with political objectives, active in 1832–68   22

Table 2.1 Combinations of the club memberships of MPs, 1832–68, amongst selected clubs   78

Table 2.2 Data on acceptance and rejection in Carlton Club candidates, books vols 1–12   85

Table 5.1a Club memberships of Liberal Whips, 1830–68   159

Table 5.1b Club memberships of Conservative Whips, 1832–68   160

Table 6.1a Liberal party agents, as identified by Cook and Keith   178

Table 6.1b Conservative party agents, as identified by Cook and Keith   178

Table 6.2 Most frequent proposers and seconders for the Junior Carlton Club, for ballot dates in 1866–7 with surviving records, including all Whips and party agents   184

Table 6.3 Conservative Associations in receipt of payments from the central party fund, 1855 and 1859   192

Graphs

Graph 2.1 Proportion of MPs known to have belonged to at least one club, 1832–68   55

LIST OF ILLUSTRATIONS

Graph 2.2 Percentage of MPs belonging to a club, broken down by Parliament, 1832–68   56

Graph 2.3 Aggregate membership of London clubs among MPs who sat in the period 1832–68   58

Graph 2.4a No. of MPs belonging to political clubs, 1832–68, broken down by Parliament   58

Graph 2.4b No. of MPs belonging to the four most popular political clubs, 1832–68, broken down by Parliament, with linear averages shown   59

Graph 2.5 Political composition of the House of Commons, 1832–68, using *Dod's* (New Parliament Edition) party labels for each MP sitting in selected years   59

Graph 2.6 Percentage of Conservative and Liberal Conservative MPs belonging to the Carlton Club, broken down by Parliament, 1833–65   60

Graph 2.7 Percentage of Conservative and Liberal Conservative MPs belonging to White's, broken down by Parliament, 1833–65   61

Graph 2.8 Percentage of Liberal MPs of various denominations belonging to the Reform Club, broken down by Parliament, 1837–65   63

Graph 2.9 Percentage of Liberal MPs of various denominations belonging to Brooks's, broken down by Parliament, 1833–65   65

Graph 2.10a No. of MPs joining selected clubs for the first time, 1832–6, all data points   68

Graph 2.10b No. of MPs joining selected clubs for the first time, 1832–6, with the values of the first year at the Athenaeum and the Reform Club removed   68

Graph 2.11 Political composition of selected clubs, by MPs' party affiliation, 1832–68, using the *Dod's* New Parliament Edition party labels, in absolute numbers   75

Graph 2.11a Reform Club   75

Graph 2.11b Brooks's	75
Graph 2.11c Carlton Club	76
Graph 2.11d White's	76
Graph 2.11e Athenaeum Club	77
Graph 2.12 Proportion of successful applicants to the Carlton Club, 1834–66	84
Graph 2.13 Proportion of successful applicants to the Reform Club, 1836–68	88
Graph 2.14 Supply of available places at the Carlton Club by year, 1836–68, accounting for the distorting effect caused by the supernumerary membership of MPs	90
Graph 2.15 No. of candidates on the Carlton Club waiting list, 1834–67	91
Graph 2.16a Political affiliations of MPs who did not belong to any club, in absolute numbers	96
Graph 2.16b Political affiliations of MPs who did not belong to any club, in percentage terms	97
Graph 5.1 No. of Conservative MPs subscribing to the whip through the Carlton Club subscription book, 1837–41	167

ACKNOWLEDGEMENTS

Every book of this kind is the product of extensive research, incurring numerous debts. This book would be materially poorer if I had not been able to secure an extraordinary degree of co-operation from many of the London clubs covered, being granted a sometimes unprecedented level of access to surviving documents and permission to quote from them. I owe huge thanks to Lord Lexden and Jonathan Orr-Ewing for their proactive help in examining the previously largely-inaccessible Carlton and Junior Carlton Club archives in the Carlton attic (now safely transferred to the London Metropolitan Archives), and Simon Blundell for welcoming me into the treasure trove in the Reform Club's basement. The Committee of the National Club oversee a remarkable archive in the Bodleian Library, and Lord Cormack and Jennie De Protani of the Athenaeum were good enough to grant me a level of access to the Club's records normally reserved for members. Christopher Palmer-Tomkinson and David Anderson of White's were also most helpful with enquiries about the fate of the White's archive. Further thanks are due to the archivists and staff of the British Library, British Postal Museum and Archive, Buckinghamshire County Record Office, Cheshire and Chester Local Studies Centre, Flintshire Record Office, Hertfordshire Record Office, Kent History and Library Centre, London Metropolitan Archive, National Archives, Somerset Heritage Centre, and University College London.

This book would not have been possible without substantial support from the History of Parliament Trust, which elected me as the recipient of its first PhD scholarship, and I owe a huge debt of thanks to Paul Seaward and the Trustees. Not only has their financial support been considerable, but the Trust's offices in Bloomsbury provided an incredibly fertile atmosphere for this research, as they shared a number of their resources with me, not to mention the invaluable thoughts of the outstanding 1832–68 team, Stephen Ball, Henry Miller, James Owen and Kathryn Rix. Each has provided their own deeply helpful insights on this eccentric endeavour.

For sharing their thoughts on issues emanating from this research, I would like to thank Eugenio Biagini, Marcus Binney, Ian Bradley, Piers Brendon, Matthew Cragoe, James Golden, Heather Hamilton, Boyd Hilton, David Howarth, Anthony Howe, Richard Huzzey, Shashank Joshi, Mark Knights, Austin Lovegrove, Bill Lubenow, James McBennett, Peter Mandler, Andrew Mell, Joe Mordaunt Crook, Jonathan Parry, Jennifer Regan-Lefebvre, Joe Simpson, Simon Skinner, Peter Sloman, Lord Smith of Clifton, Tim Stanley, Miles Taylor, Richard Vinen, Francis Wheen and Ed Young. Paul Readman has been a persistent fountain of good advice, even if not all of it has been heeded as much as it should have been. As fellow PhD students in very different disciplines, David Blunt, Linda Briggs, Alec Corio, Mary Cox, Dion Georgiou, Jessica Hambly, Julie Hipperson, Dave Hitchcock, Mike Humphries, Horatio Joyce, Dave Monger, Daniel Morgan, Chris Parkes, Simon Radford, Fern Riddell, Antonia Strachey, Chris Thompson-Walsh, Martha Vandrei, Jennifer Wellington and Igor Zurimendi all shared much coffee and many tears (the tears were mainly after my laptop blew up) throughout the thesis on which this book emanated. Michael Crick has been highly encouraging of this book, even when it has taken me away from our work on David Butler – he has been a stimulating colleague, with every meeting a masterclass in tirelessly seeking out facts, with an all-important impish sense of humour. The inimitable Brian Blessed provided characteristically larger-than-life encouragement for the whole undertaking, not to mention more than a touch of surrealism. Martin Andrews could not have been more enthusiastic in drawing on his extensive experience as an architect and restorer of heritage buildings to discuss Clubland architecture, but sadly did not live to see this work completed – I would have loved to have seen what he made of it. Amy Milne-Smith provided not only some valuable insights into gender in clubs, but also a much-needed

Acknowledgements

precedent in having also pursued a PhD on the history of nineteenth-century London clubs, and her assurances that this was not an act of professional suicide were most useful. To Arthur Downing I owe an enormous debt, particularly for first steering me in the direction of social network analysis; while the incomparable Luke Blaxill's advice on statistical analyses has been beyond praise.

I also owe huge thanks to all at the Rhodes Project, particularly Ann Olivarius, Susan Rudy and Jef McAllister, for providing such a supportive working environment in which to carry out research while balancing out my remaining PhD commitments, in the latter stages of the doctoral research. I would like to thank Peter Francis and all the staff at Gladstone's Library for awarding me a scholarship at the library, which proved to be one of the most productive periods of writing, and I greatly benefitted from the library's unique intellectual and spiritual atmosphere.

I would furthermore like to thank many of the staff and students alike at Goodenough College for providing me with such a supportive home in central London for the bulk of my PhD research, and for awarding me a bursary during part of my stay there; I certainly think I benefitted intellectually from living in the heart of the University of London's faculties and departments, but even as a lifelong (suburban) Londoner, it was not until I lived within walking distance of 'Clubland' that I was fully able to appreciate the spatial dimension of this topic, usually taking several walks a week through Clubland to remind myself of what I was trying to capture, visualising the living patterns of Victorian legislators.

I wish to thank my former students at Warwick, as they invariably made the week far more interesting than it would have otherwise been. I am also willing to forgive one class for laughing a little *too* loudly at my wistful observation that 'Karl Marx didn't get out much, he spent his whole life in the British Library – a bit like me, really.' You know who you all are.

When I first began researching this project in 2010, I took the unorthodox step of standing for the General Committee of the National Liberal Club, where I have been a member for thirteen years (consider this to double as a declaration of interest), in order to get a better perspective of the functioning of one of the few remaining political clubs; and since 2013, I have served as the Club's Honorary Librarian. While we live in a very different age from that covered in this book, the Club's rules have not materially changed since the reign of Queen Victoria. It has been an enlightening and rewarding, if at times frustrating, experience, extremely helpful in gaining empathy for the organisational pressures on and functioning of 'Clubland', and I would like to thank my fellow members of the General Committee for making the undertaking so enjoyable, particularly Janet Berridge, Michael Meadowcroft, Rupert Morris, and the late, lamented Michael Burrell. My thanks also go to Rupert and Kitty Morris for lending me their charming house in France for much of the final write-up of the book's manuscript.

My family have helped with some of the hardship which is an inevitable part of any postgraduate research, and particularly in the latter stages of the PhD work, Veronique and Jacqueline Thévoz swooped in with support when I really had no time to think of anything else; and the original PhD thesis version of the project would never have been completed without Mary O'Hagan and Antonia Strachey's support towards the end, not to mention their generosity in throwing open their home in Astypalia as a tranquil haven for writing.

My two PhD supervisors, Sarah Richardson and Philip Salmon could not have been more supportive, and deserve tremendous praise. Both have been incisive and unrelentingly constructive in their comments. Sarah has patiently and energetically guided me through the hoops of an often-perplexing PhD process at Warwick, while Philip has combined supervisions with acting as host at the History of Parliament Trust's 1832–1945 section, where he presides with enormous flair, knowledge and passion. My editor at I.B.Tauris, Tomasz Hoskins, has also been a stalwart champion of this subsequent book. Stuart Hal Smith produced an excellent index on a tight turnaround.

More prosaically, one of my biggest debts is to the late, great Conrad Russell to whom this book is dedicated. Conrad died well over a decade ago, and I never discussed any part of this topic with him (unless you count his telling a few fanciful tales about his great-grandfather). Yet I would never have chosen to study history without the inspiration of his colossal intellect and impish charm, and he left me with an abiding passion for parliamentary history. He is sorely missed, and not just by me: 'missing Conrad' is a common bond that unites a number of people named here. I am sure this work is poorer for not having been scrutinised by his razor-sharp wit and polymath's mind.

Finally, I would like to thank my fellow club members – not just in the National Liberal Club, but in all the clubs that have welcomed me in the twenty-first century. They are closer to their Victorian forebears than they might think, and I mean that as the highest compliment.

Naturally, any inaccuracies, errors or omissions are entirely my own.

INTRODUCTION

At the height of the 2009 parliamentary expenses scandal, Prime Minister Gordon Brown fumed that, 'Westminster cannot operate like some gentlemen's club.'[1] Parliament had come full circle – for a century and a half, many of the ways in which Westminster operated were indeed based on private members's clubs, and quite consciously so. It was not without reason that Dickens called the House of Commons, 'the best club in London.'[2] This is the story of how and why that came to pass.

In recent decades, clubs have been hampered by a poor image. Picture a gentleman's club, and you invariably think of a group of clapped-out old farts sat by a roaring fire, sunk in deep leather armchairs, hiding behind newspapers before passing out from a surfeit of port; 'a country house with the Duke lying dead upstairs', as has been said of several clubs.[3] And this is probably a fairly accurate image of the self-parody some clubs have veered into.

Yet today's clubs are very different from their Victorian heyday. Whereas London once housed some 400 clubs, today less than 40 of these have prevailed. The survivors spent much of the twentieth century hampered by a cycle of decline: a dwindling number of ageing members, paying rising fees, gradually becoming ever more reactionary caricatures of themselves, fuming at the iniquity of the world as they have gradually been marginalised into irrelevance – a venue for hire, nothing more, nothing less.

The era of 'club government' could scarcely have been more different. It was a time of unprecedented power and influence exercised in clubs, and by clubs, at one of the critical junctures in the making of modern Britain. The Whig Whip Edward Ellice first coined the phrase 'club government' in a letter to solicitor and election manager Joseph Parkes in 1836, when cautioning against the probable backlash in the country if newly-founded political clubs like the Reform Club were to be extended any further; and the expression was popularised by Norman Gash in the 1950s.[4] This book analyses how clubs had become so inseparable from politics in the mid-nineteenth century as to make 'club government' resonate as a concept well beyond Westminster, not only in the proceedings of Parliament but also in the conduct of parliamentary elections. It is a concept which has been frequently invoked by political and social historians of the period, yet has never received its own full-scale study.

The notion of the club was nothing new in 1832. Clubs had evolved from the aristocratic gaming and coffee-house culture of London since the seventeenth century, and their history on both sides of the Atlantic has been chronicled in detail by Peter Clark, while a further French-language study by Valérie Capdeville has expanded our knowledge of the early London clubs of the eighteenth century.[5] From the earliest days, some clubs had been overtly political, the earliest recorded example being the Rota Club founded in 1659, so called because it rotated its membership amongst MPs.[6] Over time, clubs multiplied dramatically, with the process reaching a new level of intensity in the last third of the nineteenth century, as the basic club model spiralled in popularity throughout Britain, particularly with the growing popularity of working men's clubs, and political clubs in the constituencies. This book concentrates on the involvement of London clubs in politics between the first two Reform Acts. It is not a study of London clubs, or of Reform-era politics, but of the interaction between the two.

Before proceeding further it is perhaps helpful to define precisely what is meant by a 'club'. Ashton and Reid, the premier legal textbook on the issue, notes that every club exhibit six specific characteristics:

(1) it must comprise two or more persons who are voluntarily bound together for an agreed and common purpose;
(2) it must exist for a lawful purpose other than simply for the purposes of trade or making a profit for its members;
(3) it must not be of a temporary nature;
(4) it must have a constitution or a set of rules which fairly regulates the conduct of its members towards each other;
(5) there must be a defined process for the admission of members;
(6) it must possess what can best be described as collegiality, that is, the process of making decisions or agreeing on actions shared by all the members.[7]

Additionally, it is worth observing that clubs are inherently social institutions in which membership around a common interest or group is usually paid for by subscription. The word 'club' can be (and has been) used far more widely than in the sense meant here, and can describe practically *any* leisure society; an approach adopted by Peter Clark in studying an era when fewer clubs existed. The mid-Victorian profusion of clubs and societies makes such an approach impractical. Where existing studies of mid-Victorian clubs embrace such a broad approach of encompassing *any* society, they tend to focus on one strand of such clubs – as is the case in William C. Lubenow's recent analysis of clubs as an intellectual arena.[8] This book refers to one particularly prominent type of club, based in central London, in one physical set of premises at a time. As will be elaborated, the permanent physical presence of a club in one place was critical in moulding the attitudes of its members towards such a club, and the characteristics of these establishments differed considerably from societies without permanent premises that would meet in pubs and taverns. Aside from the markedly higher subscriptions that were charged by such clubs, their use by members as a *de facto* second home with a strictly codified set of rules made the social dynamic of such clubs unique.

It is worth justifying the London-centric focus of this book, which runs counter to the dominant trend of the last half-century of scholarship in moving our understanding of parliamentary politics beyond a 'high politics' approach focussed on senior politicians at Westminster, and particularly on the trend of writing (and often comparing) political experiences in the constituencies.[9] Indeed, the approach of this book is to attempt to fuse together elements of 'high' and 'low' politics which have long been viewed in isolation. There are three main grounds for focussing on the clubs of London rather than a broader approach which would analyse clubs across Britain. The most obvious justification is that no full-length study has been written on the topic before. The second reason relates to the sheer concentration of clubs in London – there were nearly 100 in this period, of which at least nine were considered to be overtly political.[10] By comparison, most provincial towns had at most two or three clubs (and usually just one), meaning that London's clubs tended to capture a far larger slice of the enfranchised electorate than was the case anywhere else in the United Kingdom.[11] The more diverse nature of London's clubs was recognised by H. J. Hanham, who observes that

> Few of the provincial clubs which had been founded in the [eighteen] thirties and forties on the model of the Carlton and Reform had survived [for long], and those few, like the Eldon Club at Norwich, were too exclusive to be of any political value.[12]

Thirdly, it is impossible to adequately comprehend the political role of London clubs without looking at their national role in the constituencies; and so accordingly, the last chapter will examine London clubs' constituency interventions. Finally, in justifying why this topic should be tackled at all, one need look no further than the existing state of confusion on the subject. Such is the degree of misinformation in printed sources that even some of the most eminent scholars of the period have sometimes seemed confused about political club history and its chronology; for instance, Richard Shannon has cited the Carlton Club as 'the Tory response to the Reform Club' when the reverse was true (the Reform Club was not founded until four years *after* the Carlton's creation); an assertion subsequently repeated by John Ramsden.[13] Thus by addressing this historiographical gap, it is hoped to provide a degree of clarity missing from existing work on the relationship between clubs and politics.

A further way in which this study apparently runs counter to the trends of recent scholarship is in its relative neglect of the role of gender in British politics. This is not to imply that women were marginalised in post-Reform politics, for much scholarship of the last three decades has showed that contrary to previous assumptions, women actively participated in politics in many parts of mid-Victorian Britain.[14] Indeed, the all-male environment of 'Clubland' unsurprisingly offers a rich harvest for historians of masculinity, as Amy Milne-Smith has shown in her writings on the topic, whilst Barbara Black's subsequent work has shed much light on fleshing out the role of women's clubs in the late Victorian era.[15] However, the role of women in pre-1868 clubs was largely peripheral. There were no mixed-sex London clubs before that date, and there is scant evidence that the few all-women clubs of the period played any active role in politics, although some were involved in philanthropic ventures.[16]

As I have alluded to the term 'Clubland', it is worth briefly touching on its etymology, and particularly its historical context. As a term, Clubland (sometimes spelt 'club land' or 'club-land', either with or without capitalisation) originally denoted the area around St James's, with its high concentration of clubs. Yet the *Oxford English Dictionary* notes that it has grown into short-hand for 'any area in which there is a large number of clubs', identifying the first usage of the term in this wider context in 1885, in *Whittaker's Almanac* (Although the noun 'club' in this context is dated by the *OED* to 1775, and the adjective 'clubbable' to 1791.)[17] Indeed, whilst this book embraces a peculiarly nineteenth-century notion of Clubland centred on St James's, it must be recognised that it was an evolution of a series of long-standing concepts. The word 'clubbable', and the notion of clubbability, is believed to originate with Boswell's *Life of Johnson*, and is defined by the OED as meaning 'sociable' and/or 'Having such qualities as fit one to be a member of a club'; although Boswell noted that Samuel Johnson had previously used the word 'unclubbable', indicating that the concept was rooted in a negative, and was defined by what was *not* clubbable.[18] Additionally, the linguistic recognition of a 'Club' dates to at least the mid-seventeenth century, with the word having had its first recorded use in this context by Robert Sherwood in his *Dictionary of French and English Tongues* of 1633, and more notably by John Milton in 1641, and with a number of other, related uses of 'Club' having evolved by the 1650s.[19] Furthermore, although this study is centred on the distinctive political appropriation of clubs and Clubland in the nineteenth century, there is still a need for further research into the political roots of the concept of clubs in the Interregnum years. Whilst a quantification approach to the corpus of the several million books scanned into Google Books confirms that the 1880s was indeed one of the decades in which the term 'Clubland' grew in prominence, it is clear from other sources that the expression in its original, specific, St James's-centred form had been in circulation over seventy years earlier, and was already established well before the Great Reform Act. The specific geographical area is easy to define: Figure 1.1 makes it clear that by the 1832–68 period, Clubland occupied a tightly-drawn grid, bound by Piccadilly to the north, Pall Mall to the south, St James's Street to the west, and Haymarket to the east. Most clubs were concentrated in an 'L' shape along St James's Street and Pall Mall. There were always 'outliers' beyond this grid, but it recognisably remained the core of London clubs.[20] Later generations of clubs from the 1880s onwards would bring further concentrations of clubs extending beyond this space, including the full length of Piccadilly to the west, and on adjacent streets north such as Dover Street and Albemarle Street.[21] Early instances of the word 'Clubland' in popular culture can be found in such fiction as the 1828 satirical play *Noctes Ambrosianae*, with its listing of London districts including 'Club-Land',[22] which tallies with the 1820s redevelopment of the Pall Mall area on the Carlton House site; and the 1841 novel *Cecil, a Peer: A Sequel to Cecil, or, The Adventures of a Coxcomb*, with its reference to 'the frontiers of Club land' around St James's.[23] Guides to London also used the phrase, a widely-circulated example coming from a frequently reprinted 1853 travellers' guide which described the intersection between Waterloo Place and Pall Mall as representing 'the heart of Club-Land'.[24] The notion of 'Clubland' as a recognised area of London was thus already firmly established by the time of the political transformations of the Great Reform Act, several decades before the word's more abstract meaning came into use – although it must be conceded that the newly-minted term had not yet evolved into a standardised spelling.

This book examines club politics in relation to the House of Commons, but not the House of Lords or municipal politics – this focus has been dictated by the nature of the source material. I have not come across a single instance of interference by London clubs in municipal politics in this period, making it a redundant field. Excluding the House of Lords was a more controversial decision, as its political overlap with clubs has its champions. Angus Hawkins asserts that 'Around the social hub of the Carlton Club, Conservative peers, after 1858, reasserted their dominance in the Upper House.'[25] Indeed, when this study into clubs and parliamentary politics began, the original intention was to include the House of Lords. However, in sifting through the membership records of political clubs, it rapidly became apparent that, barring the small aristocratic citadels in White's, Brooks's and Boodle's, the proportion of peers belonging to London clubs was markedly lower than the proportion of MPs. E. A. Smith estimated the proportion of peers amongst members of the Carlton Club was between 14 and 18 per cent for the period 1836–41. This is entirely consistent with the research carried out here and the tallies of peers found in club candidate books, and a conservative estimate based on the records of the three most popular clubs with parliamentarians would place the proportion of all peers belonging to clubs at between a third and a half.[26] In itself, this is by no means insignificant, given the relatively low proportion of peers who were politically active. However, as Chapter 2 notes, the House of Commons' club membership was of a different magnitude, with some nine-tenths of MPs being club members. Furthermore, even basic information on the Lords in this period – for instance, regarding whipping arrangements – is far more fraught with difficulty, and would considerably complicate any such study.

The case for beginning this study with 1832 is self-evident: the new political environment after the First Reform Act is frequently cited as a landmark in British political history. Although numerous historians, most notably Frank O'Gorman, have questioned the degree to which Reform itself changed the nature of parliamentary politics from the Hanoverian *status quo*, there can be little doubt that the broader changes of the 'Age of Reform' *did* represent something of a turning point in the political system.[27] Wide-ranging reforms such as Catholic Emancipation in 1829, the 1835 Municipal Corporations Act, changes in the procedural rules of the Houses of Parliament (particularly in the wake of Sir Thomas Erskine May's codification of such rules in 1844), and the great fire of 1834 which destroyed Parliament, all resulted in substantial changes in the organisational and geographical environment in which government – and particularly 'club government' – was conducted.

The case for 1868 as a bookend date for 'club government' was made in 1959 by H. J. Hanham, who argued that the implementation of the Second Reform Act saw a transformation in the intended membership of political clubs, and that 'in London a new era opened in 1868.' He elaborated:

> Before 1867 there were very few clubs, social or political, for ordinary business men, country politicians, or working men. The great London clubs, Brooks's, the Carlton, the Conservative, and the Reform, had no room for City men or for party workers from the provinces who might come up to London on political business.[28]

Thus the electoral reforms implemented in 1868 present a convenient cut-off point for the study of the post-1832 environment. Such periodisation is not uncontroversial, with previous historians having selected other 'bookend' dates. Norman Gash's own study of 'club government' was presented in his reinterpretation of 1830–50, while other books covering the political history of the period have selected 1783–1867, 1796–1865, 1815–85 and 1815–1914, not to mention innumerable monographs which have stressed much shorter periods.[29] For this topic, 1832–68 collates the broadest possible examples of a directly comparable electoral environment.

Several factors make this long-overdue study particularly timely. An important component has been the co-operation of several surviving clubs in granting archival access. Some of the collections used, such as those of the Carlton, National and Reform Clubs have seldom been consulted by more than a handful of historians, whilst some like the Athenaeum and Junior Carlton had remained sealed to outside historians until I completed my research; the Athenaeum has only previously opened its archives to members writing authorised histories of the Club, whilst no part of the Junior Carlton archive has ever been reproduced in print.[30] Even more crucially, the recent trend towards digitisation in historical research has resulted in nothing short of a revolution in the last decade, the full implications of which have yet to be assessed, and this project has enormously benefitted from it.[31] Additionally, the book benefits enormously from recent trends in scholarship, particularly the 'cultural turn', which James Vernon argues has 'far-reaching implications for the study of nineteenth-century English politics.'[32] Accordingly, this book adopts a range of approaches and methodologies in attempting to address the role clubs played in politics in this period.

INTRODUCTION

A necessary prerequisite to any such study is an overview of the existing literature on London clubs, and of their political role in particular – admittedly a small and under-researched field. This neglect is baffling when contrasted with the fiercely-contested historiography of politics in the aftermath of the Reform Act, and is even more bewildering when one considers the far more widespread study of working men's clubs from the 1850s onwards, explored by such writers as Richard Price, John Davis and Stan Shipley.[33] Shipley in particular has focussed on the political side of such clubs from the 1870s, and their role as an arena for socialist thought; a task which involved reproducing contemporary catalogues of London's working men's clubs.[34] Historians have not matched such scrutiny with their West End counterparts. The few works specifically on the topic are much-invoked but seldom-queried. Nor is most work in this area particularly lengthy, generally extending to at most an essay or a chapter. Far more common are the passing observations by historians of some related field, such as histories of London, heavily couching their points in caveats, citing a paucity of sources. In addition to these, much writing belongs to the realm of 'club histories', often officially sanctioned, which can be a problematic genre.

The Reform and (particularly) the Carlton Clubs dominate most accounts, whilst practically nothing exists on political activity in ostensibly *non*-political clubs – several of these, like Boodle's, have 'never sought public attention.'[35] It is perhaps no coincidence that in previous decades, historians who tended to focus the most on clubs, including Robert Blake, Norman Gash, Robert Stewart and (fifty years before them) R. L. Hill, tended to be conservatives with either a large or a small 'C', with the consequence that the Carlton Club enjoyed considerably more attention than its Liberal counterparts.[36] Indeed, the Carlton Club appears to have had more written about it by political historians than all of its contemporaries combined. Yet historians differ as to what degree the Carlton's organisational supremacy was ever challenged by the Reform Club. Philip Salmon provided some detail on the Reform's earlier efforts at registration activities, although Ronald K. Huch and Paul R. Ziegler believed the Reform Club to have been only 'a marginal success' in achieving its original aims, possibly explaining the smaller interest generated; and this latter interpretation was shared by James Vernon, who asserts that 'despite the arbitration of the Liberals' central organisation at the Reform Club ... the selection of candidates was effectively a free-for-all' by the 1860s.[37]

The first serious study of such clubs in a political context was in W. Fraser Rae's 1878 article 'Political Clubs and Party Organisation'. It is perhaps a damning indictment of the topic's neglect that Rae's article written nearly 140 years ago remains one of the best studies. With an insider's perspective which would become a hallmark of much Clubland writing, Fraser Rae provided copious insights into his own club, the Reform, whilst his coverage of the Carlton was mostly restricted to speculation as to whether the Reform Club's activities were matched there.[38] Fraser Rae's pioneering efforts were followed over 20 years later by the work of Moisei Ostrogorski, whose early sociological landmark *Democracy and Organisation of Political Parties* continued to treat clubs as a serious component of the political process, identifying them as a powerful symbol of central intervention in local political contests, whether real or imagined.[39] As a foreign national, Ostrogorski also brought a distinctive 'outsider' perspective (which I can instinctively empathise with, as a Swiss expatriate in London for much of my life), that was quite different from the casual name-dropping that later writers such as Anthony Sampson would deploy when describing 'my own club'.[40] For much of the twentieth century, however, the early promise of Fraser Rae and Ostrogorski's work was followed by a lack of dedicated monographs. Instead, clubs enjoyed little more than footnotes from historians, and the occasional chapter in a wider work.

A marked exception to this neglect was the work of Norman Gash, which still heavily influences the way the topic is framed. Over 60 years ago, Gash popularised Ellice's term 'club government'.[41] Clubs recurred throughout Gash's output, being particularly pronounced in his two-part article on Conservative party organisation, and his chapter 'Club Government' in *Politics in the Age of Peel*.[42] Gash went beyond a mere outline, and set out a range of party activities which clubs engaged in, from the matching of candidates with those seats which requested one, to the ways in which the Carlton would organise reminders for Conservative MPs to vote.[43] In particular, Gash emphasised how it was no coincidence that an expansion in London clubs, and of club membership among MPs, coincided with a sharp rise in the greater organisation and whipping of voting blocs among MPs. If Gash's work has dated, then it has generally dated well. Working from largely antiquarian sources, he developed an argument on the political role of clubs which is often cited but has seldom been seriously contested. His argument has been echoed by historians such as Robert Blake, who wrote of the mid-nineteenth century as 'the era ... of the great political clubs, the Reform and the Carlton, the effective headquarters of the two sides.'[44] Some writers such as Ian Newbould have queried Gash's broader thesis on party management, contending that Tory organisation was never matched by the same level of Whig organisation, but this was not with reference to the specific role played by clubs.[45]

Gash clarified the precise role of Francis Robert Bonham in working from a desk at the Carlton, and detailed his responsibilities as the Conservatives' *de facto* first national agent, while Robert Stewart further elaborated on this account.[46] With the Carlton election committee and Bonham's desk being the closest the Carlton had to an office, the question of whether the word 'headquarters' is an appropriate description has been raised. R. L. Hill, noting that 'the Carlton Club professed to be a party headquarters', preferred the description 'centre of gravity' (which broadly matched Llewelyn Woodward's later description of it as 'a centre of Tory interests'), observing, 'The Carlton never paraded as a National Registration Society. Tory hatred of centralisation in all its forms would not have tolerated it for one moment.'[47] Hill was also sceptical of contemporary claims that the Carlton was responsible for the new Conservative Operative Societies of the 1840s, but inferred, 'The work of the Carlton Club in the provinces was limited to the management of elections; beyond that its authority was at an end', and argued that the growth of Operative Societies and Working Men's Conservative Associations in the 1840s was an unrelated development, owing more to the growing popularity of Sir Robert Peel in the country than to any new emphasis on organisation.[48] Hill's belief that the Carlton's significance was marginalised after 1846 is, however, contradicted by several historians. Robert Blake asserted in his history of the Conservative party that 'in the 1850s and 1860s [elections] the pattern has but slightly changed ... the Carlton Club is still very important',[49] and argued it was only with the foundation of a Conservative Central Office in 1870 that 'The Carlton Club had faded out as a political headquarters.'[50] Michael Rush has also demurred from Hill's analysis, not with regards to the Carlton's role in the country, but at Westminster. In his study of the evolution of backbench MPs, Rush noted that in the 1830s, 'inside Parliament there already existed a degree of party organisation', and went on to place clubs in the context of how 'the parties now began to extend their organisational activities beyond Westminster'.[51]

Whether political clubs represented anything wholly new has been questioned. As part of his landmark reappraisal of the pre-Reform political environment, Frank O'Gorman sought to emphasise the continuity of clubs as an institution with the late eighteenth century local election clubs found in areas like Liverpool and Berwick-upon-Tweed.[52] O'Gorman offered extensive evidence in support of his claim that such pre-Reform Act clubs in the constituencies served as election headquarters, and provided a robust challenge to long-held claims that the Carlton and Reform Clubs were their parties' first election headquarters. However, Robert Stewart's earlier conceptualisation of the clubs' political role had allowed for this, noting of such earlier constituency clubs, 'it is significant that none of them bore a party label and that each of them was called a club. Their most important function was the annual dinner', simultaneously confirming the strength and weakness of the parallel with post-Reform Act clubs; and as I have written elsewhere, until the 1880s, many local political clubs were dining societies rather than campaigning organisations.[53] Margaret Escott has also concluded that pre-Reform Act clubs had a political role, albeit among some regional groups of MPs, and of a more transient nature – she highlights how 'the pocket books of Sir Thomas Mostyn and Sir John Nicholl record "Welsh Club" meetings [of Welsh MPs] on 10, 24 June, 15 July 1820, 20 May 1821, 1 Apr., 17 May, 19 May 1829, and 2 May 1830, when the future of the Welsh judicature was a parliamentary issue. There were doubtless others.'[54] It should be noted that the Welsh Club for MPs was not the only example of regional politics finding expression in London club gatherings. Andrew Shields records a meeting of 'between thirty and forty' Irish Tory MPs at the Carlton Club. Shields concludes, 'The vast majority of [Irish Conservative] MPs [were] members of at least one' club, and he provides a detailed statistical breakdown and comparison of London and Dublin club memberships among this group.[55] Shields' conclusions provide a strong riposte to the notion of London clubs as representing a Londoncentric expression of society and politics, and suggest a more complex composition. Combined with this, Gash's own earlier admission that there were separate whipping arrangements for English, Scottish and Irish Conservative MPs raises questions on whether club membership was more or less prevalent among these groups.[56]

Shields' work is a rare example – along with Antonia Taddei's MSci thesis and subsequent 1999 paper on 'London Clubs in the Late Nineteenth Century' – of quantitative rather than qualitative analysis of London clubs by historians.[57] Precise Clubland statistics have seldom been provided. The patchy, anecdotal nature of available sources has traditionally led to a qualitative approach, yet Shields and Taddei have demonstrated the potential for drawing conclusions from collated club membership statistics which have been compared with parliamentary activity – a course which this book extends even further.

Clubs have also drawn scrutiny for their link to evolving concepts of party in the post-Reform environment. A recurring trend in many accounts of the period is the treatment of club membership as the closest approximation to party membership. Early Whig accounts, such as that of G. M. Trevelyan, repeatedly used 'Brooks's' as an interchangeable shorthand term for the Whigs, asserting that 'all sections of the party belonged' to the Club.[58] This identification of political clubs with party affiliation has been an enduring trend, with Donald Southgate in the 1960s believing Gladstone's 1860 resignation from the Carlton Club signified his final break with Conservatism, a judgment which Gary W. Cox shared in the 1980s.[59] Alexander Llewelyn clarified this common assumption on defectors and clubs with his point that 'Membership of the Carlton was an earnest of allegiance to the Tories', citing Graham and Stanley joining in 1841 'as a public and final break with Whiggery and alliance with Peel'[60], and Robert Blake having concurred with Llewelyn's judgment on Stanley.[61] More recently, Jonathan Parry has read some significance into the way in which 'Ministers did not join' one of the Reform Club's predecessors, the Reform Association, emphasising this point in his chapter on the emergence of the Liberal party.[62] Furthermore, this translation by historians of club membership as *de facto* party membership is apparent in readings of the *pre*-Reform Act environment, with D. R. Fisher correlating the Conservative-inclined Marquess of Blandford's 1818–20 flirtation with the Whigs with his joining Brooks's in 1817.[63] Nonetheless, Gash downplayed the conflation of club membership and political support among Victorians, writing '"Membership" of a party did not in fact exist in any technical sense; and therefore "expulsion" could not exist either ... not until 1912 was it definitely laid down in the rules of the Carlton Club that new members should belong to the Conservative and Unionist Party.'[64] Gash inferred that equating party membership and club membership would be ahistorical.

A further complication arises from the conflation of 'party' with 'faction'. Joanna Innes has been most explicit in drawing out the relevance of this to the Reform Club, emphasising the difficulty of identifying the Club as being synonymous with either the totality of a party, or with any one faction of a party. She stressed how 'Reform' became a term hijacked by an 'elite, moderate faction' of Whigs, but the Reform Club was actually initiated by 'the radical wing of the governing coalition [who] liked to think of themselves as true reformers', and who styled their ambitions as 'organic reforms', while even more confusingly, 'symptomatically, the club was embraced by the Whigs'.[65] Thus in the case of the Reform Club, the notion of *who* maintained ownership over the Club was symptomatic of a wider dispute over whose concept of 'Reform' one shared.

The last two decades have seen an increase in historical interest in clubs, beginning with several pieces of work appearing in 1999. Antonia Taddei wrote about clubs from an economic history perspective, but with reference to the late Victorian period, only describing the mid-nineteenth century in passing (and even then only with reference to later events); but her work did provide some novel quantification of how club membership worked, particularly in how one sought election to a club. That same year, Jane Rendell also published 'The Clubs of St James's: Places of Public Patriarchy – Exclusivity, Domesticity and Secrecy'. Although released under the auspices of the *Journal of Architecture*, as the title implies, it covered a broad sweep of cultural and social issues.[66] Similarly, J. Mordaunt Crook's work on the architectural manifestations of the Victorian *nouveaux riches*, published the same year, contained a section acknowledging clubs' part in the Victorian rise of 'new' money, but his work focussed primarily on the private realm of the country house.[67] Since then, Amy Milne-Smith has pursued the topic, with a book based on clubs and masculinity, and articles on domesticity in London clubs, and the role of gossip in club culture.[68] Yet as with so much that has been written on clubs, her research covers the period after 1880, when London clubs were at their most numerous.[69] Given the considerable body of work on gender politics in the aftermath of the first Reform Act, Milne-Smith's gender-based approach offers a long-overdue contribution to the topic. Barbara Black's *A Room of His Own*, published in 2012, is subtitled *A Literary-Cultural Study of Victorian Clubland*; my review of which elsewhere makes it clear that the book has much to say on the literary dimension of Clubland, but is somewhat limited in its coverage of and familiarity with the cultural dimension.[70] More comprehensively, Benjamin B. Cohen's *In the Club* (2015) draws upon an impressive frame of reference – no less than 100 clubs across the Indian subcontinent – to clarify the all-important imperial dimension to Clubland, up to and including the post-colonial legacy. Cohen's work benefits from a particularly sure-footed grasp of club administration, and the wider culture surrounding this.[71]

A work of colossal importance, also a product of recent years, is Peter Clark's exhaustively detailed *British Clubs and Societies 1580–1800: The Origins of an Associational World*.[72] This survey considered how the club model evolved from an obscure concept to a major form of sociability across the English-speaking world, and looked at its economics, impact and implications through a wide variety of organisations; from dining societies to freemasons, benefit societies and voluntary organisations. It is likely to remain the standard work in its field for many years. However, its central strength – its sheer scope and breadth – would be logistically impossible to sustain beyond its nineteenth-century cut-off point, given the further profusion of clubs and societies in ensuing decades. Clark's approach suits the period admirably, but any post-eighteenth century work must necessarily take a far narrower focus; and indeed, Clark's embrace of the broadest possible definition of 'clubs' overseas, across the English-speaking world, means that much of his book's emphasis rests well beyond the scope of this book. The key value of Clark here is in setting out the background of clubs when so many club histories have disagreed as to what the precise forerunner of the London club was.

Any overview of club literature would be wholly incomplete without touching on that curious literary sub-genre, the club history. They are impossible to ignore, and they contain much unique material which is not to be found in other sources, yet they have considerable drawbacks. The authors of such institutional club histories tended to be club members, but not historians, as exemplified by retired Major-General Sir Louis Jackson, who inauspiciously began his wildly meandering history of the United Service Club confessing, 'I will not attempt any apology for the defects of this book. Only a practised historian could have made a harmonious pattern.'[73] The primary drawback of author-members is the concept of 'club loyalty', and the self-censorship this brings. Ian Bradley complained that a 1982 centenary pamphlet on the history of his own club, the National Liberal, carefully airbrushed out any mention of the financial and sexual scandals which had recently engulfed it.[74] More subtly, club histories often perpetrate self-aggrandising claims of having hosted apocryphal incidents which could not possibly have happened there.[75] Many of these works are limited edition 'vanity' publications of a few hundred subscription copies.[76] (Although admittedly, this is a print run greater than many academic monographs!) Their approach has not fundamentally changed over the decades, and barring some books examining the social history of certain clubs, many twentieth century club histories could easily have been written in the nineteenth century. The manner in which many such club histories are published to tie in with club anniversaries means that their development is often rushed to meet deadlines – Almeric Fitzroy's history of the Travellers' Club includes a major source on the building of the club-house, which was 'RECEIVED TOO LATE FOR INSERTION' into the main body of the text, and has had to be reproduced as a photographic plate instead.[77] Additionally, club histories are by no means comprehensive in their coverage, and can be extremely short.[78] Thus club histories are often highly problematic.

They suffer further drawbacks in their selection of clubs covered. They have tended to be written about the longest-surviving institutions rather than those of the greatest interest. While many of the key political clubs *have* had numerous official histories (the Carlton has had two, White's has had three, and Brooks's and the Reform have had four), some influential clubs such as the Guards' Club and the National Club have never enjoyed a full-length published history, whilst others such as Crockford's and the Junior Carlton have had the dubious distinction of sharing a chapter apiece in books on other clubs.[79] Crockford's (unusually for a defunct club) later merited a whole book of its own,

INTRODUCTION 17

which proved to be a rich slice of social history by A. L. Humphreys that was unusually strong for the genre.[80] However, Humphreys' book is very much the exception to the rule, and was in no small part helped by the short lifespan of the Club (1828–44 in its most famous premises), which more or less imposed a tight structure on the book. By contrast, most London club histories have to cover several centuries, and a combination of patchy archives, and authors whose expertise is often only focussed on one period, means that the resultant genre is often characterised by bluster, generalisation and padding.

A further problem with traditional club histories is how these books fall prey to bouts of 'Chinese whispers', as the same tales are repeated, embellished and distorted – for instance, a staple of the Clubland literature describes the Garrick Club's 1850s dispute between Yates and Thackeray – but Anthony Lejeune changes the protagonists to Dickens and Thackeray, while Phelps feels the need to begin his history of the Carlton Club by rebutting the common misconception that the story ever happened at the Carlton (where neither Yates nor Thackeray were members).[81] Clearly, even basic matters of chronology and location have become disputed. Such distortions are problematic in political coverage: there are at least three versions of how the Reform Club came to be founded, with it being argued that it grew out of the primarily social Westminster Reform Club, or from the Reform Association with its emphasis on electoral registration, or that it was the brainchild of Edward Ellice.[82] There are also at least two versions of the Carlton Club's founding, with Petrie crediting F. R. Bonham (whom he incorrectly identified as Tory Chief Whip) in 1833, and Phelps highlighting the role of the Duke of Wellington in convening meetings and collecting funds in 1831, both of which dates are at odds with the club's 'official' 1832 foundation.[83] Whilst these counter-claims are not necessarily mutually exclusive, they establish a historiographical framework of dispute still in need of resolution.

The very earliest comprehensive club history spanning multiple clubs, and in many ways the most influential, was *Club Life of London* by the journalist John Timbs, which built on work from his 1855 book *Curiosities of London*.[84] *Club Life* passed through four editions between 1866 and 1908, being indicative of the persistent commercial demand for such a title. Timbs helpfully provided a short two-to-three page summary of some 50 London clubs, including many which have otherwise evaded attention. Timbs placed clubs in the context of coffee-houses, inns and pubs, with half of the two-volume work devoted to taverns, setting the tone for clubs being written about more for their sociability than their politics. Numerous subsequent histories took a similar journalistic approach in focussing on gossip, personalities, and incidents; and coincided with the Edwardian boom in club-building. Arthur Griffiths' *Clubs and Clubmen*, Henry Shelley's *Inns and Taverns of Old London*, and Ralph Nevill's *London Clubs* were comparable travelogues from the Edwardian era.[85] T. H. S. Escott's *Club Makers and Club Members* took journalistic club histories in a new direction, owing more to the thematic approach of W. Fraser Rae. Instead of offering reviews of each club, he extrapolated themes such as 'clubs, cliques and coteries', and particularly focused on the motivations of club founders.[86] What Escott captured particularly well for the mid-nineteenth century was the blending of the social and the political into one. Accounts such as Louis Fagan's 1880s history of the Reform Club seem to jar when abruptly turning from 'high politics' to the reputation of the Reform's head chef Alexis Soyer; by contrast, Escott explicitly outlined why these two were so connected, establishing the background of a neo-classical revival that drew precedents for merging sociability and politics.[87] A drawback Escott shared with his journalistic predecessors, however, was a neglect of clubs' histories beyond the first few years after their foundation. A characteristic feature of these early histories was to chronicle club foundations in detail, and then to add some notes on the clubs at the time of writing – but with relatively little on the decades (or centuries) between. Thus the club-founding harvest of the 1830s and 1860s is richly documented, whilst the 1840s and 1850s largely escape attention.[88] Furthermore, one can discern that the primary purpose of such background details was merely to lend some verisimilitude to the 'here and now' – the treatment of club history was a means to a contemporary journalistic end, not an end in itself. This approach further evolved in the twentieth century with the first two editions of Anthony Sampson's *Anatomy of Britain*, which fused journalism with contemporary sociology in presenting a chapter on clubs in relation to a 1960s concept of 'the Establishment'. However, with the rapid passing of the old 'Establishment' amidst the 'satire boom' of 1962, the chapter was already of questionable topicality in 1962, and it was phased out in later editions of Sampson's work.[89]

The journalistic approach reached its apotheosis in Anthony Lejeune's sumptuously illustrated *The Gentlemen's Clubs of London*, which first appeared in 1979.[90] Despite being touted by the publishers of Lejeune's later history of White's as 'an acknowledged classic', the book is riddled with inaccuracies and embellishments, and is perfectly representative of the 'club history' genre in offering little context for the 300 years covered. An updated edition came out in 2012 and, if anything, it is even less reliable.[91] Yet the book has enjoyed a monopoly as the only wide-ranging multi-club history of recent years.[92]

To dedicate so much attention here to such a patently flawed genre is no mere indulgence. These books are not just worthy of study for their dominance of the topic. They are also of immense interest as primary sources in their own right. Many of them reproduce archival material verbatim; material which is now either difficult to access, or in some cases completely lost.[93] The most notable example is the reproduction of a complete betting book, as in the 1892 history of White's.[94] This records every bet made by Club members on the premises, often on current affairs, and such books are a seldom-tapped yardstick for measuring Clubland attitudes on political questions. In the study of mid-nineteenth century British politics, only G. M. Trevelyan made any use of betting books, and even then in extremely limited form, with his citing just three examples from the Brooks's betting book in his Earl Grey biography.[95] Thus if one is suitably cautious about the archaic and reverential approaches of club histories, they can still offer historians much valuable and original material.

It is also worth noting that beyond club histories, primary source material on clubs has already gone to press over the years. Published diaries can vary considerably in relevance, but from the brief references in the future fifteenth Earl of Derby's diary, touching on his opinions of the Carlton Club's election committee, to Sir Denis Le Marchant's more detailed diary description of what was said at a closed meeting of Conservative MPs at the Carlton Club on 13 May 1832, many of them record telling details of political activities in clubs.[96]

Another abundantly-published genre is the remarkably popular 'club fiction' of the nineteenth century. Whilst a review of fiction lies outside the remit of this overview, it is worth noting that its profile has been considerable. The novels of Trollope, Thackeray and Disraeli all featured clubs as centres of political intrigue, and have formed enormously enduring popular images of the 'Tadpoles and Tapers' managing elections from Pall Mall, raising serious questions as to where fact and fiction blurred.[97]

In short, in spite of the tantalisingly promising work of Gash (and in his wake, Blake and Stewart) several decades ago, and the even earlier efforts of Fraser Rae and Ostrogorski, the political influence of London clubs in this period remains a largely elusive question. Despite the topic attracting considerable journalistic interest, and widespread academic acknowledgment that there was *some* political role for clubs in this period, much of our knowledge until now has been piecemeal and vaguely defined. Yet with the existence of so much material in both published and unpublished form, and the availability of new analytical techniques, the time is ripe for the first sustained, full-length study of clubs and politics in the years between the first two Reform Acts.

CHAPTER 1

THE DEVELOPMENT OF POLITICAL CLUBS

Introduction

Norman Gash identified the 1830s and 1840s as 'the age of club government', seeing those decades as the peak of clubs' influence in politics.[1] This chapter sets out the institutional history of the most prominent clubs, insofar as it is relevant to their political role. It is not a narrative of club histories, for which the reader is better served by the works of John Timbs, T. H. S. Escott, or Charles Graves.[2] Despite a large volume of published material, the lack of any one full-scale study of club politics in the period makes it common for simple factual and chronological errors to persist, even in recent major works on this era by established authorities.[3] Furthermore, the origins and founding political objectives of several key clubs are still disputed within the existing literature, and so these inconsistencies must be resolved before embarking further.

The clubs of the era with political objectives are relatively easy to identify, although several such as the National Club and the Free Trade Club have largely evaded the attention of historians.[4] (See Figure 1.1) Whilst these establishments can be viewed in isolation, it must be stressed that such political clubs were far more commonly viewed in

Table 1.1 London clubs with political objectives, active in 1832–68

Name	Political affiliation	Founded (Closure dates marked, if prior to 1868)
White's	Tory (loosely)	1693
Brooks's	Whig	1764
Carlton Club	Conservative	1832
Westminster Reform Club	Radical	1834 (closed 1836)
Reform Club	Liberal	1836
Conservative Club	Conservative	1840
National Club	Protestant (broadly Conservative)	1845
Free Trade Club	Free Trade Radical	1845 (closed 1849)
Junior Carlton Club	Conservative	1864

the context of 'Clubland' – the physical, geographical expression, with the concentration of clubs focussed around the 'L' shape of St James's Street and Pall Mall. All the clubs named are included in Figure 1.1, which shows the physical location of the political clubs (sometimes at several successive addresses) in the context of neighbouring apolitical clubs. From the 1860s, further clubs would be founded in other parts of central London, including north of Piccadilly and west of Regent Street, but as noted in the Introduction, the political clubs were sharply focussed in the St James's area, a short distance from Westminster.

Political clubs were thus only a small part of 'Clubland', and so although this book focuses on the political clubs named in Table 1.1, it is necessary to draw upon instances from ostensibly apolitical clubs as well, especially the two which had a noticeable proportion of their membership drawn from the House of Commons – the Athenaeum Club (usually known simply as 'the Athenaeum') and the Travellers' Club. Both had more MPs amongst their members than several of the smaller political clubs combined. Additionally, the organisational similarities between clubs are such that some comparisons with non-political clubs are revealing: clubs emulated one another's business model, and the shape of political clubs was in great measure influenced by transformations in apolitical clubs throughout the nineteenth century.

The Development of Political Clubs 23

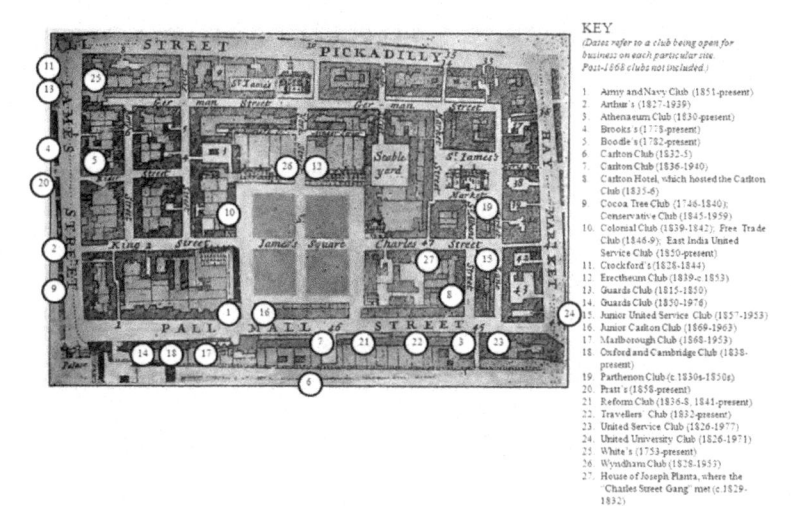

Figure 1.1 Map of London clubs in the St James's area 1832–68, including all the political clubs.
Source: Author's research, overlaid on Richard Bowles, *Plan of Pall Mall, St James's Square, etc*, in Fagan, *The Reform Club, 1836–1886*, p. 9.

The Traditional Clubs

There are numerous accounts of the origins of the earliest clubs and societies, yet beyond Peter Clark's major study and Valérie Capdeville's scholarship, there is little by way of historiography offering different interpretations for the *raison d'etre* of the earliest clubs.[5] It is almost universally accepted that they were primarily social institutions, although the standard journalistic accounts have taken at face value the claim that early clubs evolved from 'chocolate houses' – whilst this was technically true, it overlooks that such a description was often a euphemism for the legitimate front operation of these clubs, concealing the illegal gambling which went on in the back rooms, out of sight of the shop or coffee room which dominated the facade. The legal standing of being a private members' club thus complicated matters for authorities seeking to raid establishments where gambling was suspected of taking place. Gambling remained illegal throughout this period and, until the Gaming Act 1845 made it easier for authorities to shut gaming houses down, the popularity of gambling continued to be a major factor in the growth of clubs, where such activities could take place with added discretion.[6]

White's is generally accepted to be London's oldest club, but even the universally-cited 1693 foundation date is misleading; it would be more accurate to record that today's White's is the London club with the earliest roots, for it only gradually evolved into a club in the mid-eighteenth century.[7] The White's precursor shop moved between different premises along St James's Street in its first few decades, finally settling on the present location in 1755.[8] It is usually presented as a Tory heartland; an assertion which is challenged through much of this book.[9] The standard caricature of White's as a home of Pittites, and Brooks's opposite as a rival haven for Foxites overlooks the fact that both Pitt and Fox had in fact been members of both clubs.[10] (For that matter, Fox also belonged to Boodle's, which had no overt political ties.)[11] Neither Brooks's nor White's originally had any professed politics – their original apolitical character was preserved for decades, and the anonymous authors of the first history of White's believed that, as late as 1781, the club 'still preserved its character for neutrality in politics'.[12] Such speculation sounds plausible, even if the extrapolation of a later White's historian of 'Whigs and Tories living together quite happily' sounds exaggerated.[13] The anonymous authors of the first White's history cite Pitt the Younger's 'use of the club as a place of meeting with his supporters' as the turning point in its politicisation, and the driving force for Charles James Fox's alienation from the club, and his turning to Brooks's for meetings of his Whig supporters.[14]

Between the age of Pitt and the onset of the Great Reform Act, White's' link to Conservative politics was extremely informal. An anonymous member interviewed by the *News and Sunday Herald* recalled in 1835 'White's was formerly, and indeed until three or four years ago, the grand rendezvous of the Tory party', the word 'rendezvous' being an interesting distinction, emphasising the club's value as a venue rather than as an organisation.[15] By the 1830s, the conservatism of its membership was in doubt, and Thomas Raikes complained in 1832 that 'Brookes's [sic] ... is purely a Whig reunion [but] ... White's, which was formerly devoted to the other side, being now of no colour, [is] frequented indiscriminately by all.' Subsequent historians have largely agreed with this verdict, with Robert Stewart writing that by the 1830s it had 'lost most of its political flavour.'[16] If this was the case, then the practicality of White's as a venue would have been compromised.

The anonymous member from 1835 described it as 'more of a Club of political gossip and private scandal than a gambling Club'.[17]

White's' rival, the oldest of the Liberal-affiliated clubs, was Brooks's, which was founded in 1764, and has since 1778 been located almost opposite White's on the west side of St James's Street. G. O. Trevelyan wrote that Brooks's, 'the most famous political club that will have ever existed in England ... was not political in origin'.[18] The club's first official history noted that as with White's, its focus 'certainly for the first forty years of its existence, was the unlimited gambling which there prevailed'.[19] Its reputation for Whiggery came through its association with Fox, something which was emphasised in late eighteenth century popular representations of the club. (Figure 1.2) What has been written of politics at Brooks's has tended to focus on the club's Foxite connections, as with John Timbs, who wrote the longest of any of his accounts of London clubs on Brooks's, dedicating over half of it to incidents involving Fox.[20] By the onset of Reform, the Foxite personality cult was strong at the Club, which hosted a dining society of Foxite MPs memorialising their late lamented icon, the Fox Club.

Whilst the political connection at White's waned with time, it seemed to grow stronger at Brooks's. 'The 1830s saw the apotheosis of Brooks's as a political club', asserts Philip Ziegler in his study of the club's involvement in the Reform Bill. He argues that the framing of the Bill, and the subsequent decade of Whig supremacy, led to the optimum involvement of the Club in cabinet (but not parliamentary) politics, citing Clarendon's protest that one might as well go to Brooks's as a cabinet meeting, as they amounted to the same thing.[21] Certainly, nineteen out of the twenty-one members of Earl Grey's cabinet were members.[22]

A noticeable characteristic of the pre-Reform Act clubs, both political and apolitical, was their modest size. Early clubhouses varied from the small converted townhouse (i.e. White's) to the purpose-built construction in the image of a townhouse (i.e. Arthur's, Boodle's, Brooks's, Crockford's and the Travellers' Club). Even the largest rooms in such buildings, like the first-floor Subscription Room of Brooks's, were not conducive to large-scale political meetings, being relatively cramped, and more likely to be set aside for gambling or dining than politics.

Amongst the nearby clubs which flourished in the late eighteenth and early nineteenth centuries were Arthur's, Boodle's and Crockford's – all popular with parliamentarians. Despite numerous references to

Figure 1.2 James Gillray, *Promis'd Horrors of the French Invasion* (1796) depicting a Fox-led army from Brooks's on the right invading White's on the left, flagellating Pitt the Younger, and absconding with private wealth. Gillray, who lived on St James's Street, frequently referenced clubs in his work.

Source: James Gillray, *Promis'd Horrors of the French Invasion, or Forcible Reasons for Negotiating a Regicide Peace* (London: Hannah Humphrey, 20 October 1796)

significant political members in the eighteenth century, there are relatively few instances of their having had any political impact in the post-Reform era, their main interest being as venues for gossip.[23] Conservative MP William Mackworth Praed recorded how Boodle's, a social club founded in 1762, was part of the nineteenth century parliamentary world, but in a purely apolitical sense, with his rhyme,

> In Parliament I fill my seat,
> With many other noodles;
> And lay my head in Jermyn Street,
> And sip my hock at Boodle's.[24]

One exception to the marginal importance of apolitical clubs was the Union Club. Its foundation in 1799 was to have far-reaching consequences for the independence of all clubs. Despite the Club being apolitical in the period covered here, its name marked a time 'when the Union of Parliaments ... was in agitation'.[25] Until the Union Club came into being, all clubs had been proprietary; their premises being leased from a landlord who drew a profit from the running of such clubs, and members had a legal status akin to tenants. The Union Club was the first club to own the freehold of its premises, and each of its members also became a shareholder.[26] Almost all the political clubs followed suit, although it was still the norm for establishments such as the Carlton, Reform and National Clubs to rent interim premises for their first few years until their purpose-built premises were completed. Some of the short-lived clubs which closed after only a couple of years – namely the Westminster Reform Club and the Free Trade Club – did not last long enough to realise their ambition to move out of rented accommodation. Such was the extent that club ownership of premises became the norm that even the longest-standing proprietary clubs eventually raised the funds among members to 'buy out' the freehold of their premises and belatedly became members' clubs, as happened with Brooks's in 1880, White's in 1891, and Boodle's in 1896.[27]

The nineteenth-century switch from proprietary clubs to members' clubs had profound implications for how members related to the newer political clubs. Since members were now shareholders, they had a strong economic incentive to see their club flourish. As Bernard Darwin observed in a 1943 history of Clubland, 'Whatever a club possesses ... there is an immense difference between enjoying these things on sufferance as a guest or owning some minute fraction of them as a member.'[28] Conversely, the collapse and bankruptcy of a club would mean that members were liable to cover club debts – a serious disincentive to establishing new clubs, with Benjamin Disraeli cautiously citing the case of the closure of Crockford's in 1844 (of which he had been a member, left liable for the Club's debts) as a possible reason to *not* establish a Junior Carlton Club in the early 1860s. Indeed, the Junior Carlton Club only achieved adequate backing when it was made clear that members would not be held liable in the event of the Club's collapse.[29] Members also had an economic incentive to keep club membership numbers capped, since increases in club membership would reduce each member's proportion of a club's assets. Increases in membership numbers would also reduce each member's voting strength at open meetings. There were thus strong incentives in place to restrict the number of new members recruited in member-owned clubs. In short, the new model of a club that was owned by the members encouraged its members to behave in a markedly different way to the members of eighteenth century clubs.

The strong influence of the Union Club's example can be traced in the archives of clubs which were founded in the nineteenth century, as newer clubs consciously emulated its structure. When the Reform Club was established in 1836, its founding members read aloud the regulations of the Union Club, and voted clause by clause as to whether to adopt each regulation as their own.[30] It is unlikely that this was an isolated example, for if one compares contemporaneous club rulebooks, one finds the exact phraseology of many rules to be identical.[31] Indeed, as Benjamin B. Cohen has noted, this same pattern was found abroad in British colonies, with newly-established clubs typically adopting 'a modified copy of another club's rules' at their inaugural meeting.[32] Thus whilst the Union Club may not have had any major political role, it had a considerable impact on the emerging shape of the major political clubs of the nineteenth century.

The expansion of clubs began early in the century, in the 1810s and 1820s. The anonymous authors of the first history of White's noted the high number of blackballs registered in rejecting applicants – 'five balls', 'eight balls', and even 'fifteen balls' – and speculated 'We think that the ultra exclusiveness of White's under the Dandies was a protest by those gentlemen against the great expansion of club life which was taking place.'[33] Such an expansion was decidedly apolitical, and as well as the Union Club it encompassed other clubs based around professions and interest groups such as the United Service Club (1815, for senior military officers above the rank of Major or Commander), the Guards' Club (1815, for Guards officers), the Travellers' Club (1819, for travellers to locations over 500 miles from London), the Athenaeum (1824, for those involved in the arts), plus several purely social clubs such as Crockford's and the Wyndham Club (both founded in 1828). Indeed, the expansion of 'apolitical' Clubland can be seen as a delayed response to the expansion of the professions in the late eighteenth century, and the resultant formation of professional groups in the early nineteenth century such as the Institute of Civil Engineers (which received its Royal Charter in 1828). Some professional groups, such as the Law Society on Chancery Lane, formed in 1825, overlapped with the functions of Clubland, even incorporating a short-lived Law Club in the 1830s, while other organisations attempted to straddle the divide as both professional pressure group and club rolled into one, like the Land Surveyors' Club founded in 1834 on Whitehall, which moved to Great George Street in 1837, where it has remained ever since, merging with the Institute of Civil Engineers.[34] Thus whilst the new professional organisations were noticeably club-like, Clubland adapted by embracing the professions in the new clubs of the 1810s and 1820s.

The expansion of clubs after the eighteenth century was also a physical phenomenon, as the boundaries of 'Clubland' moved beyond St James's. St James's Street was a logical home for such establishments as Arthur's, Boodle's, Brooks's, Crockford's and White's, being a well-known thoroughfare through one of London's more affluent districts, where the aristocracy had their grandest London townhouses around St James's and Piccadilly (now almost all long demolished). Clubs rooted in the eighteenth century remained an ill-defined overlap between an inn, coffee house, salon and private home, and so this proximity to the homes of so many members reflected their ambiguous state. As clubs developed more specialist facilities in the nineteenth century, larger clubhouses were required for ever-larger professional groups of members, necessitating large plots of affordable land in central locations close to the established clubs. The *Illustrated London News* remarked in 1844 on the opening of the new Conservative Club, 'until a comparatively recent period, the club-houses of St James's were plain, unostentatious mansions, with little architectural embellishment in contrast with the palatial edifices reared for club-accommodation in the present day.'[35] Conversely, it was admitted by one White's member in 1835 that the establishment of 'The Carlton Club has woefully injured White's ... [because] White's ... has few of the appliances and means of more modern Clubs.'[36]

The redevelopment of Carlton House by King George IV in the 1820s was of immense importance in moulding the shape of Clubland.[37] As J. Mordaunt Crook argues, it 'created an urban vacuum', which was filled in 1827–30 by the construction of Carlton House Terrace on former gardens, and then by the building of a string of clubs on what is now the south side of Pall Mall.[38] It coincided with a boom in club formation, and offered prime real estate close to St James's, in which large new clubhouses could be built. It also coincided with the existence of the Department of Woods, Forests, Land Revenues, Works and Building between 1832 and 1851, still committed to implementing a late eighteenth century legacy of 'redeveloping crown land in London ... at a time of royal extravagance and unprecedented wartime expenditure.'[39] Within barely two decades the Athenaeum, Carlton, Guards, Oxford and Cambridge, Reform, United Service and Travellers' Clubs had all appeared on one side of the street. It is notable that at one time or another, every single building on the south side of Pall Mall (plus many of those on the north) has been a club, something reflected in Figure 1.1, which does not even cover the post-1868 half-century when clubs were largest in number. As Figure 1.3 shows, by the 1840s, one could literally walk past a non-stop procession of clubs on the south side of the street.[40]

Figure 1.3 Thomas Shotter Boys, *The Club-Houses etc., Pall Mall. 1842*
Note that on the right (south) side of the picture, one can see side-by-side (l-r) the United Service, Athenaeum, Travellers', Reform and Carlton Clubs. The vista remains mostly unchanged today, save for the Carlton Club, which is the original building by Sidney Smirke that stood from 1838 to 1854.
Source: Thomas Shotter Boys, *The Club-Houses etc., Pall Mall. 1842* (London: T. S. Boys, 1842).

The Carlton and Reform Clubs

The significance of clubs changed dramatically in the aftermath of the First Reform Act, with the foundation of two rival political clubs, both of which were to dominate subsequent nineteenth century political club discourse: the Carlton Club, and the Reform Club. Both were deemed to be inseparable from their respective parties. Lord Lexden has argued that the Conservative party and the Carlton Club 'were completely fused during the first phase of the Club's existence. Indeed, for some twenty years after its foundation in 1832, the Club was the Party', arguing that despite local differences 'it was the Club which gave the Party its identity at national level'.[41] The Reform Club was similarly often presented as 'a party political headquarters in the organisational sense', for the Liberals.[42] Yet how closely both clubs were related to the Great Reform Act itself has been a matter of some disagreement, with some accounts stressing different factors in their foundation.

Varying accounts exist of the precise timing and purpose of the Carlton Club's origins. The Carlton Club is generally assumed to have held its inaugural meeting on 10 March 1832 at the Thatched House Tavern on St James's Street – that this meeting took place is fairly uncontroversial, as a surviving document sets out the original committee elected at this meeting.[43] With the timing of its inauguration having so closely coincided with the Reform controversy, its foundation is usually cited as a symptom of the Reform Act. Yet Norman Gash argued that it had different roots – he made a case for the Club having been a continuation of the 'Charles Street Gang' of defeated Conservative ministers from the earlier Duke of Wellington ministry.[44] Certainly, this is consistent with contemporary press accounts, which attributed the Charles Street Gang with a pre-Reform Act role in elections in selected constituencies such as Berkshire, Beverley and Cambridge; in the latter in 1831, *The Times* accused the Gang of having 'transferred themselves bodily hither in the persons of their most active members ... who are "at work" in every possible way'.[45] However, these were 'members' in the sense of belonging to an informal group – there is no evidence that the pre-Carlton 'Gang' had the characteristics of a club. Furthermore, the formation of the Carlton Club coincided with the exhaustion of the Charles Street Gang's funds in March 1832, and threats of litigation from an unpaid former staff member, indicating a clear organisational break.[46]

Gash acknowledged the role of 'various discussions in January 1832' in the Carlton's eventual shape, when formed two months later.[47] Gash's interpretation was further elaborated upon by Barry Phelps in his 1982 history of the Carlton, in which he dated the first 'Carlton' meeting as having been on 16 June 1831, and named the group as having consisted of the Duke of Wellington, Chief Whip William Holmes MP, Charles Arbuthnot [an MP until February 1831], Sir Henry Hardinge MP, J. C. Herries MP, and Lord Ellenborough, all hosted by Joseph Planta MP. Phelps asserts that they were hosted by Planta himself, whereas Gash believed that they merely rented Planta's house as an office.[48] However, in the contemporary press, this 1831 gathering did not signify the founding of a new club, but was merely an ongoing gathering of the Charles Street Gang. To these individuals, *Figaro in London* later added in January 1832 the Duke of Cumberland, Lord Eldon, Lord Lyndhurst, Sir James Scarlett MP, Sir Charles Wetherell MP, John Wilson Croker MP, 'and other individuals equally illustrious.'[49] The *Sheffield Independent* repeated all of these names, adding that the Marquis of Londonderry, the Earls of Aberdeen and Harrowby, Lords Eden and Wharncliffe, Alexander Baring MP, Henry Goulburn MP, Sir Robert Inglis MP, Alexander Perceval MP, and William Mackworth Praed MP were also involved.[50] The Gang was thus a highly influential group of Conservatives, most of them having held office under Wellington and/or the first Peel administration. Highlighting the largely ignored role of the Duke of Wellington in the Club's foundation, Gash and Phelps made a case for viewing the Club foundation not as a response to the Reform Act, but as a delayed response to the organisational challenges posed by the collapse of the Duke of Wellington's government in 1830. There is certainly much circumstantial evidence to support this interpretation among press reports of the Charles Street Gang's activities between 1830 and 1832. It also echoes the much earlier insistence by John Timbs in 1866 that the Carlton was founded by Wellington in Charles Street in 1831.[51] Additionally, if one accepts the Carlton as having had roots in the Charles Street Gang, its origins may stretch back further. The *Illustrated Times* in 1856 argued that others

> will tell you that the Carlton Club was founded by the Duke of Wellington in 1831. No such thing. The Carlton Club was founded in 1828, the first year of his Premiership, by the Iron

Duke, in association with the late Sir Robert Peel, the Marquess of Salisbury, the Earl of Jersey, the late Messrs. [Henry] Goulburn and [Sir Henry] Herries, Billy Holmes (so long the Tory Whipper-in), and [F.R.] Bonham, afterwards of the Ordnance, of painful notoriety.[52]

The significance of such lists of principals is in establishing that, from the outset, what evolved into the Carlton Club enjoyed considerable support from senior Tories – unlike the decidedly acrimonious birth of the Reform Club. They also emphasise that what grew into the Carlton most likely had several informal incarnations which preceded the institution's eventual evolution into a political members' club. Such varying accounts over chronology disagree over the exact starting point of the Carlton, but today, 1832 is recognised by the Club itself as its foundation date.[53]

1832 is a plausible foundation date for the Carlton but, fittingly for a Conservative club, its evolution was organic and incremental, both before and after that date. 1832 marked the year in which the first Carlton clubhouse was opened for members, as opposed to the occasional informal meeting largely held in Planta's house. Again, contemporary accounts did not see the opening of a clubhouse as a new departure for the Carlton. Instead, early in the Club's existence *The Times* would refer to 'upwards of 50 members of the Charles Street Gang' meeting at 'their rendezvous in Carlton [House] Terrace'.[54] The premises on Carlton House Terrace (from which the Club took its name) opened in 1832, and were leased from Lord Kensington. They were temporary, with the club terminating its lease over a rental dispute in December 1835 – although contrary to accounts which cite this as having been the only factor for the move, it appears that, as early as April 1834, the Carlton had *already* planned to move out of Kensington's small house in favour of larger purpose-built premises, and the rental dispute affected only the timing of the premature move.[55] From 23 December 1835 it was then housed in rooms in the nearby Carlton Hotel on Waterloo Place until the Club's first purpose-built premises were completed in 1837.[56] None of the surviving accounts of this initial purpose-built clubhouse are particularly flattering, and it is little surprise that after the decidedly palatial Reform Club was completed for the Liberals next door in 1841, the Carlton first expanded its building in 1846, and then demolished it altogether to replace it in 1856 with a new building even larger and grander than the Reform's.[57]

The Carlton Club never had a formal position on the Reform Bill (even though most of its members were opposed to it), which is a curious feature for a Club allegedly founded by the Opposition. Even if one inclines to the view that it was the electoral setbacks of 1830, 1831 and 1832 which were more significant in the Carlton's foundation than the resignation of Wellington's government in 1830, a constant feature throughout both attributed reasons for creating the Carlton is the incentive to regroup and reorganise in the wake of defeat and the loss of office. Whilst there was political activity by the Carlton's founders before 1832, there is no evidence that they turned to formalising their gatherings into a club until January of that year; and when they did so, it was contemporaneous with Reform agitations, yet still preceded the passage of the Reform Act. It can thus be viewed in the context of the recalibration of political organisation which became necessary around the Act – but not as a direct consequence of the Act. Although not explicitly wedded to opposition to Reform, the Carlton's earliest surviving rulebook declared its attachment to 'Conservative principles', committing itself to the Conservative parliamentary cause – a logical objective in a club founded over Conservative defeat.[58]

The Carlton Club's neighbour and great rival the Reform Club, also allegedly tied to currents of Reform, has possibly the most heavily-contested historiography of any political club foundation. Unlike the Carlton, the basic chronology is uncontested – the Club opened its doors in April 1836 in a temporary clubhouse on the site of the present building in Pall Mall. In 1838, it moved to Gwydir House (now the Welsh Office) on Whitehall for the three years that it took to construct its current building, which has remained open since April 1841. J. Mordaunt Crook, in his study of the Victorian *nouveaux riches*, contrasts the membership of the Carlton ('aristocratic, professional or plutocratic, generally capitalist and imperialist, but above all establish-mentarian ... many were landed men ... the membership list of 1836 was still dominated by the landed aristocracy and gentry; four dukes, five marquesses, seven earls, and half the squirearchy of England') with that of the Reform: 'not exactly exclusive ... the Reform Club's "back-benchers" contain[ed] a striking proportion of parvenu business men', and notes that the latter's membership symbolised the evolving Liberal party's uneasy coalition of utilitarianism and collectivism.[59] To this, it can be added that whilst the Carlton's initial membership resembled that of the eighteenth century clubs, the Reform Club more closely resembled the newer professional clubs of the early nineteenth century.

More fiercely disputed are the motives and personalities involved in the Reform Club's origins. The version of events most widely disseminated originated with Louis Fagan's 1887 account of the Reform Club's history, which credited the Whig Whip Edward Ellice as 'the founder of the Reform Club'.[60] Yet despite this account having been superseded, Fagan's original version has remained widely quoted, with accounts such as those of Mordaunt Crook and Anthony Lejeune repeating Fagan's assertion that the Club owed its existence to Ellice's efforts.[61] The Reform Club celebrated its centenary in 1936 by commemorating Ellice as its founder, and even the configuration of the Reform Club's artwork today lends some credence to this, with Ellice's portrait prominently displayed in the main gallery.[62]

In fact, Ellice's alleged enthusiasm for the Club was disproved as early as 1906 with the publication of the Earl of Durham's letters. These portrayed a very different sequence of events, with the Club being the brainchild of Durham as a means of uniting Radical MPs. Durham's letters showed Ellice (along with Lord Stanley) to have been actively involved in attempts to avert the Reform Club's creation altogether, seeing it as a challenge to the Whigs in Parliament. It was only after a meeting with Sir William Molesworth and Joseph Parkes that Ellice gave his blessing to the project, and even then with some reluctance.[63]

As for the rationale behind the Reform Club, numerous reasons have been given. None of the reasons is mutually exclusive, but their relative importance is unclear. Firstly, there is the statement set out in the Club's founding resolution of 8 February 1836, at a meeting in Ellice's house at 14 Carlton Terrace. It resolved 'That a Club be formed to comprise all classes of Reformers', understandably fuelling the debate over foundation in Ellice's favour.[64] It is only when viewed in conjunction with the letters of Durham and Ellice that it becomes apparent this statement was the somewhat fudged outcome of a compromise, rather than an enthusiastic statement.

The second possible rationale is not explicitly stated anywhere, but is repeatedly inferred in recording the deep divisions in Brooks's at the time, implying that the Club was intended to supersede Brooks's.[65] If so, it did not wholly succeed in this, for Jonathan Parry observes that it 'never supplanted more familiar meeting-places like Brooks's'.[66] As an explanation for the creation of the new club, this does not quite ring true, since numerous well-known Radicals – including Daniel O'Connell, who was a founder member of the Reform Club – were already members of Brooks's and, as we shall see, there was in fact considerable overlap in the memberships of Brooks's and the Reform, and this continued for decades.

More convincing is the explanation that the Reform Club was an attempt to rival the Carlton Club. Just as the Carlton can be viewed in the context of wide-scale Conservative recalibration after the Reform Act, both ideologically (in redefining as 'Conservatives' rather than 'Tories'), and organisationally, so the Reform Club can be seen in the context of changes in Whig and Radical organisation in the 1830s, from the formation of the Political Unions by Radical Reformers, to the reassertion of aristocratic Whiggery in government after 1830. These were separate developments for Whigs and Radicals, and so in this context, the Reform Club's inception as a club encompassing all factions of Reform made it a unique institution in the post-Reform environment.

A further theory about the Reform Club's origins was proposed by David A. Haury. Acknowledging the common misattribution of Ellice as the Club's founder, Haury also sought to downplay Durham's role, and instead argued that Philosophic Radicals, particularly Joseph Hume, played a leading role. He wrote that 'The Radicals sought to improve their organisation in order to enhance their bargaining position with the Whigs. Several efforts of the Philosophic Radicals in the early 1830s to form a political club had failed', which was presumably a reference to the failed Westminster Reform Club, although Haury does not specify this. He added that 'The club actually evolved out of an initiative by the Philosophic Radicals, who at first hoped to attract all Radical and Liberal members of the Reform party and to isolate the Whigs, who would be excluded from the club. Eventually, and not without bitterness, they agreed to allow Whigs to join the club.'[67] There are two problems with this interpretation. The first is that it involves accepting Gash's view that the Westminster Reform Club *was* a first attempt at a Reform Club, rather than an unrelated phenomenon (see below). The second is that it underestimates the degree of Whig engagement with the Reform Club from its launch. Whatever Ellice's initial reluctance to give the enterprise his blessing, Edward J. Stanley was active from the Club's launch as a recruiting sergeant for Whig MPs.[68]

The final explanation posited is that the Reform Club was some form of successor to the short-lived Westminster Reform Club (WRC), and can be seen as a resurrected incarnation of that club.[69] The grounds for projecting direct continuity from one club to the other are doubtful. The 1,400-member Reform Club embracing Liberals of all factions was a far larger body than the 105-member WRC which was almost exclusively Radical in composition.[70] The members of the WRC were also reputedly overwhelmingly Irish.[71] The Reform Club's launch coincided with the collapse of the WRC, with the result that many of the older, smaller club's members moved to the newer club, but the wholly different scale of the new club meant that the Radicals of the WRC were hugely outnumbered by other members of the new Reform Club.

The Westminster Reform Club has largely evaded study, yet its short and largely unhappy history makes a stark contrast with the more successful Reform Club, and provides clues as to why the post-Reform Act clubs were noticeably larger than their forebears. The Westminster Reform Club was originally formed by a gathering of Radical MPs. The Club's own minute book dates its first meeting on 10 March 1834, and subsequent accounts accepted this.[72] It was initially styled the Westminster Club, before becoming the Westminster Reform Club at the suggestion of Joseph Hume MP.[73] In fact, discussions of launching the Westminster Club dated back to April 1833 at a meeting in the house of the Radical MP Charles Tennyson d'Eyncourt. (A further reason to doubt continuity between the two clubs is that d'Eyncourt was a founder member of the Westminster Reform Club, but did not join the Reform Club until 1843.)[74] The Club took nearly a year to launch; and even though it had already identified a suitable townhouse on Great George Street, close to Parliament, prospective members feared that this would not be an appropriate location outside of the parliamentary session, and were already divided as to whether it was to be a political club, or 'merely one for eating and drinking'.[75] The *Satirist* described it as 'a kind of antagonist to the Conservative [Carlton] Club, a re-union of the liberals...to combine political as well as social purposes'.[76] Throughout its two year lifespan, the club rented the lower two floors of the townhouse of Alderman Charles Wood MP at 24 Great George Street, a few hundred metres from Parliament, for 650 guineas a year.[77]

Alderman Wood was a far from ideal landlord, and the Club complained to him about everything from 'deficiencies' in the 'unfurnished state of the house', to a plaque on the front door brandishing Wood's name rather than the Club's.[78] The Club never realised its early ambition to be a mass-membership establishment, as signified by its early resolution 'that its Members be not limited to any definite number.'[79] It offered MPs among the membership the priority use of the Club's main drawing room, with the result that it had a limited appeal outside MPs, with less than a third of its 105 members *not* being MPs.[80] It is difficult to imagine non-parliamentary members wanting to pay a full subscription for a political club whose drawing room they were banished from whenever Parliament sat. Unlike most other political clubs described here, it is not recorded to have recruited a single peer; given the Earl of Durham's central role as cheerleader for a broad Reform Club, this is a further reason to doubt any continuity between the two clubs.[81]

More seriously, the Westminster Reform Club's handling of its own finances seems to have been woeful. Its outgoings were considerable, and were unmatched by its income. On 23 May 1835, the club had £253 18s 9d in savings, compared to £1,315 9s 10d in outstanding debts.[82] The situation only grew worse, and a tone of desperation was noticeable as the Club resolved the following month to increase its membership, to little effect.[83] By 30 March 1836, the Club's debts had risen to nearly £1,500, and the committee voted to disband the Club, making an appeal to members for contributions to settle its debts. The Club's doors closed to members on 23 April 1836 – days after the Reform Club opened on Pall Mall – but its committee continued to meet until 9 May 1838, to settle its debts.[84] The superficial resemblance of the Club's name to the Reform Club, the timing of its closure just after the Reform Club opened, and the donation of its minute books to the Reform, all appear to have contributed to the misapprehension that it had something to do with the newer club.[85]

Whilst the post-Reform Act clubs themselves may have been a response to the electoral reorganisation necessitated by Reform, there is no evidence that the larger club *memberships* of the new political clubs were any kind of a response to the Reform Act. Instead, there is some evidence that larger club sizes were borne out of financial considerations. The Westminster Reform Club provides an illustration of why the nineteenth-century political clubs took the larger shape they did, with memberships of between one and two thousand, compared to traditional clubs like Boodle's, Brooks's and White's, which maintained memberships around five hundred. Since the 1820s, clubs like the Athenaeum, the Travellers' and the Union had all occupied increasingly large and expensive premises. Members of newer clubs increasingly came to expect such vast, prestigious purpose-built premises, yet the experience of the WRC showed that even the costs of a relatively modest club occupying two floors of a small townhouse were far larger than could be covered by a small membership. Accordingly, one of the main pressures for larger membership was financial, in order to generate the income necessary for the additional expenditure of building and maintaining ever-larger club facilities.

Interest in the Westminster Reform Club has evaded all of these issues, and been almost entirely limited to the short-lived and anomalous membership of Benjamin Disraeli, first publicised during the 1835 Taunton by-election (see Chapter 6), later recounted by W. Fraser Rae in 1878, and subsequently retold by Louis Fagan when rebutting the common Victorian perception that Disraeli had been a member of the Reform Club.[86] Surprisingly, for such an oft-retold anecdote, none of the printed versions entirely tally with the original version in the Club's minute book. According to this, Disraeli signed up for the Club early in its foundation, before the character of its politics were widely known. He was elected on 2 July 1834, proposed by Liberal MP Henry Lytton Bulwer and seconded by Dr. J. Ellmore. Disraeli was one of several members who never paid their subscriptions and, after multiple reminders about this, on 14 March 1835 he enclosed a cheque for his overdue subscription of £15 15s with a letter of resignation which cited pressing social engagements which prevented him from using the Club. (No mention of politics was made in the letter.) The Club returned his cheque, insulted by the slight.[87] Whilst the tale is entertaining, it does little other than illustrate the poor record of some members in paying their club subscriptions.

Worries about subscriptions, and the dependence of clubs on them, were rife amongst the fledgling new organisations, as illustrated by the experience of the Charles Street office that was the forerunner of the Carlton Club. Whilst not a club in the strictest sense, Norman Gash observed that one of its main shortcomings was its reliance on subscriptions for the office's rent, and 'that as a permanent establishment it called for recurrent subscriptions at a rate that could not be maintained in the absence of any personal advantage to the subscribers.'[88] The new clubs, with their carefully-defined memberships that were linked to tangible membership benefits, could be far more effective at ensuring a steady stream of subscriptions were paid.

Political Clubs after the Carlton and Reform

None of the subsequent political clubs played as important a political role as the Carlton and Reform Clubs, yet several more were founded between the 1840s and 1860s for a variety of reasons. This pattern contradicts Antonia Taddei's analysis of statistical trends in post-1870 clubs, in which she notes the apparent absence of clubs formed between 1840 and 1864, and speculates that this lull in club foundations was the by-product of 'vague' party distinctions (a point which would surely be just as true before 1840, if not more so), and there being 'no political reform' in those years (despite Reform remaining on the political agenda, with numerous bills being presented before the successful passage of one in 1867).[89] Taddei had reached the impression of a gap because of the nature of the source material used – she was reliant on club listings in almanacs after the 1870s. Several 1840s clubs such as the Free Trade Club were short-lived, whilst others which *did* survive into the 1870s, including the Conservative and National Clubs, were not deemed prestigious enough to be listed in almanacs – a good indication of their marginalisation in later years.

Most of these post-1830s political clubs were Conservative. The first was the appropriately-named Conservative Club, founded in 1840. This appears to have almost entirely been created due to demand for the oversubscribed Carlton. The Club suffered from a reputation for marginalisation, with John Timbs recording that even its highest-profile trustee 'Sir Robert Peel is said never to have entered this club-house except to view the interior.'[90] Indeed, such was its relative obscurity that Charles Greville wrote a letter to *The Times* in 1854 inadvertently confusing it with the Carlton Club; he confessed in his diary 'I had imagined the two clubs were the same.'[91] (Confusingly, before the Conservative Club was founded, the Carlton Club had been informally known for much of the 1830s as 'the Conservative Club'.) From 1845, the Club was housed in an imposing building on St James's Street, close to the junction with Pall Mall, on the site of the demolished Thatched House Club (see below).[92] The minutes of the Carlton Club indicate that this site was first offered to the Carlton for use as a second club-house, but that a special meeting of the Carlton's committee on 29 February 1840 decided that, in view of the sum requested, 'it is not expedient to enter into any negotiations with Mr. Willis for the purchase of his premises'.[93] It was only thereafter that the premises were bought for the new Club, and were developed into a separate, breakaway club. The Conservative Club does not appear to have played any political or organisational role, and seems to have been far more of a social club for Conservatives, with MPs holding a range of views on touchstone issues like free trade. Its primary historical interest lies as an indicator of its members being out of favour with mainstream conservatism.[94]

A subsequent Conservative club of significance was the Junior Carlton, an altogether more politicised endeavour. Like the Conservative Club, most accounts agree that it was a response to the spiralling waiting list of the Carlton, but a key difference lay in its having received the blessing of the Carlton, whose Committee noted in 1864 that 'Having considered the prospectus of a new political club, to be called the Junior Carlton, [the Committee] do most cordially approve of the project, and will give it every assistance in its power.'[95] Indeed, the Junior Carlton was the brainchild of many of the Carlton's most prominent members. Its trustees were the Earls of Derby and Malmesbury, Lord Colville, Disraeli, and the Conservative Chief Whip Colonel Thomas Edward Taylor.[96] Its creation had long been discussed, and finally proceeded in February 1864. The Club was even more explicitly tied to the Conservative organisation than the Carlton; while the Carlton merely required members to declare 'Conservative principles' (a situation that had led to MPs no longer taking the Conservative whip still retaining their membership of the Carlton), the Junior Carlton specified that members 'must profess Conservative principles, and acknowledge the recognised leaders of the Conservative party'.[97] The Junior Carlton's records – which survive almost intact, yet have never been cited in print – indicate that the Club played an active role in politics in at least its first decade. The tone of several minutes strongly implies that the Club aimed to supplant the Carlton in numerous electoral activities, after the Carlton suffered setbacks in being publicly implicated in electoral corruption; a situation which will be discussed in more detail in Chapter 6. From 1864, the Club was housed in temporary quarters at 16 Regent Street, until the completion of its palatial clubhouse in 1869, almost directly opposite the Carlton Club on Pall Mall (which necessitated the demolition of the St James's Theatre as well as the purchase of several neighbouring houses). It contained 2,000 members and dwarfed every other club building up to that time.[98]

Of the remaining political clubs with MPs among their members, several were far more closely aligned to a strongly held position on a single issue than to a broad party position. The National Club and the Free Trade Club, both founded in 1845, were organisational responses to the controversies over Maynooth and the Corn Laws. The existence of such clubs tells us not only about the totemic significance of these two issues, but also indicates that, at least as late as the 1840s, the demand for such single-issue political clubs meant that MPs who were already members of the better-known Carlton and Reform Clubs still joined these smaller, more specific clubs. It is also intriguing that with their strong allegiance to one side of their respective debates, there was never any rival club that was either pro-Maynooth or pro-Corn Law; a state of affairs which cannot easily be explained, unless one accepts that these sentiments were already well catered for in existing clubs. The National and Free Trade Clubs have long escaped sustained analysis from historians, with John Wolffe's recognition of the National Club's importance in the light of the mid-nineteenth-century 'Protestant crusade' being a rare exception.[99] Despite considerable contemporary press coverage of its foundation and proceedings, the Free Trade Club has all but escaped detection by historians.[100]

The more successful of the pair was the National Club, which still exists today, albeit as a dining club for conservative Anglicans, hosted within the Carlton Club. It was built on a reasonably modest scale, never extending to more than 500 members in the 1860s, and well over half of its membership consisted of Anglican clergy, yet it was on the political stage that it remained outspoken. During this period, the clubhouse was closer to Westminster than any other (until 1852 it was based inside New Palace Yard itself, and thereafter on Whitehall Gardens), and it offered the use of its facilities for MPs and peers wishing to raise Protestant issues in Parliament. It made several early attempts at setting up a network of constituency associations directly answerable to the

Club, and whilst these were largely unsuccessful, their ambitiousness in developing a central political organisation from a London club foreshadowed later developments.[101] Although the Club's hard-line approach to Catholic emancipation, Jewish emancipation, and the use of state money for Catholic education ensured that it would retain some following among Conservatives, the Club also enjoyed support from some Liberals, and it overtly stressed that it never sought to endorse any one particular party, vowing that 'In the debated questions of party or commercial politics, the National Club takes no part; on these, therefore, the Committee offer no opinion.'[102] The Club was by no means successful at fulfilling its stated aim of recruiting Protestant MPs who primarily saw politics through the prism of defending Anglican institutions. MPs such as Lord Robert Pelham-Clinton, who described himself to *Dod's Parliamentary Companion* as an 'unflinching friend to our Protestant institutions', never joined.[103] This was symptomatic of the Club's often intemperate rhetoric, for while the substance of its views were broadly within the mainstream of conservative opinion, pronouncements such as an 1851 letter condemning clergy for innovations in ritual had a tendency to alienate support from the very groups to which the Club hoped to reach out.[104] Nonetheless, the Club did succeed in sustaining a rump of parliamentary support, with MPs such as Charles Newdegate, Richard Spooner and J. C. Colquhoun using the Club as a political base in denouncing the perceived encroachment of Catholicism (and later Judaism) on 'the Christian character of the legislature'.[105]

Less successful than the National Club was the short-lived Free Trade Club, which folded in 1849, only four years after its foundation. The Club spent its first two years on Regent Street, and then from 1847 rented the house of Lord Clanricarde in St James's Square, which had also been rented out to several apolitical clubs both before and after its Free Trade incarnation.[106] In parallel to the National Club's loose affiliation to the Conservative cause, the Club was never explicitly linked to the Liberals in Parliament, but having been founded by Richard Cobden it was mostly composed of Liberal Free Traders including John Bright and Charles Villiers, whilst excluding Peelite Free Traders such as Gladstone. Like the Westminster Reform Club, its membership seems to have been of a Radical disposition, and much of the contemporary press coverage of it adopted a sneering tone. *Blackwood's Magazine* revelled in the closure of 'this mangy establishment ... great is the joy of the denizens of St James's Square at being relieved from the visitations of the crew that haunted its ungarnished halls'.[107] Its dissolution occurred abruptly, being notionally concealed by its replacement in September 1849 with a 'National Reform Club', which lasted less than four months.[108] Almost two decades after its closure, a Cobden Club was formed in 1866, going on to act as a rallying point for free trade radicalism well into the twentieth century, and becoming prolific in pamphleteering; yet despite often being regarded as a 'club' by parliamentary almanacs, it had no premises of its own, and so was not a club in the sense of the establishments discussed here.[109]

Aside from the Free Trade Club's short life, there were no new Liberal-affiliated clubs founded in London to parallel the creation of the Conservative and Junior Carlton Clubs. Despite some extended talk of a 'Junior Reform Club' through much of the 1860s, this was not belatedly realised until the 1870s, when it was founded as the Devonshire Club in November 1874.[110] There is no obvious reason for this lack of impetus, but one might speculate that much as Reform had necessitated a recalibration of party political machinery, so the loss of office after the electoral defeat of 1874 provided a strong motive for political reorganisation – including in Clubland. This explanation is consistent with the Carlton Club having been founded after the fall of Wellington's government, the Reform Club after Melbourne's majority was severely slashed in 1835, and the Junior Carlton after the Conservatives had been in opposition for five years in 1864. While it is difficult to prove that these club formations were a direct outcome of election results, they can be viewed as an indirect consequence of the composition of Parliament. A comparable pattern could be observed continuing until at least the 1880s, with the Devonshire Club founded after the Liberal defeat of 1874 and the Conservative-affiliated Constitutional Club being founded during the opposition year of 1883. Yet the pattern does not fit every case, and so cannot be seen as the sole determinant of club foundations: when the Conservative Club was founded in 1840, expectations were high that the party would soon return to office. The National Club of 1845 and the Free Trade Club of 1846 were both symptomatic of the massive upheavals caused by Maynooth and free trade, yet both were founded whilst their affiliated parties were in office. Post-electoral defeat reorganisation could have contributed a motive to club foundation, but offers no easy explanation for the growth of clubs. A further non-political factor, the creation of new clubs to avoid the lengthy waiting lists in existing clubs, will be addressed in the next chapter.

Politics in 'Apolitical' Clubs, 1832–68

Whilst this book focuses on political clubs, political activity was also present to some extent in several ostensibly apolitical clubs. That politics was a staple of supposedly apolitical clubs is evidenced by such accounts as that of James Smith, a member of the apolitical Union Club, who described a typical day there in 1853:

> At three o'clock I walk to the Union Club, read the journals, hear Lord John Russell deified or diablerised, do the same with Sir Robert Peel or the Duke of Wellington, and then join a knot of conversationists by the fire till six o'clock. We then and there discuss the Three per Cent Consols [sic] (some of us preferring Dutch Two-and-a-half per Cents.), and speculate upon the probable rise, shape, and cost of the New Exchange...when politics happen[s] to be discussed, [we] rally Whigs, Radicals, and Conservatives alternately, but never seriously, such subjects having a tendency to create acrimony.[111]

Similarly, the bearing of political grudges in ostensibly apolitical clubs was not uncommon – at least one prospective member's blackballing from the Union Club in 1832 was credited to 'a variety of placemen and others of the old Charles-street-gang' on the grounds that the applicant favoured the Reform Bill.[112] Whilst it would be impossible to adequately detail all of the apolitical clubs of London in this period, it is worth noting that two such clubs, the Athenaeum and the Travellers' Club, were particularly popular with MPs, being the clubs with the fifth and sixth largest number of MPs, behind four political clubs.[113]

Explaining the popularity of these two clubs amongst MPs is problematic, but both were regarded as exceptionally prestigious, and their memberships tended to be socially well-connected. Both occupied prime sites on Pall Mall, the Travellers' Club being founded in 1819 and the Athenaeum in 1824. Both of them were strongly influential on subsequent club-house design.[114] The Athenaeum in particular, as the first club to be built around a large central lobby, and as a club-house with far larger rooms than most of its forbears, and blessed with the largest private library of its day, was perennially oversubscribed.[115] Caroline Shenton has linked the Athenaeum's creation with the demands of one of its founders, John Wilson Croker MP, for more accommodation for parliamentarians, but this does not fully explain the Club's popularity as the Club did not actually contain any accommodation until the construction of an additional floor in the 1850s and, by that time, both the Carlton and Reform Clubs had been offering MPs overnight accommodation for some years.[116] The popularity of the Travellers' Club amongst MPs may be attributed to its entry requirement that all candidates must have travelled to a location at least 500 miles from London. This automatically meant that the Club consisted disproportionately of aristocratic men, since a simple 'Grand Tour' of Italy would have qualified someone for membership.[117]

In addition to these clubs, there were numerous apolitical clubs which contained several dozen MPs between the first two Reform Acts. The remaining ones which tallied over fifty MPs were the United University Club, the Oxford and Cambridge Club, the United Service Club, Boodle's and Arthur's.[118] The first two, though independent of one another, were related: the United University Club had been founded in 1822 for graduates of both English universities then in existence, Oxford and Cambridge.[119] One of the benefactors of its new building in the 1830s was the young W. E. Gladstone, who sponsored pews in the local church so that club servants could attend services, and continued to correspond from the club well into the 1860s.[120] As the club became oversubscribed, a second club was established in 1829 to deal with the overflow, the less prestigious Oxford and Cambridge Club.[121]

Some MPs with military backgrounds conformed to the stereotype of belonging to military clubs, including the Guards Club (founded in 1815), the Junior United Service Club (1828) and the Army and Navy Club (1837); yet in each case, the number of MP members per club was small. The one military club to have had a sizeable parliamentary presence, the United Service Club, had been founded in 1815, and was informally known as 'the Senior' Club for its criteria of admitting only senior officers ranking above Commander or Major.

The remaining popular clubs with MPs fit into the apolitical social mould of eighteenth century clubs. Boodle's, which dates to 1762 and faces Brooks's, has largely been free of politics since the turn of the nineteenth century (though it remains understudied in general); while Arthur's, a gambling club founded in 1827, resembled the clubs of the eighteenth century, and contained a similar aristocratic clientele.[122]

When new clubs were being created, they were keen to list as many influential figures as possible as patrons and founder members, so as to rapidly establish their prestige. Browsing the names of founder members can thus be highly misleading, suggesting a greater degree of political overlap and influence than was actually the case. For instance, founder member MPs included Sir George De Lacy Evans at the Oriental Club, the Marquess of Hartington at the Garrick Club, and John Masterman at the City of London Club.[123] Yet none of these was a club with any documented political role (the Oriental Club was for East India Company officers, the Garrick for those interested in the arts, and the City of London for those with financial interests), and in each case, the actual number of MPs who belonged to these clubs was extremely low. It is thus only through a comprehensive study of the club memberships of all 2,588 MPs who sat from 1832–68 – undertaken in the following chapter – that it is possible to fully appreciate the extent of the overlap between clubs and members of the House of Commons.

Finally, it should be noted that not all of Clubland overlapped with the parliamentary world. Some clubs contained no MPs. These tended to be newer, apolitical clubs built on a smaller scale. The East India United Service Club founded in 1849, for example, catered for officers of the East India Company and those with Indian service connections, overlapping with the Oriental Club founded by the Duke of Wellington twenty-six years earlier for exactly the same purpose, and it had no MPs in this period. Likewise, for all its subsequent aristocratic appeal in the twentieth century, Pratt's seems not to have enticed a single MP through its doors in the eleven years after its 1857 foundation.[124] Similarly, with the wealth of well-established and well-located military clubs all existing in the shadow of the United Service Club, the creation of a new Naval and Military Club in 1862 did not inspire any MPs to join until after the Second Reform Act.

More complex were the cases when MPs probably did belong to a club, but there has been a lack of surviving records, which has made it difficult to assess the political impact of such a club. Aside from instances of lost archives, sometimes MPs did not wish to draw attention to their club membership. Certain clubs, such as the Cocoa Tree had a double-edged reputation as a 'fashionable hell'.[125] Not a single MP is on record as having publicly admitted to membership of the popular Cocoa Tree Club – an understandable situation, given its louche reputation, and its being the only club in St James's to incorporate a brothel into the premises.[126] The National Club suffered from a reputation for political extremism, and so only a third of its MPs publicly admitted to membership in *Dod's Parliamentary Companion*, compared to over two-thirds of MPs at the Carlton Club admitting their membership to *Dod's*.[127]

Conclusion

The physical and geographical expression of 'Clubland' clearly predated the political environment of the Reform Act, and was simply the latest stage in the evolution of centuries of changing cultural norms and habits among those whose social life revolved around the St James's district. Yet despite clearly non-political roots in such shared activities as gambling, conversation, and drinking both coffee and alcohol, the shape of these social activities was to have a profound effect on the form of political clubs of the nineteenth century.

Political reorganisation after the First Reform Act paved the way for the first purpose-built political clubs. These cannot be examined in isolation, but must be viewed in the context of the traditional clubs that lent the St James's district much of its prestige, and the newer wave of professional clubs (and organisations) which began proliferating from the 1820s. With the exception of the Westminster Reform Club and the National Club – both of which were politically and socially marginalised and located themselves off Parliament Square – the new political clubs located themselves in the heart of existing Clubland. Thus by the mid-nineteenth century, St James's had become a distinctive space in central London, filled with ostensibly private clubs, in which hundreds of members would share semi-public, semi-private space. The uses of that space will be examined in Chapter 4, but the very relationship which MPs had to that space owes much to the growing wave of professional organisations, the accompanying growth in Clubland and, crucially, the precedent of members-owned clubs set by the Union Club. This precedent was paramount in setting a tone of entitlement and engagement with the club as a unique space; one which would be essential in how MPs treated their clubs, particularly after the Great Fire of 1834 was to necessitate parliamentarians becoming more reliant on Clubland.

CHAPTER 2

CLUBS AND THE MPS' WORLD I: A QUANTITATIVE ANALYSIS

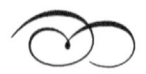

Aims and Approach

This chapter seeks to address, through the use of quantitative analysis, the question of how widely Members of Parliament used their clubs, and how well-represented MPs were in key clubs. Contemporary political literature is replete with references to the supposed importance (or lack thereof) of individual London clubs; but the intention here is to analyse the club memberships of MPs. Whilst Chapter 4 will focus on the mechanics of MPs' use of clubs with illustrative examples, this chapter seeks be the first ever quantitative analysis of the trends involved.

Quantitative approaches to history are nothing new, and their application to parliamentary history is particularly apt. Ever since sociologist W. O. Aydelotte's pioneering work in the 1950s and 1960s, using early computers to analyse parliamentary division lists in the 1840s, historians have sought to use quantitative techniques to analyse the febrile party political environment of the mid-nineteenth century;[1] subsequent research by John R. Bylsma and R. G. Watt, which used division lists to analyse politics in the 1850s, can be seen as a continuation of this trend.[2] In a landmark 1980 article, J. M. Kousser termed such developments as 'Quantitative Social-Scientific History' (QUASSH), and much debate has followed since on the applicability of such techniques.[3] The late John A. Phillips argued that 'Few areas of historical research seem more amenable to QUASSH than any modern parliamentary history. From the eighteenth century onward, the records of ... large numbers of active M.P.s in Westminster frequently require computer assistance to permit researchers to make sense of the vast array of available information.'[4] The vast quantity of data drawn on here stands as testament to this assertion. Although the data is new, the approach taken has already had its pioneers: One of Kousser's former students, Gary W. Cox, was instrumental in further refining such techniques, combining them with more traditional approaches to produce his own influential study of the role of cabinets in nineteenth-century government.[5]

The above examples primarily revolve around parliamentarians' voting records, and what this tells us regarding notions of party, principle and political issues. Data on MPs' clubs has never been treated in the same way, even though clubs are particularly well-suited to quantitative analysis, retaining membership data with many of the same characteristics which Cox has identified regarding parliamentarians. Antonia Taddei's 1999 Oxford paper on *London Clubs in the Late Nineteenth Century* represented the first use of statistical methods to analyse trends across Clubland of membership, subscriptions and entry fees, as well as an analysis of membership trends among a random sample of 200 individuals taken from *Who's Who* (twenty-nine of whom were MPs or ex-MPs). Taddei's findings on the 1870–1910 period raised a number of questions pertinent to this chapter: she found that political clubs were the most numerous club type (compared to, say, social or military clubs), and that they had the largest memberships of any clubs; although she notes that much of this growth occurred in the 1880s and 1890s.[6] While Taddei reveals much about late Victorian developments, it is hoped here to shed some light on the use of clubs by MPs in the preceding four decades.

The basis of this chapter is a database I compiled, recording all known club memberships of the 2,588 MPs who sat between the first two Reform Acts.[7] Over fifty archival and print sources have been used to identify their club memberships, with frequent cross-referencing with various almanacs and guides to ensure the correct individuals have been identified. The process began by using the History of Parliament Trust's own complete list of MPs for the 1832–68 period, and then mining the Trust's run of contemporary *Dod's* guides, using at least one copy from each Parliament after 1836 (the year in which *Dod's* began recording MPs' clubs as a category in their own right – although prior to 1836, some MPs residing at their clubs had already furnished *Dod's* with their club as their London address). Other sources were then mined, including digitised copies of the James Marshall and Marie-Louise Osborn Collection at Yale, which contains the original questionnaires answered by MPs replying to Charles Dod in the 1830s and 1840s.[8] The details on MPs were then cross-referenced with other sources, including party labels extracted from the New Parliament Editions of *Dod's*. As Joseph Coohill makes clear in his analysis of parliamentary companions, despite widespread assumptions as to the total fidelity of these guides, much of the material in the original forms was subsequently edited or altered, with 60.7 per cent of the final entries being literal transcriptions and 6.2 per cent of entries having undergone 'significant' or 'major' editing.[9] Thus numerous nuances and details in the questionnaire material remained unpublished. At this stage of the research, interim records of the club memberships of some 1,200 MPs had been gathered, displaying a noticeably high concentration of membership around certain clubs. All of them, barring two (the Athenaeum and Travellers' Club), were political clubs, and so I used this initially-compiled data on clubs with a high concentration of MPs to inform the next stage of research, which was to mine all surviving archival data from the archives of nine selected London clubs.[10]

It is hoped that the use of so many hitherto untapped sources in compiling this data can compensate for the scarcity of published sources on the topic, building up a dataset from which numerous conclusions could be drawn. In particular, given the wealth of existing qualitative examples in print on how clubs were used by MPs, it is hoped that the use of such extensive quantitative data herein contained will set existing anecdotal accounts into perspective, contextualising the typicality and accuracy of the many 'tall tales' circulating on 'club government'; and the comparison of such club membership data with voting data in the following chapter seeks to achieve similar ends.

Before presenting the data, one important caveat should be made about combining so many different sources: a small but persistent minority of MPs appears to have lied about (or exaggerated the number of) their club memberships. In such instances, it is impossible to be absolutely certain, because the patchy nature of most surviving club records has made it conceivable that some MPs joined and then swiftly resigned in one of the years for which no membership records survive.[11] While this may sound improbable, it is something which undeniably happened on at least some occasions: short-lived 'under the radar' club memberships by MPs occurred in such cases as the pro-Reform MP Robert Dillon Browne, who was elected to the Reform Club on 8 June 1836 – too late in the year to appear in the 1836 members' list published in April – but he had evidently resigned by the time of the 1837 members' list, in which he does not appear.[12] The only club which *does* uniquely hold complete membership records for the post-1832 period is the Athenaeum. Of the 320 MPs who declared Athenaeum membership in contemporary sources, only 299 appear in the Club's membership lists. Thus up to 21 MPs (6.6 per cent of the alleged tally of 320) may have lied to contemporary sources such as *Dod's Parliamentary Companion* (or in some instances, memberships may simply have been misreported), although the figure is probably smaller, and most likely closer to 16 (5 per cent).[13] In discussing the large number of MP club members, it is worth recognising that deception from MPs makes such figures at best close estimates rather than precise counts.

Why MPs should have lied about their club memberships is an interesting question. One can understand why they may have been loathe to volunteer membership information in the first place, but claiming a false membership is less easily understandable. There may have been the cultural cache and 'snob value' of claiming greater political connections.[14] This phenomenon was most easily identifiable amongst MPs who embellished the number of clubs they belonged to. Walter F. Campbell MP boasted to Charles Dod that he belonged 'To most of the London Clubs but belongs to no Political Club except Brooks's.'[15] With over a hundred social clubs extant in London at the time, this was clearly a hyperbolic statement and, of the two major non-political clubs sampled in this chapter, neither the Athenaeum nor the Travellers' Club had any record of Campbell. A further possible reason for such deception may have been related to the poor record of some individuals at paying their club subscription and outstanding bills. Despite sometimes resulting in their resignation, this may not have prevented them from continuing to use club facilities and maintaining the fiction of membership.[16] Another source of misinformation is suggested by Coohill's analysis of parliamentary companions: reluctance by MPs to co-operate with such almanacs, as when Conservative MP Thomas Frewen Turner responding to Dod's queries 'I am not very willing to enter into the particulars you ask'.[17] (Turner is not known to have belonged to any clubs, so this may have been one of the details he was reticent to share.) Coohill provides examples of MPs only co-operating with the greatest reluctance, but one can also verify from the data gathered here that there were cases of misinformation by MPs. William Baird MP listed his clubs as 'None' on his original questionnaire form to Charles Dod, yet he had actually been fast-tracked to Carlton membership less than a month after entering the House of Commons, on 24 August 1841.[18] MPs could also be disconcertingly vague, as in the case of Benjamin Disraeli who replied to his 1837 *Dod's* questionnaire by listing his clubs as 'Carlton Club, etc'.[19] Given that Disraeli had already been blackballed from the Athenaeum, the Travellers' Club and Grillions, that he had been ejected from the Westminster Reform Club for non-payment of his subscription, and that his only other club at the time was Crockford's, this wording was highly disingenuous.[20]

Despite the numerous possible causes for deception by MPs, it is still important to supplement internal club membership records with other records such as parliamentary almanacs, because of the gaps in club archives. Given that the only club for which full records exist from 1832, the Athenaeum, suggests a margin of error of around 5 per cent accounting for MPs' embellishment, we may still examine this data for trends, as there is no evidence to suggest that such inaccuracy favoured any one club or any particular group of MPs.

MPs and their Clubs

The vast majority of MPs sitting in the 1832–68 period belonged to a club (Graph 2.1); only an aggregate of 307 (11.9 per cent) did not. In other words, at least 88.1 per cent of MPs had a club. (The actual figure was almost certainly higher, owing both to some small gaps in the archives examined, and to some MPs having belonged to some clubs for which internal records have not been examined.) If the data is broken down over time, showing club membership among MPs across each Parliament (Graph 2.2), one finds that the Parliament of 1837–41 showed the most substantial increase in known MP club members, with the proportion rising from 82.1 per cent to 93.4 per cent, and not varying by more than 1.9 per cent per Parliament thereafter; indeed, the mean proportion of MPs belonging to clubs in the twenty-one years *after* the 1837 general election was 94.3 per cent, compared to a mean of 82.7 per cent for the two Parliaments covering 1832–7. We can thus observe that club membership was already widespread among MPs in the first post-Reform Parliament, but that the parliamentary intake of 1837 presented a shift in MPs' club membership habits. (It could, however, simply be that this is attributable to shortcomings in the available data. *Dod's* guides only began recording MPs' clubs from 1836, so MPs who ceased serving by 1835 will not have had their memberships recorded in this source, and the Carlton Club's missing membership records for 1832–3 may also account for some missing data.)

Regarding their individual choice of clubs, Graph 2.2 provides a summary of the complete club memberships of all MPs who sat throughout the 1832–68 period. The Carlton Club, often cited for its 'immense prestige', was confirmed as clearly the most popular club amongst parliamentarians, with some 1,024 members – an impressive tally, given that according to *Dod's*, the total number of

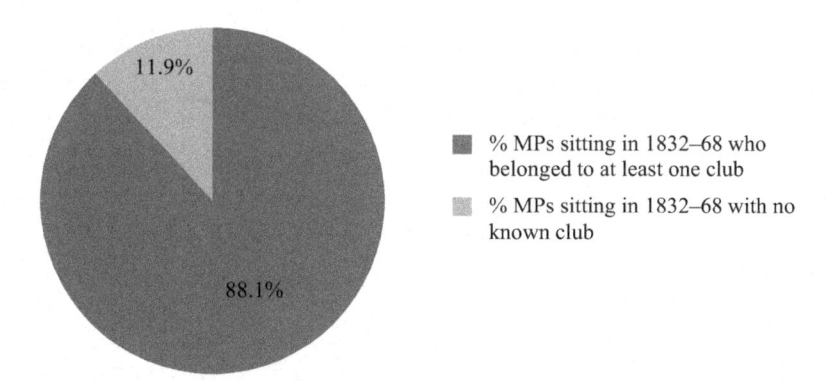

Graph 2.1 Proportion of MPs known to have belonged to at least one club, 1832–68. Source: Seth Alexander Thévoz, 'Database of MPs' Club Memberships, 1832–68'.

MPs on the Conservative benches in this period was 1,045.[21] By contrast, some clubs had surprisingly few MPs in this period. The East India United Service Club and Pratt's are not known to have had a single MP between them in the 1832–68 period. Both of them (founded in 1849 and 1857 respectively) were recent creations, and their lack of popularity amongst MPs contrasts with several clubs which we shall find were oversubscribed from their launch. Certainly the latter, aimed at the predominantly lower middle-class men 'on the make' in the East India Company, catered for a group which was not over-represented amongst parliamentarians, and duplicated the aims of the 1824-founded Oriental Club established by the Duke of Wellington for East India Company veterans, which nonetheless contained twenty-three MPs.

Unsurprisingly, Graph 2.3 shows that the four most popular clubs with MPs were all political clubs. (Denoted in the chart by black for Conservative clubs and white for Liberal clubs, with the apolitical clubs in grey.) Of these political clubs, Graph 2.4a shows the varying strength of MP membership at these institutions throughout the 1832–68 period, broken down by Parliament, with Graph 2.4b plotting the linear gradient of the four most popular (political) clubs' MP membership. Brooks's and the Reform Club, the two preferred clubs for Liberals, both showed a small but steady decline in their parliamentary representation, with the rate of decline in the Reform

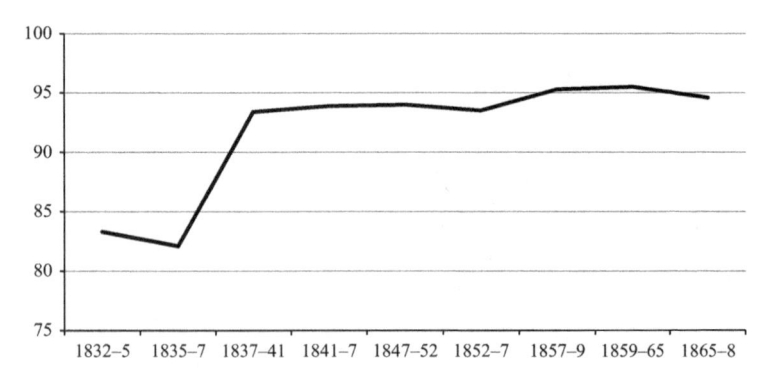

Graph 2.2 Percentage of MPs belonging to a club, broken down by Parliament, 1832–68. Source: Seth Alexander Thévoz, 'Database of MPs' Club Memberships, 1832–68.'

Club's MP members being slightly greater than that of Brooks's.[22] White's membership among MPs virtually 'flatlined' in this period, with the rate of increase being negligible. The Carlton, by contrast, showed much variation after an initial sharp rise between 1837 and 1847.

Given that one of the variables involved was the number of MPs, and that the composition of the House of Commons varied considerably throughout this period, the changes to this variable could result in significant oscillations in the number of MPs in a particular club, depending on how well-represented each party was in each Parliament. (The figures do not include ex-MPs or future MPs.) Graph 2.5 sets the context of this, illustrating the *Dod's* 'New Parliament Edition' party label data on the composition of the House of Commons for the Parliaments of 1832–68. Several party groupings were so small that observing trends would be of limited value when the sample size was so small; specifically, this applies to the Liberal Conservatives before 1852, the Whigs and Reformers from at least 1857, and the Radicals and Repealers in general, all of whom constituted 5 per cent of MPs or less, and so this should be borne in mind when viewing subsequent graphs in this chapter. However, by broadly grouping together Conservatives and Liberal Conservatives as 'Conservatives', and the Liberals, Reformers, Whigs, Radicals and Repealers as 'Liberals', it is possible to look at club membership of MPs, as a proportion of Conservatives and Liberals; and in recognition of the controversial assumptions that such groupings involve, a more detailed breakdown is possible where sample sizes of parliamentary parties are large enough.

Before examining the conceptual implications of club membership among MPs, it is worth systematically looking at the key trends of MPs in each of London's four main political clubs. Graphs 2.6–2.9 look at the popularity of these clubs with MPs of one party. Graphs 2.6–2.7 show the percentage of Conservative MPs in each Parliament who were members of the Carlton Club and White's, while Graphs 2.8–2.9 show the percentage of Liberal MPs in each Parliament who were members of the Reform Club and Brooks's.

The Carlton Club data for 1832–3 is not exhaustive in the way that it is after 1834, so the first data points in Graph 2.6 covering the Parliament of 1832 should be treated with caution.[23] After a strong start, with at least two-thirds of Conservative MPs joining in its first year, the Carlton further consolidated its popularity over its first

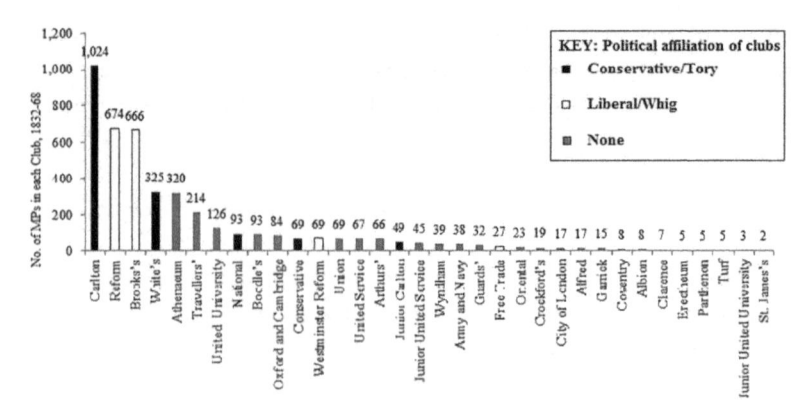

Graph 2.3 Aggregate membership of London clubs among MPs who sat in the period 1832–68. Source: Seth Alexander Thévoz, 'Database of MPs' Club Memberships, 1832–68.'

decade, exceeding 85 per cent of all Conservative MPs when the party achieved its overall majority in the Parliament of 1841 – though suffered a setback in the Parliament of 1847–52. However, it increased its share of Conservative MPs thereafter, so that by the 1865–8 parliament, 96 per cent of Conservative MPs were members. A different trend could be found in Carlton membership among Liberal Conservatives, whose numbers according to *Dod's* only became

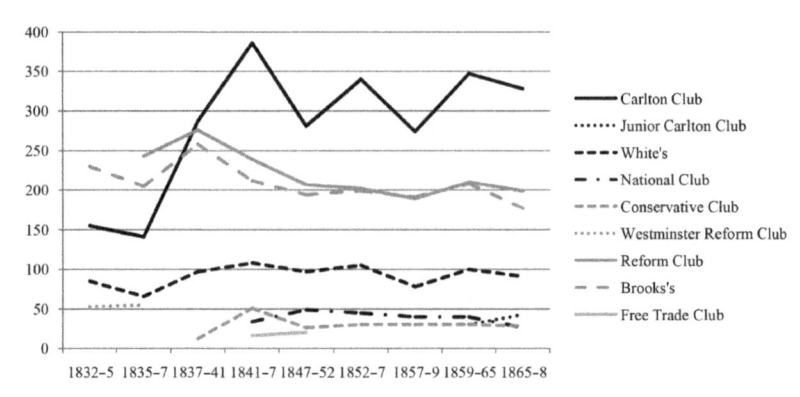

Graph 2.4a No. of MPs belonging to political clubs, 1832–68, broken down by Parliament.

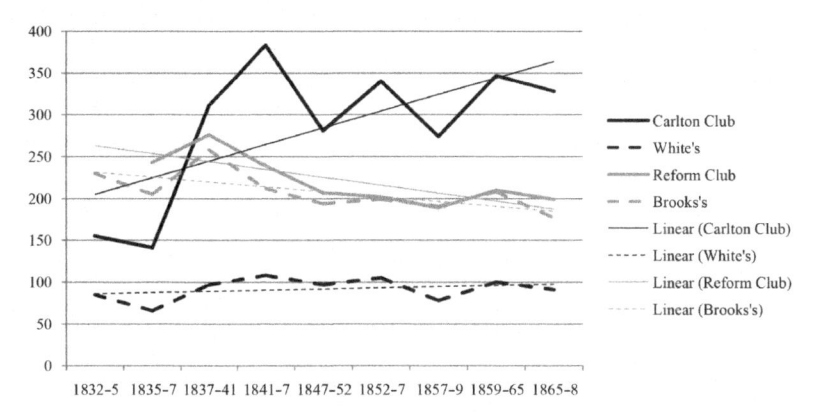

Graph 2.4b No. of MPs belonging to the four most popular political clubs, 1832–68, broken down by Parliament, with linear averages shown.

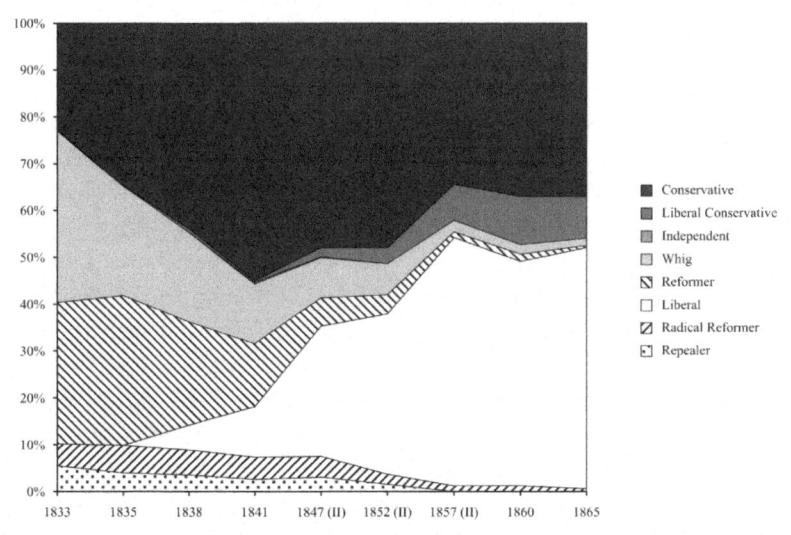

Graph 2.5 Political composition of the House of Commons, 1832–68, using *Dod's* (New Parliament Edition) party labels for each MP sitting in selected years. Source: Charles Dod (ed.), *Dod's Parliamentary Companion* [originally *Parliamentary Pocket Companion*] New Parliament Edition, *1833, 1835, 1838, 1841, 1847 (II), 1852 (II), 1857 (II), 1860 and 1865* (London, 1833–65).

Graph 2.6 Percentage of Conservative and Liberal Conservative MPs belonging to the Carlton Club, broken down by Parliament, 1833–65.[24] Source: Seth Alexander Thévoz, 'Database of MPs' Club Memberships, 1832–68'.

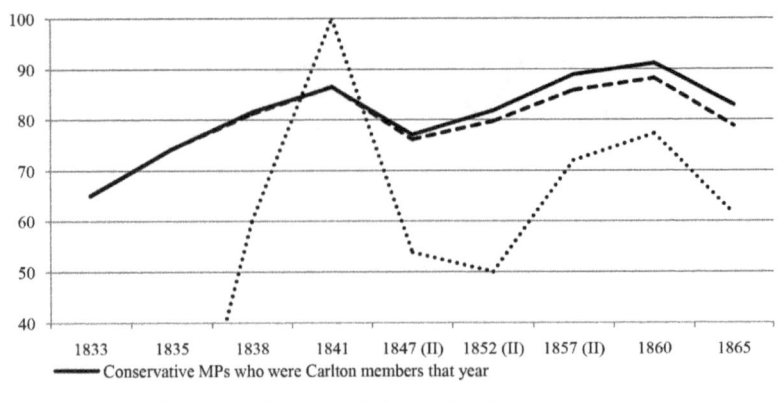

significant from the Parliament of 1852 (and so pre-1852 proportions should be ignored due to the small sample size): the proportion of MPs joining was always lower than Conservatives (though it still constituted a majority of Liberal Conservatives), and although it initially rose (most strikingly in the Parliament of 1857–9), this was not the case in the Parliament of 1865–8, where the original Liberal Conservative intake actually saw a 17 per cent drop in the share of Liberal Conservatives at the Carlton, though successful recruitment later in that Parliament meant that the share of Liberal Conservatives stabilised thereafter around the level of the 1859 Parliament. While such smaller percentages can be seen as reflecting Liberal Conservative marginalisation from Conservative party politics in the 1850s and 1860s, they should not be exaggerated, as they still represent a clear majority of Liberal Conservative MPs.

Unfortunately, this graph illustrates the limitations of such information – although it can tell us whether the overall share of a party grouping increased or decreased over time, it cannot tell us *why* this happened. This is particularly the case with the Liberal Conservatives, whose own share of Carlton membership (while they were a significant

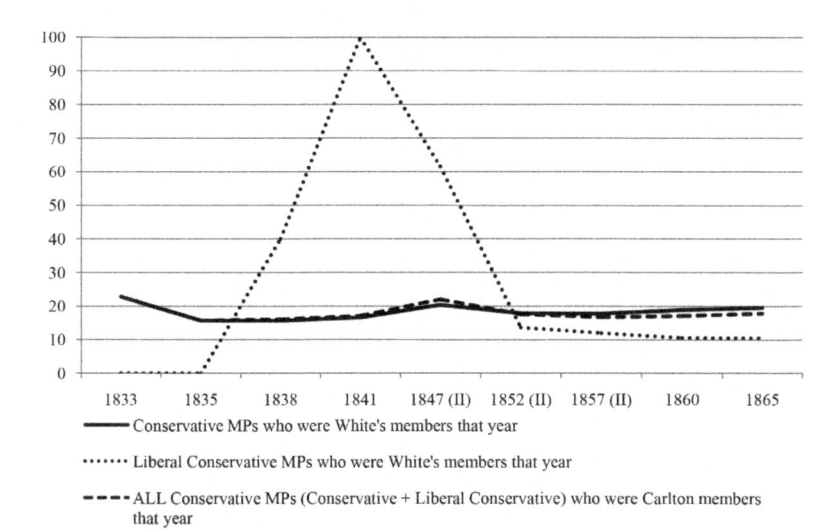

Graph 2.7 Percentage of Conservative and Liberal Conservative MPs belonging to White's, broken down by Parliament, 1833–65. Source: Seth Alexander Thévoz, 'Database of MPs' Club Memberships, 1832–68'.

grouping) was greatest in the Parliaments of 1857 and 1859; while a number of theories can be devised, perhaps correlating Carlton membership with Conservative identification, the above figures alone cannot prove or disprove such explanations.

As a club with a long-established Conservative political reputation, it is perhaps surprising to find that White's actually attracted a substantially lower proportion of Conservative MPs than the Carlton. Starting on a peak of 23 per cent of Conservative MPs in the Parliament of 1832–5, the share of Conservative MPs belonging to White's dropped by nearly a third in just one Parliament, and remained low through the 1830s, in the wake of the establishment of the Carlton. However, White's experienced a modest rise in the share of Conservative MPs from the 1840s, particularly in 1847–52 (after which it declined slightly for a decade), and then again in 1865–8. Yet beyond the dramatic drop of 1832–5, none of these variations produced a sizable change of more than 4 per cent between any two adjacent Parliaments. As with the Carlton Club, it is unsurprising to find that it was never as popular among Liberal Conservatives as it was among Conservatives. (As with the Carlton Club, pre-1852 data on the Liberal Conservatives can be largely ignored, due to the small number of self-identified Liberal Conservatives in those years.) From the four post-1852 data points available, a slight Liberal Conservative decline is perceptible from the 1850s to the 1860s. Nonetheless, with 325 MPs throughout this period, White's remained popular with parliamentarians, and if we are to reconcile this with its surprisingly low share of Conservative MPs, then the weakness of its political affiliation must be acknowledged. Its Pittite reputation had not endured in the same way that the Foxite reputation of Brooks's had ensured a continued Whiggish presence at Brooks's well into the nineteenth century; as we shall see across this period, at any one time between a quarter and a third of White's MPs were either Whigs, Liberals or even Radicals, casting doubt on the strength of party feeling at the Club. In examining who joined White's, it is striking how aristocratic its membership list was – indeed, Percy Colson's observation that Victorian White's had 'a list of members like a *Debrett* in miniature' is borne out by the membership data, which is littered with peerages and courtesy titles.[25] Thus one may speculate that family ties may have been *at least* as important as party ties – again, a theme which will be returned to.

A meaningful graph is not possible for the other major Conservative clubs. In the case of the Junior Carlton Club, this is because of the narrow range of available dates – it was founded in 1864, and so an analysis based on only two data points for the last year of the 1859–65 Parliament and the 1865–8 Parliament would invariably be misleading. Nevertheless, several trends emerge from the club's first four years. The Junior Carlton had recruited 49 MPs by 1868; a respectable number given its short existence to that point, but it still failed to equal the initial burst of parliamentary enthusiasm which one finds greeted the Athenaeum and Reform Clubs. The Club lacked prominent 'big name' Conservative MPs, beyond those who had been brought in early on as the Club's trustees but whom seldom frequented the Club.[26] As a large club initally capped at 2,000 members (compared to the Carlton's 600–800), its intended relief of pressure on the Carlton Club waiting list would not have had any discernible effect on parliamentarians, who could have bypassed the Carlton waiting list anyway, as supernumerary members not subject to the waiting list. Forty-seven of the Club's 49 MPs were already members of the Carlton. Thus of the Conservative MPs who did join, the Junior Carlton was merely a supplement to the Carlton.

The Junior Carlton's lack of success was shared by the Conservative Club that had been founded in 1840. Of its 69 known MPs, 63 were Carlton members. However, these 'second clubs' of choice for Conservative MPs did not complement one another – only five MPs were members of both the Conservative and the Junior Carlton Clubs, and each of them was a Carlton member as well.[27] The remaining Conservative-inclined club of the period, the Protestant-affiliated National Club, is not suitable for a similar analysis because of the sizeable proportion of MPs for whom a precise joining date is known – some half of its intake of 93 MPs. Yet the pattern which most clearly emerges from these MPs is one of a steady trickle of new members from the 1845 launch of the Club in the wake of the Maynooth controversy, only to dry up in the mid-1850s.[28] Not a single new MP joined the National Club between 1855 and the Second Reform Act, although some of its long-standing members such as Charles Newdegate remained active in both Club and Commons into the 1880s.

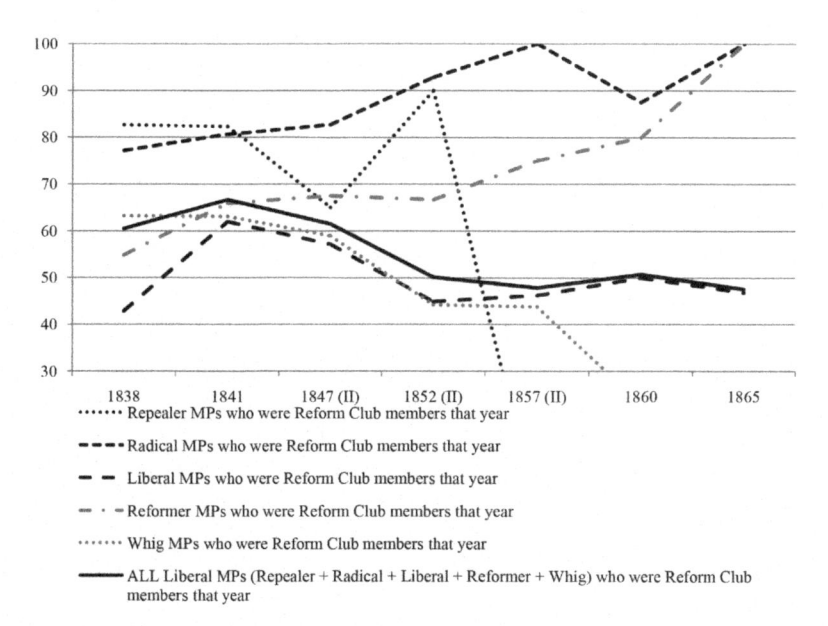

Graph 2.8 Percentage of Liberal MPs of various denominations belonging to the Reform Club, broken down by Parliament, 1837–65. Source: Seth Alexander Thévoz, 'Database of MPs' Club Memberships, 1832–68'.

The greater diversity of shades of opinion which could be described as 'Liberal' makes the popularity of the Reform Club with Liberal MPs a more complex phenomenon. As noted, 'Radical' and 'Repealer' representation was sufficiently small as to make the above trends of doubtful significance, even in the years in which they have been included – though it is intriguing that amongst such small groups, the share of Reform Club members was higher than more 'mainstream' Liberals and Whigs. The rapid diminution in Whig numbers from the 1850s means that beyond the 1852–7 Parliament the Whig figures are not statistically significant, but it is notable that the share of Whigs, which rose through the 1830s and 1840s, appeared to stabilise at a time when Reform Club membership had declined among most Liberals and Reformers. Thus given that the highest proportions of Reform Club membership were to be found among those Liberal shades of opinion with the smallest absolute numbers, then the greatest inference that can be made (from an admittedly already small sample size) is that the Reform Club presented an appealing prospect to those on the fringes of Liberal politics. Revealingly, from 1841, the trend among both Reformers and Liberals was surprisingly similar in each Parliament. (Note that in the Parliament of 1837–41, the number of self-declared 'Liberals' was small, which may go some way to explaining the divergence in this first data point for Liberals at the Reform Club.) Reform Club membership peaked among both Liberals and Reformers at over six-tenths in the Parliament of 1841, declining by a third over the next decade. Thereafter, the number of Reformers remaining in Parliament became statistically insignificant, while among the more prevalent Liberals, Reform Club membership experienced a modest rise to just over half of all MPs, peaking in the 1859 Parliament, but declining thereafter. The aggregate figure for all shades of 'Liberals' shows a very similar trend (partly reflecting the dominance of Liberals in the numbers that made up 'Liberals' of all shades of opinion); the gradual decline of Reform Club membership among Liberals from the 1840s thus contrasts greatly with the above observations on Carlton Club membership among Conservatives, which broadly increased in popularity.

For the Reform Club's semi-predecessor the Westminster Reform Club, analysis along the lines of the above examples would be meaningless, since the club's doors were only open for two years in 1834–6.

However, a quick glance at its parliamentary membership of 69 MPs gives some indication of why the Club was so unsuccessful as to end in bankruptcy. The Club enticed some of the more prominent Radical names in the Commons, such as Thomas Attwood, Daniel O'Connell, Feargus O'Connor and Josiah Wedgwood. Yet the Club was generally unsuccessful in recruiting beyond the Radical shade of opinion, notwithstanding the controversial short-lived membership of the young Benjamin Disraeli.[29] Many clubs of a non-political character thrived with such small memberships; yet given the Westminster Reform Club's minuscule *non*-parliamentary membership of 36, and the cost of maintaining its premises, it is little wonder that such facilities could not be sustained by such a small membership base.

As with the Reform Club, Brooks's presented some complex trends relating to the membership of Liberal MPs. Unlike the Reform, the modestly-sized parliamentary contingent of Radicals and Repealers were not well-represented at the Club. Despite the membership of some well-known individual Repealers, their absolute numbers were not enough to be significant; while for the Radicals, in all but one

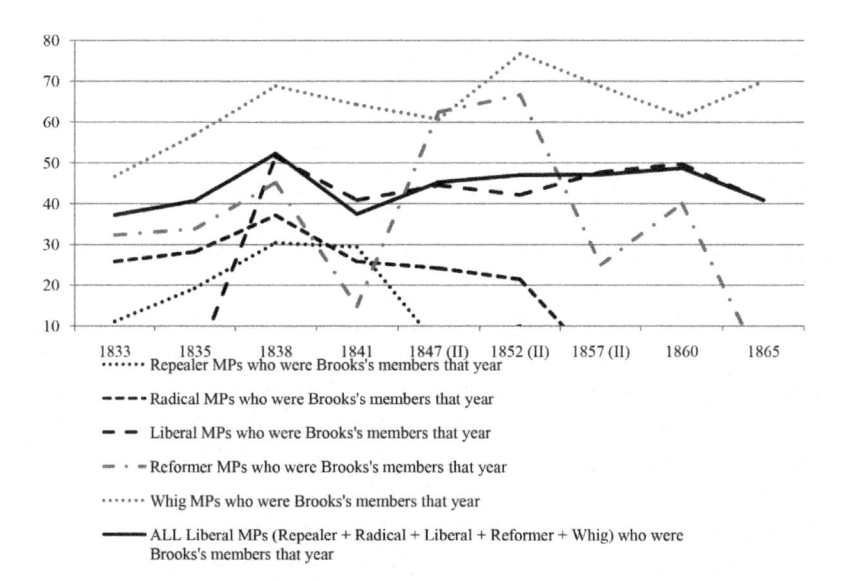

Graph 2.9 Percentage of Liberal MPs of various denominations belonging to Brooks's, broken down by Parliament, 1833–65. Source: Seth Alexander Thévoz, 'Database of MPs' Club Memberships, 1832–68'.

sample year (1841), they had the smallest share of any 'Liberal' party at Brooks's. Unsurprisingly for a club reputed to be a Whig institution, the Whigs were indeed the Liberal faction best represented at Brooks's, and this trend noticeably increased over time – although the gradual drop in Whig numbers must be borne in mind when considering the Club's increasing importance for the diminishing Whig rump. What is perhaps more surprising is that when the Whigs were better represented in Parliament, the Club was much less successful in attracting Whig MPs. In 1833, when there was no rival Reform Club yet in existence, the share of Whig MPs who joined Brooks's was barely half. The greatest variation in Brooks's membership was amongst Reformers; in the 1830s, when they were best represented in Parliament, they were the group least likely to join. As their absolute numbers reduced in the 1840s, their rate of Brooks's membership oscillated wildly – having stood at just under half in the Parliament of 1837–41, it plunged to 15 per cent in 1841–7, before rising to over three-fifths of the Reformer rump in 1847–52, and rising further still the following Parliament among the few remaining Reformers. The aggregate figure for *all* Liberals shows some variation, but mostly within a fairly limited range; only two of the nine data points (1833 and 1841) fell outside the range of 41 to 52 per cent, and then to record Liberal membership rates of 37 per cent in both years. Yet the overall picture is one of broad stability, with the Club retaining slightly under half of all Liberals of various shades of opinion.

The nuanced MP membership data on Brooks's seriously challenges the widely-accepted narrative of decline of the Club's popularity amongst Liberals, which is frequently attributed to a combination of two factors: rivalry from the Reform Club, and the reputedly aristocratic flavour of Brooks's having limited appeal amongst the increasingly Radical flavour of Liberal opinion after the Reform Act. Both of these make simplistic and flawed assumptions. Anthony Lejeune perpetuates both of these ideas in crediting the Reform Club's creation to how 'Brooks's, the headquarters of the old Whig aristocracy, was not prepared to open its doors to a flood of new men', while J. Mordaunt Crook sees the Reform Club as a 'middle-class annexe' to Brooks's, with the older club remaining 'a bastion of the great Whig grandmotherhood'.[30] Admittedly, Brooks's attracted more 'Liberal' MPs than any other club before the Reform Club was formed in 1836.[31] The assertion about the surpassing of Brooks's by the Reform Club should however be tempered by the observation that the parliamentary membership in Brooks's throughout the entire 1832–68 period (666 MPs) was almost precisely tied with that of the Reform Club (674), and it should be noted that, if Brooks's declined in popularity among Liberals, so did the Reform Club, and the latter did so at a more noticeable rate in the 1840s after its initial burst of success in the 1830s. Yet the notion that Brooks's remained a predominantly Whig club still endures, with Ian Newbould categorically stating that from 1836 'Whigs remained at Brooks's, Radicals at the Reform, proto-Liberals at either'.[32] Despite the Whiggish reputation of Brooks's, as will be seen in Graph 2.11b, from 1835 Whigs actually made up a minority of MPs who were Brooks's members. In the decades following Reform, as its parliamentary representation rose, the spiritual home of Whiggery was conspicuously successful at recruiting MPs from beyond its Whig hinterland.[33]

Further insights can be gained into the changes in MP club membership over time by looking at the joining dates of MPs who served in 1832–68; this has been done in Graphs 2.10a and 2.10b for the four largest political clubs, along with the most popular apolitical club among MPs, the Athenaeum, which is included by way of contrast. A crucial caveat is that Graph 2.10 does not show the total number of MPs in each club at any given time; such data is impossible to gather, because of the large gaps in records about how long MPs remained a member of a club. Instead, it merely shows the number of MPs joining each club for the first time, and so highlights 'peak' recruitment years.

The defining characteristic of the Athenaeum's parliamentary membership was how little it changed after the initial burst of membership on the club's foundation. 110 of its original 1,067 members in 1824 were parliamentarians. (The overall figure of parliamentarians among the membership would have been slightly higher, since this figure does not include MPs who only sat before 1832.) From this, one can infer that the Athenaeum's membership was politically well-connected from the outset, albeit as members of the club in a non-political capacity. Unlike the Carlton and Reform Clubs, there were no regulations in the club rulebook expediting the fast-tracking of MPs to Athenaeum membership.[34] Given the huge burst of members who joined the Reform Club and Athenaeum in their first year, Graph 2.10b projects the same data as Graph 2.10a, only without these two plot

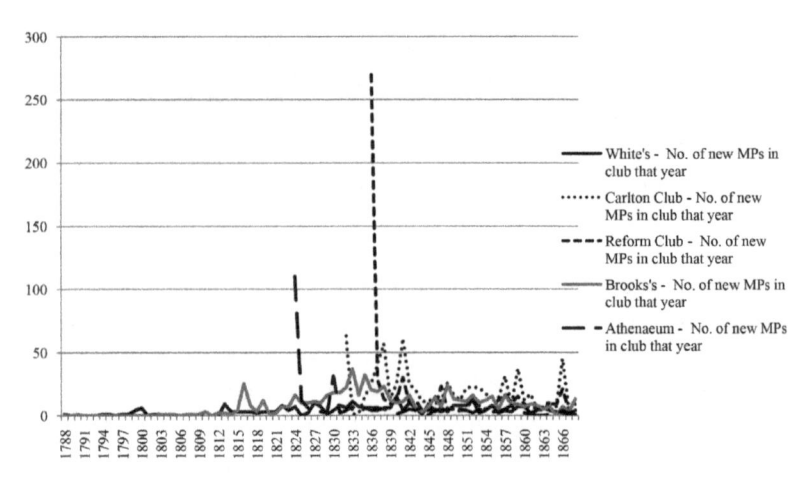

Graph 2.10a No. of MPs joining selected clubs for the first time, 1832–6, all data points. Source: Seth Alexander Thévoz, 'Database of MPs' Club Memberships, 1832–68'.

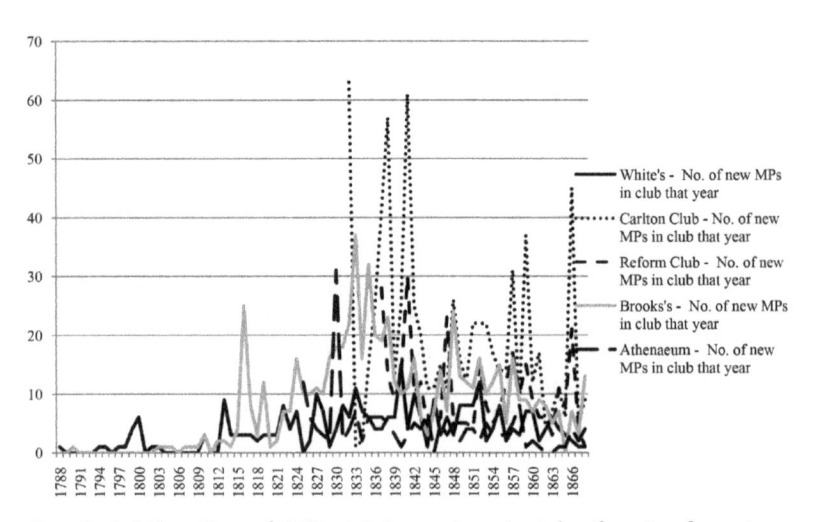

Graph 2.10b No. of MPs joining selected clubs for the first time, 1832–6, with the values of the first year at the Athenaeum and the Reform Club removed. Source: Seth Alexander Thévoz, 'Database of MPs' Club Memberships, 1832–68'.

points, so as to avoid skewing the graph. After 1824, the low number of MPs admitted to the Athenaeum each year (typically between three and seven) was symptomatic of the low supply of places available at any one time, rather than indicative of the level of demand which was – anecdotally – high.[35] (Candidates' books do not survive for the Athenaeum, so precisely measuring the demand for Athenaeum membership is impossible.) What is apparent from working through the Athenaeum's membership lists, and from the club's low number of overall admissions, is that existing Athenaeum members do not seem to have resigned so readily as members of other clubs subsequently examined, therefore places generally only became available on the death of an existing member. Admittedly, some parliamentary members, such as Disraeli, could become members under Rule II, which admitted 'distinguished persons' as supernumerary members who were not prone to the usual waiting list. However, the arbitrary limiting of 'Rule II' members to a maximum of nine per year meant that this was not a common path for parliamentarians to take, with just three recorded cases of MPs in 1832–68.[36] This was a rule designed for eminent authors, not politicians.

Like the Athenaeum, the most notable feature of the Reform Club's parliamentary membership was the enormous initial intake on its foundation. The club's spectacular success at recruiting 270 pro-Reform MPs in its launch year of 1836 was no coincidence. In February 1836, William Ord MP chaired a small sub-committee of two other MPs, Edward J. Stanley and George Grote, whose task was 'to ascertain what Liberal Members of Parlt had not joined the Club' and 'to direct the [Club] Secretary' accordingly.[37] The choice of MPs as diverse as Stanley and Grote, respectively classified by *Dod's* as a Reformer and a Radical, indicates the breadth of support which the Club sought. Such activity clearly points to a conscious attempt at complete overlap between the Club and Liberal parliamentarians – Reform Club membership was intended to be almost *de rigeur* for pro-Reform MPs.

If one overlooks the sheer scale of the Reform Club's recruitment of MPs in its first year (which admittedly dwarfed all other clubs' recorded MP recruitment for any single year), then it is easier to appreciate the Club's sizeable and sustained parliamentary influx after 1836, which correlated precisely with election years. As with Brooks's, an influx of new MPs joined in either the year of each general election or the year after. From 1837, there appeared to be a pattern of Reform Club recruitment from parliamentarians; recruitment underwent a series of peaks, which coincided either with the year of a general election, or with the year after a general election. This would seem to suggest that when a large cohort of new MPs entered Parliament after an election, many would join the Reform Club within a year. Closer scrutiny of Graphs 2.10a and 2.10b shows that this trend appears equally true of the Carlton Club and Brooks's; but not of White's or the Athenaeum. This observation will be returned to later.

Explaining MPs' Links to Clubs

In considering the multiplicity of available clubs for MPs, it is worth considering why they joined specific types of club. In particular, three factors deserve consideration: ties of family, geography and party. There were clear family connections between parliamentarians and some clubs, which can be most easily observed in families that returned numerous parliamentarians, mainly from aristocratic backgrounds, joining the two most aristocratic clubs White's and Brooks's. Donald Southgate compiled a guide to the families on the Liberal side involved in electoral contests 1832–85, singling out the main Whig families, and so their names can easily be identified.[38]

The two largest Whig parliamentary clans were the Duke of Bedford's family, the Russells, and the Duke of Devonshire's family, the Cavendishes, with eight family members apiece in the Commons in 1832–68.[39] Seven of the Russells were members of Brooks's; only Sir Charles Russell (who sat as a Conservative) shunned Brooks's for the Carlton, Guard's and Garrick Clubs. For the Russells in Brooks's, the strength of the family connection was most obvious in their unusually young ages when elected to membership; between 19 and 25 years old.[40] Indeed, it is unsurprising that the Russell clan, with its deification of the Foxite legacy, should have maintained strong ties with Brooks's, which housed the Fox Club, a dining society in commemoration of Charles James Fox.[41]

The Cavendish attachment to Brooks's was no less remarkable, with the Hon. Colonel Henry Frederick Compton Cavendish – a cousin of the Duke of Devonshire – being the only Cavendish family MP during this period to have *not* been a member, although his brother the Hon. Charles Compton Cavendish was. Again, the ages at election were all noticeably low, with Brooks's providing an open door to six Cavendishes between the ages of 18 and 25.[42] The seventh, Lord Edward Cavendish, was not elected until he was thirty. Noteworthy is that the youngest Cavendish to be admitted, not yet having come of age at 18, was the future Marquess of Hartington, also the heir presumptive to the Duchy of Devonshire. This suggests that social rank certainly went some way to expediting early entry into aristocratic clubs, but the same cannot be said of political clubs. Five Russells and three Devonshires in the Commons were also members of the Reform Club, but all joined much later in life, usually in proximity to their entry to Parliament, as per Graphs 2.6–2.9. The major difference between the Russell and Cavendish club memberships was the popularity of White's with the latter – six out of eight Cavendishes were members, and in four cases they joined White's within a year of joining Brooks's.[43] Thus the degree to which entry to this traditionally-Tory club had become something of a rite of passage for one of the great Whig dynasties of the age goes some way to explaining both the political dilution of White's by the 1830s, and the subsequent necessity for a separate Carlton Club for Conservatives to gather in, away from the prying ears of fellow members who did not share their politics.

The prominence of such Whig families in Clubland is doubly important if one considers Peter Mandler's argument for the reassertion of aristocratic rule in at least the first decade – and arguably the first two decades – after the Great Reform Act.[44] With many of these MPs joining at young ages well into the 1840s and 1850s, it seems that aristocratic methods of sociability in clubs did not appreciably change during the period; although the absence of pre-1832 data here makes it impossible to determine whether this represented a change from the pre-Reform era. Nor were these patterns restricted to the Russells and Cavendishes. Other notable Whig families included the Fitzwilliams, with six MPs, all of whom were members of Brooks's, but none of whom were members of the Reform Club. On the Conservative benches, such patterns were repeated, as with the Earl of Lonsdale's family, the Lowthers – six of them sat in the Commons, and all of them were Carlton Club members, with three of them also joining White's.

Amongst the 'family' MPs with fewer relatives in the House, the most noticeable trend was for subsequent generations of MPs to amass more club memberships than their forbears had possessed. This could be interpreted as a symptom of both social progression and of the expansion of clubs, which continued to multiply as the century progressed. For instance, County Kerry MP the Hon. William Browne (brother of the second and third Earls of Kenmare) did not belong to any clubs, but his younger cousin Viscount Castlerosse who succeeded him in the seat belonged to both White's and Brooks's. Yet inverse examples occurred, too: Henry Charles Sturt MP belonged to the Athenaeum, Brooks's, the Carlton and White's, yet his son Henry Gerard Sturt MP belonged only to the more partisan combination of the Carlton and White's.

Family ties had their limits in explaining the link between clubs and politics. Firstly, as stated above, these trends could only meaningfully be observed amongst families with a sizeable number of MPs in Parliament, which automatically means only analysing a minority of the post-1832 parliamentary intake − Southgate places the number of members from the grand Whig families in the Commons at 161, plus a further 165 MPs related to other MPs on the Liberal side.[45] Even though these numbers do not take into account the parliamentary allies of such MPs (particularly those occupying seats in the gift of Whig grandees), this still formed only a small rump of the approximately 1,400 MPs on the Liberal side of the House in 1832−68. Furthermore, the aristocratic nature of Whiggery meant that by the 1860s, the Whigs may have remained a sizeable force in the House of Lords, but in the House of Commons their numbers dwindled to under a dozen in the Parliaments of the 1860s.[46] Thus whilst the family dimension was most likely linked to the selection of clubs by those families with multiple MPs, it is of limited use in explaining the prevalence of club membership amongst almost nine-tenths of the House of Commons.

Secondly, there were structural reasons why an MP's position − and the perks in club rulebooks which allowed MPs to bypass the waiting list − did not transfer to relatives. Despite the eighteenth-century stereotype of a father putting his son's name down for his club, this practice was actually almost unheard of by the nineteenth century. It was specifically barred by the rules of some clubs, such as White's.[47] An examination of proposers and seconders at Brooks's, the Carlton, the Junior Carlton and Reform Clubs (where such records survive) reveals the reality was that close friends of the family would often be asked to propose a prospective member, rather than relatives. For instance, Sir Francis Thornhill Baring Bt MP, part of the Baring clan which frequented Brooks's, was nominated for the club in 1828 by

Viscount Althorp from the Spencer family, who had previously nominated Sir Francis' cousins William Bingham Baring MP in 1824 and Francis Baring MP in 1825.[48] Such patterns in shared or even swapped proposers and seconders for family members may be observed in multiple instances, but constituted informal, ad hoc arrangements; whereas, as we shall see, club rules according special status to MP applicants meant that far stronger club ties existed simply by virtue of being elected to Parliament.

It is less easy to extrapolate any trends between clubs and the geographical ties of MPs. Whether or not one accepts Jonathan Parry's notion of a broad pre-1859 parliamentary Liberal party with diverse wings, all shades of MPs who sat on the Liberal (and Radical) benches were well-represented at both Brooks's and the Reform Club, from every part of the United Kingdom.[49] Likewise, the Carlton Club also encompassed MPs from all four nations of the United Kingdom. Where MPs from a region may have been under-represented, one may infer that this was more a symptom of a club failing to attract many MPs in general, as opposed to one failing to attract a particular region's representation of MPs, as was the case with the modest parliamentary contingent in the Westminster Reform and Conservative Clubs. Where political clubs were well-represented amongst the MPs of one region, this was more attributable to the personal ties of the members than to any institutional ties. For example, it is unsurprising to find that the Hon. George Charles Henry Byng MP (later third Earl of Stafford) was a member of Brooks's, for he would have already moved in social circles that overlapped with Brooks's, as his seat of Tavistock was in the gift of the Russells.

What yields more substantive findings than geographical tie is the link between club membership and party affiliation. The data on MPs' memberships of politically-aligned clubs contributes new evidence to the debate over party affiliation and the evolution of parties. Given that several political clubs required their candidates to sign declarations affirming either party principles or specific policy principles, membership can be taken as strong evidence of party affiliation. The Carlton, Conservative and Junior Carlton Clubs all required members to sign up to 'Conservative' principles, the National Club's members had to assert 'Protestant principles', whilst the Reform Club required its members to sign up to the principles of the Reform Act. Even clubs like the short-lived Westminster Reform and Free Trade Clubs (of which there is no evidence of stipulating such formal declarations), were clearly targeted at recruiting members from a particular end of the political spectrum.[50] Of the political clubs, only longer-established institutions such as White's and Brooks's retained no formal requirement to endorse a policy or party. Until the Junior Carlton Club's creation, the Carlton was closest to specifically endorsing a party; John Wolffe argues that the National Club's emphasis on 'Protestant principles' rather than party principles was a deliberate attempt to build a factional political base among the Club's membership.[51]

A strong indication of the strength of party feeling in clubs can be gained from the political composition of their parliamentary representation, as shown in Graph 2.11, outlined in the absolute numbers which changed each Parliament. As with Graphs 2.5–2.9, the party labels have been extracted from the New Parliament Editions of *Dod's Parliamentary Companion* which appeared between 1833 and 1865. Admittedly, there are numerous difficulties in using these labels (or indeed *any* set of labels for the period) not least with many MPs who defied categorisation, and with MPs who changed their affiliation over time. Such labels also employ some questionable generalisations, as when using the term 'Liberal Conservative' as a synonym for 'Peelite'. Nevertheless, they do offer a comprehensive data set to compare to club membership.

Several observations can be made from the above data. In the ostensibly apolitical Athenaeum, there was usually an approximately three-to-two split favouring Liberals over Conservatives, although crucially, this was proportionate with the overall number of MPs who served during the period, with the Conservatives being particularly well-represented after their strong electoral performances of 1841 and 1852. Indeed, although various shades of Liberal opinion were generally better represented, as we shall see, it appears that those Conservative MPs who belonged to the Athenaeum tended to combine their membership with Conservative clubs far more than Liberal MPs did with Liberal clubs; 36.9 per cent of Athenaeum MPs also belonged to the Carlton, compared to 30 per cent who also belonged to the most popular Liberal club, the Reform (Graph 2.12), and this is reflected in the social network generated in Graph 2.14. The Carlton Club was unsurprisingly an overtly partisan club in its parliamentary representation, with an overwhelming majority of its MPs being Conservatives or Liberal Conservatives. The small but

Graph 2.11 Political composition of selected clubs, by MPs' party affiliation, 1832–68, using the *Dod's* New Parliament Edition party labels, in absolute numbers. Source: Seth Alexander Thévoz, 'Database of MPs' Club Memberships, 1832–68'.

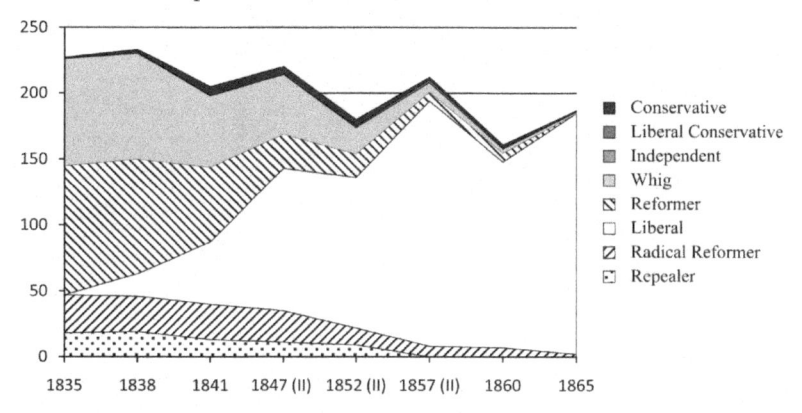

Graph 2.11a Reform Club.

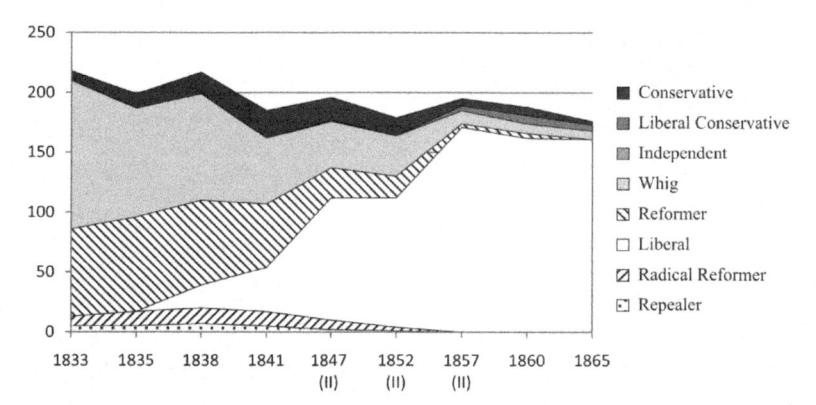

Graph 2.11b Brooks's.

consistent proportion of Carlton Club MPs from the 'Liberal' end of the political spectrum was largely explained by changes of allegiance; for example, in the Parliament of 1835–7, by including members of the 'Derby Dilly', who would have been labelled as Conservatives early in the Parliament, and would have joined the Carlton later in the Parliament. However, the use of changing labels for each MP, updated for each Parliament, has reduced the instances of such inconsistencies to changes of

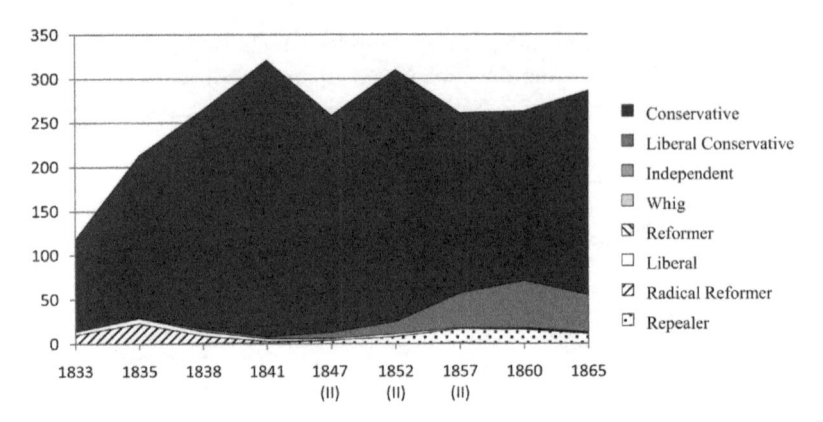

Graph 2.11c Carlton Club.

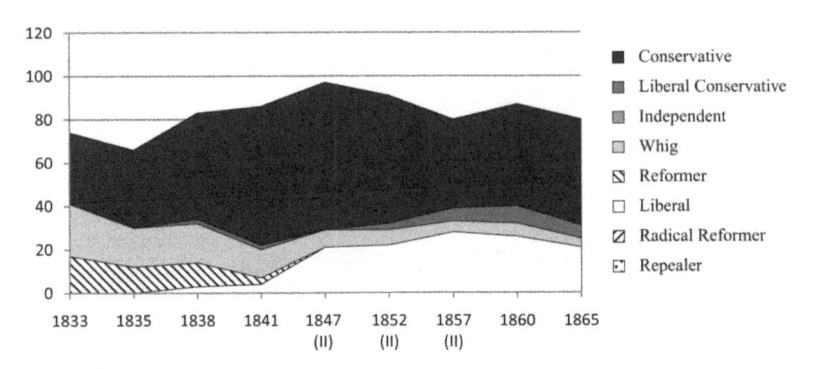

Graph 2.11d White's.

allegiance within one Parliament. Thus William Ewart Gladstone, who made extensive use of the Carlton from the 1830s to the 1850s, is categorised as a Conservative for the period 1832–47, and as a Liberal Conservative for the period 1847–68.[52] Like the Carlton, the Reform Club and Brooks's both demonstrated an overwhelming party affiliation, with the great majority of their respective MPs being Liberals of various denominations; although the *breakdown* of those denominations – Liberals, Radicals, Reformers, Repealers and Whigs – varied, and broadly reflected the changing ratios of those denominations in Parliament, as outlined in Graph 2.5. By contrast, the supposed political affiliation of White's seems weak at best, with over a quarter of its MPs at any one time

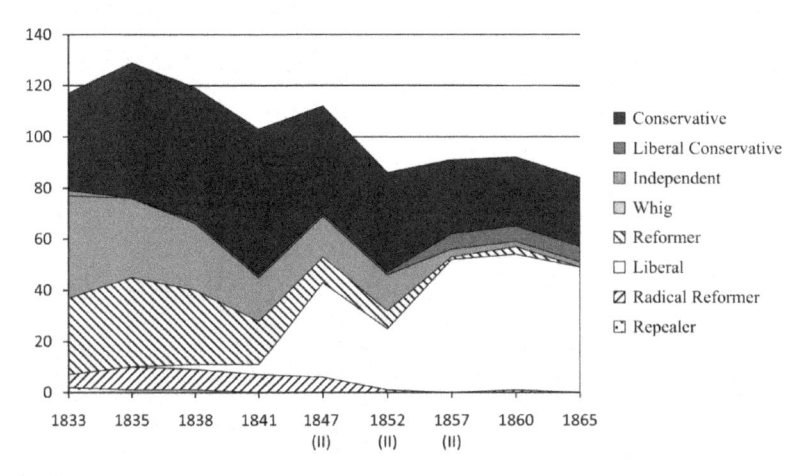

[Graph showing membership composition 1833-1865 with legend: Conservative, Liberal Conservative, Independent, Whig, Reformer, Liberal, Radical Reformer, Repealer]

Graph 2.11e Athenaeum Club.

having been Liberals of various denominations, and in many ways its composition came closer to resembling the cross-party make-up of an apolitical club like the Athenaeum than any of the three premier political clubs of the period, Brooks's, the Carlton and Reform Clubs.

Membership of Multiple Clubs by MPs

So far clubs have largely been examined in isolation, but many MPs belonged to more than one club, and Graph 2.12 looks at the combinations of club memberships amongst MPs. Many improbable-sounding combinations were possible, including 21 MPs who belonged to both the Reform and Carlton Clubs (usually at different times; as above, this is a product of analysing data drawn across a 36-year span when no comprehensive data survives on resignation dates, and so is an inevitable outcome of the necessary assumption that MPs retained all club memberships unless otherwise stated). Given such unusual combinations, it is unsurprising that some MPs could be noticeably silent about all of their club memberships, such as W. B. Beaumont, who entered Parliament in 1852. As a Liberal, he had joined Brooks's in 1851 and the Reform Club in 1855, along with the apolitical Travellers' and Oxford and Cambridge Clubs; yet he had also

Table 2.1 Combinations of the club memberships of MPs, 1832–68, amongst selected clubs

Club	Athenaeum	Broooks's	Carlton	Conservative	Junior Carlton	National	Reform	Travellers'	Westminster Reform
Brooks's	109								
Carlton	118	65							
Conservative	3	5	62						
Junior Carlton	2	1	47	5					
National	7	4	74	9	3				
Reform	96	289	21	3	0	4			
Travellers'	37	94	95	4	3	8	36		
Westminster Reform	4	23	2	0	1	0	51	0	
White's	37	105	195	3	14	7	34	65	3

Source: Seth Alexander Thévoz, 'Database of MPs' Club Memberships, 1832–68'.

joined Tory-inclined White's in 1852, declining to mention this in the list of clubs he publicised in *Dod's*.

Just as analysing party affiliations of MPs tells us much about the strength of political feeling at clubs, comparing the *shared* club memberships of MPs reveals something of each club's political character. What becomes significant is not so much the characteristics of individual members as the bonds between the members; an area particularly open to social network analysis.

Social network analysis is a relatively recent concept, having come to the fore in the last decade from the modern explosion in online social networking, and consequent attempts by sociologists to adequately measure complex webs of social interactions. Social network metrics seek to visually map social relationships between vertices and edges (otherwise known as nodes and the links between them). Methodologically, it has its roots in the eighteenth-century efforts of Leonhard Euler to represent different paths around the seven bridges of Konigsberg, and the mathematical work of Paul Erdos and Alfréd Rényi in the 1950s, and as a recognised discipline it has existed since the early 1970s, but has only fully evolved in the twenty-first century, with the explosion in social networking data generated.[53] Social historians have been quick to apply social network metrics to analysing social clubs. As medium-sized groups of interconnected individuals with recorded characteristics, such clubs offer precisely the kind of data which social network analysis was developed for. The ongoing work of Jennifer Regan-Lefebvre and Arthur Downing are just two examples of this evolving approach applied to historical research.[54] Thus the data from Graph 2.12 can be projected as the social network in Graph 2.13.[55] In this instance, with a comparison of overlapping club memberships of MPs, the clubs form the nodes while the members' data forms the links.

In the network in Graph 2.13, the thickness of the edges (lines) corresponds to the number of members shared by any two clubs (nodes), but the social network web projection allows for other patterns to emerge. The positioning of the clubs is important, with each club's position being dictated by its relationship to the whole network, rather than to any one other individual club; thus for instance, the Carlton's positioning in relationship to White's is not just dictated by the 195 members the two clubs had in common, but by the strength of the ties of both clubs to other clubs across the network. The closer clubs are projected to one another, the more significant their bonds. The result of this is to highlight the notion of 'core' and 'periphery' clubs. 'Core' clubs are centred in proportion to their centrality to the whole network. In many ways, Figure 2.1 projects the classic 'core'/'periphery' model, with the more significant, well-connected clubs in the centre, and less well-connected clubs consigned to the periphery. Much of this network speaks for itself, with the Reform Club and Brooks's sharing the strongest (i.e. thickest) link near the centre, and the Carlton and White's being the most central Conservative clubs; but the positioning of the apolitical clubs is noteworthy. Despite the Liberal-oriented political composition of the Athenaeum's MPs noted in Graph 2.11e, it remains almost equidistant from the Carlton, Reform and Brooks's. The Travellers' Club, by contrast, is firmly within the Conservative sphere, being closest to the Carlton and White's, and being closer to the ultra-Protestant National Club than the Reform Club. Again, none of this suggests anything fundamentally new, but it does illustrate points made above, with the minority of Conservative MPs at the Travellers' Club being better-embedded in overlapping Conservative clubs than the majority of Liberal MPs at the Travellers' were with Liberal clubs.

The two sample apolitical clubs seemed to have had a roughly even political divide – at the Athenaeum, 36.9 per cent of MPs were members of the Carlton, but 34.1 per cent and 30 per cent belonged to Brooks's and the Reform respectively. At the Travellers' Club, 44.4 per cent and 30.4 per cent belonged to the Carlton and White's, with 43.9 per cent belonging to Brooks's – but only 16.8 per cent were Reform Club members, perhaps indicating a more Whiggish trend amongst the well-heeled Liberal MPs who joined the Travellers'.[56]

Club membership combinations offer an insight into which political clubs could be viewed as offshoots of the membership of larger clubs. The findings confirm the prominence of the Carlton, Reform and Brooks's clubs, in showing just how many members of smaller political clubs overlapped with the major ones. As noted, the Carlton shared many members with other Conservative-leaning clubs. Amongst these, 95.9 per cent, 91.2 per cent, 80.4 per cent and 60 per cent respectively of the Junior Carlton, Conservative, and National Clubs and White's were also members of the Carlton Club, yet because of the generally smaller sizes of these four clubs, only White's contributed more than a negligible proportion of Conservative MPs at the Carlton (in its case,

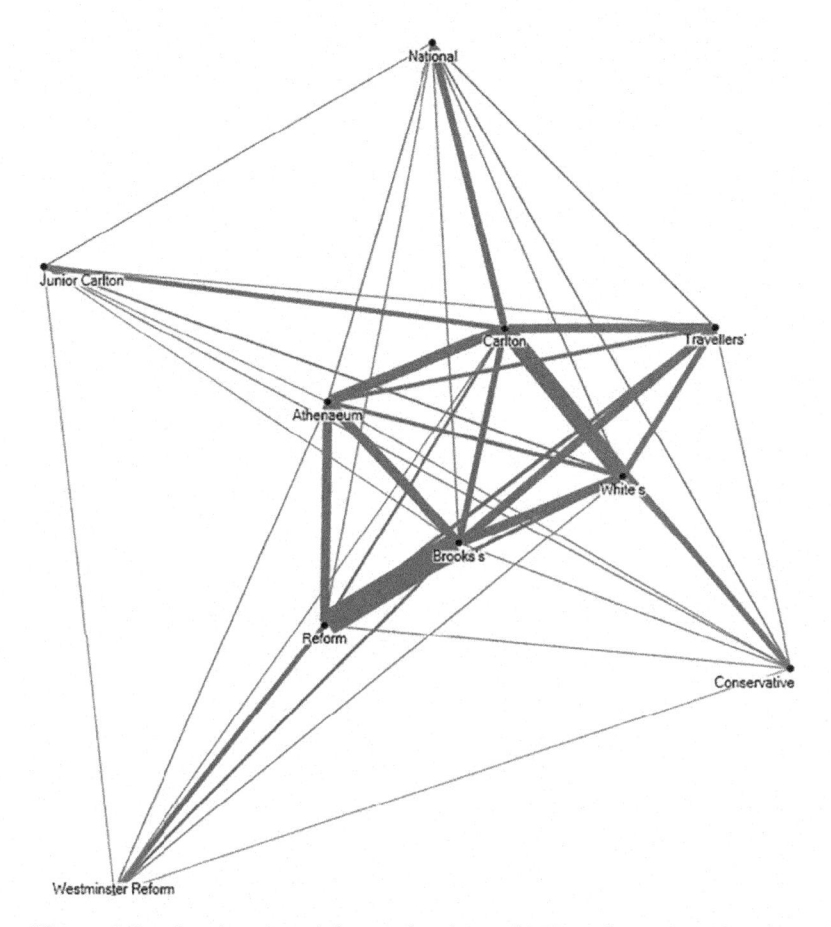

Figure 2.1 Overlapping club memberships of MPs in key selected clubs, as a social network. Source: Seth Alexander Thévoz, 'Database of MPs' Club Memberships, 1832–68'.

19.2 per cent of its members were Carlton members). On the Liberal side, 73.9 per cent of MPs in the Westminster Reform Club belonged to its successor the Reform Club. Appraising the short-lived Free Trade Club in such terms is difficult because of the small sample size available (just 27 MPs), yet it is still indicative that 23 of its MPs were Reform Club members, whilst not a single one belonged to the Carlton – a confirmation of its reputation for recruiting Cobdenite Free Traders (including Cobden himself), but not Peelites. The 42.9 per cent of both the Reform Club and Brooks's which each club shared with the other may have seemed a deceptively small proportion, but was an extremely significant result. The 289 MPs who belonged to both clubs made this by far the most common combination of clubs in the mid-Victorian House of Commons. In particular, despite the narrative of the Reform Club superseding Brooks's, it provides yet further evidence that for many Liberal MPs, there was still value in maintaining Brooks's membership in the post-Reform environment, even in tandem with the Reform Club – and with the expense which that entailed. It is revealing that the second most common combination was with the two equivalent clubs on the Conservative side, with 195 MPs belonging to both the Carlton and White's, indicating a trend of the eighteenth century clubs of Brooks's and White's still maintaining some shadow of their former popularity, but as supplements to the newer, more actively political clubs.

Trends in MPs' Elections to Clubs, Blackballing and Fast-Tracking

In the case of six clubs (the Athenaeum, Brooks's, the Carlton, the Junior Carlton, the Reform and White's) it has been possible to identify the year of joining for most MPs. With three of those clubs (the Carlton from 1834, the Reform from 1836, and the Junior Carlton in 1864), specific and comprehensive records survive, detailing *all* candidacies for club membership, whether successful or not. This data records an area long shrouded in mystery: elections to club membership. Equipped with this data, it is now possible to make several observations on three aspects of how MPs related to the election process: fast-tracking, blackballing, and resignation. Of these, blackballing has received the most attention, and deserves some explanation, for the blackball has taken on an almost iconic status, with the word entering the lexicon.[57] Bernard Darwin wrote in 1943 'The word "blackball" has a sinister ring and suggests all sort of dark and secret possibilities', while as recently as December 2012, the *Financial Times* confidently but incorrectly asserted 'Just one [black ball] was sufficient not only to halt the applicant in his tracks but to force the resignation of his proposer.'[58] The process actually varied considerably from club to club, but whether the voting was done by the entire club membership or was delegated to a committee, the shared features were that voting was done in secret using black and white balls instead of ballots, and a certain proportion of black balls (typically ranging from one in three to one in ten) meant the rejection of a membership application, and long-running feuds of retaliatory blackballing could lead to so-called 'blackballing scandals.'[59] Blackballing rules could be stringent: the Athenaeum rulebook stipulated that just 'one black-ball in ten shall exclude'.[60] At Brooks's, where just two blackballs were enough to exclude, the young Edward H. Knatchbull-Hugessen noted in his journal that a fierce row erupted in 1848 when seven candidates were rejected, including one who polled 'between 30 & 40 white balls, & only two black'. A proposal was submitted by 26 members, including Whig grandees Sir John Shelley and Lord Frederick Cavendish, that the Club should reconsider setting the bar to membership at two blackballs when a candidate collected so many whiteballs; the proposal was unanimously rejected by the Club's Managing Committee.[61]

It should be noted that MPs' familiarity with the anonymity granted by voting with blackballs predated the widespread use of the ballot in the 1872 Ballot Act – something which Lord John Russell defended, since 'choosing representatives and electing members of clubs are entirely different', arguing that club membership was not a question of being the 'sole representative' of the club, but of selecting a convivial acquaintance.[62] The whole process acquired much mystique and so MPs could go to great lengths to evade the blackball. One common tactic was to seek prestigious proposers, as was the case with Viscount Brackley MP who was proposed and seconded for Brooks's in 1847 by the Duke of Bedford and Earl Spencer.[63] However, with unprecedented access to the Carlton Club candidates' books and Reform Club ballot books of the period, it is finally possible to write with some certainty about the speculation surrounding blackballing for London's two most popular political clubs, and to apply this to parliamentarians.[64] What is striking is how rare blackballing was. Despite the considerable column inches dedicated to the dread which tormented many a candidate, the figures involved were only a small minority of cases.

Graph 2.12 shows the success rate for applicants to the Carlton Club. Each data point corresponds with one volume of the candidates' books – containing around 300 applicants – which in turn corresponded to between two and four years of applicants. The chart demonstrates a gradual decline in successful applications, from acceptance rates of 88.4 per cent and 90.2 per cent in the first two volumes (covering 1834–8), to acceptance rates of 68 per cent and 71.8 per cent in volumes 11 and 12 (covering 1861–6). In short, over time the Carlton Club became harder to join. However, the pattern was not quite as simple as these figures suggest.

Clearly identifying blackballing is problematic; one is likely to overestimate rather than underestimate it. Graph 2.12 only shows the rate of *successful* applications. The breakdown in Table 2.2 demonstrates that the reasons for unsuccessful applications were more diverse than might at first be assumed.

As can be seen, whilst outright rejection for membership *did* happen, it made up a small minority of unsuccessful applications – anything between 0.4 per cent and 11 per cent of cases in each volume. Indeed, the occasional (but by no means exhaustive) margin notes in candidates' books commenting on a rejection make it clear that some of these were not cases of blackballing at all, but of being rejected on a technicality, such as having omitted to include a seconder. (As with the case of MPs being immune to the club's membership cap, they could occasionally be immune to the problem of lacking proposers or seconders. John Barneby MP lacked both in 1838, yet remained in the Carlton candidates' book without being struck off, and was eventually elected in 1840 – a situation unthinkable for any non-parliamentary applicant.)[65]

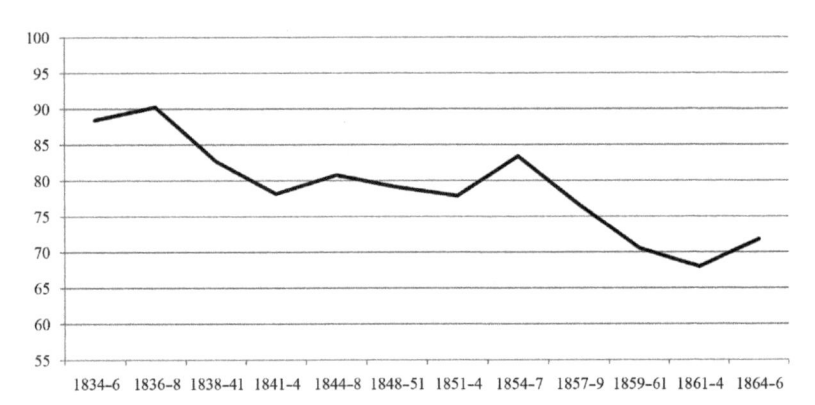

Graph 2.12 Proportion of successful applicants to the Carlton Club, 1834–66. Source: Carlton Club archive, Carlton Club, London, MS 'Carlton Club Candidates' Book', vols. 1–12 (1834–69).

Table 2.2 Data on acceptance and rejection in Carlton Club candidates, books vols 1–12[66]

Volume	Period	Total no. of candidates	No. elected	No. withdrawn	No. rejected	Died	Declined
1	1834–6	294	260	27	6	1	0
2	1836–8	287	259	25	3	0	0
3	1838–41	283	234	40	6	3	0
4	1841–4	293	229	58	1	5	0
5	1844–8	291	235	39	8	6	3
6	1848–51	292	231	48	6	7	0
7	1851–4	289	230	48	5	5	0
8	1854–7	295	246	40	5	3	1
9	1857–9	291	223	35	20	3	0
10	1859–61	285	201	47	22	15	0
11	1861–4	281	191	60	11	19	0
12	1864–6	294	211	47	10	25	1

Source: Carlton Club archive, Carlton Club, London, MS 'Carlton Club Candidates' Book', vols. 1–12 (1834–69).

By far the most common reason for failure to join a club was the withdrawal of an application. This may seem surprising, given the far more established focus on blackballing. Withdrawal of an application could be by the candidate himself, or by one of his proposers. This becomes far more understandable when one considers the convention that if a candidate was blackballed, their proposer would be expected to resign their club membership as a matter of honour.[67] Accordingly, if a candidate looked likely to be blackballed, both he and his proposer would be minded to withdraw rather than risk the proposer being forced to resign. Thus the fear of blackballing was a far greater determinant of a failed application than the blackball itself.

Naturally, the acceptance figures only reflect those who had made it into the candidates' books, that is, those who had secured a proposer and seconder in the first place. There is no way of gauging the breadth and depth of interest in membership among those unable to be formally proposed. By contrast, some candidates could accumulate some quite extraordinary surpluses of nominators. Whilst it was rare for a candidate to accumulate anything more than three or four seconders, some MPs like Edmund Lechmere Charlton could gather no less than thirty-seven supporting signatures for the Carlton Club.[68]

Up until 1866, the Reform Club's instances of blackballing were even rarer than those at the Carlton (Graph 2.13). In the Club's first year it accepted 97.9 per cent of candidates, and in its first volume of candidates (far lengthier than the equivalent Carlton Club volumes), spanning 13 April 1836 to 16 December 1852, only 105 out of 1,907 candidates were rejected by the Committee – a success rate of 94.5 per cent – and where blackballs were deployed, it is difficult to discern any pattern. For instance, the club's first 333 applicants met with only seven blackballs, until 15 December 1837 saw four blackballs being dispensed for four (seemingly unrelated) candidates.[69] Considering the relative ease of joining the Club, the *New York Times'* London correspondent wrote in 1860 that 'the Reform Club is not particular, so long as a man is of value to the cause, what his antecedents, character and banking account may be'.[70] Yet despite the correspondent singling out the Reform Club, it demonstrated a similar pattern of blackballing to the Carlton Club around the same period; high rates of acceptance at the outset, which gradually dropped over 30 years from over 90 per cent to around 70 per cent. (The Reform Club's acceptance rate then further dropped to 59.7 per cent in 1868, having stood at 73.6 per cent two years earlier.) In the absence of other political clubs with comparable detailed records over the same equally long period covering balloting, blackballing and candidacies, it may be speculated as to whether this trend was considered normal; and, if so, whether this offers an explanation as to why so many new clubs were set up in the nineteenth century. Certainly, the experience of the Junior Carlton Club would have been even starker – whilst membership was capped at 2,000 (excluding parliamentarians), when the Club was established in 1864, the Committee had the right to elect the first 500 members 'without the ordinary formalities of a proposer and seconder'.[71] With new clubs letting in the vast majority of applicants, and established clubs being increasingly selective, a strong incentive would have existed for prospective club members to set up new clubs of their own which they could join immediately, instead of facing a lengthy waiting list followed by an uncertain ballot. In the absence of further datasets covering club candidacies in this period, this is difficult to prove, but the Carlton and Reform Club acceptance rates of 1834–68 would certainly be consistent with this.

The phenomenon of blackballing can only be fully comprehended in conjunction with waiting lists, and an appreciation of the supply and demand of available spaces. Waiting times could be lengthy for non-MPs. By the 1870s, a candidate dying of old age whilst waiting to be elected to a club was a surprisingly common occurrence, being the fate of almost one in ten candidates at the Carlton. This had not always been the case: in the 1830s, non-parliamentary candidates for Carlton membership could expect to wait only three to four years to be put up for election. Yet the 1860s saw an eruption in the size of the waiting list, with most candidates not coming up for election until eleven or twelve years later, explaining the sudden jump in candidates dying whilst on the waiting list (19 and 25 candidates respectively in volumes 11 and 12 of the Carlton candidates' book). It is difficult to definitively establish why the 1860s saw such a growth in candidates for political clubs, although a perfectly feasible hypothesis would be that the debates around successive Reform Bills may well have enthused the prospective electors who would have most benefitted from successive proposed enfranchisements, and encouraged them to join a political club as a means of an entrée to the political world.

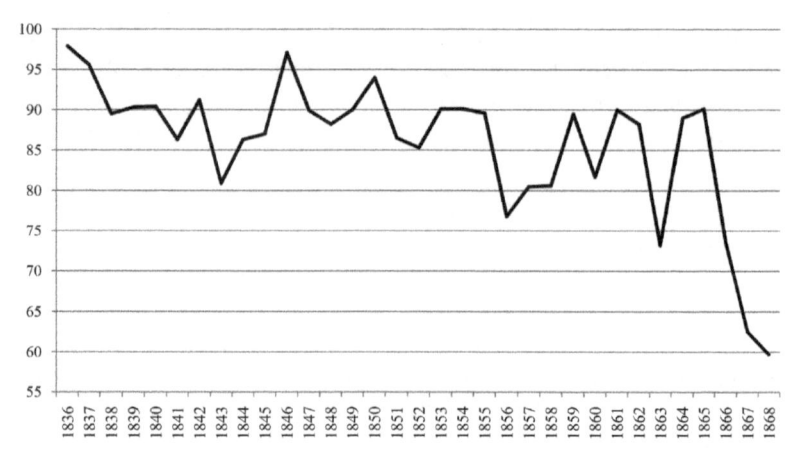

Graph 2.13 Proportion of successful applicants to the Reform Club, 1836–68. Source: Reform Club archive, London, Reform Club ballot books, vols. 1–2 (1836–78).

The length of the waiting list was determined by the availability of places, which in turn was determined by a club's cap on membership numbers, and the rate at which existing members would either resign or die. All the major clubs of the period had a cap on membership, varying from 500 to 2,000. Resignations are difficult to trace or quantify; there are sporadic references to them in club minutes, but not on any comprehensive basis.[72] Some indication is given when an applicant to a club was re-joining, and so it can be inferred that they had resigned at some earlier date – but it was far from 'typical' for those who resigned to rejoin.[73] Archival shortcomings also make it difficult to pinpoint when resignations occurred – John Collett MP was fast-tracked into the Reform Club in 1843, the same year that he entered Parliament, and he remained in Parliament until 1869; yet the precise date of his resignation is unknown because of missing Reform Club membership lists for 1855–7, and his disappearance from the lists by 1858. A further difficulty occurs when the only existing membership record was of the initial date of election, and a subsequent change of party affiliation may well have brought about a probable (but by no means certain) resignation. Certainly, after the events of 1846, the only Peelites to immediately withdraw from the Carlton were Sir James Graham and Colonel Sibthorpe; others, like Gladstone, remained members throughout the 1850s.[74] Nonetheless, MPs joining differently aligned clubs several decades apart strongly implied a resignation in the interim. Henry James Baillie joined Brooks's in 1824, having at least two relatives already there. Yet he did not enter Parliament until 1840, when he took his seat as a Conservative, joined the Carlton Club, and was an active participant in Disraeli's 'Young England' movement. His continued membership – and use – of Brooks's in the 1840s seems improbable, but there is no recorded resignation.

Whilst the non-existence of data on resignations and deaths poses a problem, this can be circumvented by taking a simple supply-and-demand model on membership in one sample club. Using the complete run of candidates' books of the Carlton Club from 1834 – a hitherto untapped source – it has been possible to estimate the supply of places.[75] This has been done in Graph 2.15. The size of the club varied, being determined by the cap of 600 members (raised to 700 in 1837, and 800 in 1862), plus the variable number of parliamentarians who had joined as supernumerary members. Whilst supernumerary membership included all parliamentarians, and so could theoretically include peers, the actual number of peers who joined as supernumerary members was low, because it is evident in the candidates' books that most of them joined when they were *future* peers using courtesy titles, and so their joining did not increase the size of the membership – therefore the number of MPs was the main determinant of the size of the Carlton above its cap, even though a negligible number of peers would have added an extra variable.[76] Graph 2.14 accounts for the total number of new members elected after 1836 (the solid line). From this figure, the number of MP-members (the dashed line) is deducted, since these were supernumerary members. What remains (the dotted line) are the number of non-parliamentary vacancies filled up by new members each year, that is, the supply of places available that year, from the resignation or death of existing members.

Calculating the demand for places has been much easier, through keeping a tally of applicants in the candidates' books. By extrapolating the accumulated number of successfully elected members (supply) from the accumulated number of candidates (demand), and factoring in the remaining variables such as the number of applicants already rejected, and expansions in the size of the membership, it is possible to calculate the excess demand for Carlton Club membership, that is, the exact size of the Carlton Club waiting list Graph 2.14).

The exponential growth of the waiting list can thus be seen. Even the Carlton Club's expansion of 1862 to accommodate an extra hundred members only resulted in a reduction of 27 on the previous year's waiting list, from 776 to 749. By the following year, the waiting list was rising again. Given this context of high competition for places, growing waiting lists, and the fear (if seldom the reality) of the blackball, the experience of MPs in joining political clubs was different from that of most other members because of one process: fast-tracking. Many MPs were able to bypass the waiting list entirely, and were elected within well under a year of nomination.

A search through the Carlton Club candidates' books for 1834–68 gives an idea of the non-parliamentary member's plight on the waiting list. Even the socially well-connected were not immune to the waiting list. Six years before he was elected to Parliament, John Henry Campbell was nominated for the Carlton by no less than twenty-four different signatures, with seconders including F. R. Bonham and the Earl of Arundel; yet Campbell still had to wait the then standard three years for membership.[77] Even the future third Marquess of Salisbury (as Lord Robert Cecil) had to wait over a year for admission to the Carlton, as he was neither an MP nor a peer when he joined the Club in 1850.[78] The contrast with fast-tracked MPs is stark.

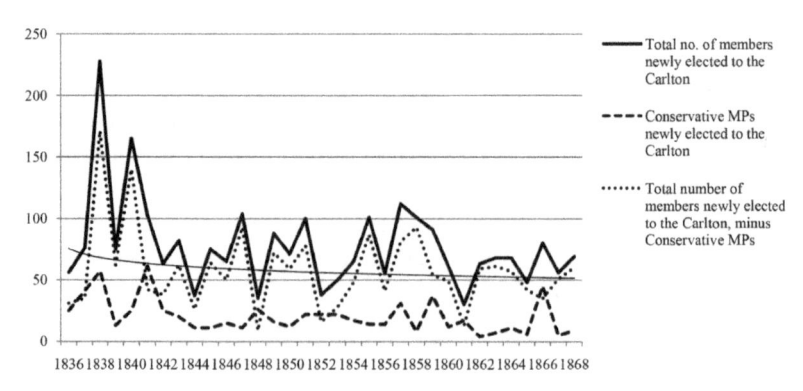

Graph 2.14 Supply of available places at the Carlton Club by year, 1836–68, accounting for the distorting effect caused by the supernumerary membership of MPs. Source: Carlton Club archive, Carlton Club, London, MS 'Carlton Club Candidates' Book', vols. 1–13.

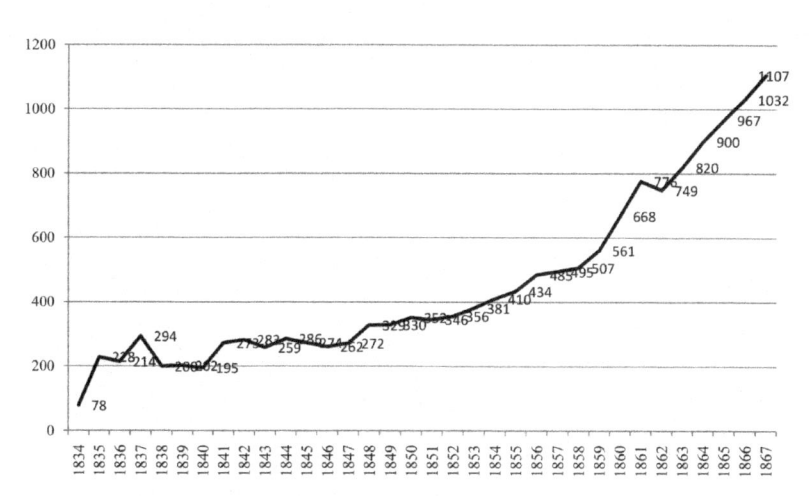

Graph 2.15   No. of candidates on the Carlton Club waiting list, 1834–67. Source: Carlton Club archive, Carlton Club, London, MS 'Carlton Club Candidates' Book', vols. 1–13.

Fast-tracking is of interest because it almost entirely happened to parliamentarians. The reasons for this were structural. The Carlton Club may have had a tight cap on membership numbers, but this cap explicitly did not apply to parliamentarians, who could be elected in unlimited numbers as supernumerary members. The Reform Club followed suit, and granted the same supernumerary status for MPs, with Rule III of the Club permitting its Committee to elect MPs and 'distinguished foreign members' without their having to go through the usual procedure, and this resulted in large numbers of newly elected MPs joining; on 17 May 1837, 17 new MPs were admitted in this way by the Committee.[79] Indeed, so confident was the Committee that MPs applying for membership would be admitted as a matter of course, that in 1839 they resolved 'That Lord Gasford and Mr. Pigot MP be allowed the use of the club House until elected by the General Committee on Friday next.'[80] Amongst relatively newly established clubs, the formalities of being put down in the candidates' book could be overlooked altogether, as happened in 1836 to Conservative MPs Richard Alsager and Thomas Balfour at the Carlton Club.[81] When the Junior Carlton Club was established, it was even more frank about the rights of parliamentarians to forgo the waiting list, stating that MPs and peers were 'at all times entitled to immediate ballot'.[82] As previously observed, newly elected MPs were most commonly elected to a political club around the time of their election to Parliament. A by-product of this behaviour was that an active Conservative supporter who had languished on the Carlton Club's waiting list for several years could find that upon his election to Parliament, his election to the Carlton Club was hurried through, and the numerical cap no longer presented an obstacle. This was the experience of Alexander Beresford-Hope, who had applied to join the Carlton Club in 1840, spent a year on the waiting list, and was promptly elected in 1841 after entering Parliament.[83] Indeed, such fast-tracking could even apply to candidates who had previously been unsuccessful. John Alexander, Conservative MP for Carlow in 1853–60, had not been in urgent need of a club, as he was one of the Athenaeum's founder members.[84] Nonetheless, he applied to join the Carlton on 22 May 1840, only to see his proposer swiftly withdraw for unspecified reasons on 6 June. Eventually, on 21 March 1854 Alexander was elected to the Carlton at the second attempt, being fast-tracked just a month after applying for the second time, and one year after entering Parliament.[85] That fast-tracking was dependent on an applicant's status as an MP is evident from the case of one MP who applied to join the Carlton on 6 April 1859. He was entered into the candidates' book as 'Sir Robert W. Carden MP', but was promptly defeated in the general election the following month. The 'MP' in his name was accordingly struck off in the book, and so he was not elected to the Carlton until five years later.[86]

Fast-tracking could also serve to correct anomalous political club affiliations, particularly in the case of existing members of White's (and to a lesser extent, Brooks's) with their inclusion of MPs whose membership owed more to familial than political connections. Conservative MP John Attwood entered Parliament in 1841, but had been a member of Brooks's since 1839. His fast-tracked admission to the Carlton on 24 August 1841, the same day as his nomination, ensured his access to a Conservative club.[87]

Within the aristocratic citadels of Brooks's and White's, fast-tracking of MPs did not happen for structural reasons, as these two clubs did not have special rules to elect MPs as supernumerary members. However, there is anecdotal evidence that such fast-tracking happened for social reasons, with Sir James Graham noting of his election at Brooks's 'I was not aware that this honour was so near at hand; but I fancy Lord Cawdor and Lord Morpeth have been so kind as to forward it of their own accord.'[88]

Precisely identifying fast-tracking is problematic, but I have chosen to define it as election to a club within less than a month of nomination. Most clubs held monthly membership meetings to elect new members, and so election within a month was a clear indication of an applicant having been moved to the front of the queue. Although the fast-tracking of MPs was widespread, it was by no means universal. There were several possible causes for such limitations. One was simple ignorance by a committee of the applicant's status as an MP. Many MPs did *not* include their post-nominal letters, and there were some cases where a committee was apparently unaware of the candidate's status as an MP. Sir James Dalrymple-Horn-Elphinstone Bt applied to join the Carlton in 1859, two years after entering Parliament. Yet he neglected to mention that he was an MP and, despite twelve supporting signatures, he unnecessarily languished on the waiting list for eight years when he could have been fast-tracked, only being elected once he was out of Parliament.[89] There were also instances of MPs on the waiting list who belatedly penciled in the letters 'MP' to their application, presumably in order to improve their chances of swift election.[90] Indeed, the practice of fast-tracking, whilst largely reserved for MPs, was *not* the norm amongst MPs – only 265 of the Carlton Club's 1,024 MPs were fast-tracked in under a month.[91]

MPs who were not Club Members

Only a small minority of MPs did not have a club. For the 11.9 per cent of MPs without one, it could be a matter of embarrassment, as with the case of Henry Mitcalfe, newly elected for Tynemouth in 1841, who could not bring himself to write 'None' in the 'clubs' field of his *Dod's* questionnaire, and instead wrote the excuse 'Seldom in London except on business only for a few days, & then live with my Brother in Fitzroy Square.'[92] Other MPs who were initially without a club did not remain clubless for long. John Collier did not originally belong to any club when returned for Plymouth in 1832, and answered Charles Dod's 1836 questionnaire by crossing out the 'club', yet joined the Reform Club later that year.[93] As might be expected, clubless MPs tended to be self-made men, with limited contacts in London society. Of those MPs who were clubless, their political affiliations can be seen in Graphs 2.16a and b, in both absolute numbers and percentage terms.

As can be seen, these MPs were disproportionately on the Liberal side of the House of Commons – a testament more than anything else to the success of the Carlton Club in recruiting the vast majority of Conservative MPs, which was a feat neither Brooks's nor the Reform Club matched. Indeed, it is striking how both the absolute number and the share of Conservative MPs without a club – already quite low in the 1830s – consistently dropped thereafter. Given that the Reform Club's foundation in 1836 filled a gap in Clubland, it is also perhaps unsurprising to find that the two largest absolute numbers of clubless MPs were both in the Parliament of 1832–5, amongst Reformers and Whigs, at 42 and 35 MPs respectively, and that these figures tumbled thereafter – although intriguingly, with the gradual increase in the number of Liberals, this brought about the phenomenon of dozens of clubless Liberal MPs, peaking in 1852, declining thereafter. Indeed, the 1852 Parliament saw the number of clubless Liberal MPs more than double, from 14 to 33, but the successive decline of clubless Liberal MPs through the 1850s and early 1860s meant that, by the Parliament of 1865, this figure had been reduced to zero. More broadly, although the general trend across the 1832–68 period was a fall in the number and share of clubless MPs, successive intakes of 'Liberal' MPs of various denominations showed considerably more oscillation than Conservative MPs did. Additionally, these figures for clubless MPs should be considered in conjunction with Graphs 2.6–2.9. The prevalence of Carlton Club membership among Conservative MPs was high (rising from 66 per cent to 96 per cent across this period), and so fluctuations in the number of clubless Conservative MPs were overwhelmingly (but not exclusively) dictated by the extent of just one club's membership among MPs. Indeed, in aggregate terms, the Carlton alone could claim among its membership 85.1 per cent of all Conservatives and 72.6 per cent of all Liberal Conservatives who sat between 1832–68. This was not reflected amongst Liberal MPs being concentrated in one club. As is made clear by the rate of Liberal MP membership of Brooks's and the Reform Clubs in Graphs 2.8 and 2.9, and by the demonstrable overlap in Brooks's/Reform Club membership in Graphs 2.12–2.13 (289 MPs, accounting for 43.4 per cent of Liberal MPs at Brooks's, and 42.9 per cent of Liberal MPs at the Reform Club),

Liberal MPs were far more diverse in their club-joining patterns. Indeed, this did not apply exclusively to the 'big two' Liberal clubs, Brooks's and the Reform, which jointly claimed between them 1,050 MPs, compared to the 1,024 MPs at the Carlton alone. It applied more broadly to Liberal MP club membership in general, for, as the Liberal bias in absolute numbers at apolitical clubs such as the Athenaeum and the Traveller's shows, such clubs could attract the surplus of Liberals who did not join one of the 'big two' Liberal clubs. It is thus perhaps unsurprising that with so many more variables, and less of a strictly-defined party link to parallel the Conservative bond to the Carlton, the excess of clubless Liberal MPs thus showed considerably more oscillation than that of clubless Conservatives.

It is less easy to generalise about meaningful trends among smaller parties such as Repealers and Radicals, since the sample size of the party groupings are so small as to be effectively meaningless; although anecdotally, it could be observed that the relatively high proportion of Repealer MPs without a London club was a symptom, perhaps, of their relative disengagement from London society.

As noted, the largest major party affiliation to have a non-club minority was that of Reformers in 1832–5. This was consistent with the limited number of club options open to Reformers. The term was a broad one, embracing everything from Whiggery to radicalism, and was gradually supplanted by a number of other terms, most notably 'Liberal'. The term was at its height in the 1830s, within recent memory of the 1832 Reform Act controversies, yet until the foundation of the Reform Club in 1836, Reformers did not have a natural club to join; Brooks's continued to have a highly aristocratic reputation (even if the reality of this is open to question), while the short-lived Westminster Reform Club's membership was Radical to an almost sectarian degree, so the vacuum in corresponding political clubs for Reformer MPs in the early 1830s may explain why so many of these parliamentarians had no recorded club – this would have been particularly relevant among MPs elected in the 1832–5 Parliament.

The next most marginalised grouping was that of the Radicals and, as with the Repealers, the relatively limited sample size (33) means that one should treat this figure with caution. Radicals were relatively well-catered for from 1834 onwards; not only were they welcomed in smaller clubs such as the Westminster Reform (which

12 of them joined) and the Free Trade Club (where seven of the Club's 27 parliamentary members were Radicals), but the broad embrace of the Reform Club meant that 22 of *Dod's* 33 Radicals were members of the Reform.[94]

Finally, Conservatives and Liberal Conservatives had the smallest share of non-club membership, with Conservatives dropping from 12.1 per cent to 0.8 per cent across the period (and although the number and share of clubless Liberal Conservative MPs rose throughout the tumultuous 1850s, as their absolute numbers became more significant, as a share it never rose above 4.5 per cent), which compares with a generally-higher share and absolute number of clubless Whig and Liberal MPs, most notably with 14.5 per cent of Whigs in the 1832 Parliament and 14.7 per cent of Liberals in the 1852 Parliament being clubless; although it must be recognised that the 1865 Parliament presented a curious development with the share of clubless Liberals being reduced to zero. In absolute numbers, only the 1841 Parliament saw Conservatives outpace the Liberals and Whigs for clubless MPs; and even this figure is misleading, as adding together the Liberal factions yet again shows an overall majority of

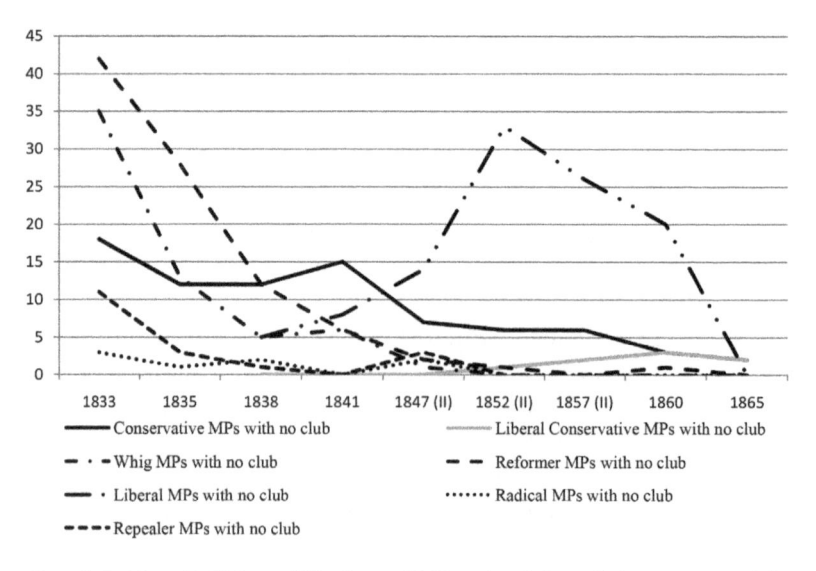

Graph 2.16a Political affiliations of MPs who did not belong to any club, in absolute numbers.

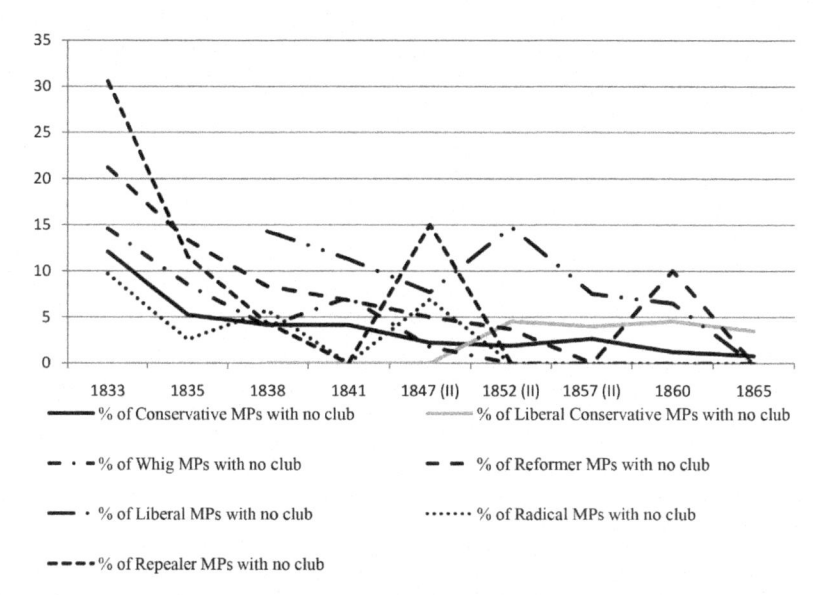

[Graph showing declining percentages from 1833 to 1865, with legend:]
— % of Conservative MPs with no club
— % of Liberal Conservative MPs with no club
— · — % of Whig MPs with no club
— — % of Reformer MPs with no club
— · % of Liberal MPs with no club
······ % of Radical MPs with no club
— — — · % of Repealer MPs with no club

Graph 2.16b Political affiliations of MPs who did not belong to any club, in percentage terms.

clubless Liberals, whilst as a share of Conservative MPs, it was still smaller than with numerous Liberal factions.

Conclusion

The wide range of data presented on club memberships here bears out a number of observations. The preponderance of club membership among MPs – consistently over 90 per cent from the late 1830s – was simply too great to be ignored. MPs belonged to a diverse range of clubs, but a few political clubs predominated; the Carlton Club for the Conservatives, and the Liberals were almost evenly divided between the Reform Club and Brooks's. Over time, the Carlton's popularity with Conservative MPs grew even further (notwithstanding a gradual dropping-off of Liberal Conservative MPs' membership), while the Reform Club and Brooks's experienced a slight decline among Liberal MPs. White's, long assumed to be a major political force, deserves some reappraisal, particularly in the light of its far more mixed political composition than the three main 'party' clubs, with more of a resemblance to a prestigious social club like the Athenaeum than to the political headquarters which the Carlton and

Reform Clubs presented themselves as. Links between political clubs and parties could be extremely strong; however, links to other factors such as family or geographical area are more difficult to prove.

The overlapping club membership of MPs is extremely revealing in emphasising the notion of 'core' and 'periphery' clubs, with political clubs like the Westminster Reform, the Free Trade, the Conservative, the National and the Junior Carlton all being confirmed in their status as offshoot establishments of three principal political clubs, albeit each with their own distinctive political culture and composition, often linked to a particular political faction. Network analysis of such overlapping club membership also stresses hitherto unsuspected links between politicians and apolitical clubs: despite most of the Athenaeum's MPs being 'Liberals', it was equally popular with members of 'Liberal' and 'Conservative' clubs, whilst the second most popular apolitical club with MPs, the Travellers', displayed far more overlapping memberships with MPs belonging to 'Conservative' clubs.

In spite of the near mythological status accorded to blackballing, the data presented here suggests much by way of club joining habits. In their early years, new clubs like the Carlton and Reform very rarely rejected candidates, but with the passage of years, clubs became more selective. The blackball, much written about as a social phenomenon in 'blackballing scandals', was extraordinarily rare, and most unsuccessful candidacies were due to a withdrawn application rather than a blackball. In political clubs, MPs were almost entirely exempt from these constraints, as they were granted supernumerary status, and so did not have to go on a potentially decades-long waiting list; instead, they could come up for the ballot immediately. However, they did not enjoy such a status in apolitical clubs, and so numerous major clubs that were popular with MPs still necessitated joining a waiting list, including the Athenaeum, the Travellers' Club, the United University Club, Boodle's, the Oxford and Cambridge Club, the Union Club and the United Service Club. (Unfortunately, with gaps in data relating to club membership, less can be said with any great certainty about club membership retention by MPs, and so much of the data simply covers joining habits.)

Finally, there is much evidence to suggest a rush by MPs to join political clubs within the first year or so of their being elected, particularly in the case of the three 'core' political clubs, though the relationship was much weaker in other clubs like White's and the Athenaeum. Whilst MPs may not have belonged to these clubs before being elected (since club intervention in election candidacies was not limited to existing club members), they were quick to join once elected, and frequently used rules existed to ensure that MPs were fast-tracked ahead of long-standing candidates for membership. Given the numerous trends of MPs belonging to clubs, and in particular political clubs, there is much evidence here to support the view that such clubs formed a significant feature of the mid-nineteenth century parliamentary landscape.

CHAPTER 3

CLUBS AND THE MPS' WORLD II: EXPERIENCES IN CLUBLAND SPACE

Introduction

This chapter concerns the geography of power; namely, how club spaces were an integral part of the fabric of mid-nineteenth century Westminster. The preceding chapter has presented much data to support this notion, but less by way of detail. It is intended to supplement the preceding quantitative data with a qualitative approach, to set out how MPs used their clubs.

This is no easy task, for even nineteenth-century sources were confused about precisely what role clubs performed in political life, and agreed far more on what functions clubs did *not* perform than what they did. In 1876, the *Saturday Review* refuted 'the pretentions of the Reform Club to be accepted as the representative and organ of the Liberal Party', and yet the same report conceded 'the Reform Club, like the Carlton, is certainly not carried on for purely social purposes: each has a political object'.[1] To the fresh perspective of foreign observers, it seemed plain that London clubs *did* play a critical role in the evolving party system: the *New York Times* observed in 1856 'In England political affairs are managed by Clubs as here by conventions', identifying the Carlton and Reform Clubs as 'where the wires that ring the call to political parties in England are pulled'.[2] If such claims were true, then the political clubs had a unique overlap of social and practical functions. To explore the range of Clubland activities in Westminster, five key themes will be examined: the clubs' flexibility as a space (a recurring theme relevant to all the subsequent themes), their meetings both in public and in private, Clubland masculinity and the flow of information and gossip in clubs. Through these, it is hoped to better explain the practicalities of how clubs formed a vital part of the party system which evolved through the period.[3] Given the patchy, anecdotal nature of much of the material from club archives and private archives, it is intended here to pick out examples that signify a broader trend in how club spaces functioned as part of the system, particularly in the absence of a fully-functioning parliamentary estate for much of the period.

One of the most important reasons for the rise of clubs in a parliamentary context from the 1830s onwards had nothing to do with currents of reform or party developments, but with practicality: there were few alternative places to go. On 16 October 1834, a vast conflagration burned down most of the old Houses of Parliament. The subsequent neo-gothic edifice, constructed largely to the designs of Reform Club and Travellers' Club architect Charles Barry, took over 30 years to complete. In the interim, from 1835 temporary accommodation was provided for the Commons in the former House of Lords (the old Court of Requests), and for the Lords in the Painted Chamber, the latter renovated by the Carlton Club's original architect Sir Robert Smirke. (Smirke had also briefly tried to take control of Parliament's redevelopment in the 1830s.)[4] Until the 1852 session, there was no permanent purpose-built Commons chamber on the site, aside from the 'experimental' Commons sittings of May 1850 in an acoustically ill-suited chamber.[5] Even after 1852, the chamber was frequently noisy and impractical being close to a construction site throughout the 1860s; consequently MPs could no longer rely on the lobbies of Parliament to conduct much of the discussion, lobbying and recreation which had formerly taken place within the old Palace of Westminster.[6] Proximity to the sewage-strewn Thames also made the parliamentary estate an unappealing dining prospect for MPs and peers. Parliamentarians at Westminster were repeatedly dogged by foul odours from such varied causes as faulty ventilation, the dumping of parliamentary kitchen waste outside the Commons, and poor sanitation.[7] Instead, MPs and peers sought more palatable alternatives for entertaining nearby, but there were few reputable alternatives in mid-Victorian London.

The emergence of parliamentary alliances around broad issues of principle such as reform, protection and religion (as opposed to smaller factions based on family and patronage) also meant a growing need for larger venues to house all of these parliamentarians. The majority of aristocratic preserves along Piccadilly and St James's Street – such as Holland House, and the traditional clubs of White's and Brooks's – were inadequate to the task of accommodating such large meetings, while the cost of their maintenance fell disproportionately on one patron, landlord or family.[8] Accordingly, the need to accommodate MPs in an adequate space assumed a paramount importance.

A feature of this chapter is that it mostly treats the period as one; although the political context changed significantly over time, the role of clubs did not appreciably change after the 1830s. The club 'system' was still evolving in the 1830s as the Carlton and Reform Clubs were founded, and acquired their traditions. There were short-term arrangements in the 1830s which proved ramshackle and temporary, such as the Charles Street office that predated the Carlton Club, considered by Norman Gash to be a 'hasty and amateurish improvisation'.[9] Likewise, after the founding of the Carlton and Reform Clubs in the 1830s, there were numerous other offshoot establishments such as the National Club and the Free Trade Club, with overlapping MPs. Yet these can be viewed as supplemental (and sometimes short-lived) additions to the club 'system'. It is contended here that by the Parliament of 1837–41, a clear pattern had emerged in how MPs engaged with their clubs, and the broad rhythm of how and why 'clubbable' MPs used their club spaces did not appreciably change thereafter. Changes in the expectations of clubs, proximity to Westminster, and campaigning activity would all take place – but not until after the Second Reform Act.[10]

Space: Its Politics and Dynamics

The concept of space has been discussed at length by historians in recent decades. One of the ramifications of the belated translation of Jürgen

Habermas's *The Structural Transformation of the Public Sphere* has been to open a debate among English-speaking scholars on the precise parameters of public and private spheres.[11] Habermas's own writings on eighteenth century culture have paved the way for much subsequent work on the relationship between space and politics in a pre-industrial context; Beat Kümin has argued that in pre-industrial Europe, space 'no longer appears an inert shell or "container", but ... a relational construct and, in turn, a factor with a potential to shape subsequent forms of human exchange', and it is hoped here to look at how space was used, not only being shaped by the political activities of Clubland, but also in shaping those activities.[12]

The clubs of St James's have often been overlooked for their significance as a space, and some historians actively refuted their importance in such terms. W. A. Munford thought the Radicals 'not a Party at all, not even a tolerably organised Group', because 'they had no common policy and *no common meeting place outside the House*' (my italics). Regarding the existence of the Reform Club, Munford conceded it was founded 'to meet this obvious need but by [1836] the flood tide of reform was beginning to recede and the Club soon had far more Whigs than Radicals among its members', adding dismissively that 'some Whigs were possibly attracted at least as much by [Alexis] Soyer's cooking as by Barry's architecture'.[13] Furthermore, Mike Crang has deprecated 'the temptation so often evident in the geographic literature to end up privileging one space, scale or relation as the arena of the political'.[14] Certainly, Crang's warning can be seen as a counterpoint to the spatial turn being taken too far. The spatial turn in history has afforded historians the opportunity to draw far-reaching conclusions about seemingly marginal points. In an overwhelmingly penetrating and original analysis of the influence of space on radical politics up to 1845, Christina Parolin likens the 'Rose and Crown' pub on the Strand to a working-class parliament. At first this may seem a far-fetched assertion, but she argues persuasively in its favour, citing the pub's visitors drawn from around Great Britain, its hosting national meetings of plebeian radicals, its focus for demonstrations outside Parliament, and the clear procedures laid down for discussions and debate.[15] Whilst caution needs to be exercised in not over-extending the argument, the use of space by clubs is thus a hugely neglected dimension to studies of the period.

Clubs form a strong counter-argument for the privileging of a particular space in the political process and, beyond Parolin's work, numerous studies have used physical spaces as the focus of social and political developments.[16]

The writings of Henri Lefebvre have long been influential in French but, as with Habermas, it is only in recent years with their wider translation that they have begun to inform an English-language understanding of spatial theory, particularly in their emphasis on flow in space. In a landmark essay, Lefebvre contended 'There is an ideology of space ... Because space, which seems homogenous, which appears given as a whole in its objectivity, in its pure form, such as we determine it, is a social product.'[17] Lefebvre argued that the concept of space cannot be measured by 'one formal method, logical or logistical; it can only be, a *dialectical method*, that analyzes the contradictions of space in society and social practice', and so much of spatial theory concerns the debate over how space is used, and its wider significance.[18] In particular, it 'deals with flows: of energy, raw materials, money, the labor force, various goods, mixtures of people and things, signs, information and understanding, symbols, capitals, etc.'[19] Lefebvre has influenced other writers, such as the approach taken by Nirmal Puwar, in her work on politicised spaces. Puwar has outlined the way in which ostensible social changes have physical manifestation, notably by charting how the growing role of women in politics is physically defined by the spaces to which they are granted access.[20]

Lefebvre's emphasis on flows stresses the importance of temporal factors; in this context, how club spaces were used in different ways at different times.[21] As well as combining elements of public and private spaces, the club could be used as a theatre for conspicuous demonstrations of power – which will be more explicitly outlined in the section on dinners below. And as we shall see, club floor plans encouraged circulation around the clubhouse through set routes and main entrances, which in turn encouraged meetings and interactions in defined corridors, function rooms and atriums.

Clubs were by no means the only Victorian leisure space to demonstrate this crucial spatial dimension, as evidenced by Peter Bailey's trailblazing work on the use of space across Victorian leisure, which has prompted others such as Pamela Horn to follow his study of these areas.[22] Bailey himself has also looked at working men's clubs in some detail, but the so-called 'gentlemen's clubs' have not enjoyed the same level of scrutiny.[23]

Clubs served as a semi-public, semi-private space; one which carefully controlled the admission of members and guests, and which tightly controlled what information was disseminated to the public. There were some facilities that were shared by all clubs, political and apolitical: a hall guarded by a porter, a dining room (which was usually a 'coffee room' in the early Victorian vernacular), and some form of living room (which would invariably be known as a 'smoking room' from the 1850s, coinciding with the rising popularity of tobacco after the Crimean War). Bernard Capp has identified 'the twin spatial significance of the law – both institutional and "occasional"', and it is precisely this boundary that clubs straddled.[24] Capp argues that there was a long tradition of 'political sites intended (in part) to reinforce the established order of government', the most clear of which in an early modern context were churches and law courts, and on a less formal level these included carnivals and petitioning.[25] Political club spaces should be viewed in such a context, both in their 'official' capacity as gathering points for those sharing political principles, and in their ability to place themselves at arm's length through stressing the independence of their institution. Combined with this, Angus Hawkins has singled out how club membership necessitated 'a closely-knit social and intellectual world reinforcing shared opinions'.[26] Clubs thus had a distinctive ability to grant a physical focus for this mindset, being a meeting point in which membership served to regulate access to a layer of political activity.

In the 1820s and 1830s, clubs underwent several transformations from their eighteenth century forebears. The first and most obvious was the larger size of new clubs. As we have seen from the Westminster Reform Club's growth, this owed far more to the need for economies of scale to match the increasingly lavish clubhouse ambitions of members, and the larger number of subscription-paying members needed to raise funds, rather than any desire to embrace the newly expanded electorate after the Reform Act.[27] Georgian-built clubs like White's, Brooks's and Boodle's all had relatively small clubrooms; the front hall of each, for instance, was scarcely larger than a domestic corridor, with the hall of White's measuring less than five square metres. By contrast, the scale of Victorian clubrooms was noticeably greater, as with the Reform Club (built in 1838–41) with an atrium of approximately one hundred and seventeen square metres and the Junior Carlton Club (built 1864–9) with an atrium of one hundred and eight square metres. Evidently, there was no clear linear progression, for each clubhouse depended for its dimensions on several variables, not least the area and shape of the available plot of land. Nevertheless, from the mid-nineteenth century, purpose-built clubhouses were being constructed on a larger scale than their Georgian predecessors. The two most influential club buildings in this respect were the Union Club on New Square (subsequently Trafalgar Square, with the building still surviving today as Canada House) built in 1821–2 and the Athenaeum on Pall Mall built in 1824–30. Both represented a substantial expansion on the cramped clubhouses beforehand, and glancing at the floorplans of mid-nineteenth century clubhouses it is apparent that this remained the case in the wake of these two trailblazers.[28] Whilst the newly-expanded clubhouses were not the only large rooms in central London, being supplemented by those in large private houses such as Devonshire House and Lichfield House, they represented a substantial advance in accommodation for large meetings.

Large rooms were an asset for clubs hosting MPs. If that seems an overly simplistic point, it needs to be stressed that it has not been made before. There was, of course, already a tradition of factional meetings in clubs before the Reform Act. Amongst the Whigs, parliamentarians met in the cramped confines of Brooks's, where the largest room could fit no more than 100 people at most, and only 50 or so could be comfortably seated. Memories were still fresh of the tempestuous Whig meetings at Brooks's on 9 and 13 May 1831, which revealed the depth of Whig divisions over Reform provisions.[29] With the opening of the Reform Club's palatial new clubhouse in 1841, the expanded accommodation afforded the opportunity for larger parliamentary meetings to convene than in Brooks's. (The Westminster Reform, the National, and Free Trade Clubs never evolved beyond renting pre-built premises, but at their establishment, each had aspired to a purpose-built clubhouse.) The Athenaeum was apolitical, but its large, central atrium (Figure 3.2) was subsequently imitated by political clubs including the Reform in 1841 (Figure 3.1, centre), and the Carlton Club building of 1854. (Figure 3.3) Such atriums stood in contrast to the small corridors of Brooks's and White's, and allowed groups of several hundred to gather in one space. Indeed, Sir Robert Smirke's original purpose-built Carlton Club of 1836 was demolished and entirely rebuilt by Sidney Smirke after

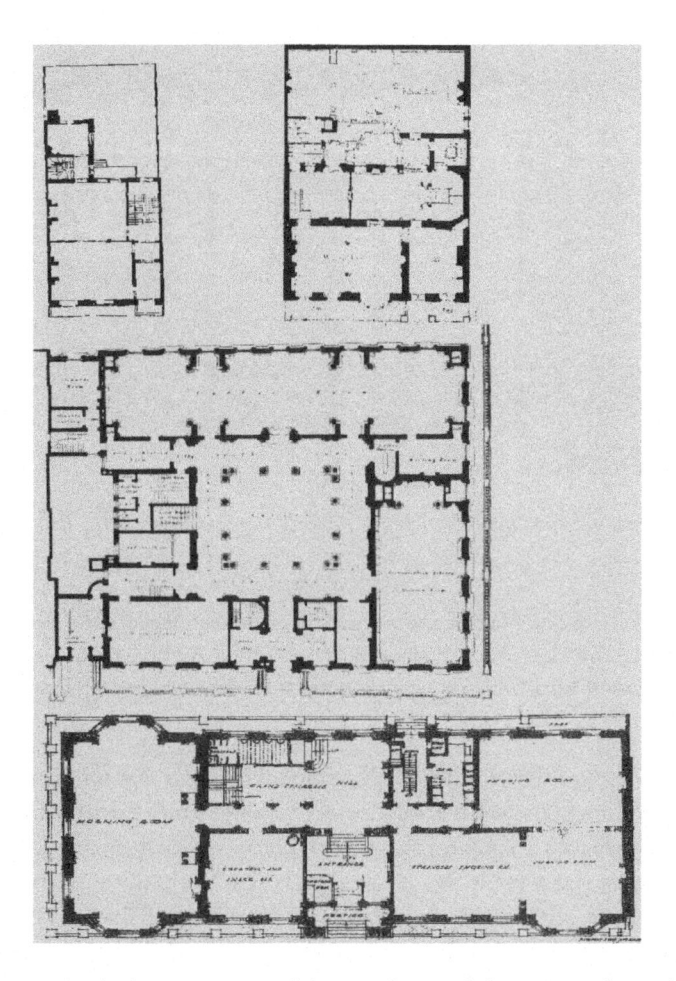

Figure 3.1 Scale comparison of the ever-larger clubs, using a floor plan of their ground floors. The original premises of White's (1778, top left), the expanded and altered White's of the early nineteenth century (top right), Sir Charles Barry's Reform Club (1841, middle), and David Brandon's Junior Carlton Club (1866, bottom) give a sense of the growing scale of club architecture before, during, and at the end of this period. Sources: London Metropolitan archive, accessed at http://www.british-history.ac.uk/report.aspx?compid=40621 and http://www.british-history.ac.uk/report.aspx?compid=40611 (accessed on 14 May 2011); Junior Carlton Club archive, Carlton Club, London, unmarked MS of Junior Carlton floorplan, c.1935, but reflecting a design laid down in 1866–9.

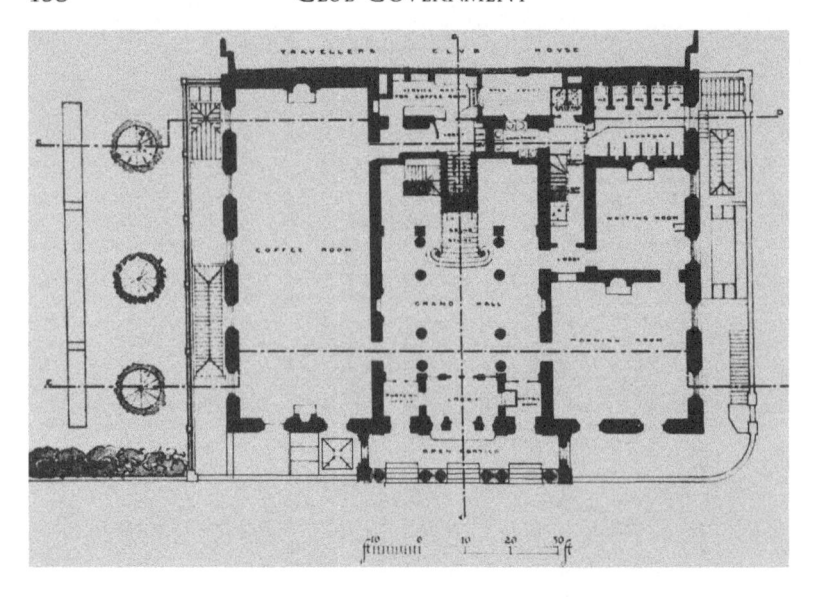

Figure 3.2 Floor plan of the ground floor of the Athenaeum. Note the pillared Grand Hall. Source: London Metropolitan Archive online, accessed at http://www.british-history.ac.uk/report.aspx?compid=40609 (accessed on 14 May 2011).

only 18 years, following multiple complaints about the impracticality of the building, and John Timbs noted 'it was of small extent, and plain and inexpensive'.[30] Looking at the plan (Figure 3.4), one is struck by the lack of open space available for members, particularly in contrasting the stairway area with the atriums apparent in Figures 3.1–3.3. The use of such atriums for parliamentary party gatherings can be seen in Figure 3.5.

Additionally, in glancing at these floor plans, one is struck by the size of the main club rooms, which were commandeered for meetings of members.

Central to the clubs' use of space was the tight control over inclusion and exclusion. Hall porters were deployed to debar unwelcome visitors, and even visitors who were admitted found themselves kept from most club rooms by strict regulations. In an architectural survey, Peter Marsh observes 'No one who enters the Reform Club can mistake it for a setting for democracy', but this argument can be taken yet further to convey the exclusivity of clubs in general.[31] It was this

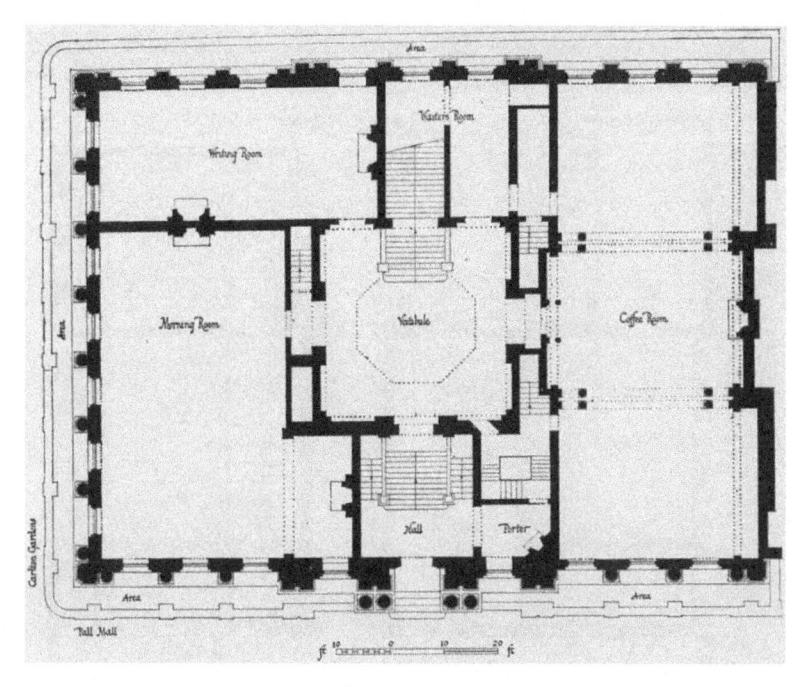

Figure 3.3 Floor plan of the ground floor of the Carlton Club (second building, by Sidney Smirke, 1854). Source: London Metropolitan Archive online, accessed at http://www.british-history.ac.uk/report.aspx?comp id=40592 (accessed on 14 May 2011).

characteristic – the exclusion of democracy – which made political clubs so appealing for parliamentarians requiring a combination of privacy and sociability close to Parliament. This was by no means a unique process: James Vernon has already identified how in contemporary constituencies, electoral politics moved out of the 'public' space of pubs, and into the private space of rented halls, as well as moving from the open spaces of outdoor public meetings to the confined spaces of indoor meetings, where tighter control over ticket admission was possible.[32] Jon Lawrence has subsequently traced the trajectory of this movement after 1868, presenting such developments in the context of politicians' increasing drive to control and minimise the 'moments of social levelling' that occurred when politicians would meet the public.[33] Yet prior to 1868, the creation of a borderline public/private space in Clubland did not appear so much a political

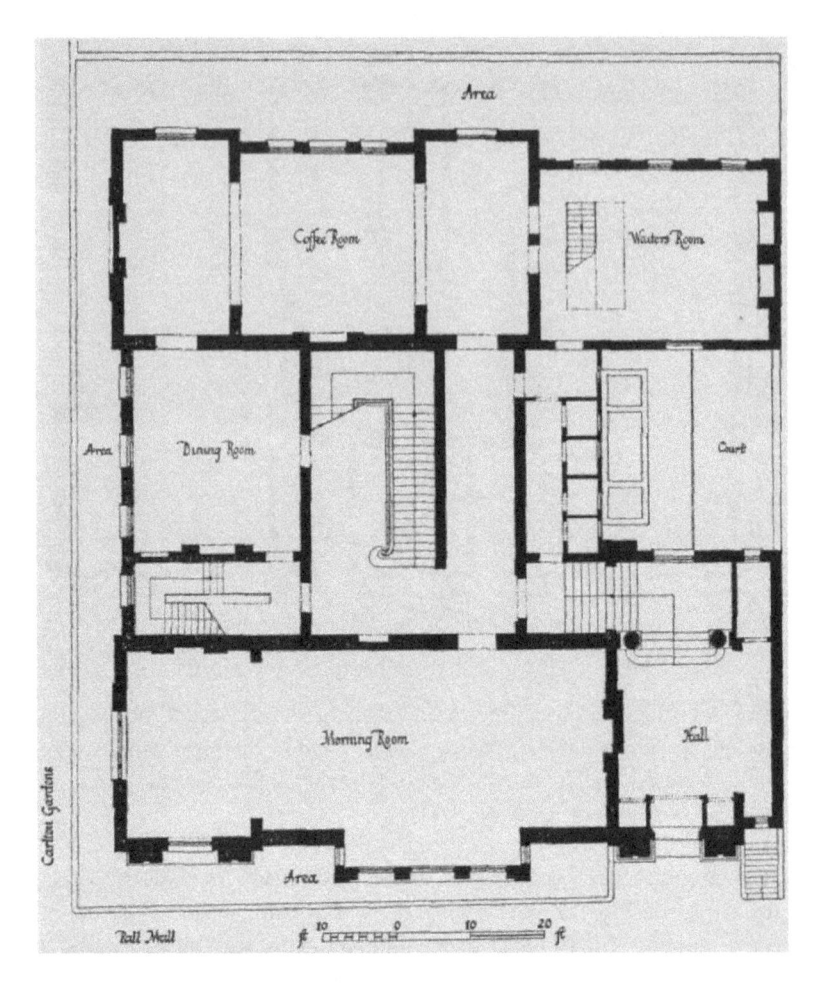

Figure 3.4 Floor plan of the ground floor of the Carlton Club (first building, by Robert Smirke, 1836). Source: London Metropolitan Archive online, accessed at http://www.british-history.ac.uk/report.aspx?compid= 40592 (accessed on 14 May 2011).

development as a social one, necessitated by a natural desire for privacy. Among a club's own members, the club was to all intents and purposes a public space; it is significant that in 1845 the Radical MP Joseph Hume described the Carlton and Reform Clubs as 'public spaces'.[34] Yet to the outside world, they were private property, out of bounds.

Figure 3.5 Posthumous print of Disraeli, portraying him addressing an unidentified meeting of Conservative MPs (c.1867) in the vestibule of the second Carlton Club building. Source: *The Graphic*, 23 April 1881, p. 416.

The very fact of club membership automatically granted privileged use of a space, as being a member meant access to the social networks contained within a club's membership. It also involved a certain element of patronage, since members could themselves decide who would be proposed and seconded, and could decide who to admit as guests. The latter point should not be exaggerated, however, because of the codified restrictions on club spaces, most of which remained strictly 'members only' in this period. Until the second half of the nineteenth century, the status of a guest was precarious at best. Most clubs did not admit guests into the main club rooms until the 1850s and 1860s; the first Earl of Kimberley and his teenage son 'dined at the Traveller's [Club] under the new rule admitting strangers', when it was introduced as late as 1863.[35] Rooms for receiving guests were invariably smaller and less sumptuously decorated than members-only areas. Even then, guests would have to be accompanied by their host member at all times, severely restricting their degree of social engagement with other members. This was the case with men, but even more so with women. Barring rare setpiece banquets, even the rooms for receiving guests remained off-limits to women, and it was not until the latter part of the century that men-only clubs would admit women visitors to selected rooms. Furthermore, the opening up of any club space to guests could be contentious. At the Junior Carlton Club in 1866, a proposal by Captain Meller MP 'to allow Members to introduce a Friend for the purpose of partaking of a Glass of Sherry and a Biscuit or Sandwich when needed' proved sufficiently subversive a challenge to the exclusivity of the club's space that it failed. Sir Thomas Bateson MP, a member of the Junior Carlton's Committee, responded by cautioning about 'the large number belonging to the Club and the confined space available [in the temporary club-house] for carrying on the Business'.[36]

Whilst all club spaces were united by their exclusion of the outside world, they were anything but homogeneous. The close proximity of so many factions among both Liberals and Conservatives led to inevitable friction. As Asa Briggs has noted of the Conservatives in the 1860s, they 'did not make up one single team. There were many different groups in 1867, although most of them used the Carlton Club as a common social and political centre.'[37] Under such circumstances, it is inevitable that such diverse factions, closely socialising in a relatively small set of rooms competed for that space; a theme particularly apparent in the use of meeting spaces.

The increased constitutional primacy of the House of Commons in this period – and the corresponding emphasis on support drawn from it – gave an added incentive for sociability to take on an additional level of importance in club spaces. As Angus Hawkins has argued, each government between 1835 and 1867 fell on the basis of a loss of Commons support; and each Parliament in that period contained at least two (sometimes three) governments, regardless of the share of the vote in general elections. Consequently, the forging of strong Commons alliances, actively lobbying for ministerialists, became a prominent feature, with the principal settings being 'in the drawing rooms of the great hostesses, at dinner parties, and *in the clubs around Pall Mall* [where] these elites merged'.[38] (My italics.) In advancing sociability amongst MPs, it must be admitted that while clubs played a critical and distinctive role, they must be viewed alongside salons and the grand private houses of the surrounding St James's and Piccadilly district, and the distinctively masculine flavour of this will be expanded below. This context of extra-parliamentary sociability as an integral part of parliamentary government led party managers to seek some measure of control over ostensibly social occasions: Conservative Whip Sir Thomas Fremantle MP kept a supply of 'personal' invitation cards to dinner with Sir Robert Peel, for distribution to other MPs.[39]

The importance of clubs was identified by Kim Reynolds as providing 'a physical location for extra-parliamentary political activity ... necessitated ... by the inadequacy of the buildings of the houses of parliament for social and informal contact between members', with their 'severe pressure on space'.[40] Private sociable spaces such as salons offered a range of social facilities, and at the upper end they could rival a club, as demonstrated by the space given over to gambling. Even the smaller clubhouses like Brooks's had a room dedicated to gambling, as with its Subscription Room, where card games proliferated. Within townhouses that entertained, 'everyone had at least one card table', and the larger houses could have six.[41]

It has become something of a cliché to liken the Houses of Parliament's facilities to those of a London club – Dickens's description persists, and M. H. Port has cited numerous references (mostly from Victorian parliamentarians) to the Commons as a club, and an 1869 committee examining Edward Barry's plans for a revamped Commons dining room recorded that the plans were 'very similar to that of the Reform Club' designed by Edward Barry's father, Charles.[42] Indeed, if some parts of Parliament seemed 'clubbable', they were actually more suited to certain club purposes than the clubs were: the House of Commons' smoking room was better designed for its purpose than its Clubland counterparts, being built with a tiled floor and partly-tiled walls to minimise the retention of tobacco odours by the furniture.[43]

Clubs would not match such technology until the 1880s, when the National Liberal Club and the Constitutional Club experimented with ceramics in their smoking rooms, and the Royal Automobile Club followed suit in the 1910s.[44] Older clubs could be reluctant to adapt to the new vogue for smoking: a dispute at White's over permission to smoke persisted as late as 1882, by which time subscribing membership had dwindled to just two hundred.[45] Thus by the end of the period of club government, Parliament's facilities were not being compared with those of the pre-1834 Palace of Westminster, but with the rival facilities which clubs offered.

Yet if there is some overlap in the functions of club spaces and the social facilities of the new House of Commons, the debt was to the broader social context of mid-Victorian society than to Clubland specifically. In his study of the Houses of Parliament building, Port does *not* consider what influence Charles Barry's Reform Club might have had on his later parliamentary design, but does argue that Barry's earlier Travellers' Club building – which Port believes marked his 'maturity' as an architect – was a less significant influence than that of having designed King Edward VI Grammar School, Birmingham, with its elongated narrow spaces.[46] Port identifies the Travellers' Club and the school as 'the antecedents' of Barry's parliamentary design, which 'required an enormous club, replete with service quarters, meeting rooms, restaurants, libraries, chambers of state, corridors and offices', and management of the circulation around these facilities.[47] Of each of these features, only one – the chambers of state – was not shared by club architects, and clubs were undoubtedly consistent with this style. A major contrast between clubs and parliamentary architecture is apparent from Roland Quinault's observation that 'There is little iconographic evidence that the new Houses of Parliament were conceived as a temple to Whiggism', despite Barry's debt to such Whigs as Lansdowne, Russell, Hallam and Macaulay in advancing his career, and Quinault argues that the Palace of Westminster was conceived as a politically neutral arena – in stark contrast to the partisan iconography of political clubs lined with portraits of party heroes.[48] A further opinion on the newer, larger, purpose-built post-Reform Act clubs is offered by Tristram Hunt, who sees such clubs as responsive to the tastes of the new electorate rather than established politicians and 'old' money: most notably, with an Italianate *palazzo* form that signalled a departure from the Greek Revival tastes of the Regency, the Reform Club building 'was exactly the type of design the Manchester money men were after.'[49]

Much could be made of the cartographical dimension of Clubland spaces; the relatively small distances involved between St James's 'Clubland' and the Houses of Parliament, which were some 800 metres away by road, or 500 metres in a direct line.[50] Yet much of this is self-evident, and needs little further comment. What is of most interest in the distances involved is the relatively narrow range of roads available when travelling between Clubland and Parliament. There were some opportunities for short cuts across smaller streets such as Carlton Gardens, but MPs travelling by cab would have invariably had to go through Whitehall (or else undergone large diversions around St James's Park), although on foot they could have cut across St James's Park, not necessarily saving much time, as MPs would have had to skirt the edge of the park, around John Nash's lake dug in 1827–8, there being no bridge across until 1857.[51]

Overall, surprisingly little attention has been paid to club spaces, particularly in light of their applicability to many of the characteristics of the 'spatial turn' noted by Habermas and Lefebvre. Their expanded dimensions during this period, their control over access, their location, all made them uniquely appealing to legislators, and were consistent with the trend towards conducting politics in private (or semi-private) locations. The use of their internal space also made them exceptionally well-suited to certain specific uses – particularly meetings.

Meetings: Use of Club Space and Purpose

Meetings were a crucial use of club space; for both formal and informal meetings. Where and how these were held tells us much about the value of clubs to parliamentarians. In holding such meetings, space continued to be an important factor, with Peter Marsh labelling the Reform Club as 'a great stage in the theatre of politics' – a term which not only emphasises the public side of clubs, but also the stilted, controlled nature of what was presented to the outside world. However, such an emphasis on hosting large-scale meetings should not obscure the equal importance of secluded, conspiratorial alcoves as well as the grand set-piece rooms and atriums of clubs described above, especially given the off-the-record nature of many club meetings.[52]

It is important to stress that political meetings by clubs fell into two broad categories: official, and unofficial. Official meetings, in which a club publicly put its name on an initiative, were rare. Clubs were loathe to advertise any political intervention. As T. M. Parssinen noted of the late eighteenth century, 'Many politicians doubted from the beginning whether extra-parliamentary associations, regardless of their tactics and goals, were constitutional. They often saw little difference between an association and an anti-parliament', and this attitude prevailed into the mid-nineteenth century.[53] Instead, unofficial meetings were far more common – although an initiative may not have been formally sanctioned by the committee of a club, the names carrying out these activities on club premises and with club resources were often the same as those involved in the running of the club. As we shall see in the final chapter, this was particularly the case during fundraising for electoral activities, some of them illegal, when clubs actively shunned the limelight.

One of the reasons club meetings have traditionally avoided scrutiny was the lack of reporting of their proceedings; but this was not always the case. Sometimes, when a non-club element was important at a meeting, it was felt appropriate to hold a preliminary meeting of MPs at a club, but to then call a full-scale public meeting nearby where outsiders could be admitted; this happened in August 1836 when eight MPs called a public meeting at the Crown and Tavern Inn on the Strand after meeting at the Reform Club first.[54] Similarly, clubs could sometimes voluntarily invite publicity for some of their proceedings. When the Reform Club held a banquet for newly appointed Crimean War naval commander Sir Charles Napier in 1854, Fitzstephen French MP described how it was 'attended by reporters from all the morning papers, for the purpose of making public the proceedings'.[55] Yet such press invitations to club proceedings were the exception rather than the rule, and remained remarkable for their atypicality.

Despite the lion's share of Clubland political meetings being 'unofficial' and off-the-record, there is some evidence that such meetings could be sanctioned by club authorities – who could not, after all, have been in ignorance about such initiatives. In 1852, Richard Cobden wrote to Sir Joshua Walmsley about pro-ballot initiatives, and how 'I urged upon some men in the Reform Club, whom I met there (such as Torrens, McCullagh, Haly, &c.) to work in this matter, and I advised them to try to bring [George] Grote out of his shell.'[56] The proposed involvement of Grote – one of the Club's founders, and a member of its Committee – suggests that no attempt was made to conceal the existence of such meetings from the Club.

The nuances of club attitudes to meetings can be observed in the furore surrounding two meetings at the Carlton, one in 1840, the other in 1844. As the first has hitherto escaped description by historians, it is worth relating in some detail.

After a house dinner of sixty Carlton members 'representing agricultural constituencies' on 31 March 1840, a Tuesday, it was unanimously agreed to call a wider Carlton meeting on the following Saturday, for members 'favourable to the principle of protection to agriculture'. The meeting was intended as a response to the Anti-Corn Law League, and was advertised by a notice on the chimneypiece of the Carlton's Reading Room.[57] On the morning of the meeting, the notice was taken down by the Conservative Whip Lord Redesdale and, after a low turnout ensued, the Duke of Buckingham rued how 'the Object of those who represent agricultural districts was in a great measure frustrated', and demanded an inquiry. Lord Redesdale, then Chairman of the Club's Committee, admitted to being responsible for the note's removal after being contacted by 'some Members connected with the manufacturing districts who were exceedingly hurt by what they considered a Club meeting being called on such a subject which they deemed injurious to their interests with their constituents',[58] and so he had removed the 'irregular' note under the pretext that it ran the risk of provoking a counter-meeting of Conservatives favouring abolition of the Corn Laws. Redesdale decreed that 'such counter-proceedings would be most injurious to the Club, and that it is a most wholesome rule that such proceedings should be declared irregular', adding his assurance that 'I am personally a strong supporter of the existing Corn Laws.'[59] The Carlton's Committee subsequently passed the following resolution:

> To private meetings for political or other purposes of Members assembling by mutual agreement at the Club there can be no objection, but when Notices are publicly placed in the rooms, the assembly takes in a great degree the Character of a Club Meeting, & the objects there advocated may be represented out of doors as those to which the Members are considered to be pledged.

This may lead to Counter Notices being issued to remove such impressions, the posting of which might cause much ill feeling & injury to the Club. The Committee feel it to be their duty to check all proceedings which may be in the slightest degree disagreeable to either the majority or minority of the Members, & especially when they are of a character which may render the continuance of individuals as Members of the Club inconvenient in influence to the Opinions which may be entertained by their constituents, of the obligations imposed upon them by their connexion with the Club.

No notice therefore in future can be allowed to remain posted in the Rooms which has not received the sanction of the Committee.

It has also been represented to the Committee that much inconvenience has arisen from Notices being improperly placed on the Parliamentary notice board. The only persons authorised by the Committee to post those Notices are [Conservative Whips] Lord Redesdale, Sir George Clerk MP, Sir Thomas Fremantle MP & Mr Henry Baring MP.[60]

The incident offers several insights. Most obviously, the Club had no objection to hosting controversial political meetings *per se*, but wished to maintain a sufficient distance to plausibly disclaim responsibility. Secondly, it reveals the Club's principal sensitivity being to the *reporting* of club meetings. Thirdly, the protectionism controversy was recognised as being deeply divisive among Conservatives even before Peel's second premiership. Certainly, the activities of such a meeting signify that Norman Gash's reference to 'the agriculturalists at the Carlton' was no empty figure of speech.[61] Finally, it shows that the issue of sensitive meetings was not restricted to protectionism alone but, as we shall see, the principle extended to other issues, such as when Conservative MPs met at the Carlton two years later to proclaim support for the construction of Irish railways.[62]

The second major instance of discord at the Carlton came in the aftermath of a 'quarrelsome' meeting of Conservative MPs on 16 June 1844, a Sunday. 'A requisition by five members' (presumably without the authorisation of the Committee) had convened a meeting of between sixty and seventy MPs 'who ordinarily vote on the Ministerial side', in which they urged a reversal of the previous Friday's vote on the West

India sugar duties. The outcome was a vote the following night (proposed by Philip W. S. Miles MP) in favour of reducing the duties, with the rebellious motion (which was lost by 233 votes to 255) which was accused by the *Morning Post* of being 'the decision of the Carlton'.[63]

What angered the Carlton was not so much the meeting's content, as the reporting of it. After an accurate description of the meeting appeared in *The Times*, it was deduced that the details could only have been passed on by one of the members present, generating 'an extraordinary sensation in the Carlton'. *The Times* justified its report of the proceedings by arguing 'the meeting was not of the usual [club] kind, but ... was fully attended by Members of Parliament', itself an admission that 'official' meetings of this kind were rare.[64] Recriminations ensued, with the *Spectator* reporting that Benjamin Disraeli was widely suspected as the source of the leak, but his guilt could not be proved. As club rules did not permit a member's expulsion without proof of wrongdoing, there was talk of dissolving the entire club and then refounding it, minus the offending member.[65] Disraeli himself wrote to *The Times* categorically denying having been the MP to leak the contents of the meeting, condemning it as 'an act of gross impropriety'.[66] Similarly frowned upon had been an incident ten years earlier in 1834, in which Sir Henry Hardinge MP had told the Commons of a private conversation he shared with Richard Sheil MP at the Athenaeum, which Sheil disowned as 'a conversation after dinner, never recollected, even by the narrator, for eight months'.[67] The condemnation aroused by Hardinge in 1834 and the anonymous Conservative MP in 1844 illustrates the degree of seriousness about maintaining the reputation of clubs, and particularly club meetings, as sanctuaries of anonymity.

As a proviso, it should be added that there was no stigma attached to conveying private conversations held on the *steps* of a club, for example, as Maurice O'Connell MP did when speaking in the Commons in May 1853; quite the reverse, for it communicated a sense of importance.[68] The crucial difference was that, as one was not physically located inside the club space, the same standards of confidentiality did not hold.[69]

Michael Sharpe has highlighted 'official' club action by the Reform Club in his pamphlet on its Political Committee.[70] However, with his study being based on a chronicle of the activities of that committee (founded in 1868) rather than the Club's broader political actions, it is predicated on the assumption that the Club's 'unofficial' pre-1868 political activities were minimal. Sharpe identifies just three pre-1868 political initiatives, all sourced from the Reform Club archives. In February 1845 'an unofficial committee of seven members of the Club recommended an examination of measures to improve the attendance of MPs at debates and divisions, and to promote the objects and principles (not detailed) of the Liberal Party'. Sharpe claims this was 'the first recorded attempt at collective independent political action by the members of the Reform Club', yet it is difficult to believe that the members of this political club waited nine years to take their first political action when numerous instances of meetings of MPs in the 1830s are recorded.[71] Equally improbably, Sharpe conjectures 'a second initiative was not taken for a further fifteen years', referring to a proposal for the Club to play some role in the new Liberal Registration Associations founded in March 1860 – a proposal which came to nothing due to the fifty-one supporting members falling short of the necessary quorum of sixty. Sharpe does, however, concede that the Club had a 'political role ... but not an actively Reformist one', briefly outlining several uses of the Club by politicians.[72] Clearly, even in a dedicated account such as Sharpe's, the Reform Club's pre-1868 political activity has long been underestimated.

Meetings at political clubs displayed a tension between parliamentarians desiring to hold meaningful gatherings, and party leaders and managers hoping to control, or at least to influence, them. In the above-cited discussion of the 1844 sugar duties meeting at the Carlton, one can find great reluctance among government supporters to recognise the Club's legitimacy as an agent for such events. At the meeting on 16 June, several government supporters led by Disraeli challenged 'by what authority' the meeting had been convened, and it is possibly for that reason that the Carlton went out of its way to use the meeting to simultaneously pass several glowing resolutions expressing 'unlimited confidence' in the government.[73] At the Reform Club, similar tensions were evident as members used the facilities to call meetings that could be injurious to senior Whig politicians. Dr John Allen recorded in his diary on 26 November 1837:

> There was a meeting yesterday at the Reform Club at which 50 members of Parliament were present. Molesworth made a speech against Ministers, O'Connell answered him and said that if they

wished to bring in a Tory Government they must not count on the support of the Irish members, and that he in particular would do his utmost to expose them to the indignation of all true Reformers ... there were only five – Molesworth, Leader, Wakeley, Grote and Whittle Harvey – who were for withdrawing their support from the Ministry. Brougham is supposed to have had some share in setting them on these proceedings.[74]

Yet such was the influence of the Carlton and Reform Clubs, MPs working through the club appeared to acquire added layers of authority. When the 1838 Irish Municipal Corporations Bill caused concern among Conservatives, a committee was set up to negotiate concessions from the government. The committee reported its findings to a full party meeting at the Carlton on 21 May. The agreed amendments were then moved when the Commons went into committee a week later.[75]

Clubland meetings could cover standard parliamentary business, sometimes with measurable outcomes, such as an 1839 Carlton Club meeting chaired by Thomas Langlois Lefroy MP, which promised 'warm support' for the proposed construction of Irish railways.[76] However, the 'inconvenience' of this meeting was unanimously condemned by the Carlton's Committee, and a follow-up meeting was abandoned at the Committee's request, with their adding that all advertised meetings should in future meet with their approval first.[77] Nonetheless, such Clubland meetings did have tangible outcomes. Conservative MP John Hardy observed that 'it was not until after' a key meeting of MPs at the Reform Club that Whig MPs became outspoken in their opposition to Peel's reintroduced Income Tax in 1842 – something which was confirmed by John Bright.[78] Such meetings around parliamentary business need to be viewed as an extension of parliamentary debate, but it would be a mistake to see them as invariably instrumental in any outcome. They could be unsuccessful, as was the case after the fall of Derby's second ministry in 1859, when the members of the Carlton 'declared against a dissolution' – although one was still triggered within days.[79] Club meetings should thus be seen as a dimension of parliamentary debates, not a determinant of their outcomes.

It would also be inaccurate to characterise party leaders and managers as being inherently opposed to club meetings. On the contrary, effective party leaders 'worked' the clubs, just as they 'worked' the nearby salons and private houses of St James's where large and small groups of MPs could be found – but leaders were often personally reticent to 'work' the clubs in too systematic a manner. Among party leaders in this period, only Peel and Disraeli were particularly conspicuous in 'working' the clubs, and Disraeli's level of activity in holding large- and small-scale Carlton and Junior Carlton meetings in the 1860s was far more modest than his Carlton activities when scaling the 'greasy pole' in the 1830s and 1840s. However, it is apparent from Disraeli's correspondence that he looked in on the Carlton and Junior Carlton most days, to collect mail.[80] Peel was particularly active in the clubs through the 1830s and 1840s – for instance, on 14 November 1837, as MPs gathered for the new parliamentary session, he 'spent much of his time at the Carlton, welcoming supporters and issuing invitations to small House of Commons club dinners where old and new MPs could get to know each other and their leader.'[81] Peel also did the same at White's, with a member there noting in 1835 that the Conservative leader 'frequently' visited the Club 'on a Wednesday when out of office, and oftener still on a Saturday'.[82]

Of the remaining Conservative leaders, an aloof distance was maintained from the Carlton. Wellington openly held the Carlton in contempt (despite having founded it), and famously stated late in life that the two most valuable lessons he had learned were to 'Never write a letter to your mistress, and never join the Carlton Club.'[83] The 14th Earl of Derby, while being a user of the Carlton Club, preferred to entertain at home, where there was even greater control over the company he kept, and where his wife reliably acted as hostess – although he was not averse to calling setpiece meetings of parliamentarians in clubs. In opposition in November 1846 – two years after the rebellious 'requisition' at the Carlton – the then Lord Stanley convened a party for Conservative MPs at the Carlton ahead of the fractious first meeting of the new parliamentary session.[84] Amongst the Whigs, party leaders were also found in their clubs, but made relatively infrequent use of them. In September 1836, the third Baron Holland recorded 'At Brookes. Palmerston and Glenelg [sic] and Mr Bulwer there' but this entry was a relative rarity.[85] Earl Grey, Viscount Melbourne and Lord John Russell all made use of Brooks's, which they were all long-standing members of, but were almost never seen at the Reform Club, despite being members. Palmerston frequented the Reform Club more than any of his predecessors, but was still more notable for turning up at setpiece banquets than making regular use of the club. The Earl of Aberdeen was not a diligent user of clubs during his ministry. Finally, Gladstone did not even bother to join the Reform Club until after attaining the premiership in 1868, and resigned in 1874, Richard Shannon believing that his membership was 'taken up at convenience and dropped without compunction'.[86] Clubs may have been a theatre of 'high politics', frequented by cabinet ministers, backbenchers and party managers, but they were not much of a theatre of the 'highest politics'. It was not until H. H. Asquith made a daily habit of reading for hours in the Athenaeum and Reform Clubs in the Edwardian period that Clubland participation by a party leader would peak.[87]

Clubs, Public Meetings and Protests

As clubs became increasingly synonymous with Westminster, the post-Reform period saw them becoming a focus for protest for the first time. Their rising prominence, and the assorted apocrypha of electoral corruption attributed to them, made them a natural target for protestors. Such a process would not reach its apex until the 1880s, when the Trafalgar Square riots resulted in the smashing of several clubs' windows in 1886, and 1888 saw the throwing of a bomb in the Junior Carlton Club. (Terrorist action targeted at political clubs would continue until the 1990s.)[88] Yet by the pro-Reform protest of Trafalgar Square on 29 June 1866, clubs had already emerged as a suitable foci of public protest, with 10,000 protestors marching past the Carlton Club.[89] Observing the procession, Lord Stanley recorded: 'They went off pretty quietly, only shouting and groaning at the Carlton.'[90] A press account contradicted this, and stated that the crowd which 'raised a storm of hisses' outside the Carlton also 'indulged in the most uproarious cheering' outside the Reform, 'which was renewed when some of the members waved their handkerchiefs and gave other signs of approval.'[91] Later that year, a December protest for trades reform also targeted the clubs of Pall Mall, there being 'considerable interest' in the demonstration from the 'balconies and upper windows' of the Athenaeum and Reform Clubs. The Reform Club 'was specially marked out by the trades for a demonstration of applause', as 'hats and caps were raised and lusty cheers were given'. In contrast to the July Reform protests, the *Penny Illustrated Paper* thought it 'most noteworthy' that 'there was no attempt to hiss the few gentlemen stationed at the windows of the Carlton Club'.[92] A further pro-Reform protest marched through Pall Mall on 11 February 1867, the procession lasting an hour and a quarter.[93] Thus we see that by the 1860s, the political clubs were attracting a level of attention unknown in previous decades.

Protests thus made a marked contrast in their use of space compared to that of the clubs themselves. Free from the careful codification of space and its uses inside a club, public protest could be chaotic, even anarchic. Yet the proximity of a protest to a club could inspire affection, and public salutes as well as violent demonstrations. In time, the proximity of the St James's clubs to the new Trafalgar Square, with its crowds, would underline their vulnerability.[94]

By comparison, the meetings behind the closed doors of clubs continued to be dominated by the available space, and the way access to that space was restricted. The ability to host 'unofficial' meetings in clubs was a significant asset in allowing MPs the organisational and social centre of a members-only club; a privilege denied to those hosting unofficial meetings outside, either in the open air, or in a tavern. It also maintained some ambiguity as to the extent that such gatherings were functions for a set party or cause. This very ambiguity could lead to nuanced conflict as some parliamentarians contested the legitimacy of club meetings, and the right to use club spaces for such meetings could be a battleground between different factions for the physical heartland of conservatism, liberalism, radicalism and whiggery.

Masculinity and Sociability: Clubs' Single-Sex Spaces and their Rival Social Spaces

In recognising clubs as a meeting space, it is also worth considering their rivals for communal spaces – private meeting rooms, such as Almack's (later renamed Willis's Rooms), located on King Street in St James's. Such subscription rooms were not clubs, but rather venues available for private hire. Instead of membership, admission was gained through tickets, although these were highly sought-after and frequently traded on the basis of personal acquaintances, thus meriting some comparison with club membership. Peter Mandler notes that that the

'Lady Patronesses' who controlled ticketing 'were spoken of as virtual despots'.[95] Subscription rooms could also be financially dependent on women, as with Almack's which was run by Viscountess Palmerston.[96] Yet the relationship between members, space and meetings was extremely different to that of a club. Membership of a club conferred the right for members to call meetings (unless expressly forbidden by the club's committee). Any lobbying to gain admission needed to be done only once, to acquire membership, and the role of women was usually peripheral or non-existent. By contrast, the constant coaxing and persuading of Lady Patronesses required to gain admission to a string of events at salons – like the weekly balls of Willis's during the London season – led to a very different political climate both inside and outside the salons; one in which women played a decisive 'gatekeeping' role.[97]

Despite the absence of membership through subscriptions, Almack's and Willis's Rooms are still of interest here for their importance as a space, since they were one of the few central London spaces outside of Clubland to be able to accommodate mass meetings of several hundred people, including those of the emerging parliamentary parties. They were also physically located in Clubland, being just off St James's Street. On 2 May 1846, the National Club held its first open meeting there.[98] Most famously, as recognised in the previous chapter, the meeting of 280 Peelite, Whig, Liberal and Radical MPs at Willis's Rooms on 6 June 1859 is frequently cited as a turning point at which the formation of a parliamentary Liberal party was consolidated.[99] The demonstration of demand for occasional but high-profile political meetings by MPs in Willis's Rooms shows what political clubs could offer almost all year round, without the rental costs associated, or problems over ticketing: large, semi-public spaces with adjacent private spaces, and party managers' control over access and privacy.

John Tosh argues that such assembly rooms were already in decline by the 1830s, attributing this to their mixed-sex environment compared to the 'separate grooves' of the 'associational life of men and women'; a pattern wholly consistent with the single-sex character of the political clubs.[100] Peter Mandler takes a somewhat different view, arguing that Almack's 'was replaced – literally as well as figuratively – by a public space in which aristocratic women both had more real power and were less likely to draw criticism', noting that the physical transformation of Almack's premises into Willis's Rooms was accompanied by a formalisation of women's roles at dinners, concerts and lectures, and that this was 'not a descent from authority to powerlessness'. Thus although clubs and subscription rooms were not in direct competition, there was some overlap between all-male political Clubland and the mixed salons in this period.

In addition to subscription rooms having borne some superficial resemblance to clubs, many of the social activities supporting Westminster politics continued to exist in long-established salons and drawing rooms (although they were in decline from the 1830s), and of heavily codified private dinners. These formed an essential part of the political Clubland context, yet the greater involvement of aristocratic women in their running highlights how much more they shared with subscription rooms than with clubs. One of the main appeals of the increasingly popular clubs among MPs was their avowed masculinity: club spaces presented an almost entirely masculine world. They excluded women as both members and (for much of this period) as guests, with their participation being limited to acting as servants.[101]

Less prestigious clubs did admit women visitors, but only at certain hours – in 1852, Conservative agent Henry Edwards Brown visited Norwich candidate Colonel T. S. Dickson at the Conservative Club, bringing a young lady (introduced as a niece of his), and Dickson thought little of Brown's request to show the woman around the clubhouse. Dickson subsequently told Brown 'I showed you no more civility than I would any stranger, or any person that I did not particularly like ... who brought a lady in, and asked me, "Colonel Dickson, perhaps you will be kind enough to show me and this lady over the Club, as you are a member of the Club". I do not call that civility'.[102]

Only in exceptional circumstances could women guests set foot in the major clubs – as with Wellington's funeral in 1852, when black-draped clubhouses offered a viewing platform for the procession, and the presence of numerous women was noted; or else during Garibaldi's breakfast visit to the Reform Club in 1864.[103] In normal circumstances, a woman merely waiting for a member on the premises was frowned upon. It is noticeable that when former Conservative MP Peter Borthwick was pursued to the Carlton Club by a creditor, a Mrs. Bates of Richmond, the Club responded with a rebuke which did *not* refer to his using the club as a forwarding address for his indebted business transactions, but which did refer him to a resolution 'That the Porter have orders to prevent females waiting in the Clubhouse'.[104]

The position of women in clubs did not appreciably change during this period, and even female club servants were only employed in the most junior capacities. The first women-only club to exhibit the same distinctive use of space as the male clubs, the Ladies' Institute, was founded in 1860, but floundered after seven years, and no comparable successor emerged until the 1880s. Despite publishing the *English Woman's Journal*, it avoided political involvement.[105] Mixed-sex clubs would not be trialled until the launch of the Albemarle Club in 1874, and even then would remain strictly apolitical. It was not until the launch of the Ladies' Carlton Club in the early 1920s that a political club which welcomed women was established.[106] Throughout this period, Clubland spaces remained overwhelmingly masculine.

This separation of sexes, which can be seen in the context of a number of other spheres familiar to MPs of the period, including the public schools, Oxbridge, and Parliament itself – and exclusion of feminine input into at least parts of British political and cultural life – contrasts sharply with Kim Reynolds' portrait of aristocratic women in politics, in which she argues that 'Unlike middle class feminists, aristocratic women did not perceive the political system as a closed world from which they were excluded and into which they demanded admittance'.[107] Reynolds asserts that amongst the Victorian aristocracy, 'separate spheres' did not apply to 'politics' and 'society', citing extensive examples of the role of women in politics. However, clubs were noticeably absent from this analysis; such an argument should be considered in conjunction with the exclusion of women from political clubs. Aristocratic women were indeed an integral part of the wider political context of Trollopean country-house parties and London dinners held by such hostesses as Ladies Palmerston, Waldegrave, Jersey and Stanley of Alderley.[108] As such, it is important to stress that the exclusion of women from club spaces did not equate with the exclusion of women from the wider world of the political club member. Peter Mandler notes that, as well as the high-profile role of women in electioneering, 'in an age when politics was largely conducted in private, women on terms of intimacy with powerful men could also exercise – in the salon, in the dining room, in the bedroom – considerable influence over public life'. Clubland's masculinity diminished the social opportunities for female involvement in 'high' politics, but it certainly did not eliminate it altogether.[109] Some dinner hostesses could be shrewd and systematic political operators, as with Lady Palmerston, who kept a list of thirty-one Irish MPs, labelled 'to be invited to dinner 1862'.[110] Yet as Mandler has outlined, while the input of aristocratic women was certainly a 'distinctive contribution', such political activities 'were privileges of their class rather than of their gender', with limited applicability beyond social elites.[111]

Within the physical space of the Westminster area, the status of even the most aristocratic women was clearly separate and subordinate. At private dinners, etiquette was often a barrier, requiring women to retire to a separate room after dinner, excluding them just as drink was likely to make conversation more candid. Kathryn Gleadle notes the case of Katherine Plymley, sister of the Archdeacon of Shrewsbury, who could 'dispute with house-guests' at informal meals such as breakfast and before lunch, but who was 'an onlooker and not a participant' at her brother's political dinners. Gleadle portrays political dinners as inviting women 'not because of their contribution in their own right but because they might enable men to enjoy the occasion better', and concludes 'domestic-based political activity did not necessarily erase conventionally understood boundaries of gender behaviour'.[112] Within Parliament, women could only observe House of Commons debates from behind the grille of a segregated gallery in the new House (itself an improvement on the cramped 'ventilator-cum-peepholes' in the old Commons' ceiling which female observers had to huddle around). Political clubs presented even more opportunities to exclude women from the world of Westminster, not just because of the physical barrier to involvement, but also because of the taboos on reporting club affairs to non-members, which by implication included all women. Thus despite the wider context in which early Victorian women engaged with politics, there were clear limits to the degree of participation.

Kim Reynolds has stressed the primacy of political hostesses because of the distinctiveness of their role – she asserts that 'The political situation itself created a need for political hostesses', and to a great extent, this holds true. She thus identifies the vacuum which political hostesses sought to fill:

In the absence of any highly structured party organisations, either within or outside parliament, there was no formal method of communication between members, between front and back benches, or between opponents; still fewer were the means of communicating with supporters outside parliament.[113]

With the exception of providing communications between parliamentary opponents, clubs attempted to fill *all* of these roles, some highly effectively.[114] It is thus worth emphasising that what Reynolds calls hostesses' 'service to party' in bridging these divides were often accomplished in tandem with Clubland.[115]

The notable exception to the above was in communicating between parliamentary opponents. Clubs were wholly ineffectual at this, whereas Reynolds and Mandler have both identified the 'extra-parliamentary' element of salons and dinners, and their 'extra-party', nature. Reynolds asserts that this quality made Lady Palmerston's dinner parties 'invaluable in the unstable years from 1846 until Palmerston's death in 1865, during which time her parties reflected the shifting coalitions that made up the governments of the day'.[116] By contrast, the most notable political clubs were inherently wedded to a *party* (as with the Carlton, Junior Carlton and Reform Clubs) or a *faction* (as with the Conservative, National and Free Trade Clubs), although the distinction was usually ambiguous as club rulebooks stressed their attachment to *principle*. Such attachments to party, faction or principle were seldom shared by salons for any protracted length of time (and were never codified in writing), although such salons could be dominated by factions for a while, as with the Whigs at Holland House in the 1830s. Even in such cases, a far more ambiguous, cross-party usage of space persisted, unlike the strict membership barriers in place in clubs.

Mandler identifies salons as having often been synonymous with whiggery, noting their distinctive 'cosmopolitanism, philosophy and feminity', and indeed many of the more remarkable instances of politics in salon spaces were by Whig hostesses.[117] Yet the world of salons encompassed Conservatives as well as Liberals. Radicals MPs, the legislators least likely to feature in salon politics, were also those least likely to belong to a club,[118] and so the world of salons was truly cross-party, if culturally dominated by whiggery. Disraeli wrote after attending a particularly male, Whiggish gathering: 'At Lady

Palmerstons on Saturday there were so few ladies & so many men, that Lady Dufferin, as she came in ... [stated] that she thought it was a meeting of the Reform Club'.[119] The cosmopolitanism of salon spaces was made possible by the bond of aristocracy, and the absence of formal membership. As we have seen, familial links were present but far from omnipotent in determining the political composition of Brooks's.[120] Mandler recognises 'the throngs of unoccupied noblemen' from across Europe involved in Holland House.[121] Their involvement was not paralleled in the clubs, where the long waiting lists for membership served as a disincentive for those visiting London for short periods. Thus the cultural composition of most clubs, though less avowedly aristocratic than salons, was also less cosmopolitan.

Further major differences to salons had little to do with space, and everything to do with personalities. As private spaces owned by individuals, salons were subject to the preoccupations of their patrons. After the death of the third Baron Holland in 1840, Holland House ceased to occupy any notable role in Whig politics. By contrast, a political club's dispersal of decision making between its member-shareholders,[122] committee, chairman and full-time professional secretary ensured that even with wavering political commitment from one quarter, there was bound to be some demand for a continued political role.[123]

The importance of gossip in the political process is discussed below in greater detail. One of the reasons why clubs were so conducive to gossip was because of contemporary notions of 'clubbability', which in turn emanated from contemporary notions of masculinity, and masculine interactions in a single-sex environment.[124] Whilst this has been apparent to other writers examining clubs before and after the mid-nineteenth century, the meaning of masculinity in a club environment changed in this period. As Amanda Vickery has noted, 'Georgian masculinity flourished in the clubs and coffee houses', yet the expression of such masculinity had changed since the Georgian era.[125] For Vic Gatrell, the masculinity of eighteenth century clubs reflected a combination of bawdiness and physical brutality, sometimes in a cross-class setting in which the 'journeyman' and the 'gentlemen' met. Gatrell recognises that such behaviour in clubs was often fêted in Georgian political circles, with tumultuous scenes such as Isaac Cruikshank's much-imitated *Breaking up of the Union Club* (1801), in which Charles

James Fox is engaged in a rowdy brawl, and its pastiches Samuel De Wilde's *The Reformers' Dinner* (1809), George Cruikshank's *Dinner in the Four in Hand Club at Salthill* (1811), Thomas Rowlandson's *Breaking up of the Blue Stocking Club* (1815), and George Cruikshank's particularly brutal anti-abolitionist *The New Union Club* (1819). Gatrell argues 'These were "laughing" not "savage" satires – or less satires than *celebrations*' of such bawdy masculinity.[126]

Post-Reform Clubland displayed a very different kind of masculinity. There was still a certain devil-may-care *braggadocio*, but it was verbal rather than physical, and was most evident in the emphasis on gossip and indiscretion. Open displays of emotion were positively frowned upon; it was more clearly contained in the stricter codification of manners in keeping with the times; Marjorie Morgan has argued that such codification of rules and manners up until the mid-nineteenth century regulated aristocratic and middle class social habits alike, and clubs which embraced both aristocratic and middle-class members were no exception.[127] Facilities which had been so easily open to abuse a century earlier – such as all-night opening that had been notoriously exploited by gamblers – were now justified and even regulated by the respectability of parliamentary hours. In contrast to Georgian St James's, Victorian Clubland appeared relatively staid, and its 'respectable' masculinity was well-attuned to playing a role in Westminster politics.

Confident assertion of masculinity was a central part of the club environment, shunning the input of women who were involved in other aspects of political culture. While women may have served parties, the overlap between club and party ensured that women were necessarily marginalised from the organisational activities in which clubs engaged, and from any direct participation in the discussions within them. A rising emphasis on 'respectability' in Clubland further cemented this, by giving male politicians an excuse to preserve the exclusively male character of their political clubs; setting in motion a political club culture which would be continued into the late twentieth century.[128]

Gossip

The physical layout of clubs lent itself to the personal interchange of news and, in particular, gossip. Yet because of its transitory nature, the importance of gossip has remained underestimated. As has been noted, the Athenaeum was the first club to be centred on a large, capacious central lobby, with the Carlton, the Reform, the Conservative and the Junior Carlton Clubs all following suit. Consequently, communal areas such as the central lobby and the steps leading to it functioned as a central meeting point for exchanging the latest information, as evidenced in Figure 3.6. The lobby also served as an interception point, offering members the chance to 'buttonhole' passing members. There were various ways of circulating around a club – but members could only use the front entrance to arrive and leave, as can be observed by Figures 3.1–3.4, and there are no documented instances of members entering or leaving by a service entrance; members would only access a club by its main entrance. Thus to loiter in the precincts of the lobby by the front entrance was to occupy the space that all members would cross, and gave ample chance to monitor the parliamentary traffic going by. The presence of seats in the lobbies points to a demand for members to spend time in that one place. (Figure 3.7) That Figure 3.6 was not merely the product of the artist's overactive imagination is attested to by William Keogh MP, who visited the Reform Club in December 1852, and who recalled its central lobby as 'that great hall which, when Ministries are changing, is a sort of political encampment'.[129] Similarly, the Earl of Malmesbury recalled an important conversation with Robert Knox, Editor of the *Morning Herald* 'in the hall of the Carlton'.[130] Indeed, just as Figure 3.6 demonstrates the clubs being used to spread news of the birth of the Aberdeen coalition, so they were used to report the advent of that administration's collapse. In January 1855, Lord Stanley maintained that the government's fall 'was kept secret to the last moment', but that he first heard of it at the Carlton, one hour before the news was made public.[131]

The value of gossip at Westminster has long been recognised.[132] As noted above, political clubs were ideal for the proliferation of gossip; not only because of the value placed on indiscretion among members, but because of the physical layout of club spaces, which concentrated circulation of members into a few narrow routes around the clubhouses, maximising the opportunities for members to interact. Figure 3.8 demonstrates just how well-suited clubhouses were to gossip in their use of three-dimensional as well as two-dimensional spaces, with members separated from eavesdroppers by vertical as well as horizontal distance (something underlined by the height of most club-house ground floors well above external ground level, minimising potential eavesdropping and lip-reading from outsiders). Club gossip could be particularly useful for parliamentarians, in offering a testing ground for political opinion, as when Charles Villiers wrote to John Bright in January 1859 and was able to extrapolate that feelings against war in Italy were 'universal', based on his conversations in London's clubs.[133] Clubs could also amplify popular anecdotes and myths, like the salacious joke about Palmerston's mistress ('She is Kain, but is he definitely Abel?'), the spread of which through Clubland in 1865 was blamed by Disraeli for actually increasing Palmerston's popularity before that year's general election.[134]

Yet members could also mistrust views expressed too forcefully in Clubland, exemplified by Greville's suspicious complaint about Sir Edward Codrington MP telling 'everyone who would listen to him' at Brooks's of a conversation he had had with the Duke of Wellington.[135] MPs could be cautious in volunteering too much gossip in clubs,

Figure 3.6 'The Reform Club-House: Members awaiting intelligence of the formation of the new ministry'. Source: *Illustrated London News*, January 1853. The central lobby can also be observed in the floor plan in Figure 3.1.

Figure 3.7 Members talking in the main hall of the Carlton Club. This hall can also be observed in the floor-plan in Figure 3.3. Note the seats. Although this picture is from 1890, the seats were built in from the lobby's completion in 1854. Source: *Illustrated London News*, Saturday, 24 May 1890, p. 649.

mistrusting those who might draw out their opinions. In August 1866, Lord Stanley was suspicious of his conversation with Baron Baude at the apolitical Travellers Club: 'he found great fault with, and criticised in a decidedly hostile tone, the policy of his own government, whether to draw me out I don't know'.[136] Furthermore, the traction of such gossip among MPs depended on the varying rate with which they frequented their clubs – whilst some lived in them, others like Richard Cobden would only look in once a week.[137] Clearly, there were limits to the seriousness with which gossip was regarded.

Nonetheless, Clubland gossip was eagerly consumed by the press, for it offered a sense of urgency and of 'inside' information. Despite the Carlton Club's paranoia over the verbatim report of its MPs' private meeting in 1844, it was not unknown for journalists to report such parliamentary gossip from the clubs, often under what would

THE STAIRCASE,
CARLTON CLUB.

Figure 3.8 Members talking in the gallery above the main lobby of the Carlton Club. Source: *Illustrated London News*, 24 May 1890, p. 649. As with Figure 3.7, this picture is from 1890, but the design – and use – of the lobby was unchanged since its completion in 1854.

subsequently be called 'the Chatham House Rule', maintaining the anonymity of the speaker(s) while detailing what was said and where. In September 1855, the *New York Times*' London correspondent was able to quote the precise words of one unnamed MP in the Reform Club the night before, calling for the dismissal of General James Simpson from the Crimea.[138]

Thus given the contemporary interest in gossip, it deserves further scrutiny. A problem in appraising its importance is its transient nature. Fortunately, fragments survive. Whilst some of the more sensational examples can be found in diaries and letters, more representative examples can be found by consulting betting books, which recorded wagers and survive from this period for Boodle's, Brooks's and White's.[139]

Wagers are of course popularly associated with the Reform Club, due to the premise of Jules Verne's *Around the World in Eighty Days* (1875), yet an analysis of betting books offers a far more representative insight into their frequency and political relevance.[140] Betting books were used to record any wager, however trivial, made on club premises. As well as the topic, they recorded the individuals making the wager, the date, the amount staked, and the outcome. They provide an excellent barometer of topics of conversation on which strong views were held. Amy Milne-Smith has used betting books to analyse social attitudes in the 1880–1918 period, but throughout the 1832–68 period, one finds that the single most frequent topic of wagers was politics, making up well over half of all recorded bets.[141] If one examines these political wagers, several themes noticeably recur among members' conversation.

Wagers over political issues act as strong indicators of conversations and attitudes. Amidst agricultural controversies, George W. F. Bentinck made several wagers on wheat: in 1850 he placed a £100 wager with Lord Glasgow over the average price of wheat over the next five years, and later that year Bentinck would go on to bet Lord Bessborough £50 on the likelihood of a corn duty being imposed over the next six years.[142] Other fiscal questions prompted similar wagers. In 1833, Mr. De Horsey bet Sir Joseph Copley £5 over the national debt.[143] Another fiscal wager was for £100 in 1857, between Rainald Knightley MP and Lord Foley, arguing that Gladstone's proposed abolition of the income tax would not take place by 1860, but would be revived in some form.[144]

Of the non-fiscal issues, Jewish emancipation wagers notably recurred during the 1850s and 1860s, when Jewish Disabilities were being debated in Parliament. In 1857 there was a one pound wager between Lord Bath and Frederick Cadogan over the chances of passing the Oaths Bill then before Parliament.[145] In 1866, Bath wagered Lord de Lisle '£5 that a Jew Peer takes his seat in the House of Lords within 5 years from this date (provided always there is a House of Lords)', while later that year Lord Henry Lennox bet Lord Royston '£25 that a Jew Peer takes his seat in the House of Lords within 5 years from this date'.[146] A generation earlier, Catholic emancipation had created similar controversy within Clubland, as when Suffolk's long-standing MP Sir Thomas Gooch bet veteran Welsh grandee Sir Watkin Williams Wynn MP in 1828, 'one sovereign to receive 20 whenever there are 30 Catholics in the House of Commons'.[147]

In keeping with the tone of the times, many political wagers involved personalities rather than issues, such as the £100 bet between Lord Forester and Lord George Bentinck in June 1832 over Earl Grey's chances of remaining Prime Minister after the next election.[148] On 27 January 1846, before the Peelite split, Lord Glasgow wagered Bentinck £100 that Sir Robert Peel would continue as Prime Minister for three years – a strong indicator of Bentinck's low estimation of Peel's survival.[149] Some of these wagers could be long term, and tended to reveal deeply-held convictions: in 1847, H. W. Forrester bet Gerald Sturt £150 to £50 that Lord Stanley would be Prime Minister during his lifetime.[150] However, the shorter-term bets give an idea of the gossip sweeping through a club at a given time (and of the desire to make a profit from such insights), such as a five pound bet between Lord Munster and Lord Bath on 27 February 1859 that Messrs. Walpole and Henley would have resigned their cabinet seats by 6pm that night.[151]

By far the most popular source of political betting was the election contest. This did not, however, necessarily imply that elections were the most popular source of Clubland conversation, but that they were particularly well-suited to placing bets on. They are, however, strong evidence of electioneering conversations taking place. Occasionally, they dealt with the size of majorities in the House of Commons after general elections, such as Lord Belfast's bet to George Damer MP about Lord Melbourne maintaining his majority after the 1841 election.[152] However, most tended to be specific to one constituency.

These electoral bets over constituencies offer insights into how well-informed the proposer of the bet was; they could vary from uncannily accurate forecasts over closely-fought elections, to bold boasting that was wide of the mark.

Some bet challengers were successful. Between May and June 1837 'Lord Belfast bets Lord Ailsa £5 that two Liberal members are returned for Westminster at the next general election', and they duly were by over 1,000 votes.[153] Around the same time, 'Lord Gardner bets Lord Rokeby that no Tory sits for Westminster at the next general election (bar. Sir F. Burdet[t]). If Burdet[t] comes in with a whig this bet is off., Rokeby and Burdett was duly returned alongside one Whig.[154] During the 1856 Frome by-election, White's member N. Macdonald bet ten pounds to the Marquis of Bath's five pounds on the electoral chances of the two candidates the Hon. Major W. G. Boyle and Lord Edward Thynne – Macdonald won by backing Boyle, while Bath's kinsman Thynne was defeated.[155]

Some bets, though unsuccessful, were over contests that were sufficiently close for the bet to have been worthwhile – and therefore implied a good level of judgment or knowledge about the contest concerned. In 1836, 'Lord Rokeby bets Mr. Arden £1 (one) that two Conservative members are returned for Middlesex next general election', but had to pay up when the Conservatives only gained one of two seats in a tight four-way contest when the top and bottom polls were 4,796 to 4,273.[156] Similarly, on 27 June 1837 'Lord Rokeby, a strong Conservative, bets Sir Joseph Copley £5 to 4 that Lord Ingestre beats Col. Anson for Staffordshire [South]', only for Anson to win by forty-seven votes.[157]

There were several unwise or ill-informed bets. In 1836: 'Lord Rokeby bets Mr. Byng and Mr. Arden one pound each that Sir J[ames] Graham comes in for Liverpool if he stands at the next general election', only for Graham to not stand.[158] On 18 June 1837, Henry Baring wagered Charles Ross a (regrettably illegible) sum 'that two Conservatives are not returned for Middlesex at the next election', but the seat returned one Whig and one Conservative.[159] Other wagers seemed to reflect bravado about forthcoming elections. On 23 June 1857, the Liberal Guildford Onslow (later notorious for his keen advocacy of the Tichborne claimant) confidently predicted 'I take from Sir E. Butler five ponies to two that I walk over for the Western Division of Surrey next Election', but in the event, he did not contest the two-member constituency, instead giving a clear run for one Liberal candidate against the two Conservative ones.[160]

One MP with a penchant for consistently placing foolhardy electoral bets was Gerald Sturt. In 1851, he wagered George Tomline thirty pounds to twenty pounds that Denbighshire would return two Protectionists at the following general election, when only one was elected in 1852.[161] In 1852, he bet Lord Norreys a sovereign that the latter would not stand for Oxfordshire at that year's election, only for Norreys to stand, coming last of four candidates in the three-member seat.[162] In 1859, he bet Thomas Bateson five pounds that Gladstone would hold Oxford University at the following (1865) election, only for Gladstone to lose it.[163] In 1865, he bet on the incumbent F. W. F. Berkeley to hold Cheltenham, duly losing a five pound bet to L. Dawson Damer.[164] As Sturt's losing streak demonstrates, clubs may have been havens for gossip, but the frequency of such gossip did not guarantee its accuracy.

All this helps construct an image of mid-Victorian Clubland as being fixated with politics and political calculations. This presents a challenge to Milne-Smith's view that 'only rarely did men discuss matters of great importance or depth in their clubs', something which perhaps holds true of broader Clubland by the end of the century, but which was not true of political clubs in the middle part of the century.[165] Gossip on 'high politics' was integral to the identity of political clubs; the promise of 'inside information' added lustre to the prestige of membership.

Conclusion

In the aftermath of the Great Fire of 1834, clubs played a vital part in moulding the physical shape of Westminster politics in the nineteenth century. Whilst many aspects of clubs were not new, and have their parallels in the inns, salons and private homes that previously existed, the distinctive use of space, and the unique combination of on-site facilities, made clubs a powerful and popular space for legislators to work from, while the flow of traffic by MPs and Whips during the sitting of Parliament denotes the high level of club use. Chapter 2 proved that club membership amongst MPs was high, but it is only through the qualitative approach set out here that it has been possible to show that club use was high as well. Although grand, setpiece meetings within the clubs (and occasionally, as street protests in front of the clubs) are the most obvious manifestations of club use, the flexibility of club spaces to hold low-key, small-scale meetings should not be underestimated. A particular triumph of club architects was their success in designing buildings that could successfully hold gatherings of every scale, and the uniqueness of the clubs in this respect is significant. Consequently, clubs were a unique environment; all the more so since their distinctive masculinity stood at odds with a parliamentary system which disenfranchised women, but in which women played a number of other crucial roles around Westminster. The consequent club culture found in that space, rife with gossip and a rich anecdotal culture, formed a unique part of the evolving world of Victorian Westminster.

CHAPTER 4

CLUBS AS AN MP'S BASE: ACCOMMODATION, DINING, INFORMATION AND ORGANISATIONAL SUPPORT

Introduction

For most MPs, their club was a home from home. For at least one in ten MPs, it *was* their home.[1] Yet it could also be regarded as more than this, for as well as offering overnight accommodation, it offered affordable dining and organisational support – something that was crucial when MPs were expected to fulfil their duties without an office. T. A. Jenkins highlights how, in an era in which most MPs were not professional politicians, they expected to mix their legislative duties with a 'a fair – or more than fair – amount of pleasure', in the 'salons and clubs, dinners and balls' of London, and how this posed difficulties for Whips in corralling MPs through the division lobbies.[2] The value of the party-aligned clubs – particularly the Carlton and Reform Clubs – was in offering such pleasures in a space which crossed over with Westminster, still within reach of the Whips.[3] Feargus O'Connell recorded that a common cry of Liberal MPs retiring to the Reform Club was 'Send a cab for me to the club before the division' and that such movements were facilitated because 'there is a cab stand at the very door of the House [of Commons], and the whole process of going for, and returning with, an honourable gentleman does not occupy more than eight minutes'.[4] Thus, with a steady flow of traffic of MPs between clubs and Parliament during well-attended divisions, the clubs effectively functioned as an outlying extension of the parliamentary estate.

Accommodation

The accommodation role of clubs is often overlooked, particularly for those MPs who did not have a London home, and who were permanently resident in their club when Parliament sat. The National Club even traded on the basis of its Old Palace Yard clubhouse's accommodation, noting 'Several Members of the Club House having expressed a great desire to be allowed to engage a Bed Room in the House for the energetic Parliamentary Season', although it did not specify what proportion were attending as participants or spectators.[5] At a time when hotels were still considered disreputable, the club offered a town address that was both inexpensive and respectable, resulting in dozens of MPs at a time giving their club as a town address. When applying for the Carlton Club in 1856, recently elected MP R. J. W. Bond had no qualms about giving his home address as the Army and Navy Club.[6] However, whilst clubs provided crucial accommodation for a minority of less affluent MPs, the scope of this phenomenon should not be exaggerated. Even larger clubs such as the Carlton and the Reform had only a few dozen rooms. Some MPs chose to stay elsewhere when in London. Thomas Bunbury MP already belonged to the United University Club before joining the Carlton Club in 1841, yet Bunbury's 1838 *Dod's* entry gave his London address as the St James's Hotel on Jermyn Street.[7] Similarly, numerous MPs resident in the St James's area gave home addresses only a few metres from their clubs. Indeed, Reform Club member George Duncan MP resided at 19 Great George Street – far closer to Parliament than the clubhouse.[8] It is thus difficult to explain why MPs with such convenient London addresses would have joined a club if it were a mere boarding house. Instead, clubs had added value for MPs, beyond their accommodation.

Dining

Food and dining were crucial to the appeal of clubs, and, by extension, to the furtherance of politics within them. They were also an essential part of the Westminster system, for while the original Bellamy's restaurant provided hearty meals on the parliamentary estate from 1773 to 1834, thereafter it was increasingly the clubs to which MPs turned.[9] It was not until 1848 – after an interval of 14 years since the Great Fire destroyed Bellamy's – that a Select Committee examined the question of parliamentary dining provision. The original Bellamy's had been a small-scale, intimate pair of rooms with one butler. Prices in the old Bellamy's were high, and serving hours did not necessarily tally with late-night sittings, leading many MPs to fast during sittings, whilst others relied on bringing snacks such as nuts and pears into the chamber to fuel late-night debates.[10] For the much-expanded dining facilities of the new House, the Select Committee 'worked the department under a manager in the same way as the house committee of an ordinary club', according to one Edwardian account.[11]

Although there has been some literature on political dinners in the period – most notably in recent years by Marc Baer, Peter Brett, Matthew Cragoe and Kathryn Gleadle – this has mainly focussed on the significance and ritual of constituency dinners.[12] Club dinners in London had their own unique characteristics. Club histories have venerated their most celebrated chefs, most conspicuously Alexis Soyer at the Reform Club in the 1840s, while after Soyer's retirement, John Timbs wrote that 'The best judges are agreed it is utterly impossible to dine better than at the Carlton'.[13] Social histories of the period have singled out Soyer as one of the earliest 'celebrity chefs', part of a French gastronomic wave which swept London in the mid-nineteenth century.[14] The lure for MPs was all too apparent, as John Bright joked: 'Clubs are celebrated for their cookery, and a great number of the members [of Parliament] make preparing for their dinners and eating them the chief object of their concern during the day'.[15] The wider political dimension of such meals has been overlooked.

Club meals can be divided into two broad types – 'regular' meals, and special banquets. The serving of 'regular' meals at hours directly tied to parliamentary sittings was ideal for parliamentarians, whose sittings could be irregular.[16] Not only did it ensure that MPs had a convenient place to eat, well within a short distance of Parliament but, as has been noted, it also provided party whips with nearby venues to find large gatherings of MPs. Rule seventeen at Brooks's insisted that dinner was 'to be furnished daily, during the sitting of Parliament', being served at 7pm, 'and the bill brought in at half-past nine exactly' in good time to attend late-night votes.[17] Members wishing to attend had to give only two hours' notice, as opposed to the four hours required when Parliament was not sitting.[18] At White's, the Club's minute book recorded on 3 April 1865 'it was ordered that one joint of meat should be prepared every day at 7.30, at two shillings per head, while Parliament was sitting, and that claret should be furnished at four shillings a bottle', emphasising not only convenient mealtimes around parliamentary hours, but also affordability.[19] Furthermore, at the Westminster Club in 1834, 'half an hour after the closing of the House of Commons, be the time after which no Member shall be admitted'; members who got in before the doors closed could stay all night.[20] When the Reform Club was founded two years later, it allowed its members to enter the Club anytime between 8am and 1am.[21] Contemporary press accounts corroborate the notion that clusters of MPs would retire to political clubs for a late dinner after a sitting in the Commons.[22] Furthermore, the Reform Club codified its dinners for parliamentarians by hosting a weekly dinner for Liberal MPs from the start of the 1837 parliamentary session.[23] The Club could be relied upon to provide parliamentarians with a secure partisan atmosphere, free from prying ears, because during the parliamentary session, members were not allowed to bring guests into the Club.[24] Additionally, the eccentric hours of clubs were not limited to late nights, but to weekends as well, as recognised by the Liberal MP Sir John Shelley, who pointed out in 1860 that private members' clubs were exempt from licensing laws and that one could always drink on Sundays at the Reform Club.[25] Furthermore, a club's dinner menu was the responsibility of its governing committee, and its wine list was invariably the preserve of the wine committee. In political clubs, MPs dominated both, therefore a small number of parliamentarians heavily involved in club affairs spent more time than most sampling food and drink. (On the Carlton Club's founding Committee in 1832, thirteen of the thirty-five members were MPs, and another nineteen were peers. In 1834 the Westminster Club boasted that two-thirds of its twenty-six-strong Committee were MPs. In 1850, five of the National Club's eight Wine Committee members were MPs.)[26]

Special banquets are also revealing, for both their subject matters, and their content. Many events were organised in honour of political figures, such as a Free Trade Club banquet of July 1846, held in celebration of the passage of Corn Law repeal, which was attended by MPs including T. M. Gibson, William Ewart and George Moffett; or the Reform Club banquet in honour of Viscount Palmerston on 20 July 1854, which was attended by the entire cabinet.[27] Their scale could be impressive, like a previous Reform Club dinner for Palmerston on 21 July 1850, about which Greville observed the audience was 'a rabble of men, not ten out of two hundred whom I know by sight'.[28] That dinner was held in support of Palmerston four days after his censure by the House of Lords over Don Pacifico, demonstrating the Club's solidarity. A further Reform Club dinner was held after Palmerston's vindication by the Commons, although the Palmerston biographer David Brown records 'only a sense of decorum had dictated that a modest Reform Club dinner be held to mark the triumph; there would have been enough enthusiasm, [Palmerston] said, for a dinner for a thousand people in Covent Garden'.[29] Such meals could also send out signals of international solidarity, as with the breakfast of 21 April 1864, when 200 Reform Club members welcomed Giuseppe Garibaldi, most of them wearing Garibaldian rosettes.[30] Some, such as the Reform Club's dinner in honour of Daniel O'Connell, even offered politicised dishes from Soyer, such as *soufflés a la Clontarf*.[31] The largest dinners could be widely publicised, with reporters attending so as to provide verbatim accounts of speeches and record the extensive lists of attendees; something unthinkable in everyday club dinners. As has been noted above, setpiece dinners sometimes included women, although this was the exception, not the rule, since clubs remained mostly off-limits to female visitors in this period. Not only were the dinners predominantly all-male, but so was their promotion by professional club staff, often on club stationery – this contrasts with private salon dinners, which frequently involved women as organisers.[32] At such setpiece dinners, the purpose was to send out a clear signal of a club's approval of a defined cause or an individual; a notable example being the banquet held for William Beresford at the Carlton in December 1852. Beresford had recently been censured for indiscretion in a bribery inquiry, and Lord Stanley confirmed to his diary that the dinner was intended as 'a counter-demonstration' in favour of the embattled Conservative Whip, although

Greville mocked it as 'twenty ruffians ... [dining] to celebrate what they consider [Beresford's] *acquittal*!'[33]

Undoubtedly the most controversial – and the most heavily publicised – dinner of the period was the 7 March 1854 Reform Club banquet for Admiral Sir Charles Napier held prior to his departure for the Crimea. As it drew attention in Parliament and in the national and international press, it merits discussion here. The dinner was presided over by Viscount Palmerston, and prominent MPs present included Lord John Russell, Sir James Graham and Sir William Molesworth.[34] Even though the after-dinner speeches were not statements of policy, the personalities were sufficiently important to lend the event a sense of officialdom; the Hon. Arthur Duncombe MP later called it an 'unusual ceremony' for installing an Admiral.[35] Varying accounts exist of the dinner, but they all agree that some of the speakers made intemperate remarks with international repercussions – and reports of these speeches spread around the globe. In the United States, Napier's 'very foolish and bragging' comments were reported as a promise to resolve the ambiguity of whether Britain was at peace or war by announcing war once he was in the Baltic.[36] In New Zealand, it was reported that Graham had told Napier that the latter could declare war whenever he wanted, provided the war was short and sharp.[37] As Greville wrote in his diary, the dinner was 'unwise and in bad taste'.[38]

Such was the seriousness of the reports of this dinner that on 13 March 1854, the two Liberal MPs John Bright and Fitzstephen French triggered a parliamentary debate on what had and had not been said in the speeches. Graham's original attempt to derail the debate – that he was 'not disposed' to answer for comments made 'after dinner' – only further alienated the House of Commons.[39] Bright's censorious speech, accusing ministers of unwarranted levity, was brushed off by Palmerston's characteristically breezy admission of 'the most perfect indifference and contempt' for Bright's rebukes.[40] Palmerston also distanced the Club from any official involvement, adding that Bright 'thinks that these dinner arrangements must be Cabinet questions', but that the issues discussed were 'open questions' which were 'not discussed in the Cabinet at all'.[41] In Greville's opinion, Palmerston and Graham 'positively *disgraced* themselves' as much in the debate as at the dinner.[42]

The 1854 debate over the Reform Club dinner also brought out simmering political resentment at the embrace of the military establishment by a political club. Given that Napier and Admiral Sir James Deans Dundas had been long-standing Reform Club members, Conservative MP Sir Thomas Herbert grilled Sir James Graham about the implied political bias of Graham's words 'We as reformers may be proud' of their appointments to command the task force, and sought reassurance that their promotion was free from political motivations.[43] A cleverly divisive speech from Disraeli, portraying the 'sound Reformers' of the Reform Club as Conservative allies, further stirred the sense of discontent among the government's supporters.[44]

For the ministers present at the controversial dinner, the incident was a source of embarrassment. Ministers had been given advance notice of the debate and, although Palmerston gave a typically swaggering performance, both Graham and Molesworth appeared rattled. Graham first refused to elaborate on his politicised comment on Napier, then backtracked by denying that 'political considerations entered in the slightest degree' in Napier's appointment. A defensive Molesworth protested 'I am not aware that I said anything of which I need be ashamed' and accused Bright of 'illiberal and narrow-minded prejudices'.[45] The controversy continued for some time, and a year later Graham was still fielding questions on it in the Commons, answering 'I am not likely to make any repetition of the offence'.[46]

The Napier banquet was an atypical incident in its breadth and significance, but it highlighted the perils of holding such large-scale banquets, especially given the presence of the press. Although the rest of the period produced no banquets of comparable notoriety, it did not deter setpiece political dinners from flourishing alongside more informal dinners. Nor did it stop the press from being invited to such proceedings, as evidenced by a further Reform Club banquet for Palmerston later the same year. Indeed, a delegation of 'gentlemen of the press' at flagship club banquets became something of a fixture during this period, and if one looks several decades ahead, it is apparent that this practice thrived until at least the end of the century.[47]

Information

Clubs received a regular flow of news and information from the outside world, and sought to cater for MPs' needs to remain informed. The previous chapter documented how gossip could be conveyed using

Figure 4.1 The Reform Club banquet for Sir Charles Napier. Source: *Illustrated London News,* 18 March 1854, p. 228.

individual insights and knowledge. But on an organisational level, clubs did much to ensure that members remained as informed as possible, using the most up-to-date technology available, through the medium of newspapers, reference libraries and telegraph wires.

Newspapers were widely subscribed to in clubs. Expanding national rail links throughout this period allowed clubs to order up-to-date regional as well as London papers, and the concentration of titles offered MPs a valuable resource. Scrutinising the surviving Carlton Club minutebooks, one is left with the impression that the Club subscribed to all London newspapers, as well as any provincial newspapers which were requested by members – any single member's request needed to be rubber-stamped by the Committee, but there is no documented instance of the Club *not* approving a new subscription requested by a member, no matter how provincial or arcane the publication. As well as ordering the London newspapers, between 1835 and 1841 the Carlton successively started ordering (at the request of members) the *Parliamentary Gazette, Dublin Evening Post, Bath Chronicle, Torch, Tablet, Ecclesiastical Gazette, Greenwich Guardian, Staffordshire Gazette* and the *Salisbury and Wiltshire Herald*.[48] At the Westminster Reform Club, subscriptions in the 1830s had a more London-centric character, extending to *The Times*, *Morning Chronicle*, *Morning Herald*, *Post*, *Morning Advertiser*, *Globe*, *Courier*, *Standard*, *True Sun* and the *Sun* daily, as well as the weekly journals *John Bull*, the *Age*, *Examiner*, *Spectator*, *Observer* and the *Satirist*.[49] At the Reform Club, a specific Newspaper Committee existed to recommend titles as well as newspapers requiring extra quantities, which in the early 1860s included the *Daily Telegraph*, *Globe*, *Daily News*, and the *Dublin Express*.[50] Such a broad reflection of titles was presumably matched at Brooks's, where the accounts show that £269 2s 1d was spent on newspapers in 1842.[51] Stephen Koss noted that one of the most popular publications across clubs was the *Pall Mall Gazette*, which 'catered expressly to a Clubland clientele', and articulated broadly Palmerstonian sympathies: 'Fiercely anti-Gladstonian and jingoistic, it accurately reflected club opinion'.[52] Old newspapers were also bound for reference in club libraries, providing a historical resource for members.[53] If anything, there was a surfeit of newspaper titles, with the Carlton disposing of its regional papers and only binding the national ones.[54] Judging from the stream of political correspondence pouring forth from political clubs, it is clear that newspapers did not go unread, but were closely scrutinised on the premises. For instance, in 1838 Frederick Polhill MP wrote from the Carlton to correct an erroneous division list that had been published in *The Times*.[55] Indeed, this was a far from isolated example, and already by 1833 Daniel Harvey MP mocked the flow of 'morning letters from this Conservative [Carlton] Club-house and that Union to the Editors of newspapers, requesting them to insert a correction that Mr. so and so was in the House, and voted in the majority'.[56] Scrutiny of the letters pages of *The Times* reveals scores of such letters throughout the period, with the scanning of newspaper division lists by MPs in their clubs acquiring something of a ritualistic status. Given such activity, not for the first or last time MPs were known to treat these club newspapers as their own – in 1835 the Carlton's Groom of Chambers was appointed to the task of ensuring newspapers were not removed, yet the following year the Hon. Arthur Trevor MP was accused of stealing the Club's newspapers.[57]

As well as holding newspapers, club libraries could be well-furnished with both standard reference works and specialist tracts. White's, with a less ambitious literary emphasis than many clubs (for it had no library) was said in 1835 to contain 'a tolerably fair supply of papers, but no books, excepting a few reviews and magazines'. The anonymous White's member who offered this opinion elaborated 'as to newspapers and periodicals, no one at the tip-top Clubs reads either one or the other', the definition of 'tip-top' here presumably being 'aristocratic'.[58] Other clubs had further barriers to library use. The National Club would allow its members use of its reading room, but non-clergy members were required to pay an extra £2 2s (plus an additional entrance fee of £6 6s). In the case of the National Club, it was communicated to members that this was a rationing measure, owing to the high demand for reading room places, which were usually 'full'.[59] Yet the political focus of such club libraries could present a challenge to the theological status quo, with Radical MP Charles Buller complaining that through the windows of the Carlton he could see that members spent their Sundays reading *John Bull* and the *Age* instead of the Bible.[60]

For more up-to-the-minute news, even established Georgian clubs like Brooks's were dispensing news received by telegraph wire by the 1850s.[61] Indeed, when strong parliamentary performers such as Ralph Bernal Osborne were speaking, telegraph messages were sent to London clubs in advance, noticeably boosting attendance by MPs.[62] Additionally, the political clubs prominently displayed parliamentary information. John Bright MP, a daily user of the Reform Club during the parliamentary session, told the Commons 'In the hall of the Reform Club there is affixed to the wall a paper which gives a telegraphic account of what is being done in this House every night, and what is also being done in the other House'.[63]

Consequently, the nineteenth century clubs were able to provide their members with some of the best libraries and periodical collections in London, at a time when such facilities on the parliamentary estate were either non-existent, or in their infancy. The Athenaeum was (and remains) unrivalled among Clubland libraries in both size and scope, whilst the Carlton, Junior Carlton, Reform and Travellers' Clubs all provided members with formidable libraries. (In the case of the Travellers', the library was so capacious as to outgrow its club in 1841, and it had to be spun off into the nearby London Library, which was run along the club business model.)

Organisational Support

Whilst dinners appealed to MPs' sociability, clubs offered other, more tangible benefits – facilities which were invaluable when MPs would not be given offices on the parliamentary estate for well over one hundred years, and which were not matched by any townhouse or salon. The significance of club postal facilities should not be underestimated, particularly given the importance of the flow of letters in contemporary politics, and the mid-nineteenth century revolution in postage. The introduction of the penny post in 1840, the development of express mail coaches in the 1840s, and the distribution of post by train from the 1850s dramatically expanded the use of postage facilities, and clubs made ample use of such advances.[64] Percy Colson noted that at White's 'One popular privilege was the franking of letters, a useful one, seeing that the postage of an ordinary letter cost tenpence. A Cabinet Minister could frank fifteen a day'.[65] Given the large volume of political correspondence posted from clubs, and the evolution of a later club such as the National Liberal hosting its own branch of the Post Office in the 1880s, it would not be unremarkable to suppose that several political clubs in this period offered franking facilities along the lines of White's.[66] However, one should not overestimate the innovation of this. Duncan Campbell-Smith writes that since the eighteenth century 'Letters went free of postage for Whitehall officials and anyone connected with the army or navy, as well as to Lords and MPs at Westminster. All were now guilty of distributing "franked stationery" – often no more than a sheet of paper, bearing an eligible signature – to their family, friends and business associates in ever more outrageous quantities'.[67] If one examines the surviving correspondence between Peel and F. R. Bonham in the 1830s, one finds that most of it was franked – although occasionally letters were not.[68] Where the clubs offered something new was in *legitimately* granting party managers and agents not in Parliament the use of such facilities.

The postal environment in which clubs operated can be broadly split into two halves: pre- and post-1840. Before 1840, most mail was paid for by the recipient (making franking all the more significant), and postage costs increased with distance, with mail within London being two pence per sheet of paper, but mail to Scotland costing as much as a shilling per sheet.[69] There was thus an economic incentive for letters to be brief (one page or less) and infrequent. Furthermore, the pre-1840 use of a club as a postal address meant that one could avoid having to pay for unsolicited letters, since a club would pay for receiving them (potentially making the club subscription good value for money for the member who used it as a postal address). The 1837 publication of Rowland Hill's *Post Office Reform: Its Importance and Practicability* prompted a public debate on the topic of postage, and against this backdrop, numerous statistics were gathered which render a clearer picture of the postal environment of the 1830s.[70] Club postal routines seem to have been fairly standardised amongst political and non-political clubs alike, with the Carlton Club's servants encountering the Athenaeum's servants at the Charing Cross receiving house as they both submitted their mail for the last post at 6pm.[71] The clubs themselves would have received their daily mail no later than 11:25am each weekday, and sometimes before 10:05am.[72] Thus, even allowing for delays in club porters sorting the mail, it is likely that mail was available for members before noon.

Clubs provided a convenient postal address for writing to an MP, although there was no guarantee that MPs would actually read such correspondence, however important. In 1858, when the Earl of Derby offered Conservative MP John Mowbray the post of Judge Advocate-General, his letter offering the role lay unread with the Carlton hall porter, even though Mowbray had dined at the Carlton the previous night before going on to a vote. Only a chance encounter with Disraeli on the steps of the Carlton prompted Mowbray to check his post.[73] Additionally, the safety of mail from interception could vary within a political club. On the one hand, it provided MPs with a safe haven from domestic queries, which led Disraeli to ask his sister to send her letters to him at the Carlton instead of his house, so that Mary Anne Lewis (whom he was then courting) could not read them.[74] On the other hand, club porters could and would obey orders from party leaders and their lieutenants to intercept members' mail: when John Young MP asked the Carlton porter whether a letter to Somerset Richard Maxwell MP had been picked up, he was told that Lord Enniskellen 'had asked for it and had taken it to Sir Robert Peel'.[75]

Since clubs offered MPs some protection of anonymity by refusing to acknowledge when members were on the premises, some MPs could use this to their advantage, particularly if their outside business affairs necessitated evading creditors. The example of Peter Borthwick MP making an appointment with his creditor Mrs. Bates at the Carlton Club in 1842, only to then not turn up, presents one stark example.[76] Given the propensity of other MPs such as Disraeli to use the Carlton as a business address when writing to creditors, it is quite conceivable that such behaviour was not uncommon.

A further set of facilities for MPs were those which offered organisational assistance in highlighting parliamentary issues of particular interest. MPs at the same club joined together to form committees. One of the Carlton Club's earlier initiatives in the 1830s was to form a committee to monitor any parliamentary proceedings which might affect the interests of landed proprietors or occupiers. The effort was considered successful enough to be imitated by the Central Tithes Association in 1836, which praised how the 'Carlton Club ... system had worked most efficiently'.[77] Such groupings of MPs most likely co-ordinated joint action, as was the case with several petitions on Ireland in 1853 which were all noted to have been 'presented by members of the Carlton Club'; although when making this observation, *The Times* could provide no direct evidence of club involvement in compiling them.[78] Certainly at the National Club the annual reports to members boasted of the co-ordinated activities of its parliamentarians, particularly in presenting bills and amendments, and triggering an annual vote in opposition to the ongoing Maynooth Grant after 1845. The Club published detailed division lists in support of this.[79] One should consider such organisational groupings when observing MPs who were active club users jointly moving amendments, as when Charles Newdegate MP and Richard Spooner MP presented an unsuccessful 1858 amendment to the Oaths Bill, attempting to prevent Jews from sitting in Parliament.[80] Existing accounts of this, such as that of Angus Hawkins, are lent a further dimension if one considers the involvement of both MPs in the National Club and its parliamentary committee's efforts.[81]

Also worth acknowledgement was the organisational assistance offered by club staff. This has been noted by Peter Marsh when identifying the most salient facilities of the Reform Club:

> a large central hall where the Parliamentary Liberal Party could assemble, grand dining rooms, rooms for smaller meetings of Party members, and – this is very important – office space in the basement for the creation of a nationwide constituency organisation to register the Party's supporters as qualified under the terms of the 1832 Reform Act. [82]

These offices were primarily targeted towards fundraising, registration and candidate selection efforts in constituencies, and are examined in more detail in Chapter 5.

Political clubs thus carved a unique niche for themselves in offering active politicians – and not just parliamentarians – a wide range of facilities for everything from discreet meetings and dinners for two or three men to large-scale semi-public banquets declaring public support for political causes. The unique value of the club from the 1830s to the 1860s was in its combination of many different facilities under one roof: accommodation, dining, franking, private meetings, and all relatively inexpensively, within the party surroundings already outlined. Additionally, what must be stressed is the novelty of many of these facilities. Contrary to the staid 'Clubland' image today, Victorian clubs were viewed as highly innovative in their use of technology, and their integration of it in providing comforts for MPs. Given such convenience, and the lack of a functioning parliamentary estate, it is thus particularly understandable why Victorian MPs as a social group were more likely than most to spend a substantial portion of their lives in London in their clubs.[83]

Conclusion

Clubs proved to be an invaluable base for MPs between the first two Reform Acts, particularly in the light of the dearth of facilities offered by the Palace of Westminster at the time. For a small but significant minority of MPs, they provided central, affordable, reputable accommodation during the parliamentary session. They offered members a wide array of dining experience, from intimate dinners to grand setpiece banquets extolling party positions. Yet their importance was not restricted to leisure pursuits – the major clubs also provided MPs with a comprehensive range of periodicals and reference works which assisted with research, and the clubs themselves offered a wide array of forms of organisational support, from postal franking to physical desks. The cultural dimension of such facilities is not to be underestimated. As we saw in the previous chapter, the dissemination of gossip was central to the appeal of clubs to those involved in politics. Yet gossip was not merely disseminated in person; clubs employed every available means at their disposal to keep members informed, embracing modern technology; telegraph wires, newspapers, post and gossip. This ensured that despite the half-mile distance which separated Clubland from the parliamentary estate, they remained at least as well-equipped for members, parliamentarians and party managers to remain informed, and in many instances the political clubs offered clearly superior facilities to Parliament, which remained a building site for much of the daytime.

Clubs are often portrayed as staid, outdated institutions – an image which owes far more to the long, slow decline of Clubland across the twentieth century than their nineteenth century heyday. At their height, they integrated a remarkable degree of modern technology, from the latest building materials through to such groundbreaking technologies as telegraphs and gas lighting. Far from being bastions of traditionalism, they were tremendously innovative in the array of services and facilities offered and, in the nineteenth century, most were quick to adapt in accommodating changing leisure trends such as the rise of smoking. Until the completion of the Palace of Westminster in the 1860s, no other convenient location offered MPs such an array of facilities under one roof; and, even then, it is questionable whether parliamentary facilities could truly match the clubs until the twentieth century.

CHAPTER 5

CLUBS AND WHIPS IN THE HOUSE OF COMMONS[1]

Introduction

With the growing political role of clubs in the mid-nineteenth century, they were increasingly a popular venue for the activities of party Whips. This chapter seeks to explore how the growth in the Whips' role was intertwined with the clubs. Whips and whipping have long suffered from neglect, but in recent years, our understanding of whipping in this period has been enormously enhanced by the work of J. M. Bourne, Joseph Coohill, P. M. Gurowich, Angus Hawkins, T. A. Jenkins, John C. Sainty and Gary W. Cox.[2] As Sainty and Cox have demonstrated, the passage of the First Reform Bill coincided with a watershed in the use of Whips to secure support for parties and governments.[3] The reasons for this were not uniquely tied to the culture of reform; Sainty identifies a crucial element being the merger of whipper-in and Patronage Secretary, which had hitherto been different posts, with Patronage Secretaries frequently entering Parliament only *after* their appointment.[4] Furthermore, as Hawkins has argued, the mid-nineteenth century represented a break from the past in the new-found emphasis placed on governments commanding a majority in the House of Commons.[5]

Whereas late-eighteenth and early-nineteenth century ministries could count on support from several dozen 'ministerialists' and/or the 'King's friends' in Parliament, this would seldom constitute an overall majority, and renewed constitutional pressure to secure a Commons majority in the post-Reform period led to an increased level of importance in the role of Whips. Nonetheless, whipping was still in its infancy, and while it involved ensuring the attendance of supporters, it did not extend to some of the later activities which defined whipping in the twentieth century, such as seeking to orchestrate a parliamentary debate with prearranged speakers; far from it, the floor was still prone to being seized by parochial mavericks, and even in the second half of the century, complaints about a 'paralysis of parliament' were still widespread.[6] Furthermore, unlike their twentieth-century counterparts, Whips had limited powers of coercion; MPs did not owe their election to them, and the threat of withdrawal of the whip did not necessarily spell electoral ruin to a parliamentarian.[7] Thus the role of the Whips was still evolving.

This chapter examines the role of Whips in three key areas:

(1) Whips in clubs,
(2) Subscriptions to the Whip – and the neglected role played by clubs in administering them, and,
(3) Whips, clubs and party identity – and the degree to which club membership facilitated whipping in being regarded by contemporaries as a proxy for club membership.

Whipping was frequently attributed to clubs, or the absence of whipping to the absence of clubs. For instance, when Conservative MP Henry Kemble tried to delay Liberal MP Thomas Duncombe's anti-Income Tax petitions on a procedural point in 1842, Duncombe alleged that Kemble,'complained, he supposed, because he had not whipped up the Carlton Club for the occasion'.[8] It is the contention of this chapter that such allegations were well-merited, and that as the practice of whipping grew throughout this period, the unique facilities and membership of London's political clubs made them an indispensable component of the party Whips' world.

Whips in Clubs

As a necessary prerequisite to whipping in clubs, Whips had to have access to such clubs, through being members. Tables 5.1a and 5.1b name the principal Liberal and Conservative Whips in the House of Commons in 1832–68, and identify their club memberships, which can thus be construed as being within their sphere of club influence:

Several trends can be noted. All the Liberal Chief Whips in this period belonged to both Brooks's and the Reform Club, except Tufnell in the years 1841–50, who was not a Reform Club member, but who was assisted by Lord Marcus Hill, who was. All of the Liberal Chief Whips joined Brooks's first, although there is no obvious single reason for this. Every junior Liberal Whip belonged to either Brooks's or the Reform Club, and 11 out of 18 Liberal Whips belonged to both clubs. From the Reform Club's foundation in 1836, both Brooks's and the Reform Club contained at least one Liberal Whip at all times.

All 15 of the Conservative Whips in this period (including the seven Chief Whips) belonged to the Carlton Club. Whilst the Junior Carlton Club was only established in 1864, it was still well-covered by the Whips, with all three contemporary Conservative Whips belonging to it (as well as one former Whip). White's fared less well, with five of fifteen Conservative Whips belonging to it, and intriguingly, no Conservative Whips covering it in the years 1837–46, casting further doubt on whether it was considered to be a Conservative political club by the late 1830s. Yet while William Beresford and Colonel Taylor both belonged to the National Club, the *other* major Carlton Club offshoot of the 1840s, the Conservative Club, was conspicuous by its absence, with not a single Whip known to have joined.

Not only do the above figures demonstrate how Whips had easy access to the principal political clubs, holding membership in their own right, and presenting the opportunity to whip MPs inside the clubs, but they are also consistent with the pattern of the Carlton Club being the centre of Conservative activity, and Liberal parliamentary activity being divided between Brooks's and the Reform Club.

J. M. Bourne has outlined how Whips formed 'small ad hoc committees ... in the Carlton and Reform clubs', and 'Though chief whips had no direct control over election to membership of the clubs, their good offices were often sought and this proved a useful addition to

Table 5.1a Club memberships of Liberal Whips, 1830–68

Tenure	Liberal Whips (Chief Whips in bold)	Clubs, with year of election (if known)
1830–2	**Edward Ellice**	Brooks's (1809); Reform (1836)
1832–4	**Charles Wood**	Brooks's (1827); Reform (1836); White's (1861); Travellers'
1834–5	**F.T. Baring**	Athenaeum (1824); Brooks's (1828); Reform (1836); United University
1835–41	**Edward J. Stanley**	Brooks's (1828); Reform (1836)
	Robert Steuart (1835–40)	Reform (1836)
	Richard M. O'Ferall (1835–9)	Brooks's (1830); Reform (1836)
	Henry Tufnell (1839–41)	Brooks's (1830); Travellers'
	John Parker (1840–1)	Athenaeum (1826); Reform (1836); Carlton (1838); Brooks's (1840, subsequently resigned, then reinstated 1846)
1841–50	**Henry Tufnell**	Brooks's (1830); Travellers'
	Lord Marcus Hill	Reform (1840)
1850–8	**William G. Hayter**	Brooks's (1838); Reform (1842); United University
	Lord Marcus Hill (until 1852)	Reform (1840)
	Earl of Mulgrave (1851–8)	Brooks's (1851); Reform (unknown date)
	Grenville Berkeley (1853–6)	Travellers'; Brooks's (1855)
	Henry Brand (1855–8)	Brooks's (1846); Reform (1858)
1858–67	**Henry Brand**	Brooks's (1846); Reform (1858)
	Edward Knatchbull-Hugessen (1858–65)	Brooks's (1855); United University
	Sir William Dunbar (1859–65)	Brooks's (1857)
	Hon. Luke White (1862–5)	Brooks's (1864); Army and Navy; Kildare Street, Dublin
	William Adam (1865–6)	Brooks's (1850); Reform (1866); Athenaeum (unknown date)
1867–73	**George G. Glyn**	Brooks's (1854); Reform (1862); Travellers'
	(*Glyn's junior Whips not listed, as they only began serving in that capacity after the 1868 election.*)	

Table 5.1b Club memberships of Conservative Whips, 1832–68

Tenure	Conservative Whips (Chief Whips in bold)	Clubs, with year of election
1832–5	(*Unknown*)[9]	N/A
1835–7	**Sir George Clerk**	Athenaeum (1824); Garrick (1831); Carlton (1832)
	Charles Ross	Athenaeum (1824); White's (1827); Carlton (1832)
	F. R. Bonham	Athenaeum (1824); Carlton (1832)
1837–44	**Sir Thomas Fremantle**	Carlton (1832)
	Henry Baring	Brooks's (1824, resigned 1830, reinstated 1854); Athenaeum (unknown date, possibly 1825/6); Carlton (1832)
	James More Gaskell (from 1841)	Carlton (unknown date – before 1836); Oxford and Cambridge
1844–6	**Sir John Young**	Athenaeum (1832); Carlton (unknown date – before 1836)
	Henry Baring	Brooks's (1824, resigned 1830, reinstated 1854); Athenaeum (unknown date, possibly 1825/6); Carlton (1832)
	James More Gaskell	Carlton (unknown date – before 1836); Oxford and Cambridge
1846–52	**William Beresford**	Carlton (1842); National (1845); Travellers'
	Charles N. Newdegate	White's (1838); Carlton (1840); National (1845); Arthur's; Travellers'
	W. Forbes Mackenzie (from 1850)	Carlton (unknown date – before 1836)
1852–3	**W. Forbes Mackenzie**	Carlton (unknown date – before 1836)
	Thomas Bateson (1852)	Carlton (1844); White's (1847); Traveller's; Junior Carlton (1864)
1853–9	**William Jolliffe**	Carlton (unknown date – before 1836); White's (1840); Arthur's, Boodle's
	Col. Thomas Edward Taylor	Carlton (1841); National (1845); Junior Carlton (1864); Travellers'
	Henry Whitmore (from 1855)	Carlton (1840); Oxford and Cambridge; Junior Carlton (1864)
1859–68	**Col. Thomas Edward Taylor**	Carlton (1841); National (1845); Junior Carlton (1864); Travellers'
	Henry Whitmore	Carlton (1840); Oxford and Cambridge; Junior Carlton (1864)
	Gerard Noel (from 1866)	White's (1849); Carlton (1852); Junior Carlton (1864)

Source: List of Whips sourced from John Sainty and Gary W. Cox, 'The Identification of Government Whips in the House of Commons 1830–1905', *Parliamentary History*, 16 (1997), pp. 339–58; Club memberships of Whips sourced from Seth Alexander Thévoz, 'Database of MPs' Club Memberships, 1832–68'.[10]

their patronage'.[11] An inspection of the candidates' books of the Carlton Club and Junior Carlton Clubs finds that Whips did indeed have substantial influence over election to these clubs. Not only were F. R. Bonham, Lord Redesdale, Sir Thomas Fremantle and Thomas Edward Taylor all noticeably frequent proposers or seconders for membership of these clubs, but in the dozens of instances of their sponsored candidates, it has not been possible to find any case of an *unsuccessful* candidate sponsored by these Whips.[12] While there is no evidence of any widespread fast-tracking of a Whip's candidate (of the kind which characterised MPs' club admission), it appears that nomination by a Conservative Whip carried the very highest recommendation at the Carlton and Junior Carlton Clubs. It is also noticeable that despite the rules permitting MPs to be fast-tracked anyway, MPs still conspicuously asked Whips to nominate them as Carlton Club candidates — Sir William Jolliffe was approached by the intermediary W. Carrington in 1861 to propose Sir Michael Hicks-Beach MP (along with H. Farquhar), while in 1857 George Dundas MP had sought Jolliffe as seconder for a newly-elected MP he had proposed, John Thomas Hopwood.[13] Such requests were not atypical, and there were multiple instances of complete strangers writing to Jolliffe, seeking him as a proposer for the Carlton.[14] Additionally, the other most persistent nominators of successful members at the Junior Carlton in the 1860s were the solicitors Philip Rose and Markham Spofforth, who were responsible for much of the clubs' electoral activities, suggesting that at the Junior Carlton, Conservative agents had comparable patronage to that enjoyed by Whips at the Carlton.[15] At the Carlton Club, however, the Chief Whip's power of nomination may have been greater than a party election manager's: in 1857, Philip Rose wrote to Jolliffe that 'Mr. G. M. Colchester is anxious to be admitted to the Carlton as soon as you can arrange it. Will you let me know about how soon he may hope to be admitted[?]' The tone of this letter suggests that whatever power of nomination Rose had, his authority derived from the Chief Whip.[16] Furthermore, just as Jolliffe's tenure as Chief Whip was drawing to a close, his influence over Carlton admissions grew even stronger, for on 17 March 1859 he was appointed to the Club's Committee of Management, which met weekly on Tuesdays, and had the power to appoint club members on the merits of their service to the Conservative cause, bypassing the need for a ballot.[17]

By contrast, the Reform Club Ballot Book and the Brooks's members' lists do *not* appear to have registered a high number of candidates proposed by Whips, barring those sponsored for the Reform Club by Edward Ellice, who was an *ex*-Whip by the time the Club was launched. Nor does the Reform Club agent James Coppock appear to have nominated many candidates.[18] This suggests a different political culture between the Liberals at Brooks's and the Reform Club and the Conservatives at the Carlton and Junior Carlton, with a greater degree of patronage wielded by Whips in Conservative circles. While the role of Whips in club nomination is a trend which has been overlooked by historians, it appears to have been common knowledge at the time; in 1839 Sir George Sinclair observed in the House of Commons that Conservative MPs applying to the Carlton were often proposed by Sir Charles Wetherell and seconded by F. R. Bonham.[19]

Whips were also heavily involved in setting up the major political clubs after 1832. Lord Redesdale was one of the five original trustees of the Carlton Club in 1832.[20] Edward Ellice was the founding Chairman of the Reform Club in 1836, and later became one of its trustees, while both Edward J. Stanley and Richard More O'Ferall were founding members of its Committee.[21] Colonel Thomas Edward Taylor was one of the five founding trustees of the Junior Carlton Club in 1864.[22] Even the National Club was well-represented by Whips, with both William Beresford and Charles Newdegate being active founder members of the Club's Committee throughout their time as Derbyite Whips in the late 1840s.[23]

Hosting a high concentration of parliamentarians in the evenings, clubs were a perfect recruiting ground for Whips needing to drum up parliamentary numbers for a looming vote at short notice, and there is much evidence to support the view that this became systematised. Whips would 'work' Brooks's, the Carlton and Reform Clubs before significant votes. For instance, in 1836, after the maverick MP George Robinson proposed the introduction of a property tax, government Whips leapt into action. Journalist James Grant recalled 'When it was uncertain how soon the question might be pressed to a division, messengers were despatched to Brookes's [sic], the Westminster [Reform] Club, at 24, George-street, and the other places of resort of the Liberal members; so that in the short space of half an hour the number of members in the house swelled from forty-eight or fifty, to about two hundred'.[24] Numerous other contemporary accounts support the notion that political clubs were packed with politicians during the parliamentary session. Writing to his sister from the Carlton Club's new purpose-built clubhouse in 1836, Disraeli marvelled 'The Carlton is a great loun[ge]. I write this in the room [where there are] some 80 persons all of the first importance'.[25] Even when it was less packed, the Carlton's concentration of MPs remained high, as Disraeli noted 'The C[arlton] is not very full, but the MPs are flocking in this morning'.[26] The heavy use of the Carlton does not seem to have diminished over the years, with Disraeli complaining fourteen years later about writing in 'this noisy club',[27] and a further twelve years later about the club being 'full to overflowing'.[28] Thus by the 1830s, the clubs at the very least supplemented the grand houses of St James's as a first port-of-call for Whips, yielding a high numbers of MPs for divisions, and this does not seem to have diminished between the first two Reform Acts. What the journal of Liberal Whip Edward Knatchbull-Hugessen makes clear is that as late as the 1860s, much attention was paid by the Whips to Brooks's as well as the Reform Club; on 12 January 1866, for instance, he gauged how 'Brooks's is, as usual, full of forebodings & fears as to the Reform Bill', while six days later he dined at Brooks's with Lord Hartington and Henry Brand to share information picked up in the Club, and another six days later he dined there with Lords Clarendon and Enfield, sharing 'a long talk afterwards'.[29] Given the high concentration of Adullamite MPs at Brooks's, it is unsurprising that the Club should have remained of such great interest to Liberal Whips during Russell's last unsuccessful Reform Bill.

In their work, Whips benefitted from dedicated facilities in the purpose-built clubhouses, although these could be rather sparse. Both the Carlton and Reform Clubs included basement offices for the use of Whips, although in the opinion of a *New York Times* foreign correspondent, such Whips' offices at both clubs constituted 'a small dark cavern'.[30] If any larger-scale work was required, Whips would have to make use of the communal desks in the club rooms, for which competition could be high, and which depended on the level of crowding in each club.

By the middle of the century, Whips were aided during divisions by the installation of division bells inside clubs. It has not been possible to verify precisely when clubs first installed division bells, although they were already present by the mid-1850s, and they must have been installed sometime after 1839, when Thomas Duncombe MP openly suggested to the House of Commons that low turnouts on Commons votes could be avoided by installing division bells in locations where MPs were found; 'Why not at the Reform Club, why not at the Carlton?'[31]

Thus through their dedicated facilities and their accessibility to Whips who were both senior members and (in the case of the Carlton and Junior Carlton) often influential sponsors of membership, Whips occupied a key role in political clubs, which afforded them a remarkable degree of access to the high concentration of MPs contained therein.

Subscriptions to the Whip

The evolution of a physical 'whip' – a slip of paper outlining forthcoming divisions, underlined several times depending on the importance of the vote – has been the subject of work by T. A. Jenkins, focussing on its emergence in this period.[32] As Jenkins notes, ongoing research into this is undermined by 'the dearth of basic information about how the Whips carried out their work ... particularly on the whig-Liberal side', with the singular exception of the papers of Henry Brand.[33] Accordingly, much of what we know of the evolution of printed whips comes from Conservative parliamentarians. Nonetheless, it is possible to note a central Carlton Club role in the growth of whipping, particularly in the papers of Conservative Whip Sir Thomas Fremantle, which offer a vivid insight into the culture of whipping which emerged in the late 1830s.

A subscription was set up amongst Conservative MPs and peers to pay for 'Parliamentary Notices & Circulars, Messengers &c', at an initial cost of two pounds per annum.[34] Bank receipts show that this subscription fund was administered by Fremantle in the Commons, and Lord Redesdale in the Lords.[35] A letter from Fremantle to parliamentarians suggests the subscription was instigated in March 1837. However, it appears that the whip had already been underway for some time prior to this, since Fremantle observed the subscription was only raised since 'the expenses already incurred ... have been this year *unusually great* in consequence of Parliament meeting in November', with 'notes' (as the whips were initially called) being 'sent out almost daily'.[36] (It should be noted that this evolutionary perspective on the nature of whipping presents a possible challenge to Sainty and Cox's data on the sudden shift in whipping after 1832, with their presenting strong evidence that the year marked a turning point in whips' attendance.)[37] Subscription to the whip was initially made by signing a subscription book kept in the Morning Room (later renamed the Smoking Room) of the Carlton Club.

The placing of the subscription book in the Carlton Club is significant. The Club's Smoking Room was a strictly members-only environment, meaning that joining the Club would have been considered a prerequisite to taking the Conservative whip. Given that one would have needed a proposer and seconder at the Carlton to take the Conservative whip, and given the role of Whips in admission to the Carlton, the club's role in whipping was thus central.

The presence of the book in the Club also necessitated that Conservative parliamentarians had to actually turn up at the Club (as opposed to remaining inactive Carlton members); when William Lascelles MP was late in paying his 1840 subscription, he apologised to Fremantle, 'I have not been able to go to the Club lately where I should have found out that I ought to have booked up long ago'.[38] Furthermore, the complete, bound book being available for inspection (as opposed to a sign-up sheet with only the most recent signatories added) afforded the opportunity to 'name and shame' Conservative parliamentarians by omission from the book; a use of the Club's shared social space to political ends.

Additionally, the Carlton was directly involved in administering the whip: Fremantle wrote to MPs 'The subscriptions may be paid to myself, or sent to the Steward or Porter of the Carlton Club'.[39] Given that clubs retained the apparatus to manage large numbers of subscriptions for their own membership, it is perhaps unsurprising that this task was delegated to the Carlton. Crucially, it demonstrates that the Carlton was deemed a reliable arbiter of who was and was not recognised as a Conservative parliamentarian.

However, with Lords being less numerous in their subscriptions than MPs, Lord Redesdale wrote a chase-up letter backtracking somewhat regarding the Carlton's special status, saying that parliamentarians 'willing to contribute towards this object' could alternatively pay their subscription to the Duke of Buccleuch, the Marquises of Salisbury and Chandos, the Earl of Lincoln, Lords Hotham and Cole, as well as

Sir George Clerk MP, the Hon. George R.-R. Trevor MP, or Charles Rope. Nevertheless, Redesdale's phrasing that these individuals would 'receive' the subscription strongly suggests that they were simply passing them on rather than directly administering the payments.[40] Furthermore, such intermediaries could be less reliable than the Club; when Matthias Attwood MP found that his payment to the intermediary Henry Drummond did not reach the subscription fund, he vowed 'I will subscribe in future by applying at the Carlton'.[41]

In the early years, renewal of the Carlton whips' subscription was not automatic, and apparently had to be repeated for each new parliamentary session. Returning to London after the summer recess in September 1839, Redesdale complained to Fremantle 'When I left London the book had 317 names', but that there were fewer on his return.[42] Accordingly, the Whips kept meticulous records of parliamentarians who had paid, crossing them off from a printed list. When troublesome parliamentarians failed to pay, Conservative Whips conferred over how best to chase up payment, and with the clubs being a popular communal space for MPs, they could be used to 'ambush' those who still owed subscriptions, with Redesdale reporting to Fremantle in 1840 'I have not yet been able to see [Lord] Walford at the [Carlton] Club, to which he usually comes when in town'.[43]

The distribution of paper whips by the Carlton Club was widely known within a year of the subscription's introduction. In February 1838, Daniel O'Connell MP declared in the Commons that he had 'no doubt' these paper whips originated from the Carlton. O'Connell challenged MPs to identify 'whether a single ballot took place which was not preceded by such a canvass, by the issue of such special commands? Not one!' He then asked Conservatives to rise if any of them contested this claim. None did, and O'Connell's allegation is fully supported by documentation establishing almost daily paper whips from the Carlton in the late 1830s.[44] The whips were originally handwritten, but from February 1840 they began to be printed (the cost of which was met by the subscription), and this can be seen as reflective of the evolving mid-nineteenth century print culture.[45]

Fremantle, the instigator of this subscription, has been described by J. M. Bourne as 'one of the first recognisably 'modern' chief whips',[46] and he was also highly thought of by his colleagues, who unanimously passed a resolution at a Carlton Club meeting on 27 June 1840 thanking him and Henry Baring for 'their constant and indefatigable feat and judgment during the present Session of Parliament in arranging the attendance of Members attached to [the Conservative] cause'.[47] Ahead of divisions, Fremantle was highly diligent in ensuring attendance, and when this could not be guaranteed, he made sure that MPs were suitably 'paired' with other abstainers.[48] A year after Fremantle's appointment as Secretary at War in 1844, Sir James Graham argued that Fremantle's talents would have been better used in his previous post, which was so closely tied to the Carlton: 'I still think that Fremantle ought to go to his Chair at the Carlton. It is the office for which he is best qualified, which he would serve the Public most and be placed in his best position for himself and his Family'.[49]

The numbers in Graph 5.1 suggest that with a £2 subscription, the Carlton fund would have raised between £634 and £758 in each of these years. Interestingly, expenditure was not limited to purely parliamentary affairs – postal expenses show numerous messengers and items of correspondence by F. R. Bonham were covered by this fund in late 1838. As Bonham was no longer a Whip after the loss of his seat in 1837, and as the same account notes multiple instances of correspondence with the constituencies of Leicester, Sandwich and Great Yarmouth (all boroughs

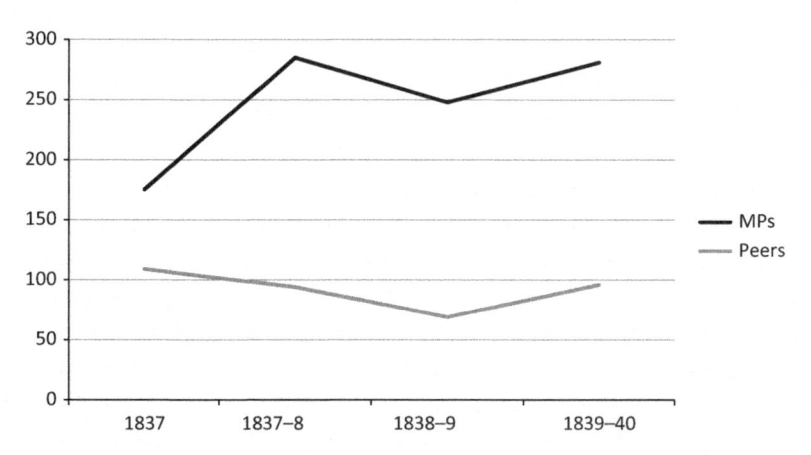

Graph 5.1 No. of Conservative MPs subscribing to the whip through the Carlton Club subscription book, 1837–41. Source: T. A. Jenkins, 'The Whips in the Early-Victorian House of Commons', *Parliamentary History*, 19 (2000), pp. 264–5.

which saw by-elections in 1838–9), this strongly suggests some overlap in expenditure on the Carlton Club's electioneering activities set out in Chapter 6.[50] This is supported by the example of the 1840–1 parliamentary session, when the subscription raised a total of £762 2s 0d, and yet actual expenditure on whips was only £338 11s 7d. Jenkins suggests that the balance of £423 10s 5d might have been spent on 'the costs for the following year', but this explanation does not account for where a comparable surplus in previous years might have been spent.[51] The above instances of the fund being debited for correspondence with constituencies holding by-elections would seem to suggest that the money may have been more plausibly diverted to fund the Carlton's electoral activities.

The system remained in place, using identical circulars, for the rest of Fremantle's tenure in Opposition although, as Jenkins has highlighted, once government funds and patronage became available, all trace of the subscription disappeared after the Conservatives took office under Peel.[52] The next Conservative Whip for whom detailed papers survive from his tenure is Sir William Jolliffe in the 1850s and, although the 1830s Carlton-initiated system was once more in evidence during the opposition stints in the 1850s, down to the phrasing of written whips, it was no longer physically centred on the Carlton Club. By the late 1850s, circulars of the kind once sent from the Carlton were being distributed from alternate addresses close to Parliament, like 5 Barton Street and 6 Victoria Street.[53]

Comparing the methods of Fremantle and Jolliffe, it can be observed that when the Conservatives were in government, special attention was paid to extracting subscriptions from ministers – a subscription list survives from 1841, with ministers (and their offices held) listed and crossed off.[54] By the time of the Earl of Derby's minority administrations, Conservative Whips regarded their own ministers with particular weariness, as is evident from the close attention paid to monitoring their record in divisions. Detailed scorecards were kept showing 'Votes of Members in office', spanning one week at a time as well as aggregate figures for several months. From this, Whips could note which ministers were failing to support the government – Sir Fitzroy Kelly, for instance, only attended five out of fifteen divisions in one week in 1858, while later in the session Sir Bulwer Lytton came bottom of one Whip's chart, attending just 57 divisions out of 108.[55]

The impression conveyed is that without a parliamentary majority, Whips for minority Conservative governments had to focus even more attention on whipping senior figures than on backbenchers.

As noted, in contrast to the detailed surviving papers of Conservative Whips, there are fewer detailed collections of Liberal Whips in this period, and it is only very recently that Joseph Coohill has unearthed evidence of a system of written whips in the 1830s, along the lines of the Carlton — although crucially, what survives does not indicate a parallel role in whipping played by the Reform Club during this period.[56] It should be noted, however, that the Conservatives' long periods in opposition were a major factor behind the instigation of a subscription, while the long tenure of office of Whigs and Liberals enabled them to use government funds to support whipping. Bourne notes that 'salaried' patronage tied to control of the Treasury continued to be a major force until the 1870s. As such, Whig and Liberal domination of office between 1832 and 1874 (aside from Peel's second ministry, and several much briefer ministries) meant that Liberal Whips enjoyed considerable leverage, while Conservative Whips had little patronage to offer for long periods out of office, and so the Carlton can be seen as an alternative organisational focus outside of office.[57] Further constraining the deployment of patronage was the observation that Disraeli 'was astonished at the amount of Patronage which was *unavailable*, i.e. that they could not get their men to take'.[58]

The Reform Club was used to raise a subscription for electioneering as early as 1837, and while this fund had little to do with the requirements of whipping, one of its administrators was Liberal Chief Whip Edward J. Stanley, indicating that the apparatus for such a mechanism *could* have existed by this point — but there is no firm evidence beyond this.[59]

Whips, Clubs and Party Identity

The listings of party Whips previously given in Tables 5.1a and 5.1b are slightly misleading, insofar as they do not fully convey the ambiguity of the Whips' responsibilities. Whips saw their role to drum up support for government or opposition votes, and surviving paper whips support the notion that they were counting support 'for' and 'against' in various categories — for instance, in 1840, Fremantle placed MPs into categories including, 'Conservatives doubtful', 'Whigs doubtful', 'Absent

Conservatives' and 'Vacant seats'.[60] The changing context of party throughout the post-Reform period made this a significantly more complicated matter than Conservative Whips simply rounding up 'Conservative' MPs and Liberal Whips rounding up 'Liberal' MPs.

Party identification among MPs, and its strength in this period, has been the topic of fierce debate in recent years. Among those stressing its significance, Jonathan Parry has sought to show how a combination of 'liberal toryism', Whiggery and radicalism can all be seen as different facets of a broad Liberal Party in the years after 1820.[61] Frank O'Gorman has added a further dimension to the debate, by querying the extent to which changing party identification was a new phenomenon in the nineteenth century, by tracing its eighteenth-century antecedents.[62] As Derek Beales has noted, the whole question of party identity was additionally complicated by the strength of the notion of 'independence' among MPs, with independence from party, interest and office being seen as virtues.[63] Angus Hawkins has consistently argued that even in the tumultuous 1850s and 1860s, there existed 'largely cohesive – though not rigid – associations of like-minded MPs, based upon voluntary subordination, recognising a degree of independence, making and unmaking governments'.[64] This independence was critical, for it made the rise, sustenance and fall of governments dependent on seeking support beyond an immediate base of Ministerialists. The importance of Whips in such a context was paramount.

Tables 5.1a and 5.1b emphasise the degree to which all Conservative Whips belonged to the Carlton (and later the Junior Carlton), and all Liberal Whips belonged to either Brooks's or the Reform Club. Yet with party lines frequently blurred, whipping operations could sometimes cross Clubland political lines. One of the most obvious examples of mixed party allegiances in this period, the Aberdeen coalition, was actually relatively straightforward for whipping: Sainty and Cox note that it 'may conveniently be taken as a unity [with Palmerston's 1855–8 Liberal administration] for the purpose of whipping', with William Goodenough Hayter, the Earl of Mulgrave and Grenville Berkeley all whipping for both consecutive administrations.[65] It was suggested by J. B. Conacher that, during the administration, Hayter was responsible for whipping the Peelites, rather than the Peelites having their own Whips.[66] If this were the case, it would have presented a problem for Whig Whips seeking to round up Peelites MPs who still frequented Conservative clubs, to which they would not have been admitted.[67]

Whips belonged to party-aligned clubs with an almost inevitable predictability. Whilst apolitical clubs such as the Athenaeum and the Travellers' Club contained Whips of all shades of opinion, there were few Whips who belonged to political clubs of a differing shade of opinion to their own — the one noticeable instance where this occurred was an expression of changing allegiances. Henry Baring had joined Brooks's in 1824; but he resigned six years later, and a further two years later he was a founder member of the Carlton, by which time he was considered to be a Conservative. Although he served as a junior Whip throughout the 1830s and 1840s, he later identified with the Peelites, which goes some way to explaining his eventual reinstatement in Whig circles as a member of Brooks's again from 1854.

Party divisions could lead to parallel whipping operations in the same club. After the Peelite/Derbyite split, Derbyite Chief Whip William Beresford set up a 'rival desk in the Carlton' to the Peelites' organisation, although F. R. Bonham reported to Peel in November 1846 that he was unimpressed by Beresford's efforts.[68] Part of the reason for the Carlton Club's endurance through this period was its ability to accommodate as many of the 'ultras' as possible while retaining Peelites and Derbyites alike, and accommodating their rival organisations. In remaining as broad a church as possible which still included the 'ultras', the Carlton may have foiled Derby's attempts to reposition the Conservatives through 'masterly inactivity', but it contributed to the Conservatives remaining united through their long years of Opposition.[69] By 1863, John Patten (usually described by most sources as a Conservative, but thought by Stanley at the time to be of 'no party') complained of how 'the Carlton is ruled by a little ultra clique, which does great mischief'.[70]

Nevertheless, despite such nuance, membership of a political club was considered by most political observers to be a visible manifestation of overall political allegiance into a broad camp. Such was the link between club and party in the mid-Victorian mindset that it was not unusual for the two to be used as synonyms for one another, and it was even necessary for parliamentarians to make distinctions between club and party. When Palmerston took the Home Office in 1852, he wrote that it signified his formally joining 'the great Liberal party (not in the

H. of Cms, nor at Brooks's nor at the Reform Club) but in the United Kingdom'.[71]

Changes in political club membership were thus accorded great significance. Whilst the defection of the 'Derby Dilly' is generally viewed as a gradual phenomenon over the Parliaments of 1835 and 1837, a crucial moment in formalising changing party allegiance was Sir James Graham and Lord Stanley's election to the Carlton Club in the summer of 1840 – although Stanley was reportedly uncertain whether 'his accession to the Carlton would reconcile or foment difficulties'.[72] Such closely monitored changes of party allegiance could apply to expulsions as well as election to a new club. Both Charles Greville and the fourth Duke of Newcastle saw the proposed expulsion of Sir Francis Burdett from Brooks's in November 1835 as a symptom of Whig tensions over relations with O'Connell's supporters. Burdett called on the Whigs to repudiate O'Connell, and challenged the members of Brooks's to expel him if they wished to continue to draw on O'Connell's support.[73] Changes of club could also signify an issue of political principle. In December 1841, when Lord Ashley believed that Peel's government would oppose the ten hours demand, his response was to contemplate resigning from the Carlton, and he consulted F. R. Bonham on whether he should do so.[74]

In each of these cases, an actual or proposed change in club membership was seen as the consummation of a change in political allegiance, and it is thus little surprise that political clubs attracted the attention of Whips. In discussing the problems with early Victorian party definitions, Jonathan Parry has acknowledged 'club membership seems about as good a guide as you can get to these [party] dimensions';[75] an opinion shared by Anthony Howe with reference to the 'Free Trade' MPs. Howe notes that the members of the short-lived Free Trade Club were 'the people who [were] the core free trade MPs', while membership of the Cobden Club founded in 1866 is a strong indicator of pro-Cobden – but not necessarily Cobdenite – sentiment.[76] Furthermore, the basic fact of membership was seen to be evidence of an MP's broad outlook, not necessarily of his taking the whip – even if it was a prerequisite to it, as with the Carlton serving as a gateway to whipping subscriptions.

The more marginalised political clubs did not necessarily escape the Whips' attention. While the Westminster Reform, Free Trade and

Conservative Clubs tellingly did not have any Whips among their memberships, the same could not be said of the ultra-Protestant National Club, whose membership focussed on a specific number of religious issues: the Maynooth grant, Catholic and Jewish emancipation, the role of religion in university reform, and diplomatic relations with the Vatican. With the Club being based on the parliamentary estate in Old Palace Yard before 1852, and in nearby Whitehall Gardens thereafter, it was difficult to ignore, and its engagement with whipping was advanced. It encouraged its parliamentarians to vote on religious issues, and the Club's annual reports to members often included division lists on how the Club fared on these issues. Indeed, it was due to the efforts of two of the Club's MPs, Richard Spooner and Conservative Whip Charles Newdegate, that a vote on Maynooth was brought onto the floor of the House of Commons almost every year from 1845 until Newdegate's retirement in 1885, primarily as a means of testing the strength of anti-Catholic sentiment in the Commons.[77] The Club would frequently record the participation rates of its own parliamentarians, as with an 1863 petition against a Bill to pay priests of all denominations in prisons. Newdegate was reported to have made 'an able speech' against the proposal, and 'nineteen members of this Club recorded their votes against that measure'.[78] It appears that Beresford and Taylor circulated whips to the (mostly Conservative) MPs at the National Club which were tailored to the Club's interests, emphasising when 'Protestant issues' were at stake in divisions.[79] Thus although the broad churches of Brooks's and the Reform and Carlton Clubs dominated the Whips' engagement with Clubland, there was scope for the more tightly focussed clubs like the National Club to concentrate their activities and organise a whip among smaller groups of parliamentarians.

Conclusion

With the post-Reform Act growth in the role of Whips, clubs played a central part in allowing Whips to discharge their responsibilities. Whips enjoyed extensive access to clubs, whether as co-founders, trustees or committee members of such institutions, or as members whose patronage and influence in sponsoring applications was highly sought after. Membership of the most significant party clubs (the Carlton for the Conservatives, the Reform and Brooks's for the Liberals) was held between a Chief Whip and their Assistant Whips, granting them easy access when rounding up MPs in advance of a division. The Carlton and Reform Clubs had dedicated (if modest) office facilities for Whips and, more importantly, the Carlton Club appears to have played a central role in the administration of printed party whips, running the subscription system which funded printed whips in the opposition years when no government funds were available to support such efforts. It appears likely that a substantial portion of the money ostensibly raised for this subscription – over half of the £650 a year – was diverted into the Carlton Club's fund for contesting elections and by-elections. This subscription system for party whips grew throughout the 1830s and, while it had outgrown the Carlton Club by the 1850s, many of the other elements of whipping remained tethered to the clubs. However, although Joseph Coohill has recently unearthed evidence of printed Liberal whips in the 1830s, paralleling the Carlton's efforts (and confirming something long-suspected by parliamentary historians), there is no evidence that the Reform Club played any role in the distribution of these whips.

What has already been documented by others is the growing importance of Whips and whipping in this period, as the practice of constitutional government in the post-Reform era gradually embraced the notion of securing an overall majority in the House of Commons – and the Whips were a crucial instrument in securing this. What has been neglected from such accounts is the full extent of the role played by clubs in supporting many of the Whips' functions: whipping in club offices, through club funds, using club networks of members, expressing identities, and on club premises. Clubs thus formed an integral part of early whipping culture in the mid-nineteenth century.

CHAPTER 6

CLUBS AND ELECTORAL INTERVENTIONS

Introduction

Much has been written about the supposed influence of clubs on Victorian elections. Popular pamphlets were replete with references to 'Carlton-Club-gold' and 'the golden showers of the Reform Club', while local and national newspapers grumbled about secret election funds.[1] Such charges were immortalised in several lasting works of fiction, most notably the novels of Benjamin Disraeli and Anthony Trollope, provoking confusion as to whether these authors were accurately documenting their respective perspectives as an MP and a former Westminster journalist, or were merely dramatic licence. Norman Gash's work has also provoked speculation around Clubland involvement in nineteenth century electioneering.

Portrayals of club electoral interference were difficult to miss in contemporary literature. The enduring image remains the manipulative election agent, based in a Pall Mall club, the most famous incarnation being in Tadpole and Taper, two unscrupulous Carlton Club agents who debuted in Disraeli's *Coningsby*, later reintroduced in *Sybil*.[2] Trollope also perpetuated the archetype, particularly in his *Pallisers* novels. First, in *Phineas Redux*, Trollope introduced agents

Ratler and Bonteen, seen by Owen Dudley Edwards as Trollope's 'answer to Tadpole and Taper, though ... more fleshed-out creations',[3] then Trollope's *The Prime Minister* presented the variant characters of Rattler and Roby, 'both good men, in their way ... [who] pass their time between the steps of the Carlton and Reform Clubs', dispensing patronage and acting as 'fixers'.[4]

As Frank O'Gorman writes, accusations of club involvement in electoral malpractice predated the Reform Act, and that such clubs merely 'systematized the uncoordinated activities of earlier, somewhat informal, bodies but they did not mark any qualitative change in the nature of party politics'.[5] However, the extent of such activities, and awareness of it, undoubtedly grew from the 1830s onwards. The Charles Street office which preceded the Carlton Club's electoral activities had closed by the middle of 1832, and yet a year later, Charles Arbuthnot confided to the Duke of Wellington 'If Charles Street should come into a court of justice it will be most injurious'.[6] The Carlton swiftly took over such electoral activities, with press reports just eight months after the Carlton's creation accusing the club of having 'advanced' £2,000 towards the 1832 general election campaign in Hull.[7]

The Carlton's electoral role has drawn scrutiny from Norman Gash, Donald Southgate, Robert Stewart, and Bruce Coleman.[8] The implicit neglect of the electoral activities of Liberal clubs has in part been balanced out in recent years as the Reform Club's overlooked electoral role has been stressed by Joseph Coohill, Matthew Cragoe and Philip Salmon, while both Salmon and Nancy LoPatin-Lummis acknowledge the role played by the Reform Club's predecessors, such as the Reform Association and the regional Political Unions set up on the model of the Birmingham Political Union founded by Thomas Attwood.[9] However, an implicit part of this revised focus towards Liberal electoral efforts through clubs and their predecessors has been to stress the variation of local efforts.[10]

Finally, while the notion of electoral interference from the centre has often been bound up with allegations of corruption, it is perhaps preferable to use the term 'organisation' rather than 'interference'. There *was* a central party fund administered by the Carlton Club through the party Whips, and the clubs *did* engage in some instances of bribery. But as John A. Phillips wrote, 'however visible corruption may have been at times, it was on the whole politically irrelevant', and Phillips provided much evidence that instances of it in the post-Reform era were highly selective.[11] As the below case studies show, while bribery was certainly alleged in some instances, much of the electoral efforts of the clubs involved the far less sensational elements of candidate selection, writing literature, and fundraising to legitimate ends.

Individuals: Agents and Central Organisation

The electoral activities of clubs were organised by a small group of individuals over several decades. Few Clubland figures were more reviled than parliamentary agents. In 1859, John Bright described this species:

> [the] party electioneering agent – you may see, I repeat, a man of this description, emerging after dark from the Carlton Club, proceeding to a pillar letterbox which stands quite near it upon the opposite side of the street, and dropping into it – unless, indeed, he should find it necessary to go as far as Charing Cross for the purpose of registering them – some ten or twenty letters about nine or ten o'clock in the evening, while the unfortunate people of Banbury are labouring under the delusion that they are carrying on a great constitutional contest.[12]

Bright, as a daily user of the Reform Club during parliamentary sessions, was well-placed to observe such proceedings from the Carlton's next-door neighbour. Existing accounts have focussed on two agents in particular, Joseph Parkes at the Reform Club and, more notoriously, F. R. Bonham at the Carlton Club, yet our knowledge of club agents beyond these two individuals is extremely limited. Both Bonham and Parkes played a key role – but it is intended here to temper an account of their activities with the equally large and important role played by solicitors acting as agents, especially James Coppock for the Liberals, and Henry Edwards Brown, Philip Rose and Markham Spofforth for the Conservatives. Each found their electoral duties deeply entwined with the Reform and Carlton Clubs, from which they operated. The very existence of these agents presented an embarrassment; when Colonel G. C. W. Forester MP testified before a Select Committee, he initially tried to say that as a non-member of the Carlton, Brown could only visit certain rooms used for receiving guests, that Brown never used the Club unaccompanied by a member, and that he had no office there. After cross-examination, Forester admitted that Brown did in fact have a key to an office (which Brown shared with Forester), that Brown did use the Club unaccompanied, and concluded, 'I shall decline any questions with regards the Carlton Club altogether'.[13]

Tables 6.1a and 6.1b highlight both the small number of known agents, and the confusion about the dates they served, not least since we shall see that the dates for Parkes, Bonham, Rose and Spofforth are questionable, and the role of Brown has been neglected entirely.

As Bruce Coleman notes, it was F. R. Bonham who was 'the figure usually associated with the Tadpole and Taper image'.[14] Extensive attention was paid to him by Gash throughout his work on the 1830s and 1840s, and it is this strand of historiography which predominates – although, in recent years, Philip Salmon has queried this orthodoxy, deducing from an accusation by Lord Chandos of Bonham's alleged 'utter incompetency' that he may not have been as unchallenged as central agent as has previously been supposed, and was 'a second-rate figure'.[15]

Existing accounts of Bonham's work portray his influence as having waned after his resignation from the government in disgrace in 1844,

Table 6.1a   Liberal party agents, as identified by Cook and Keith

????–1847	Joseph Parkes
????–1857	James Coppock
1857–1865	W. R. Drake
1865 only	J. Travers Smith
1865–1886	'Work undertaken by Chief Whips. Legal business done by firm of Wyatt, Hoskins and Hooker.'

Table 6.1b   Conservative party agents, as identified by Cook and Keith

1832–1846	F. R. Bonham
1853–1859	Philip Rose
1859–1870	Markham Spofforth

Source: Chris Cook and Brendan Keith, *British Historical Facts, 1830–1900* (rev. ed., London: Macmillan, 1984, of orig. edn, London: Macmillan, 1975), p. 95.

further reduced after the fall of Peel's second ministry, and ended altogether after Peel's death.[16] In fact, while Bonham certainly dedicated himself to the memory of his late master and refused to assist the Derbyites, there is evidence that Bonham continued to be heavily involved in the Peelites' independent electioneering efforts, still using the Carlton as a base until the late 1850s. In 1849, he could be found monitoring election results, correctly predicting to the Earl of Lincoln MP the outcome of the impending Cork by-election: 'Col. Chatterton will carry Cork as a [Derbyite] Protestant', adding ruefully 'Perhaps if we [the Peelites] had the semblance of a Party, or anyone [were] to take the trouble, we might have had some chance in this constitutional selection'.[17] Gladstone also consulted with him throughout his years as a Peelite. Gladstone's diaries highlight that, in the 1850s, his only recorded correspondence with Bonham was when he was up for re-election, as on 10 January and 17 January 1853, when he faced opposition in the Oxford University by-election.[18] As late as 26 March 1857, Gladstone wrote to his wife requesting 'Please send the inclosed [sic] to Bonham at the Carlton', seeking 'some more information' on the votes at stake in forthcoming election.[19]

Joseph Parkes of the Reform Club was almost as celebrated and reviled as Bonham. Like Bonham, he occupied a desk at his club, from which he corresponded with local associations.[20] To Richard Cobden, Parkes was 'a troubled spirit, haunting the Reform Club at midnight, holding converse with certain self-sufficient elves, or flitting to & fro in cabs', inseparable from the Club.[21] While his electoral interventions became more selective with the passage of time, Joseph Parkes' role at the Reform Club continued into the 1840s. In 1843, Richard Cobden wrote to Sir Charles Pelham Villiers stressing the value of institutional memory:

> it would be a very desirable thing to have a secret history of the last [1841] election — I mean of all the bribery & dark doings of that struggle of the factions... Will you institute some private enquiries — [William Durrant] Cooper[22] of the Reform Club? With the aid of [Joseph] Parkes and [James] Coppock[23] — could tell all, but I fear they would have much to conceal of their own doings. [Joseph] Croucher would tell all he knows for a *con-si-de-ra-ti-on* ... we can't be too well armed with facts reflecting the interference of

corruptionists at the last ... It is not of course intended to publish the acc^t, but to keep it for private use.[24]

Parkes' career as a parliamentary 'fixer' clearly predated his involvement in the Reform Club – he was heavily involved in the formation of the Birmingham Political Union in 1830, and that same year, his electoral interests seemed widespread: he wrote to former MP Charles Tennyson that he was searching for 'a seat for a wealthy man (not a politician)' and would make £4,500 available for any constituency that would have him.[25]

As previously noted, Parkes was deeply involved in the formation of the Reform Club and particularly in persuading a reluctant Edward Ellice to give his blessing to the undertaking and, even after his retirement in 1847, he continued to hold influence there until his death in 1865. But Nancy LoPatin-Lummis believes 'his work for the whigs was quite limited after the Municipal Corporation Commission [of 1833–5] and the legal work immediately following the reform measures', and was restricted to his serving as an election agent in several midland boroughs in 1837 and 1839, and for some select seats in 1841.[26]

Despite the standard narrative of Bonham and Parkes' central electoral role, the reality was that they relied upon a network of locally employed agents to implement their work in the constituencies, and also depended on the services of a solicitor to assist them in their central work. These solicitors have been underestimated in their significance. At the Reform Club, Parkes was aided and then supplanted by James Coppock, while at the Carlton Club, Henry Edwards Brown had a similar role, eventually being succeeded by Disraeli's solicitors Rose and Spofforth, who noticeably worked together as agents (not, as Cook and Keith argued, in succession to one another).

While it is Parkes who has usually been linked to the Reform Club because of his well-documented founding role, James Coppock has been relatively ignored – although Albert Nicholson and H. C. G. Matthew acknowledged that, along with Parkes and Bonham, he 'was a founder of centralised political organisation'.[27] Coppock's own role as the Reform Club's agent and solicitor made him *at least* the equal of Bonham in influence, magnified by his longevity. Instead of viewing Coppock as Parkes' successor, it would be more accurate to portray him as Parkes' apprentice, working alongside him as his legal subordinate from 1836 onwards, and eventually taking on more and more of his functions.

Coppock tried — but failed — to gain membership of the short-lived Westminster Reform Club.[28] George Woodbridge recorded simply that, at the Reform Club, 'The first [club] secretary was James Coppock, a highly successful parliamentary agent, who came close to being the Whig party manager in the mid-1830s. He undertook the work to help start the Club, and a few days after its doors opened [in April 1836] he resigned'.[29] Yet Coppock stayed on at the Reform Club for twenty-one years, performing other duties, a contemporary description of his electoral functions being 'on proper occasions to find out objections to Conservative voters, and patch up Radical ten-pounders'.[30] Throughout the 1830s, he had also worked as the paid full-time Secretary of the Reform Association, until its functions were absorbed into the Reform Club by 1841.[31]

Like all the agents described here, Coppock had a legal background. A noticeable development of Carlton organisation for the Derbyites from the 1850s onwards was the passing of the electoral machine into the hands of solicitors Philip Rose and Markham Spofforth, but this was actually a development copied from the Reform Club's working methods of the late 1830s. Both Parkes and Coppock were solicitors, while Bonham had originally trained as a barrister, and was succeeded in the 1840s by Brown, another solicitor.

Far more so than Parkes, Coppock gained a reputation for embroilment in the dark arts of politics. The *Lyttelton Times* thought him 'a personage who has at once served as both the tool and the scapegoat of the Liberal party'.[32] This was illustrated by an 1852 incident: John Arthur Roebuck — a Sheffield MP, who had previously sat for Bath — took the unwise step of publicly criticising Coppock. As *The Times* reported, Coppock's retaliation was swift, and undermined the Reform Club's own denials of electoral manipulation:

> It seems to be an understood thing that Mr. Coppock is a piece of furniture belonging to the Reform Club, which members of that club are at liberty to use first and spit upon afterwards; and that to repudiate him publicly, while maintaining an intimate private connexion with him, is at worst a mere white lie. Mr. Coppock, however, to do him justice, has at last developed some susceptibility to affront. His revenge is easy. He has but to open his desk and take from the pigeon-hole labelled 'Bath' a bundle of letters which prove

not only that he intrigued for Mr. Roebuck at Mr. Roebuck's request, but that he paid into Mr. Roebuck's own hands the amount of the election expenses which the latter proclaims were borne entirely by his constituents.[33]

Earlier that year, Conservative MP Lord Claude Hamilton had used parliamentary privilege to embroil Coppock in the bribery which led to the disenfranchisement of St Albans in 1852:

> The late Mr. Coppock was one of the most successful Liberal bribers and corruptors that ever lived in this country. He was the life and soul of the Reform Club. He was in the habit of receiving enormous sums of money from gentlemen at the Reform Club, and then he went down to the country and bribed any constituency that was willing to accept his bribes. One of the best instances of that gentleman's practices was at the borough of St. Albans. There was a very respectable gentleman of the name of Mr. Bell, who in an evil hour fell into the hands of this purist, Mr. Coppock, and who said to him – 'If you will give me £4,000, I will get you a seat in Parliament.' The boldness of the man appeared in this, that he used to send the money from the Reform Club direct, and he never sent bank-notes – he always sent sovereigns. In this case Mr. Bell's address was printed in that fine glowing tone which Ballot men use; then came denunciations of Tory bribery; then came a layer of sovereigns – then came another layer of denunciations of Tory corruption – and then another layer of sovereigns.[34]

In Carlton circles, Coppock's role was paralleled by that of Henry Edwards Brown, a partner in the firm of Thompson, Debenham and Brown at 31 Parliament Street, who emerged as a key player in the Club's electoral work by the late 1840s.[35] As previously noted, Bonham had a poor opinion of the efficacy of Chief Whip William Beresford's rival desk, but many of the Derbyites' electoral activities seem to have been the work of Brown. Lord Stanley thought Brown 'a shrewd parliamentary practitioner'.[36] At the parliamentary committee into the withdrawn 1852 Norwich election petitions, George Hadfield MP noted that Brown's 'name had come before Parliament upon various occasions', and that 'Brown and his partners are the Parliamentary agents for the

Carlton Club in electioneering matters'.[37] During the 1852 general election, Brown himself boasted 'that he had one of those dark little rooms under the Carlton Club, and that he was to be found there every day'.[38] Yet Brown was dismissed from both roles in 1853, at the same time the Whips were reshuffled, with Disraeli's allies being moved into key positions, including solicitors Rose and Spofforth assuming Brown's old post.[39]

Philip Rose had long been Disraeli's solicitor, and his help with stabilising Disraeli's personal finances after 1846 saw the firm of Baxter, Rose and Norton appointed the Carlton Club's new solicitors, and were referred to by Acton Ayrton as 'the parliamentary agents of the Conservative party', with Rose singled out by Liberal MP Henry Berkeley in 1861 as 'the agent for the Carlton Club, who managed elections for the Tory Party'.[40] In 1853, Rose took on a young new solicitor into his firm, Markham Spofforth, and the two would direct the Carlton's electoral activities, from candidate selection to petitioning, in conjunction with Chief Whip Sir William Jolliffe. *Vanity Fair* later credited Spofforth with having 'invented' a new breed of elector, 'the Conservative working man'.[41] It is generally believed that Rose withdrew from Conservative electoral organisation in 1859 after being embroiled in the controversy over the Berwick election;[42] but this seems improbable when one considers Spofforth's ongoing role from within the same legal firm, while in 1855 Rose complained to Jolliffe that as his junior in the law firm, Spofforth was not sticking to an agreement to *not* communicate daily with Whips and party leaders, which Rose saw as his own role.[43]

As well as being active members of the Carlton, both Rose and Spofforth were heavily involved in the establishment and running of the Junior Carlton Club in the 1860s. From the outset, Spofforth was in discussion with Disraeli about the nature of the Club, with Disraeli writing to him a year before the Club's launch, that he refused to allow it to be 'managed in an aristocratic spirit' like existing clubs, and 'What we want is a rallying point for our working friends in the country, & not a gilded receptacle for town loungers'.[44] While Rose and Spofforth were both occasional proposers of new members to the Carlton Club, an analysis of the Junior Carlton members' books between its 1864 launch and 1868 (Table 6.2) makes it clear that Spofforth was the joint most prolific proposer or seconder of new members (with Viscount Nevill),

Table 6.2 Most frequent proposers and seconders for the Junior Carlton Club, for ballot dates in 1866–7 with surviving records, including all Whips and party agents

Membership ballot held on	Philip Rose (agent)	Markham Spofforth (agent)	Lt. Colonel Thomas Edward Taylor MP (Chief Whip)	Hon. Gerald Noel MP (Whip)	Henry Whitmore MP (Whip)	Viscount Nevill	Lt. Colonel Edwards MP	J.R. Ormsby Gore MP	Lord A.E. Hill Trevor MP	Lord Burghley MP	Total no. of candidates proposed at that ballot
6 February 1866	1	3	3	0	0	2	1	0	2	0	28
13 February 1866	0	7	0	1	0	3	1	0	0	0	26
20 February 1866	0	0	0	2	0	4	3	2	1	3	26
27 February 1866	0	3	2	0	0	2	1	1	1	1	25
6 March 1866	0	2	1	1	0	4	2	0	2	2	24
13 March 1866	0	2	3	0	2	1	3	0	0	0	26
20 March 1866	0	3	1	0	0	1	7	0	0	3	25
27 March 1866	0	0	1	2	0	1	4	1	1	1	26

17 April 1866	1	4	1	1	1	2	1	1	0	26
24 April 1866	0	6	1	1	9	5	1	2	2	53
1 May 1866	2	7	3	2	5	2	2	2	3	51
8 May 1866	6	5	0	2	5	0	1	1	3	51
12 February 1867	0	3	0	0	4	0	1	0	0	26
19 February 1867	1	2	0	1*	4	1	0	0	0	27
19 March 1867	0	2	3	0	2	0	1	4	0	26
14 May 1867	0	1	0	0	0	0	0	0	0	5
Total	11	48	19	13	48	32	11	17	18	471

*On this occasion, Noel's candidate the Rev. H. Warburton was blackballed. There are no other recorded instances of any of these proposers' candidates being rejected among the 471 nominees; an acceptance rate of 99.8% – something which is consistent with the observations in Chapter 2, with the number of blackballs in the first few years of the Junior Carlton's existence being extremely low.

Source: Junior Carlton Club archive, Carlton Club, London, Untitled MS – scrapbook of forms for 'Candidates to be balloted' (all surviving forms included).

single-handedly proposing over a tenth of the Club's new members; and that Rose was also one of the Club's more frequent proposers, with not one of Rose or Spofforth's candidates ever being rejected (see Figure 6.2). They thus occupied an entirely overlooked role, as gatekeepers of Conservative society, as well as being electoral managers. Spofforth was eventually made to stand down as Conservative party agent in March 1870 as a direct result of his Junior Carlton activity: a clumsy attempt to install his friend C. K. Keith-Falconer as Club Secretary resulted in his becoming 'increasingly unpopular with many members', and a wave of Junior Carlton Club resignations was attributed by E. J. Feuchtwanger with triggering Spofforth's resignation as agent.[45]

Mary S. Millar singles out Rose as a man of 'probity ... pathologically horrified by corruption' who sought to reform the 'amateurish and blatantly corrupt Conservative party machine' which he inherited from Brown, but this risks both overstating the degree of Conservative corruption before 1853, and underestimating it thereafter.[46] A somewhat different view was taken by Stewart, who emphasised Rose's preoccupation with maintaining his reputation in legal circles, citing it as the reason for his refusing both a salary and an official job title, and Rose wrote that he *'could not afford to be looked upon* in the light of a paid political agent'.[47] (My italics.) In reality, as Rose never assumed a formal title (that of 'principal agent' was one retrospectively given to him), his 1859 resignation should be seen as largely symbolic, and so the management of elections by both Rose and Spofforth should be seen as marking one continuous era from 1853 until the creation of a central Conservative office in 1870.

A Central Election Fund

The widely-rumoured existence of a central election fund has divided historians. Gash, Stewart and Coleman have strongly asserted that the Carlton Club operated a political fund, although with much of the evidence on the existence of a Carlton fund relating to the 1850s, Philip Salmon has argued there is 'little support' for Liberal claims of a Carlton election fund in the 1830s.[48] As Chapter 5 has outlined, it appears likely that over £400 per annum of MPs' subscriptions to the whip through the Carlton *was* diverted to an election fund in the 1830s. Additionally, it is likely this would not have been the only source of a

Carlton-controlled central election fund, not least as the sum would have been too small to fund more than one or two constituencies. In 1844, Liberal MP William Williams alleged that Conservative peers also played a role in raising political funds through the clubs:

> it was very well known that Peers of the realm openly, and without disguise, subscribed vast sums of money – not thousands, but tens of thousands, for the purpose of buying and corrupting the electors ... there was not a Gentleman on the Treasury bench who could not point out Peers who had subscribed to the funds of the Carlton Club, and he was equally certain that Gentlemen on his own side of the House could point out Peers of their party who had done the same.[49]

Whilst accusations of other parties fundraising through clubs was common, Williams' statement, protected by parliamentary privilege, was rare for its candour in conceding that both sides of the House engaged in such practices. Nonetheless, its reference to 'tens of thousands' remains disconcertingly vague.

Fundraising for a party election fund need not have always been a centralised activity, and also took place in the constituencies in which such money was spent. At the 1847 general election, voters in Carlisle were treated to breakfast by the (ultimately victorious) Conservative candidate William Nicholson Hodgson. After the election, publicans presented their bills to Hodgson's agent but, at the same time, they were each 'called upon to give a sovereign for the Carlton Club', thus partially offsetting the Club's election debts.[50]

Yet the most comprehensive, reliable and large-scale form of fundraising appears to have been through the payment of club subscriptions. The clearest instance of this can be found in the papers of the Junior Carlton Club, which began to raise funds after the Second Reform Act and, unlike the Carlton and Reform Clubs, surviving records make it possible to state with some certainty how much money was raised. A fierce debate over the levying of a Political Fund was waged at the Club's fifth Annual General Meeting on 24 May 1869 and, as the Club was still reeling from the cost of its extravagant clubhouse on Pall Mall, the sums involved provoked discontent. One member, Hume Williams, objected that 'the proposed Political Fund would absorb funds of the Club which would be required for paying the expenses of the establishment.' A debate ensued, and the compromise reached was that 'the fund proposed to be set aside for the Political Fund would not be appropriated unless the balance at the end of the year [1869] admitted such appropriation'.[51]

At the same AGM, the Junior Carlton then underlined its political commitment by unanimously carrying a declaration, setting out the control of its political fund. The declaration and its nine points are worth quoting in detail, for it has never been cited anywhere, yet it constitutes the fullest written explanation of a club's political fund, in both rationale and administration. Noting that it was, 'a Political Club, in strict connection with the Conservative Party, and designed to promote its objects, and that to give due effect to this intention it is expedient that the Club should possess some political organisation, and be empowered to apply some portion of its funds to political purposes', the Club resolved, 'to set apart, towards a fund for political objects out of the Annual Subscription of each Member, not being a Supernumerary Member, any sum not exceeding One Guinea'.[52] The club had reached its cap of 2,000 members, and had a subscription of £2 2s, so a fund of up to £1 per member would have accounted for nearly half of the subscription, and an annual fund of up to £2,000, or £14,000 over one seven-year Parliament. The declaration continued:

> The amount so set apart shall appear in the Annual Balance Sheet, under the head of 'Political Fund' ... The 'Political Fund' shall be administered by a Special Committee to be called 'The Political Committee' appointed as hereafter described, and shall be applied for strictly legal purposes, and for none other, at its sole discretion; and a Report of the applications of the Fund shall be furnished confidentially at the close of each year to the General Committee.[53]

The reference to 'strictly legal purposes' appears to be an acknowledgment of the reputation of the Carlton and Reform Club political funds. The declaration then stipulated that this Political Committee, 'shall consist of six independent Members of the Club not being on the General Committee, six Members elected by the General Committee elected out of its own body, and the Trustees of the Club for the time being who shall be "ex officio" Members'.[54] Thus although the Club had autonomous control of the fund, it is clear that the individuals controlling the fund were not the same as those running the Club day-to-day through its General Committee. Indeed, the stipulation that the Trustees were ex-officio officers of the fund meant that Derby, Disraeli and Jolliffe were all involved as club trustees.

The resolution then confirmed that even before the new arrangements of 1869, the Junior Carlton had a functioning Political Committee, acknowledging a 'first Political Committee the Members of the Club recently acting as a Political Committee, but which has now been dissolved', and granting them the right to nominate six members of the new, post-1869 Political Committee, with the remaining Political Committee posts being made up of six General Committee nominees, and six Trustee nominees; with the six Political Committee nominees then being subject to annual election by members at their Annual Meeting, and the Political Committee having the power to appoint any interim vacancies.[55]

The resolution concluded that, 'It shall be in the sole discretion of the Political Committee, either to expend the Political Fund during the year in which it is set apart, or to accumulate the whole or any portion of it for application in any subsequent year'.[56] This allowed the Political Committee to build up substantial reserves for a general election, of up to £14,000 over a full seven-year Parliament; although the shorter lifespan of most Parliaments, and the drain of by-election expenditure, would doubtless have to be offset against this. This Junior Carlton Club document sheds much light on the running of club political funds, yet it raises a major question: was this arrangement unique? Or was it simply an adoption of the system previously in place at the Carlton and Reform Clubs in the 1830s and 1840s? Certainly, as Chapter 2 notes with the verbatim adoption of the Union Club's constitution by other member-owned clubs set up in the nineteenth century, it was common for clubs to copy the organisational procedures of one another; but in the absence of documentary evidence, it is impossible to definitively prove any duplication.

Possible corroboration of the Carlton having operated a similar system comes from when the Club denied involvement in bribery at Cambridge in 1852 (where the result was declared void on petition), the Club claiming that 'every shilling spent by the Carlton Club is published', and that any person could consult these accounts – a defence which was countered by the charge that election expenses were not met by funds from the club subscription, but by a separate election fund controlled by the Club – which is certainly consistent with the structure of the Junior Carlton's fund.[57]

The annual figure of £2,000 of Junior Carlton Club money into an election fund puts into perspective the kinds of sums involved. Even with further sources of fundraising including the Whips' subscription, contributions from peers, and money raised in the constituencies, it seems likely that an election fund was considerably smaller than rumoured. At the more extreme end, the *National* speculated in 1848 that the Reform and Carlton Clubs 'could expend 5,000*l* or 6,000*l* sterling on a contested election', which would have made them the dominant sponsors of contests in some constituencies.[58] Yet it appears from surviving records that they distributed significantly smaller amounts to constituencies.

Two known lists exist, both relating to the Carlton Club, setting out local associations which were recipients of a central election fund, administered by Conservative Chief Whip Sir William Jolliffe. The later list covers the general election of 1859, and has previously been published in Stewart's *The Foundation of the Conservative Party, 1830–1867*.[59] Yet an earlier list by Jolliffe, dated 21 June 1855 and also found in the Hylton papers, has hitherto escaped scrutiny, and gives a clearer idea of which associations were in receipt of funds outside of a general election year.[60] Both are provided in Table 6.3, showing which constituencies were shared between the two.

The comparison of the two lists yields several interesting finds. In both lists, all but one of the recipient constituencies was a borough; the only county seats funded were in Bedfordshire and Sussex. This confirms Stewart's observation that 'Rose's notebook has little to say about the counties'.[61] The 1855 list makes no mention of the amounts spent, but the 1859 list does; most constituencies received between £200 and £700 at a time, but often received two or three payments totalling over £1,000. Some illegible associations received £1,000, with one being the recipient of £1,500, and another £7,800.[62] In total, Stewart notes that the 1859 central fund adds up to between £47,100 and £52,500[63] – consistent with rumours of 'tens of thousands' of pounds spent by an election fund, but disproving the view that in individual contests 'a bill for £10,000 was not uncommon'.[64]

Though smaller than some estimates of the fund, such sums were still larger than necessary for purely legitimate purposes. An 1852 Carlton Club delegation to Canterbury (where that year's election result was subsequently overturned on petition) concluded 'that 300*l* would be enough for the legal and legitimate expenses of that election, as the parties did not appear desirous of acting on anything other than purity [sic] principles'.[65] In short, it was expected that only *il*legal and *il*legitimate expenses would account for greater spending in such a borough.

Even if such funds were partly spent on bribery as alleged, it must be conceded that a large part of them would have gone towards legitimate election expenses, including the cost of a canvass and the returning officer's fees. Furthermore, while Stewart was unsure whether the Carlton ever paid for agents in the constituencies, it appears that such expenditure did indeed take place. At the 1853 bankruptcy court proceedings of newspaper proprietor John Strutt, his creditors were identified as including £550 owed to William Beresford of the Carlton Club the 'balance of bill of costs', another £105 owed to the Carlton for unidentified 'professional services', a further £105 owed to them for 'professional services on account of Lord Maidstone's election' (in Westminster, at the 1852 general election), plus £52 10s, for the 'West Surrey election'.[66] Such sums were consistent with an election agent's salary; S. M. Cross, a Liberal election agent in Evesham in 1857, gave his wages as between three pounds and twenty guineas *per day*.[67]

Surviving correspondence confirms that this central fund was used to finance by-elections as well as general election campaigns in the 1850s; for instance, in December 1857, Rose wrote to Jolliffe discussing receipts and cheques covered from 'the special fund', to cover by-elections in Buckinghamshire, Northamptonshire and Whitehaven – but the only specific amount mentioned was a mere fifteen pound cheque, and the letter suggests that Rose was administering the fund from his office at 6 Victoria Street.[68] Thus, whilst a limited election fund was undoubtedly administered by Bonham from the Carlton twenty years earlier, it must be acknowledged that the fund did not remain at the Carlton, and as electioneering was increasingly handled by solicitors, so the financial centre of such activity moved away from Clubland.

Just as important as the reality of a Carlton Club election fund was the very public reputation of such a fund. As noted, accusations of

Table 6.3 Conservative Associations in receipt of payments from the central party fund, 1855 and 1859

1855 list	1859 list
Abingdon B *(December 1854 by-election)*	
	Banbury B
Barnstaple B *(March 1855 by-election)*	
	Bedfordshire C
	Berwick-upon-Tweed B
Bridport B	Bridport B
	Bristol B
Canterbury B *(August 1854 by-election)*	
Chatham B	Chatham B
	Chester B
Christchurch B	
	Devonport B
Dorchester B	
Dover B	Dover B
Guildford B	
Hastings B	
Honiton B	
	Hull B
	Leicester B
Lewes B *(April 1855 by-election)*	Lewes B
Lyme Regis B	
Lymington B	Lymington B
Maidstone B	
	Newcastle
Newport B	
Northampton B *(March 1855 by-election)*	
	Norwich B
Oxford B	
Peterborough B	Peterborough B
Poole B	
Portsmouth B *(March 1855 by-election)*	Portsmouth B
	Reading B
	Rochdale B
Rochester B	
Rye B	
Salisbury B	Salisbury B

Sandwich **B**	Sandwich **B**
Shaftesbury **B**	
Sussex (East) **C**	
	Taunton **B**
Wareham **B**	
	Wells **B**
Weymouth and Melcombe Regis **B**	
Wilton **B** *(March 1855 by-election)*	
Winchester **B**	Winchester **B**
	Worcester **B**
(Total: 31)	*(Total: 25)*

Seats in which a by-election was held in the preceding year are indicated.
B = Borough
C = County
Source: Figures taken from Hylton MSS, Somerset Heritage Centre, Taunton, DD/HY 24/11/39, and Stewart, *Conservative*, p. 391.

'Carlton gold' were commonplace, but they were also critical in providing a rationale for many of the central Whig and Radical organisational efforts of the 1830s and 1840s, which were frequently defended as merely being attempts to check Conservative efforts. This was not a new development to either the age of Reform, or of 'club government', and parallels can be found with arguments deployed by predecessor organisations just before the Reform Act; a Mr. Hallett, the Whig agent in Berkshire, admitted to accepting election funds from the Political Unions, but claimed that he did so only to counteract 'Charles Street Gang' funds accepted by incumbent Conservative MP Robert Palmer.[69] Palmer insisted 'not one shilling' had been contributed by the 'Gang', but the story still acted as a powerful motivator for centralised fundraising among Whigs.[70]

Similarly, in the post-Reform environment, even when Brooks's lacked any such funding apparatus, it did not prevent political opponents from suspecting that it did; for instance, in May 1835 (one year *before* the Reform Club was launched), Devon's election funds included 'Raised among the friends of Reform, per Mr. Ellice, 1,000*l*', which led one letter writer to ask *The Times* 'Is there a fund at Brookes's [sic], or whence comes this 1,000*l*?' citing the Carlton's election fund as a parallel.[71] In truth, Brooks's never had any such fund, and the efforts of the Reform Association efforts remained independent of any clubs until the Reform Club's launch the following year – and, even then, there is no evidence of a directly-handled fund.

Petitioning

Until the Parliamentary Elections Act 1868, election petitions were not a matter for the courts, but for parliamentary committees. While some forms of petitioning have attracted attention, such as Henry Miller's recent study of Corn Law petitions in the 1840s, election petitions, in which petitioning Parliament offered a major opportunity to overturn unfavourable election results, remain a largely neglected phenomenon.[72] This was not lost on the clubs, with both the Carlton and Reform Clubs making crucial contributions to petitioning culture.

Centrally organised petitioning efforts from the Carlton were already in evidence within months of the Club's foundation. In February 1833, Conservative MP William Forbes Mackenzie wrote to J. C. Herries from the Carlton Club, 'we are now getting a sum together to help the local people in the petitions of rather a peculiar character, which makes me hold to ask you to assist us – one is as the Attorney General at Southampton'.[73]

At the Reform Club, James Coppock's legal background was put to good use in the pursuit of petitioning on behalf of the Club's supported candidates. It was noted in December 1837 that Coppock filed no less than fifteen petitions against constituency results from the general election earlier that year 'at the eleventh hour', and was identified in each case as the constituency agent. The *Oxford Mail* speculated that these petitions – many on identical grounds – were 'lithographed at the Reform Club at the very last stroke of the clock'.[74] A more plausible explanation was offered two days later by 'Vigil', an anonymous letter writer. These identical 'manufactured' petitions had indeed been lithographed (presumably at the Reform Club, although the letter did not specify), but were sent to the constituencies by Coppock, who accompanied them with an appeal to be filed.[75]

By the 1850s, such efforts were matched by the solicitors of the Carlton Club, and solicitors from both the Carlton and Reform were implicated in the practice of 'pairing' petitions. After the general election of 1852, Conservatives issued two petitions against the Norwich result. The Select Committee appointed to look into the abrupt withdrawal of both Norwich petitions concluded that withdrawal 'formed part of an arrangement and compromise between ... Henry Edwards Brown and James Coppock ... in pursuance of which arrangement eight Petitions were simultaneously withdrawn, implicating the seats of 10 [MPs]'.[76] They found that both Brown and Coppock withdrew their respective petitions over the wishes of the local associations. Norwich Conservative agent W. M. Kitton found his own petition withdrawn by Brown, even though he had specifically rejected a proposal by Brown to do so in exchange for the Liberal petition against West Norfolk, believing 'the West Norfolk petition is a sham'.[77] Brown had first been introduced to Kitton before the election by Colonel George Forester MP at Brown's office in the Carlton Club, although Kitton noted 'Forester never led me to believe that the Carlton Club would take up that petition, and pay the expenses'.[78] Pointing to his light workload at the time, he indicated that a surety for the petition would have to be found locally.[79] Thus there appears to be ample reason to suspect that the accusations that the solicitors of both the Carlton and Reform Clubs were involved in large-scale petitioning were indeed well-founded.

Textual Influence

It is curious that one of the ways in which we can now most demonstrably show club organisation was seldom commented upon at the time: textual influence. The Reform Club was rumoured to operate its own printing press from its cellar, reproducing radical literature, but it is doubtful whether the Carlton resorted to print, for almost all of its surviving papers up until 1868 were handwritten (unlike the Junior Carlton, which embraced print from its inception), and Conservatives were quick to disclaim any textual links to the Carlton. In 1835, John Martin, Hon. Secretary of the Westminster Conservative Society, took strong exception to *The Times* describing one of his circulars as being linked to the Carlton Club, and insisted 'The Carlton Club has no more to do with this society than the Cockspur-street Club; nor did the words "Carlton Club" ever appear in any one of the circulars'.[80]

The ultra-Protestant National Club provides the clearest evidence of strong textual influence by clubs. From 1846, the Club spent the next six years publishing an ambitious programme of addresses at monthly intervals, proclaiming the Club's views on a number of Protestant questions.[81] From the very outset, these addresses aimed to inspire the formation of 'Protestant Associations' linked to the Club, and encouraged such associations to reproduce the Club's addresses at every opportunity.[82]

The National Club also took out public advertisements and published one-off pamphlets on ad hoc issues – for instance, in 1847 the Club's Committee allocated £150 to 'Circulation of Articles through the Public Press strongly exposing the want of Christian Principles involved in ... the admission of Jews into Parliament', and subsequently bought newspaper advertisements on the topic.[83] Furthermore, from the National Club's launch, much of its Committee's time was preoccupied with circulating and commenting upon printed articles of Protestant interest, and as time went by this occupied ever more of the Committee's attention.[84]

A drive to appeal directly to the constituencies through the medium of print made sense for the National Club for two reasons. Firstly, one can view its discourse in the context of the much broader mid-nineteenth century anti-Papal 'Protestant Crusade' by numerous membership organisations, as identified by John Wolffe.[85] Secondly, the Club's numbers at Westminster were too modest to ever win a well-attended division and, with the exception of a handful of MPs like Charles Newdegate, its parliamentarians tended to be marginal figures. With the Club enjoying limited success at Westminster, it had little choice but to mount a direct assault on the constituencies.[86] A similar phenomenon is observable with the short-lived Free Trade Club of the late 1840s; in 1866, several of its surviving members were involved in the creation of the Cobden Club, which sought to popularise Cobdenite views through its publishing imprint.[87]

The activities of clubs in using print to affect elections can be further contextualised if viewed alongside the efforts of other organisations, most notably the Radical-affiliated Reform Association which eventually merged into the Reform Club in 1841. Although their efforts were independent of the Reform Club, several key personalities overlapped – not least one of its founders, Joseph Parkes – and it can be seen that the National Club's efforts to organise in the country was nothing new in the 1840s. The Reform Association most conspicuously printed *The County Elector's Manual* and its sister publication *The Borough Elector's Manual*, distributing them to Reform Associations around Britain.[88] John Hayes Lyon, the Whig agent for South Cheshire in the mid-1830s, owned a copy of both.[89] These 'how to' guides explained simply, succinctly and clearly how the reformed electoral system worked, and what an agent's role should be within it. Printed margin notes summarised each section. Despite their slender length (twenty-two pages, smaller than modern A6 size), they were models in compressing information. Numerous passages were shared between both publications, not least in urging 'that the Election entirely depends on the Registration. Every man, therefore, who is qualified should use every possible means to have his own name, and the names of his political friends, placed upon the Register', and that 'Next in importance to placing on the Register the names of persons properly qualified, is the duty of preventing the insertion of those parties who are not duly qualified, or who, upon any grounds, are incapable of voting'.[90]

On this latter point, the Reform Association's electoral handbooks were extremely carefully phrased, presumably in case copies fell into the wrong hands. Both the county and borough manuals did not explicitly instruct agents to invent excuses for objections to rival voters being registered. Nonetheless, the manuals' idiom left the reader in little doubt what an agent was expected to do. Describing the dates of Revising Barristers' circuits and where these might be advertised locally, they noted, 'It is important to observe that a Voter is in all cases competent to give evidence before the Barrister to support his claim. He need not, however, necessarily be a witness, and any other person in possession of the facts will be sufficient to prove his qualification.' The corresponding margin note for this section cautioned 'Voter may be his own witness'.[91]

However, if we are to recognise the advanced state of electoral machinery deployed by Parkes's Reform Association in the 1830s, unassisted by any clubs, it is also worth recognising the incompetence with which distribution of these materials could be carried out. A central plank of Gash's argument for the importance of electoral interventions by clubs is the degree of communication with the centre, and the Reform Association's experience in South Cheshire demonstrates the ambition of a national headquarters communicating with the constituencies was not always effectively realised. In early August 1838, James Coppock sent John Hayes Lyon a circular, requesting that year's subscription for the Reform Association, and renewing his request for the previous year's subscription, which had not been paid.[92] Such circulars were routine, with a similar one having been sent to Liberal MP William Wilshere in Great Yarmouth two months later.[93] Lyon's brother responded to Coppock from his lodgings at the United University Club: 'My late Brother died in 1836, which accounts for the Revenue alluded to in your Letter. As Executor of my late Brother I do not feel justified that I am at liberty to pay the Subscriptions of the Reform Association'.[94] There was no indication from Coppock's circular that any effort had been made in the previous year to contact Lyon, and so it does not appear unusual for the Reform Association's contact with individual agents in the country (even those such as Lyon who covered a whole county) to have been limited and infrequent. If anything, it bears out Joseph Coohill's observation that the Reform Association, the Cleveland Square group and the Reform Club, were all characterised by 'a high level of communication between the centre and the constituencies' — but that each of these in its own way was a spectacular failure at achieving such aims.[95]

Finally, it should be noted that textual influence was not restricted to print culture. As is clear from the above-cited circulars from James Coppock to Liberals in Cheshire and Great Yarmouth, as well as surviving letters from F. R. Bonham in the Peel MSS and the Glynne-Gladstone MSS, and the handwritten whips in the Fremantle MSS, the 1830s saw the continuation of the eighteenth-century culture of handwriting repetitive, formulaic circulars, before the easy availability of print by the 1850s made this unnecessary.

Funds, Candidates and Registration

Unlike the textual influence of clubs, which was rarely cited, from the 1830s onwards allegations abounded of clubs providing funds, candidates and registration drives in the constituencies. These three areas are more difficult to assess, partly due to a relative lack of surviving documentation, and partly because they were so closely bound up with rumour and innuendo. Accordingly, these themes are explored through the following case studies, illustrating the reality of such initiatives in selected constituencies by drawing upon the club-related electoral experiences of two members of the Gladstone family, and of Benjamin Disraeli.

In recent years, Norman Gash's assertion that candidates were adopted due to club influence has come under increased scrutiny from historians such as Michael Markus.[96] Clubs *did* play a role in candidate adoption, as alleged. Yet, contrary to contemporary caricatures, instances of coercion over candidate adoption appear extremely limited. Certainly, the notion of being 'Sent down by the Carlton' does not appear to be supported.[97] The role of the Carlton and Reform Clubs was to come up with lists of suitable candidates for seats where local interests desired a contest, but were unable to find a suitable candidate of their own. The most oft-cited instance is that of Disraeli, who owed his introduction and selection in Maidstone in part to the Carlton, and it is worth reproducing at length the unpublished account of Maidstone Conservative John Monckton, for it makes it clear that, far from Disraeli having been imposed by the Carlton, the impetus for the Carlton's role in a second candidate came from the local Conservatives:

> At the General Election in August 1837 a Committee of the Conservative party in Maidstone had determined to run one candidate only, namely Wyndham Lewis Esquire (an intimate friend of the Duke of Wellington). At the end of the first day's canvas, on casting up the promises, they so far exceeded the number contemplated, that the Committee determined to apply at the Carlton Club for another Candidate, and three of our Committee went to London, and with the aid afforded at the Club, Mr. Disraeli was selected, and he consented, and went down with our three friends at once, and entered upon the canvas on the following morning. He soon became a great favourite with the Voters.
>
> I was selected to propose him on the nomination, but having engaged to propose Mr. Wyndham Lewis, I was obliged to decline a great honor.[98]

Other instances would continue to abound of candidate introductions that were entirely voluntary. In 1852, the Conservative candidates Colonel L. S. Dickson and the Marquess of Douro unsuccessfully contested Norwich, with Dickson standing 'in consequence of an introduction from "the Carlton"'.[99] However, such examples need to be tempered with the observation that clubs were not the only source of candidate introductions. Prospective parliamentarians could also go through Whips, as with Lord Edward Thynne, who had a letter of introduction to Sir William Jolliffe written by his nephew the third Marquess of Bath, who wrote that Thynne was 'very desirous to appear as a candidate for Wells', pledging 'He will work out his own call & all he wishes is to be put in communication with our parliamentary agents – "Mr. Rose"'; Thynne was duly selected for the Somerset constituency of Frome, which he won at the second attempt in 1859.[100] Thus, although agents and Whips often worked in a club context, the connection should not be overstated – they were not the only means of central involvement.

Clubs could, exceptionally, provide footsoldiers to campaign in elections, but this appears to have been the exception rather than the rule. The most notable instance was the 1837 Westminster by-election in which Sir Francis Burdett sought re-election as a Conservative and, according to Disraeli, several hundred Carlton members were involved:

> The Tories worked hard. The Carlton Club mapped the city into districts, & divided them among the ardent youth of the party. May-fair fell to me & Sir Robert Pigot, & very great fun we had. There was one street in our district entirely filled with cooks, chiefly Foreigners. Ten years afterwards, writing *Tancred*, I availed myself of the experience then obtained, & it formed my first chapter.[101]

Yet this can scarcely be seen as a typical example, both because of the exceptional nature of this by-election, and because of the extreme proximity of the constituency to the Club, which facilitated direct assistance in a manner that was not repeated elsewhere.

Clubland in the Constituencies: Disraeli and the Gladstones

One need only look at individual election and by-election contests to see how the reputation as well as the reality of London clubs could have a marked influence on such contests. This can be traced, for instance, in the electoral experiences of Benjamin Disraeli, and of the Gladstone family, each of which repeatedly intertwined with London clubs.

At the April 1835 Taunton by-election, Disraeli was selected after an introduction by the Carlton Club's F.R. Bonham, through two letters described by Gash as, 'a good example of the kind of control exercised by the central managers in many constituencies'.[102] Yet the letters show little 'control' – merely the 'soft power' of fulsome praise for the candidate. Disraeli implicitly acknowledged the Club's role in his selection, saying, 'If I have been sent down by the Conservative [Carlton] Club, this time, I shall come down by the requisition of the electors at Taunton the next'.[103] At both that by-election and the subsequent general election, there is evidence that the Taunton Conservatives received money from the Carlton Club's election fund.[104] Despite Disraeli not yet even being a Carlton member at the time, he boasted to his sister on the eve of nominations 'They have opened a subscription for me at the Carlton headed by [Lord] Chandos'.[105] Subsequent accounts placed the value of the subscription at £300.[106] Yet Disraeli's candidature was adversely affected by embarrassing press coverage around another club, alleging his recent membership of the Radical-aligned Westminster Reform Club. The allegation by the *Morning Chronicle* that he 'is actually a member of the Westminster Reform Club' proved hugely damaging to Disraeli, setting the tone for his defeat to Henry Labouchere by 452 to 282.[107]

Meanwhile, the family of Disraeli's great future rival, Gladstone, found itself deeply embroiled in club electoral interferences. Thomas Gladstone, elder brother of W.E. Gladstone, sought a parliamentary seat after falling out with his Portarlington constituency in the early 1830s, and turned to the Carlton Club's F.R. Bonham. It is clear from Thomas Gladstone's surviving correspondence with Bonham that he was not particular about where he was to stand, so long as there was a near-certainty of victory. In 1834, Bonham suggested the notoriously corrupt borough of Sudbury, and made little attempt to conceal the means deemed necessary to win the seat, noting, 'My notion is that it will be *certain* but *not cheap* ... for a seat *of this kind* there are always plenty of competitors'.[108] Gladstone did not stand in Sudbury, but he continued to press Bonham, as in 1828:

> I think the next thing I can do is to go up to Town, which I propose to do to-morrow so as to be at the [Carlton] Club on Friday mor[ning], by which time the Baronet [Sir Thomas

Fremantle} will probably be in Town. If not around when you receive this perhaps you will write to say that I am to be there on Friday in the hope of meeting him with you. I know him, which will facilitate matters.[109]

Bonham replied, offering intelligence from different seats, though it was not particularly accurate: he insisted, 'Mr. Preston of Yarmouth will take an opportunity of writing to you on the affairs of Yarmouth for which place it is known that Rumbold does not intend again to offer himself', whereas Liberal MP C. E. Rumbold did in fact successfully re-stand at the following general election.

The following year, Bonham made his most elaborate attempt at a Carlton intervention for Gladstone. The Conservative Committee in Sandwich sought a new candidate, offering to let them withdraw if they did not like the result of a fresh canvass.[110] This sparked a mounting row over the cost involved of such a canvass. Bonham pleaded for more money, 'I should think for the purpose required Four Hundred Pounds ought to suffice, and as you mentioned John's willingness to give Two hundred, I would muster the greatest exertion to obtain the other Three',[111] but Gladstone complained how much this was costing his father, Sir John Gladstone: 'my f[athe]r considers that he has already *spent* £300 – tho' all he could do has been done to keep it down. If I give £200 there may be £500'.[112] Ultimately, with the canvass proving unsatisfactory, Gladstone withdrew his candidacy – despite a last-ditch attempt by Bonham to persuade him in a meeting at the Carlton Club.[113] Bonham made it clear he circulated the canvass to other interested applicants at the Carlton: 'All participants who were cognizant of the matter have your canvass except Sir W. Goulburn who has not been at the Carlton the last two days and as you desired me to return it'.[114]

Thomas Gladstone's younger brother, William Ewart Gladstone, also had several electoral run-ins with the real or imagined power of clubs in the constituencies. As the 1841 general election loomed, W.E. Gladstone feared a contest in his Newark constituency. A day after arriving at Newark, he wrote to his wife:

There is no hard national evidence as yet of opposition: no one in the field, & the other party very much disorganised. They say however that a man will come down from the Reform Club tonight: and it cannot be regarded as very untouchable on financial grounds though we have no means of judging how far it is actually worth a visit.[115]

Gladstone's ensuing correspondence with his wife repeated his mounting dread that some last-minute Reform Club-backed candidate would stand against him.[116] In the event, a last-minute candidate did stand, Thomas Hobhouse, only to be soundly defeated by Gladstone and his running mate. There is no evidence that the Reform Club was ever involved in efforts to run a candidate, and there was nothing beyond rumour to connect the Club to Hobhouse's somewhat shambolic last-minute campaign. Nonetheless, even in the absence of such a threat, the mere rumour of a possible Reform Club intervention was enough to motivate Gladstone and Manners to fight a spirited campaign, heavily canvassing the seat. Thus even in the absence of a campaign, a club's reputation could act as a spur to action.

W. E. Gladstone went on to have notable run-ins with both the Carlton Club and the National Club in the peculiar circumstances of the 1853 Oxford University by-election. The by-election was triggered by Gladstone's acceptance of office under Aberdeen, and proved a testbed for the issues of religious reform and university reform.[117]

From the available textual evidence, one may speculate that the National Club was already involved in the 1847 general election campaign for Oxford University, when religion was a major issue. The National Club's Committee worked hard in the 1847 election to produce template literature which could be disseminated in constituencies nationwide.[118] Such literature would not typically mention the National Club by name, but would echo the Club's themes, not least the centrality of Protestantism to national identity. A pamphlet written by F. D. Maurice during the 1847 campaign urged opposition to Gladstone at Oxford, and seems a textbook example of such National Club literature, with its rallying cry 'With Protestantism I believe our national existence is bound up; everywhere the preservation of it should be our chief care', and it went on to cite all of the Club's preferred tropes of the day, including the Dissenters' Chapels Bill and the Maynooth Grant Bill. The pamphlet concluded by comparing Gladstone's voting record with the public stances of Roundell Palmer, and it urged

Gladstone's defeat.[119] Nowhere was the National Club named in this pamphlet, yet reading it alongside other National Club-sponsored literature of the period, it bears all the same hallmarks, shares their stock phrases, and seems highly likely to have been the work of their printing presses.[120] Gladstone had worked hard in 1847 to counteract the religious objections to his candidature, and published a three-page pamphlet, countering many of the charges levelled at him as misrepresentations.[121]

Going into the 1853 election, Gladstone thought that if he were to lose the seat, 'it will be on political not religious grounds'.[122] Yet against a backdrop of religious tests as a major issue for the Oxford University constituency, and the ongoing Royal Commission on Oxford University, plus Gladstone's nuanced position around Jewish disabilities, the National Club took a keen interest in running a more aggressively Protestant candidate against Gladstone.

The challenger to Gladstone was one Dudley M. Perceval, a 51-year-old Derbyite Conservative and younger son of former Prime Minister Spencer Perceval. *The Times* thought him 'dim, protean and nondescript',[123] while M. R. D. Foot and H. C. G. Matthew summarised Perceval's career as a 'controversialist and pamphleteer'.[124] Perceval was also a member of the National Club's Committee, heavily involved in its electoral and campaigning activities. It was this association which thrust him into the centre of the by-election at short notice.

It was only after the by-election that it became clear what the roles of the Carlton and National Clubs had been. At the 1852 general election, the National Club had already proposed the ultra-Protestant former MP for Kilmarnock and Newcastle-under-Lyme, J. C. Colquhoun, who was himself a founder Committee member of the Club. According to Gladstone's supporters, Colquhoun 'proved so decidedly unacceptable to the influential residents who were canvassed on his behalf, that it was found necessary to withdraw him'.[125]

When the by-election writ was moved in December 1852, the time to mount a challenge was extremely short. Two anti-Gladstone Committees were formed, one at the British Hotel, Charing Cross, with Dr. C. Lempriere as Hon. Secretary, the other at Magdalen Hall, Oxford.[126] The Charing Cross committee approached the Marquess of Chandos to stand, but he refused – not least as he already represented a safe seat. Neither of the two committees were deterred by this, and on

Saturday 1 January 1853, they optimistically resolved in a circular 'It having been decided to bring forward the Marquis of Chandos in opposition to Mr. Gladstone ... The Committee for promoting his Lordship's return sit daily at this place and at Oxford'.[127] Sir Stafford Northcote subsequently argued that in order for the '1 January' circular to have been distributed in time, it would have had to have been printed *before* Lempriere visited Chandos, on the assumption of his acceptance. Chandos recalled that the next day, Sunday 2 January, 'it was intended to propose my name to Convocation, whether I consented or not ... the proceedings would be continued irrespective of my decision'.[128] The Chandos committees released a further circular dated Monday 3 January 1853 announcing 'that the Marquis of Chandos has consented to be put in nomination for the vacant seat', apparently in the hope of leaving Chandos with no alternative, and that day's *Morning Herald* incorrectly reported that Chandos was about to stand against Gladstone.[129] Chandos met with Dr. Lempriere of the Charing Cross committee later that day at the Carlton Club, confirming that he would *not* be standing, and then wrote to Gladstone, reassuring him of his position.[130]

Gladstone's opponents were thus placed in an extremely difficult position. Monday 3 January was the eve of the first day of polling. They had announced a contest, and had already released circulars and cards for Chandos, but their chosen candidate refused to stand.[131] They required a new candidate at extremely short notice. They contacted both the Carlton Club and the National Club. The Provost of Oriel College, a supporter of Gladstone's, argued that this turn of events was the fault of Chandos' committees: 'This was, indeed, too like placing the University at the mercy of the Carlton and National Clubs'.[132] There is no record of whether the Carlton Club ever proposed a candidate – it would have been surprising if they had, for Gladstone was still a Carlton member (as was Chandos),[133] and it would have been surprising if a club had nominated a candidate to stand against one of its own members.

It is, however, plausible that there was still some level of collusion between the Carlton Club and National Club, for relations between the two were cordial enough in the 1850s. Charles Hay Frewen was an MP who was active in both clubs, sat on the Committee of the National Club throughout this period, and who was supported in his Sussex East constituency by a National Club-affiliated local association (As noted in Figure 6.3, Sussex East was also the only county constituency to receive financial assistance from the Carlton fund in 1855, with Frewen still sitting for the division then.) In March 1855, Frewen wrote a 'private' note on National Club stationery to Sir William Jolliffe, openly proposing Conservative election candidates: 'I know of *two* good men, *one* for $\frac{1}{2}$ the other for L. – One of them is cousin to the Duke of Hamilton who has great property in Scotland; – Spooner's motion about Maynooth is the card. – I will send up to you as soon as I have had my breakfast'.[134] Such a tone of easy familiarity does not suggest the National Club operated wholly independently of the Carlton's electoral machine, even though there is limited evidence of active collusion.

Whether or not the Carlton came up with an anti-Gladstone candidate, the National Club opposed Gladstone on the Maynooth grant, Jewish disabilities, and ecclesiastical titles, and proposed Perceval as their candidate – he was both a founder member of the Club, and a member of the Club's Committee.[135] As such, it does not appear that the National Club looked very far, and there is no evidence that the Club permanently maintained a list of election candidates in the same way that the much larger Carlton Club was alleged to have done. Perceval was promptly adopted, and it was only on the opening morning of the election – Tuesday 4 January – that it was announced that he would be the candidate in Chandos' place. Although Perceval led the poll by eighteen votes on day three of voting, Gladstone resumed the lead and was re-elected with a reduced majority of 124 votes. Thus the reputation of clubs for providing candidates meant that, when a new candidate was needed at short notice, Oxford's Protestant Derbyites turned to the Carlton and National Clubs, and the contest's strongly religious flavour worked to the advantage of Perceval in narrowing the gap.

Conclusion

Whilst the central role of clubs in Westminster politics is easily established, their significance in the constituencies was much more variable. They undoubtedly functioned as a vital centre of correspondence from which to co-ordinate efforts on a national basis and, for this reason alone, they deserve greater attention. Yet such correspondence and fund dispensation could be haphazard and irregular.

It was as a provider of election funds that clubs drew the most attention, yet while it is likely that structures such as that of the Junior

Carlton's political fund were in place at the Carlton and Reform Clubs as early as the 1830s, it still remains difficult to prove due to the volume of records destroyed; and from the sums disbursed in the 1850s, it seems likely that the central Carlton election fund was both smaller than rumoured (at c.£50,000), and that the activities funded were more often legal and pedestrian than illegal and colourful. Despite sensational contemporary claims as to the size of club resources, even historians who have supported the existence of a club fund have acknowledged its limitations, with Stewart conceding that, in the constituencies, 'the amounts were tiny in an age when a contest rarely cost less than £2,500 and often more than £10,000'.[136]

In providing a pool of willing candidates of independent means, often at short notice, clubs fulfilled a vital function in allowing elections to be planned on a national basis. Only the absence of a surviving club-sponsored candidates' list – and its comparison with the number of actual candidates – prevents a quantification of the number of vacancies filled by clubs, but it should be observed that with the rise in contested elections through the mid-nineteenth century, the role of club-provided candidates' lists would most likely have been an important one.

In registration drives and subsequent canvasses, clubs provided money, expertise, contacts to solicitors and agents, as well as analysing and circulating the results among senior politicians. Although many such drives occurred locally, and the earlier work of the Political Unions showed that regional organisations had already begun to organise such activities, the Reform and Carlton Clubs again co-ordinated such activities on a national scale for the first time – albeit patchily.

Clubs also played a textual role in writing and disseminating election literature, although it should be noted that the most conspicuous component of this was the National Club rather than the better-known Carlton and Reform Clubs.

The role of clubs in corruption was more controversial. Moisei Ostrogorski, one of the earliest writers to outline the political role of clubs in a Westminster context, was fully justified in writing: 'The intervention from London haunted people's minds in the provinces even when it never took place; and, in accordance with the old tradition, it was attributed to the Carlton Club or the Reform Club.' Indeed, instances of corruption were associated with clubs and vice-versa – but this needs to be tempered with recognition of the relative atypicality of corruption in the post-Reform years, and clubs were far from being the only source of corruption. Yet Ostrogorski was demonstrably wrong when he insisted that 'In reality, clubs had no share in [corruption], they had lost their influence, especially the Reform Club'.[137] Clubs continued to host a range of electoral activities through to the Second Reform Act – and even beyond, if one considers that the Junior Carlton Club did not set up its Political Fund until 1869, while the Reform Club only formed a Political Committee in 1868.[138]

Even when clubs were not involved in elections, their reputation was such that the mere rumour or suspicion of potential involvement could result in the deployment of resources and campaigns by an opponent, as in Newark in 1841.

Ultimately, clubs played a significant co-ordinating role in election campaigns between the two Reform Acts – yet this should not be overstated. Their role remains important with the benefit of hindsight, for its historic shift in the direction of party centralisation. Yet it is difficult to hold that it was the central factor in Conservative or Liberal general election fortunes. Club electoral organisation was far too limited, and deployed far too sparingly, for it to have fully matched its fearsome reputation.

CONCLUSION

Edward Ellice's oft-quoted expression 'club government' was aptly chosen, yet it did not fully capture the extent to which clubs and politics at Westminster had become intertwined by the middle of the nineteenth century. Existing debate among historians on the nature of 'club government' has often focussed on club electoral interventions, which is in some ways surprising, as in this respect clubs were frequently *less* influential than is supposed. Norman Gash, Robert Stewart, Bruce Coleman and Alistair Cooke have all spearheaded the view that clubs, led by the Carlton, were crucial in the determining of elections, while others (most notably Philip Salmon, Nancy LoPattin-Lummis and Matthew Cragoe) have countered that the counter-efforts centred on the Reform Club have been underestimated.[1] All of these views have been refuted by Frank O'Gorman, who contends that 'the experiments in central direction of party affairs, in the shape of the Carlton and Reform Clubs, should not be overestimated ... [they] ... effected little or no fundamental shift of power from the constituencies to a London-based party machine. They systematized the uncoordinated activities of earlier, somewhat informal, bodies but they did not mark any qualitative change in the nature of party politics.'[2]

Whilst Frank O'Gorman is justified in pointing to some limited pre-Reform Act predecessors of the Carlton and Reform Clubs, it is hoped that the evidence presented here makes a strong case for clubs having taken on an entirely different role *after* 1832, functioning in a number of new and distinctive ways. The case for 'club government' is only partly based on Clubland electoral activities which have already received some attention.[3] Despite the frequency of by-elections, the overall significance of elections was debateable in a period when great emphasis was placed on parliamentary government, and the securing of a majority in the Commons. As Angus Hawkins has argued, this did not necessarily mean winning an outright majority at a general election – for much of the period, parliamentary government meant the forging of shifting alliances to secure the return or survival of a government.[4] The degree to which clubs added to this culture of parliamentary government – with their unique use of space, their sociability, their facilities, and their open access to whipping – was their greatest contribution to politics.

In the aftermath of the Great Reform Act, a reorganisation of parties and their machinery became necessary for existing politicians and political groups to adapt to the new post-Reform political environment. Many of these changes were wholly unrelated to clubs, not least the gradual coalescence of numerous smaller parties and factions into two broad parties, a process which had arguably begun long before 1832. It is within the context of such change that the growth of 'club government' must be viewed.

It is not maintained that *any* club was inherently important to the political process: Pall Mall is littered with the corpses of failed clubs, and in this period alone, the Cocoa Tree, Colonial, Crockford's, Erectheum, Free Trade, Parthenon and Westminster Reform Clubs all closed their doors; other clubs were politically negligible, with membership among MPs in single figures, or even non-existent.

Nevertheless, Gash's assertion that the 1830s and 1840s was the age of 'club government' is in part borne out by the research here – depending on one's definition of the term. If 'club government' is measured in utilitarian terms by the number of individuals directly concerned with it – both inside and outside Parliament – then it may well be best assessed through a study not preoccupied with the St James's institutions covered here, but with the growth of working men's clubs from the 1850s, and their adoption as headquarters for local political parties. Although local political clubs dated to the eighteenth century, the spread of these was still in its infancy in 1868, and it was only from the 1880s onwards that they began to formally affiliate with political parties in any large numbers.[5] However, although the organisational focus of such clubs could be considerable, any such study would need to recognise the limited resources (particularly financial) at the disposal of such clubs, in contrast with the larger sums and more prominent personnel available to the central London clubs in the mid-nineteenth century in the absence of any other central organisation – a point which forms a strong argument for the financial importance of clubs in this period.

The 'big three' political clubs, Brooks's, the Carlton and Reform Clubs, all continued to enjoy mass membership by the vast majority of Conservative and Liberal MPs until at least the Edwardian era.[6] Indeed, just as these clubs had been supplemented by larger clubs such as the Junior Carlton after 1864, so the process would continue, with mass membership clubs including the City Carlton, St. Stephen's, Beaconsfield, Constitutional, City Constitutional and Junior Constitutional Clubs for the Conservatives, and the City Liberal, Devonshire and National Liberal Clubs for the Liberals, all being founded from the 1870s to the 1880s.[7] Each had mass memberships which dwarfed the clubs discussed here, extending to provincial and lower-middle class politicians, and so, if an age of 'club government' is to be identified based on simple aggregate membership numbers, then the 1832–68 period would *not* be considered the peak of club political significance.

Yet for all the merits of any such studies into the late Victorian growth of clubs into the political sphere, and their absorption of working-class and lower-middle-class political culture, 'club government' was never about maximising the number of people involved in the political process.

Instead, 'club government' should be a viewed as a cultural shift, in which the political arena overlapped heavily with the operation of clubs, resulting in major cultural and organisational changes to the practice of politics. It was during the 1830s that clubs grew to accommodate a clear majority of MPs, with over 90 per cent belonging to at least one club by the end of the decade, and that figure sustained at least until the Second Reform Act.[8] Although peers do not appear to have shared this concentration of membership, the success of the parliamentary embrace brought clubs into the heart of the political sphere as they became a shared space for MPs. Club membership should not be viewed in isolation; it is only through the use of social network analysis that it is possible to fully set out the degree to which 'core' clubs supported a number of more peripheral clubs. Such club links also explain much about the culture of clubs, not least the most common shared club membership being between the Reform Club and Brooks's, and how ostensibly apolitical clubs overlapped in membership with political clubs.[9]

Since clubs were elite institutions, it is worth posing the question of whether the most socially elitist clubs were also the most politically significant. It appears not. Certainly, the most overtly aristocratic clubs remained the smaller, longer-established clubs Boodle's, Brooks's and White's. The renewed political importance of Brooks's throughout this period acts as a powerful counter-argument to the conventional view that these older clubs faded into apolitical irrelevance, or that the Reform Club unambiguously replaced Brooks's as a Liberal headquarters. On the contrary, Brooks's continued to be central to Liberal politics at Westminster until at least the 1886 Home Rule split and, while its membership was never limited to Whigs, it still provided a natural social centre for Whiggery, meaning that it assumed great importance during later governments retaining a strong Whig element.[10] This was apparent during Russell's second ministry, when the Adullamites were of crucial importance in frustrating further Reform initiatives, and Brooks's assumed a central role as a social centre for MPs who held the balance of political power. Yet the relative marginalisation of White's, and the lack of any real political significance for Boodle's in this period, stood in stark contrast, making it difficult to interpret the success of Brooks's as part of any wider reassertion of aristocratic government through Clubland.

The principal 'success stories' from the 1830s onwards were the Carlton and Reform Clubs, part of a new breed of political club, which embraced a great many members drawn from the professions. Such clubs were rooted in the new wave of clubs themed around professions and interest groups which had already proliferated since the 1810s, but the political displacement of the 1832 Reform Act created a climate in which new institutions in this mould assumed a valuable political function, with the Carlton and Reform Clubs filling this vacuum. In addition to the principal new clubs, a number of less successful clubs – the Westminster Reform, Conservative, Free Trade and National Clubs all tell us much about the shape of smaller political factions, and their failure to sustain a successful political club reveals much about the organisational difficulties faced by groups such as the Cobdenites, Radicals and Ultras.[11]

The organisational transformation of Clubland in the nineteenth century affected the shape of the new clubs. Rather than following the proprietary model of eighteenth century clubs, the new member-owned clubs could claim to legitimately represent a cause or interest rather than a patron; making them very different to the salons and subscription rooms found nearby, or the pre-existing proprietary clubs.[12] It should be noted that the period covered here was struck by a disparity – whilst the clubs founded in the nineteenth century were almost invariably member-owned, Boodle's, Brooks's and White's remained in the hands of private landlords until the last quarter of the century; although there is no suggestion that the clubs' landlords made political demands.

The unique status of clubs and of club membership made them privileged spaces; semi-private, and semi-public. In their ability to selectively admit members and guests, they acted as gatekeepers to the political world, and the male-only preserve of the key political clubs was a significant contributor to the conspicuous masculinity of Victorian politics at Westminster, in strong contrast to the continued role of women as ticketholders at surrounding salons, hostesses at neighbouring homes, and public gallery observers in the new Palace of Westminster.[13]

The physical layout of clubs greatly facilitated politics, as a 'theatre of state', as well as a series of corridors that regulated the flow of politicians in carefully planned social interactions. Clubs offered a variety of suitable rooms for MPs to hold meetings in, varying from the atriums of the Athenaeum, Carlton and Reform Clubs which could easily host a parliamentary party meeting of 300 MPs, to the more intimate alcoves found in clubs of all sizes, suitable for smaller-scale conversations, and particularly well-suited to discretion. The scope offered for such meetings was considerable, and they included such controversial topics as planning Liberal parliamentary tactics over Peel's reintroduction of income tax in 1842, and meetings of Conservative rebels over the sugar duties in 1844.[14]

The isolation of clubs, carefully guarded by hall porters who were supposed to know each member by sight, allowed politicians some respite from the outside world; democracy and clubs stood ill at ease with one another. Clubs aggressively excluded non-members, and yet members elected one another by secret ballot, and actively craved a flow of newspapers and telegraph news from the outside world. A club offered its MP members the chance to survey the world at a safe distance, with an enviable number of facilities under one roof: accommodation, stationery, postage, and carefully regulated access to the flow of gossip through dinners and small-scale gatherings. Numerous accounts testify to the political clubs having been packed to capacity by meetings of MPs, both at setpiece meetings, and simply through use being made of Coffee Rooms (the standard term for Dining Rooms) and Morning Rooms (later 'Smoking Rooms') throughout the parliamentary session. Changing nomenclatures and facilities in clubs reflected changing social trends in the middle of the century, from the rise of cigarette smoking to the use of faster forms of communication such as the telegraph.[15]

Advances in technology were fully recognised and embraced by those who most recognised the importance of 'club government', and so it comes as little surprise that Whips were among those who paid clubs the most attention. Between each group of party Whips, membership was held at the principal London clubs where MPs could be found, facilitating the rounding-up of parliamentarians before key divisions. Whips played a central role in founding the major political clubs of the period, in some cases sitting on their Committees, and at the Carlton (but not at Brooks's or the Reform Club) they wielded a disproportionate influence over candidates who were successfully elected. The Whips' relationship to clubs was cyclical – they built them up as social centres for MPs, and in turn they were able to reap the benefits of having a convenient place to find MPs.[16] The clubs' 'gatekeeper' role further reinforced whipping activities at the Carlton, with the compulsory subscription book for the party whip being held in the club morning room, making visits to a members-only area of the Carlton almost mandatory. The Whips' activities were further systematised by the provision of modest offices in clubs, the establishment of hansom cab routes in an eight-minute round trip to Parliament and back, and through the installation of division bells in clubs by the 1850s.[17]

The Carlton Club assumed an additional whipping role. Largely deprived of the patronage and resources of office for years at a time, the Conservatives lacked government-provided funds to facilitate the more disciplined whipping necessary in the post-Reform environment. Consequently, by the late 1830s the Carlton was used to administer a system of subscriptions to the Conservative whip in both Commons and Lords. Although this system fell into abeyance during the second Peel

CONCLUSION 215

government, it was later resurrected when the Conservatives returned to opposition.

In the absence of formal party membership, club membership offered the closest approximation to a party identity, and MPs' club memberships can be uniquely helpful in suggesting political affiliation; not only in the case of political clubs offering a set of colours with which to identify an MP, but also in the rarer cases of MPs who did *not* belong to a club.[18]

That we still know so little of the central funding of political parties in this period – and that rumours of 'Carlton Club gold' and 'the golden showers of the Reform Club' have endured – stands as a testament to the success of the clubs in maintaining secrecy about their financial arrangements, as well as the vivid picture painted by invective at the hustings and captured in the frequently quoted novels of Disraeli and Trollope. Whereas the central importance of clubs to mid-nineteenth century Westminster politics remains hugely *underestimated*, their role in the constituencies, by contrast, has long been exaggerated. The Carlton, Junior Carlton and Reform Clubs did organise central election funds, dispensed by party managers, and (later, in the case of the Carlton) Whips; and their status as clubs benefitted these funds in permitting a degree of secrecy. However, the scale of these funds has been grossly exaggerated; surviving Junior Carlton Club records indicate that the political fund's income was some £2,000 per annum, and so even over a full seven-year parliament this would not have permitted more than a few hundred pounds in selected contests. Whips' records from the 1850s indicate that the beneficiaries of a central fund numbered, at best, a few dozen seats; enough to be significant, but certainly not as all-pervasive as the clubs' reputations suggest. In identifying central funds, it must also be recognised that there is some confusion as to whether the clubs sustained their involvement in the organisation of these funds. A certain amount of cross-pollination of different Carlton funds was likely, with the surplus from the whipping subscription of the 1830s having been diverted to the electoral fund; but again, the amounts (in the hundreds of pounds) did not fully justify the Carlton's fearsome reputation, and supports the notion that Carlton funds were used to supplement selected electoral contests rather than single-handedly bankrolling them.[19]

Such embellishment is typical of how a number of myths have prevailed about clubs over the years; frequently, the degree of secrecy about what went on behind the closed doors of clubs prompted speculation which bracketed them with freemasonry and secret societies, and the increased targeting of clubs by protestors can be seen as a popular reflection of this. The reality was seldom as sinister as their fearsome reputation suggested. One area prone to frequent misinformation and exaggeration was the practice of blackballing. Contrary to the widespread belief that it was rife and, talk of 'blackballing scandals', its practice was extraordinarily rare, and due to the unique rules of political clubs, parliamentarians were almost invariably exempt from it. Indeed, the 'fast-tracking' of MPs was facilitated by the central role given to whips and party managers, which ensured that new parliamentarians were granted access to the key political clubs, almost as a matter of course.[20] Consequently, the MPs of Brooks's and the Reform Club both resembled a large cross-section of the Liberals in Parliament (with both clubs embracing everything from Whiggery to Radicalism, and each club containing around half of all Liberal MPs of various denominations), whilst the Carlton included some nine-tenths of Conservative MPs.

Although Clubland myths may have been misleading, they could also be extremely potent. Even when the role of clubs was exaggerated, in itself such exaggeration was significant and, arguably, played a part in politics. As we have seen at Newark in 1841, the mere allegation (however unfounded) that a club might potentially deploy a candidate was enough to spur the opposing party to counter with repeated canvasses of the constituency, with the result that great significance was attached to intelligence of rumoured club action. Although it is not possible to accurately measure the link, it should be noted that the rising reputation of 'club government' coincided with a rise in contested elections; something consistent with the notion that fear of club intervention could be powerful in prompting counter-efforts. The resonance of 'club government' imagery was also evident from its prevalence in electoral discourse. The allegation that a candidate was imposed or funded by the Carlton or Reform Clubs was a common cry to discredit them with the electorate, calling into question their independence, and thus their suitability to sit in Parliament. Even when grounded in truth, such remarks were invariably embellished.

As noted, club electoral funds merely offered a supplement to existing sources of funding, while clubs had no power to impose candidates. Instead, the candidates introduced by clubs were an innovative way for constituencies to bid for a candidate when they required one, using a centralised network that deserves recognition for its innovation – but it was restricted to local associations which actively sought a candidate and did not wish an election to go uncontested.[21] The value of clubs' social networks could thus have national ramifications, but the organisation offered was limited.

Gash saw 'club government' as coinciding with what he called the 'age of Peel', 1830–1850. Yet the organs of 'club government' continued well beyond 1850 (and indeed 1868). What changed over time were the personalities associated with the organisation. At the Carlton Club, the alienation of the Peelites brought about the withdrawal of Bonham from the Derbyite electoral machinery in the late 1840s, while at the Reform Club, the gradual withdrawal of Parkes in the 1840s and the death of Coppock in 1856 signalled the end of an era. In each case, electoral functions continued to be carried out by the parties, but the shift towards firms of solicitors as party agents such as Rose and Spofforth for the Conservatives, and Wyatt, Hoskins and Hooker for the Liberals, necessitated a gradual shift of the electoral machinery out of Clubland spaces. With these dislocations, it would be a mistake to project the continuing presence of Clubland spaces as embodying continuity.[22] Instead, the individuals, skills, spaces and political context all evolved substantially throughout the period, and the Second Reform Act would bring further dislocation, with centralised party organisations in the 1870s which were conspicuously *not* based around clubs.

'Club government' was a clearly-definable phase in the evolution of central party organisation, tied to the conglomeration of party and transformations in the political system, both at Westminster and in the country. Yet it also left a lasting impact on the shape of British politics.

Over sixty years ago, Gash was fully justified in writing of the age of 'club government'. Yet a paucity of available sources has discouraged generations of historians from fully tackling the questions posed by Gash's provocative popularisation of Ellice's rhetoric, with the result that 'club government' has either – in the case of constituency interventions – gone unchallenged in its acceptance of contemporary embellishments about the scale of Clubland corruption, or else grossly underestimated the vital role that clubs played in the evolution of Victorian London's distinctive parliamentary culture. In analysing new sources, from seldom used (and in some cases, completely unused) club archival material to recently digitised newspapers, a very different picture emerges. Amidst the fractious political realignments in the decades following the Great Reform Act, the central role of clubs in fusing the organisational and the social into a distinctive set of spaces played a key role in shaping mid-Victorian politics.

APPENDIX

APPENDIX TO CHAPTER 2: LIST OF SOURCES USED IN THE DATABASE OF CLUB MEMBERSHIPS FOR MPS WHO SAT IN THE HOUSE OF COMMONS IN 1832–68

Archival sources

MS numbers are stated when they exist – please note that most of these archives are unsorted and/or uncatalogued, and so most documents are without MS numbers.

Athenaeum Club archive, Athenaeum Club, London
An Alphabetical List of the Members, with the Rules and Regulations, of the Athenaeum (London: William Clowes, 1826) – bound with subsequent editions from 1830, and each year covering 1832–68.

Bodleian Library, Oxford
Carlton Club, *A List of members of the Carlton Club* (London, 1836), Bodleian MS 2479 e.2 (10).

Carlton Club archive, Carlton Club, London
'Carlton Club Committee Minutes, Volume 2, 1835–9'.

'Carlton Club Committee Minutes, Volume 3, 1839–43'. *Note that these two volumes are the only ones which survive for the pre-1868 period. A first volume covering the years 1832–5 was cited in Sir Charles Petrie's 1955 history of the Carlton, but is conspicuously missing from today's Carlton archive.*
'Carlton Club Candidates Books, 1834–69', 13 vols.

Junior Carlton Club archive, Carlton Club, London
'Junior Carlton Club Candidates Books, 1864–8', 6 vols.

National Club MSS, Bodleian Library, Oxford
'Minute-book of the General Committee, 1847–54', MS Bodleian Dep. b.235.
'General Committee Minute Books, 1861–1870', MS Bodleian Dep. b.236.
'National Club Annual Reports, 1846–1960', MS Bodleian Dep. bc.683.

Reform Club archive, Reform Club, London
'Reform Club Minute Book 1836–41', Reform Club archive.
'Reform Club Minute Book, 1864–70', Reform Club archive.
'Reform Club Letter Book, 1836–48', Reform Club archive.
Anonymous, *Reform Club List of Members, August 1st, 1836* (London, 1836).
———, *Rules and Regulations for the Government of the Reform Club, with an Alphabetical List of the Members* (London, 1837).
———, *Rules and Regulations for the Government of the Reform Club, with an Alphabetical List of the Members* (London, 1838).
———, *Rules and Regulations for the Government of the Reform Club, with an Alphabetical List of the Members* (London: T. Brettell, 1840).
———, *Rules and Regulations for the Government of the Reform Club, with an Alphabetical List of the Members* (London: T. Brettell, 1841).
———, *Rules and Regulations for the Government of the Reform Club, with an Alphabetical List of the Members* (London: J. Mitchell, 1842).
———, *Rules and Regulations for the Government of the Reform Club* (London: McGowan, 1847).
———, *Rules and Regulations for the Government of the Reform Club* (London: McGowan, 1851).

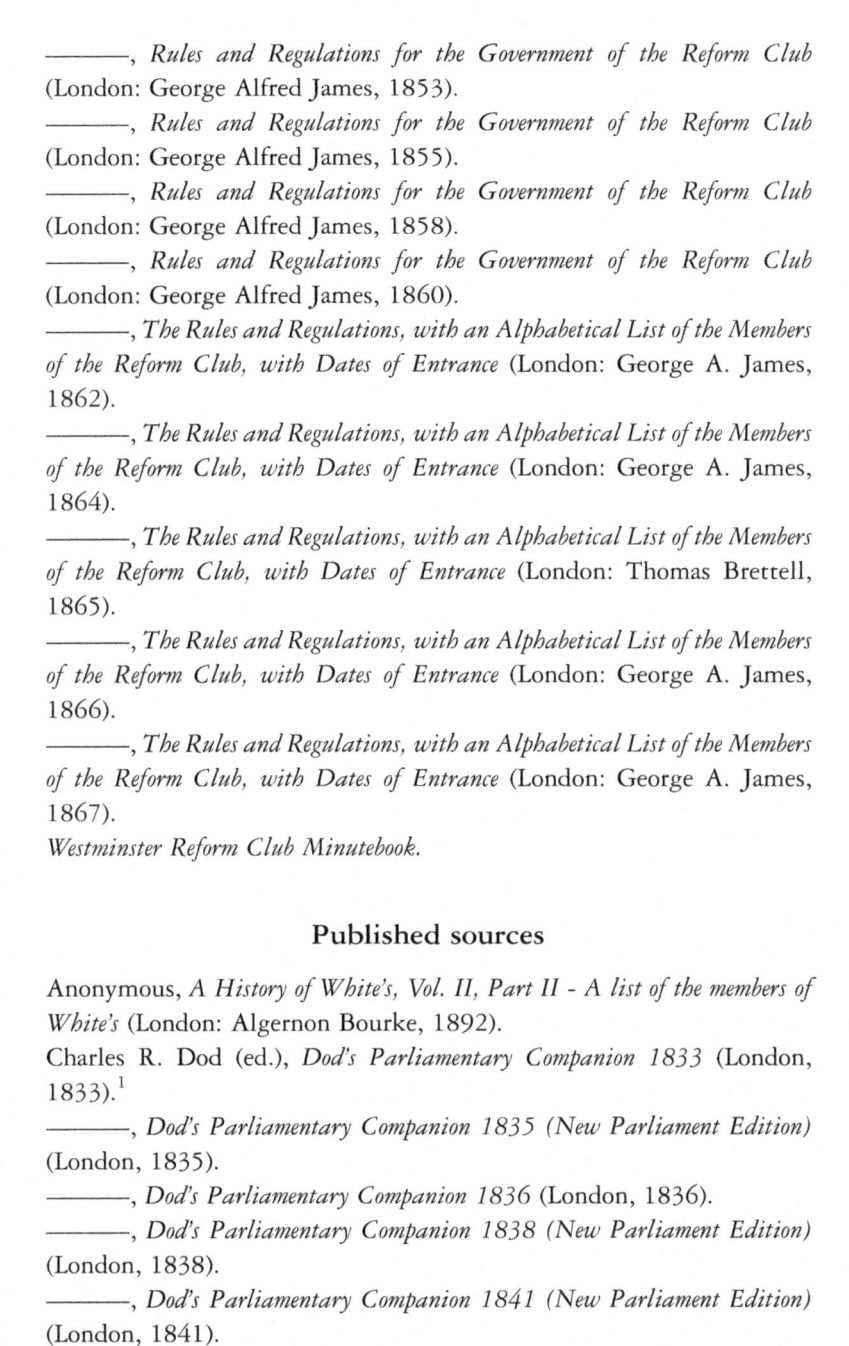

———, *Rules and Regulations for the Government of the Reform Club* (London: George Alfred James, 1853).
———, *Rules and Regulations for the Government of the Reform Club* (London: George Alfred James, 1855).
———, *Rules and Regulations for the Government of the Reform Club* (London: George Alfred James, 1858).
———, *Rules and Regulations for the Government of the Reform Club* (London: George Alfred James, 1860).
———, *The Rules and Regulations, with an Alphabetical List of the Members of the Reform Club, with Dates of Entrance* (London: George A. James, 1862).
———, *The Rules and Regulations, with an Alphabetical List of the Members of the Reform Club, with Dates of Entrance* (London: George A. James, 1864).
———, *The Rules and Regulations, with an Alphabetical List of the Members of the Reform Club, with Dates of Entrance* (London: Thomas Brettell, 1865).
———, *The Rules and Regulations, with an Alphabetical List of the Members of the Reform Club, with Dates of Entrance* (London: George A. James, 1866).
———, *The Rules and Regulations, with an Alphabetical List of the Members of the Reform Club, with Dates of Entrance* (London: George A. James, 1867).
Westminster Reform Club Minutebook.

Published sources

Anonymous, *A History of White's, Vol. II, Part II - A list of the members of White's* (London: Algernon Bourke, 1892).
Charles R. Dod (ed.), *Dod's Parliamentary Companion 1833* (London, 1833).[1]
———, *Dod's Parliamentary Companion 1835 (New Parliament Edition)* (London, 1835).
———, *Dod's Parliamentary Companion 1836* (London, 1836).
———, *Dod's Parliamentary Companion 1838 (New Parliament Edition)* (London, 1838).
———, *Dod's Parliamentary Companion 1841 (New Parliament Edition)* (London, 1841).

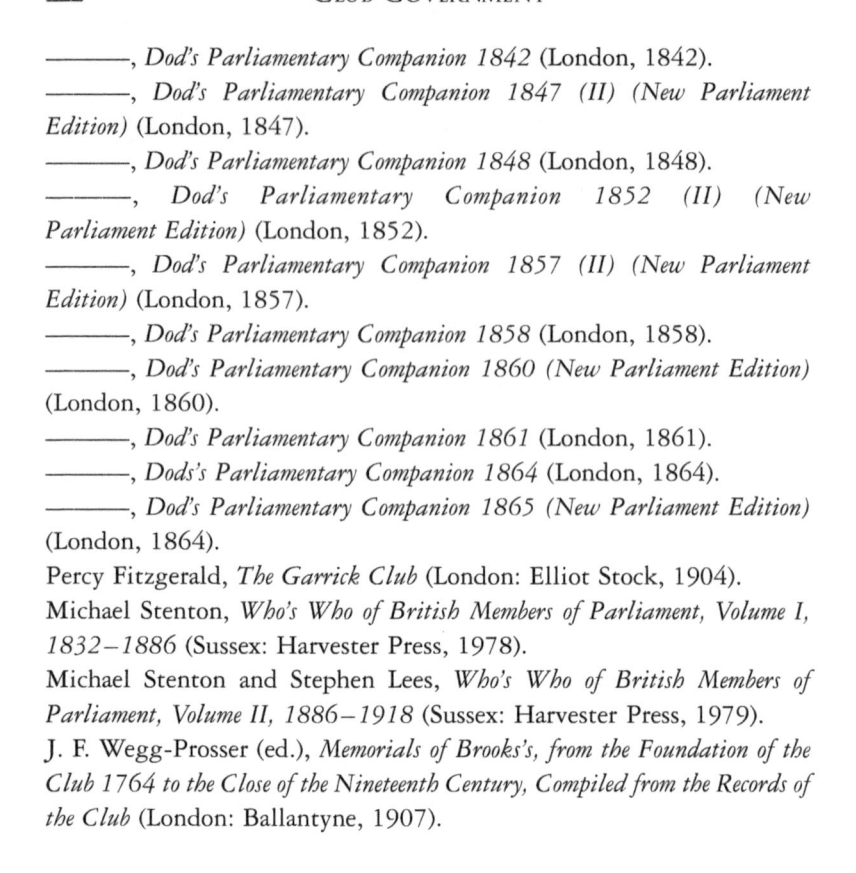

———, *Dod's Parliamentary Companion 1842* (London, 1842).
———, *Dod's Parliamentary Companion 1847 (II) (New Parliament Edition)* (London, 1847).
———, *Dod's Parliamentary Companion 1848* (London, 1848).
———, *Dod's Parliamentary Companion 1852 (II) (New Parliament Edition)* (London, 1852).
———, *Dod's Parliamentary Companion 1857 (II) (New Parliament Edition)* (London, 1857).
———, *Dod's Parliamentary Companion 1858* (London, 1858).
———, *Dod's Parliamentary Companion 1860 (New Parliament Edition)* (London, 1860).
———, *Dod's Parliamentary Companion 1861* (London, 1861).
———, *Dods's Parliamentary Companion 1864* (London, 1864).
———, *Dod's Parliamentary Companion 1865 (New Parliament Edition)* (London, 1864).
Percy Fitzgerald, *The Garrick Club* (London: Elliot Stock, 1904).
Michael Stenton, *Who's Who of British Members of Parliament, Volume I, 1832–1886* (Sussex: Harvester Press, 1978).
Michael Stenton and Stephen Lees, *Who's Who of British Members of Parliament, Volume II, 1886–1918* (Sussex: Harvester Press, 1979).
J. F. Wegg-Prosser (ed.), *Memorials of Brooks's, from the Foundation of the Club 1764 to the Close of the Nineteenth Century, Compiled from the Records of the Club* (London: Ballantyne, 1907).

Microfilm collections

Charles R. Dodd [later Dod] (ed.) (1842), *Autobiography of Five Hundred Members of Parliament; Being a Collection of Letters and Returned Schedules Received by Charles R. Dodd During the First Four Reformed Parliament, viz., from 1832 to December 1842, and Constituting Materials for Compiling the Successive Editions of the Parliamentary Pocket Companion* {microfilm] (New Haven, Connecticut: Yale University, James Marshall and Marie-Louise Osborn Collection [copy held at London: History of Parliament Trust]).

NOTES

Introduction

1. Andrew Grice, 'The Westminster Gentlemen's Club is Dead', *The Independent*, 19 May 2009.
2. Charles Dickens, *Our Mutual Friend* (London: Chapman and Hall, 1864) Book II, Chapter 3, p. 5.
3. Algernon West, *Recollections 1832–1866* (London: Smith, Elder & Co, 1899), p. 98.
4. Norman Gash, *Politics in the Age of Peel: A Study in the Technique of Parliamentary Representation, 1830–1850* (London: Longmans, 1953), pp. 393–430. Specifically, the quotation was reproduced on p. 406.
5. See Peter Clark, *British Clubs and Societies, 1580–1800: The Origins of an Associational World* (Oxford: Oxford University Press, 2000), especially pp. 71, 89, 181, 224, 228, 271 on Brooks's and White's clubs; see also Valérie Capdeville, *L'Âge d'Or des Clubs Londoniens (1730-1784)* (Paris: Editions Champion, 2008), *passim*.
6. Clark, *Clubs*, pp. 51–2; John Timbs, *Clubs and Club Life in London, with Anecdotes of its Famous Coffee Houses, Hostelries, and Taverns from the Seventeenth Century to the Present Time* (reprint, London: Chatto and Windus, 1908, of orig. edn, London, 1866), pp. 4, 13.
7. David Ashton and Paul W. Reid, *Ashton & Reid on Clubs and Associations*, 2nd edn (London: LexisNexis, 2011), pp. 3–4.
8. See the chapter on 'Making Cultural Capital: Clubs, Societies and New Forms of Binding Ties' in William C. Lubenow, *Liberal Intellectuals and Public Culture in Modern Britain, 1815–1914: Making Words Flesh* (Woodbridge: Boydell and Brewer, 2010), pp. 91–126.
9. It is impossible to summarise in one note all the political studies on local politics for this period, but notable full-length studies published in this area have included Richard W. Davis, *Political Change and Continuity, 1760–1885:*

A Buckinghamshire Study (Newton Abbot: David and Charles, 1972); Edwin Jaggard, *Cornwall Politics in the Age of Reform, 1790–1885* (Woodbridge: Boydell, 1999); and the landmark John A. Phillips, *The Great Reform Bill in the Boroughs: English Electoral Behaviour, 1818–1841* (Oxford: Clarendon Press, 1992). Also worth mentioning is the idiosyncratic and controversial 'deference theory' interpretation by D. C. Moore, 'Concession or Cure: The Sociological Premises of the First Reform Act', *Historical Journal*, 9 (1966), pp. 39–59, which was further elaborated upon in D. C. Moore, *The Politics of Deference: A Study of the Mid-Nineteenth Century English Political System* (Sussex: Harvester Press, 1976).

10. In 1900, there were 'more than 200 clubs in London, half of which had been founded within the previous thirty years.' Anthony Lejeune, *The Gentlemen's Clubs of London* (London: Macdonald and Jane's, 1979), p. 15.
11. See the chapter on 'regional and ethnic societies' in Clark, *Clubs*, pp. 274–308.
12. H. J. Hanham, *Elections and Party Management: Politics in the Time of Disraeli and Gladstone* (London: Longmans, 1959), p. 100.
13. Richard Shannon, *Gladstone: Peel's Inheritor, 1809–1865* (reprint, London: Penguin, 1999, of orig. edn, London: Hamish Hamilton, 1982), p. 43; John Ramsden, *An Appetite for Power: A History of the Conservative Party Since 1830* (London: HarperCollins, 1998), p. 47. Ramsden asserted that the Carlton Club was created to 'counterbalance the Whigs' Reform Club'.
14. Recent years have seen a growing literature on the political involvement of mid-Victorian women, including the case study by Sarah Richardson, 'The Role of Women in Electoral Politics in Yorkshire During the 1830s', *Northern History*, 32 (1996), pp. 133–51; the three studies contained in Catherine Hall, Keith McClelland, and Jane Rendell (eds), *Defining the Victorian Nation: Class, Race, Gender and the British Reform Act of 1867* (Cambridge: Cambridge University Press, 2000); and the full-length study in Kathryn Gleadle, *Borderline Citizens: Women, Gender, and Political Culture in Britain, 1815–1867* (Oxford: Oxford University Press, 2009), especially pp. 189–91.
15. Milne-Smith, 'Clubland' (2006), *passim*; Milne-Smith, 'Club Talk', pp. 86–109; Barbara Black, *A Room of His Own: A Literary-Cultural Study of Victorian Clubland* (Athens, Ohio: Ohio University Press, 2012), pp. 219–38.
16. Women's-only clubs would not flourish until the late Victorian and Edwardian eras. Elizabeth Crawford has helpfully compiled a guide to these clubs. The Ladies' Institute, which opened in 1860 at 14a Princes Street and later moved to 19 Langham Place, and which simultaneously served as the offices of the *English Woman's Journal*, was the first women's club run along the lines of their all-male Victorian counterparts, based around a permanent set of premises. But it was a short-lived venture, closing in 1867, and women's-only clubs only began to be set up in large numbers from the 1880. Elizabeth Crawford, *The Women's Suffrage Movement: A Reference Guide, 1866–1928* (London: Routledge, 2000), pp. 117–29, esp. p. 123. Furthermore, the eighteenth century presented a number of women-only clubs that were very similar counterparts

to the much earlier, smaller clubs of that age, most notably Ladies' Boodle's, which took the form of a society of ladies who met in rooms rented from Almack's, as discussed in Daniella Ben-Arie, 'A Ladies' Boodle's in the Eighteenth Century', Marcus Binney and David Mann (eds), *Boodle's: Celebrating 250 Years, 1762–2012* (London: Boodle's, 2013), pp. 177–80.

17. 'Clubland', *Oxford English Dictionary*, 2013, http://0-www.oed.com.pugwash.lib.warwick.ac.uk/view/Entry/34788 (accessed 10 November 2013).
18. 'Clubbable|Clubable', *Oxford English Dictionary*, 2013, http://0-www.oed.com.pugwash.lib.warwick.ac.uk/view/Entry/34790 (accessed 10 November 2013).
19. There are a number of meanings of 'club', with the older, unrelated definitions related to blunt instruments dating back to the thirteenth century; but the first one relevant to this book, rooted in the world of finance and found in Sherwood's 1632 *Dictionary, French and English Tongues* is 'To contribute (as one's share) towards a common stock.' The next relevant definition, 'To collect, gather together, or combine into one mass or body, to mass', is first credited to John Milton in 1641. An elaborated definition could be found by 1652's play *A Joviall Crew; or, The Merry Beggars* by Richard Brome, recognised by the *OED* as 'To combine *together* (or *with* others) in joint action; to combine as partners or members of a club.' A variation on the first definition could be found in Samuel Holland's 1656 play *Don Zara del Fogo: A Mock-Romance*, and is 'To conjoin, combine, or put together into a common stock, or to a common end.' A further definition is 'To form themselves into a club or mass', and was first found in the Richard II section of George Daniel's 1657 poem *Trinarchodia: The Several Reigns of Richard II, of Henry IV and Henry IV*. 'Club', *Oxford English Dictionary*, http://0-www.oed.com.pugwash.lib.warwick.ac.uk/view/Entry/34789 (accessed 10 November 2013).
20. Just two major clubs were to the east of Haymarket: the United University Club off Pall Mall East, which can still be seen in Figure 1.2 due to its proximity to Haymarket; and several hundred metres further east, the Union Club was on New Square (subsequently Trafalgar Square), though is not included in Figure 1.2. More clearly outside the boundaries of Clubland were the National Club in New Palace Yard (1846–52) and later located in Whitehall Gardens (1852–1913); the short-lived Westminster Reform Club on Great George Street (1834–6); and the temporary home of the Reform Club on Whitehall while its Pall Mall clubhouse was under construction. (1838–41). Nonetheless, each of these locations was still within ten minutes' walking distance of Clubland as defined above.
21. Seth Alexander Thévoz, 'Club Government', *History Today*, 63, February 2013, p. 52.
22. Anonymous, 'Noctes Ambrosionae', *Blackwood's Magazine*, May 1828, p. 794.
23. 'Mrs. Gore' [Catherine Grace Frances], *Cecil, a Peer: A Sequel to Cecil, or, The Adventures of a Coxcomb, Volume II* (London: T. and W. Boone, 1841), p. 288.
24. Peter Cunningham, *London As It Is* (London: John Murray, 1853), p. xxii.

25. Angus Hawkins, 'Lord Derby', R.W. Davis (ed.), *Lords of Parliament: Studies, 1714–1914* (Stanford, California: Stanford University Press, 1995), p. 150.
26. E. A. Smith, *The House of Lords in British Politics and Society, 1815–1911* (London: Longman, 1992), p. 104. This estimate seems consistent with my own findings in the Carlton Club's candidate's books.
27. See Frank O'Gorman, *Voters, Patrons, and Parties: The Unreformed Electoral System of Hanoverian England, 1734–1832* (Oxford: Clarendon Press, 1989), *passim*.
28. Hanham, *Elections*, p. 99.
29. A case for 1815–1885 is made by Derek Beales, *From Castlereagh to Gladstone, 1815–1885* (London: Nelson, 1969), especially pp. 13–17; Advocates of 1815–1915 have included Michael Bentley, *Politics Without Democracy, 1815–1914: Perception and Preoccupation in British Government* (rev. edn Oxford: Blackwell, 1999, of Oxford: Blackwell, 1984). Proponents of stretching back to the eighteenth century in contextualising this period include Asa Briggs, *The Age of Improvement, 1783–1867* (London: Longman, 1959), and Boyd Hilton, *The Age of Atonement: The Influence of Evangelicalism on Social and Economic Thought, 1795–1865* (Oxford: Oxford University Press, 1988), and an alternative set of dates presented by the same author, Boyd Hilton, *A Mad, Bad, and Dangerous People? England 1783–1846* (Oxford: Oxford University Press, 2006).
30. For this study, I am grateful to the Athenaeum for granting me a level of access to their archives normally reserved for that Club's own members. The only publications to have previously quoted from the Athenaeum archives are several privately published histories of the Club. I am equally grateful to the Carlton Club for allowing me access to their archives, putting up with a considerable amount of inconvenience as I daily made my way up a ladder into their attic, sending dust clouds into the kitchen below. Whilst the Carlton archives have been cited in a half dozen publications in the last century, the Junior Carlton (whose archive only transferred to the Carlton when they merged in 1977) has never been cited by any historians – not even official Carlton Club histories which also covered the Junior Carlton, due to the tight turnaround imposed by publication deadlines, for reasons subsequently elaborated upon in this Introduction.
31. Examples from the last few years include the launch of such digitisation projects as the ProQuest Parliamentary Papers website in 2006, the British Library nineteenth century newspapers website in 2007, and the extension of the latter as recently as 2012.
32. James Vernon, *Politics and the People: A Study in English Political Culture, c.1815–1867* (Cambridge: Cambridge University Press, 1993), p. 1.
33. See Richard Price, 'The Working Men's Club Movement and Victorian Social Reform Ideology', *Victorian Studies*, XV (1971), pp. 117–47; John Davis, 'Radical Clubs and London Politics, 1870–1900', David Feldman and Gareth Stedman Jones (eds), *Metropolis: London* (London: Macmillan, 1989); Stan

Shipley, *Club Life and Socialism in Mid-Victorian London* (London: Journeyman/ London History Workshop Centre, 1971).
34. Shipley, *Club Life*, pp. 77–80.
35. Anita O'Brien and Chris Miles, *A Peep into Clubland: Cartoons from Private London Clubs* (London: Cartoon Museum, 2009), p. 7.
36. See Robert Blake, *The Conservative Party from Peel to Churchill* (London: Fontana, 1970), pp. 34, 137–40; Gash, *Politics*, pp. 393–430; R. L. Hill, *Toryism and the People, 1832–1845* (London: Constable, 1929), pp. 37–41, 57; Robert Stewart, *The Foundation of the Conservative Party, 1830–1867* (London: Longman, 1978), pp. 138–41.
37. Philip Salmon, *Electoral Reform at Work: Local Politics and National Parties, 1832–1841* (Woodbridge: Boydell, 2002), pp. 55–7; Ronald K. Huch and Paul R. Ziegler, *Joseph Hume: The People's M.P.* (Philadelphia: Diane Publishing, 1985), p. 95; Vernon, *Politics*, p. 186.
38. W. Fraser Rae, 'Political Clubs and Party Organisation', *Nineteenth Century*, 3 (1878), pp. 908–32. Contrast Fraser Rae's description of 'not incorrectly inferred' Reform Club activities, p. 919, with the unsourced supposition of the Carlton Club's activities, p. 920. Although he did not mention it in the article, Fraser Rae was a member of the Reform Club – see Reform Club archive, Reform Club, London, 'Reform Club Ballot Book Vol. 1, 1832–56.'
39. Moisei Ostrogorski, *Democracy and the Organisation of Political Parties* (reprint, New York: Macmillan, 1970, of orig. edn, London: Macmillan, 1902), vol. 1, pp. 143–5, 421–2.
40. Anthony Sampson, *The Anatomy of Britain* (London: Hodder and Stoughton, 1962), p. 57.
41. Gash, *Politics*, pp. 393–430.
42. Ibid.; Norman Gash, 'The Organisation of the Conservative Party, 1832–1846, Part I: The Parliamentary Organisation', *Parliamentary History*, 1 (1982), pp. 137–59; Norman Gash, 'The Organisation of the Conservative Party, 1832–1846, Part II: The Electoral Organisation', *Parliamentary History*, 2 (1983), pp. 131–52.
43. Gash, *Politics*, p. 138. The practice was discontinued in 1839.
44. Robert Blake, *Disraeli* (London: Eyre and Spottiswoode, 1966), p. 271.
45. Ian Newbould, 'Whiggery and the Growth of Party 1830–1841: Organisation and the Challenge of Reform', *Parliamentary History*, 4 (1985), pp. 137–56.
46. Norman Gash, 'Bonham and the Conservative Party', Norman Gash (ed.), *Pillars of Government, and Other Essays of State and Society, c.1770–c.1880* (London: Edward Arnold, 1986), p. 110; Stewart, *Conservative*, pp. 136–41, section headed 'Bonham and the Carlton'.
47. Llewelyn Woodward, *The Age of Reform, 1815–1870* (Oxford: Oxford University Press, 1962), p. 88; Hill, *Toryism*, pp. 37–9.
48. Hill, *Toryism*, p. 57.
49. Blake, *Conservative*, p. 140.

50. Ibid., p. 146. Note that Robert Stewart later established that this headquarters was formed three years earlier, in 1867. Stewart, *Conservative*, p. 338.
51. Michael Rush, *The Role of the Member of Parliament Since 1868: From Gentlemen to Players* (Oxford: Oxford University Press, 2001), p. 45.
52. O'Gorman, *Voters*, pp. 289–91, 327.
53. Stewart, *Conservative*, p. 130; Seth Alexander Thévoz, 'Cambridge University Liberal Club, 1886–1916: A Study in Early Student Political Organisation', *Journal of Liberal History*, 91, Summer 2016, p. 10.
54. Margaret Escott, 'Wales', D. R. Fisher (ed.), *History of Parliament: The Commons, 1820–1832, Volume I: Introductory Survey and Appendices* (Cambridge: Cambridge University Press, 2009), p. 66.
55. Andrew Shields, *The Irish Conservative Party, 1852–1868: Land, Politics and Religion* (Dublin: Irish Academic Press, 2007), pp. xv, 7–8.
56. Gash, *Aristocracy*, pp. 154–5.
57. Antonia Taddei, 'London Clubs in the Late Nineteenth Century' (MSci thesis, University of Oxford, 1998); Antonia Taddei, 'London Clubs in the Late Nineteenth Century', Oxford University Social and Economic History Group paper (1999).
58. George Macaulay Trevelyan, *Lord Grey of the Reform Bill: Being the Life of Charles, Second Earl Grey* (London: Longmans, 1920), pp. 15, 43, 202. See Chapter 2 for supporting statistics on Brooks's membership among Whigs, which seems to largely bear out Trevelyan's argument, while showing that the membership of Brooks's was far more politically diverse than simply as a bastion of Whiggery.
59. Donald Southgate, 'From Disraeli to Law: Chapter 2 – Dogdays and Daring', R. A. Butler (ed.), *The Conservatives: A History from their Origins to 1965* (London: Allen and Unwin, 1977), p. 145; Gary W. Cox, *The Efficient Secret: The Cabinet and the Development of Political Parties in Victorian England* (Cambridge: Cambridge University Press, 1987), p. 34.
60. Alexander Llewelyn, *The Decade of Reform: The 1830s* (Newton Abbott: David and Charles, 1972), p. 59.
61. Blake, *Conservative*, p. 34.
62. Jonathan Parry, *The Rise and Fall of Liberal Government in Britain* (New Haven, Connecticut: Yale University Press, 1993), pp. 130–1.
63. D. R. Fisher, 'George Spencer Churchill, Marquess of Blandford' (1793–1857), D. R. Fisher (ed.), *The House of Commons 1820–1832, Volume VII: Members S–Y* (Cambridge: Cambridge University Press, 2009), p. 237.
64. Gash, *Aristocracy*, p. 156.
65. Joanna Innes, '"Reform" in English Public Life: The Fortunes of a Word', Arthur Burns and Joanna Innes (eds), *Rethinking the Age of Reform: Britain 1780–1850* (Cambridge: Cambridge University Press, 2003), p. 95.
66. Taddei, *Clubs* (1999), pp. 7–13; Jane Rendell, 'The Clubs of St. James's: Places of Public Patriarchy – Exclusivity, Domesticity and Secrecy', *Journal of Architecture*, 4 (1999), pp. 167–89.

67. J. Mordaunt Crook, *The Rise of the Nouveaux Riches: Style and Status in Victorian and Edwardian Architecture* (London: John Murray, 1999), *passim*.
68. See Amy Milne-Smith, 'Clubland: Masculinity, Status and Community in the Gentlemen's Clubs of London, c.1880–1914' (PhD thesis, University of Toronto 2006); Amy Milne-Smith, *London Clubland: A Cultural History of Gender and Class in Late Victorian Britain* (London: Palgrave Macmillan, 2011); Amy Milne-Smith, 'A Flight to Domesticity? Making a Home in the Gentlemen's Clubs of London, 1880–1914', *Journal of British Studies*, 45 (2006), pp. 796–818; Amy Milne-Smith, 'Club Talk: Gossip, Masculinity, and the Importance of Oral Communities in Late Nineteenth-Century London', *Gender and History*, 21 (2009), pp. 86–109 respectively. Milne-Smith, *Clubland* (2011), p. 210 graciously acknowledges the importance of the political dimension explored by this author, and of the need for further work on this topic.
69. Correspondence with Amy Milne-Smith, 16 February 2010.
70. Black (2012); See also my review, Seth Alexander Thévoz, 'Review: A Room of His Own', *Canadian Journal of History* 49:2, Spring/Summer 2014, pp. 101–3.
71. Benjamin B. Cohen, *In the Club: Associational Life in Colonial South Asia* (Hyderabad: Orient BlackSwan, 2015), *passim*.
72. See Clark, *Clubs, passim*.
73. Louis C. Jackson, *History of the United Service Club* (London: United Service Club, 1937), p. v.
74. *The Times*, 21 October 1982, p. 9.
75. One of the more demonstrably false incidents relates to the East India United Service Club. Each of the club's official histories testify that it was in the Club's one-time Ladies' Drawing Room that the Duke of Wellington's victorious despatch from Waterloo was handed to the Prince Regent in 1815, and in June 2011 the Club went so far as to rename the room the Wellington Room in honour of this event. Despite giving a long and otherwise accurate account of the building's various uses since the eighteenth century, both club historians Denys Forrest and Charlie Jacoby omit to mention that this could not have happened in the same room, as the previous building was pulled down and rebuilt to a new design in 1866, 51 years after Waterloo. Indeed, the room dimensions, positioning and even elevation of the original ballroom have little in common with those of the present-day 'Wellington Room'. For the 'official' club version of events, see Denys Forrest, *Foursome in St. James's* (London: East India Club, 1982), p. 14; Charlie Jacoby, *The East India Club: A History* (London: East India Club, 2009), pp. 18–9. Neither book makes any mention of the old clubhouse's demolition. For accounts of the building's demolition and reconstruction by the architect Charles Lee, see Arthur Irwin Dasent, *The History of St. James's Square and the Foundation of the West End of London, with a Glimpse of Whitehall in the Reign of Charles the Second* (London: Macmillan, 1895), pp. 124, 240.
76. Examples include Fitzroy, *Travellers'*; R.C. Rome, *Union Club: An Illustrated Descriptive Record of the Oldest Members' Club in London, Founded Circa 1799* (London: B.T. Batsford, 1948).

77. Fitzroy, *Travellers'*, photographic plate between pp. 30–1.
78. Roger Fulford, *Boodle's, 1762–1962: A Short History* (London: Boodle's, 1962) has just fifty-two pages of text. Note that this was recently superseded by the first full-length history of Boodle's, Binney and Mann (eds), *Boodle's*, which is some five times lengthier than its predecessor.
79. The histories of political clubs referred to are Sir Charles Petrie and Alistair Cooke, *The Carlton Club* (rev. edn, London: Carlton Club, 2007, of orig. edn, London: Eyre and Spottiswoode, 1955); Phelps, *Power and the Party*; Louis Fagan, *The Reform Club* (London: B. Quaritch, 1887); J. Mordaunt Crook, *The Reform Club* (London: Reform Club, 1973); George Woodbridge, *The Reform Club, 1836–1978: A History from the Club's Records* (New York: Clearwater, 1978); Russell Burlingham and Roger Billis (eds), *Reformed Characters: The Reform Club in History and Literature, an Anthology with Commentary* (London: Reform Club, 2005); Anonymous, *The History of White's, with the Betting Book from 1743 to 1878 and a List of Members from 1736 to 1892*, 2 vols (London: Algernon Bourke, 1892); Percy Colson, *White's: 1693–1950* (London: Heinemann, 1951); Anthony Lejeune, *White's: The First Three Hundred Years* (London: A&C Black, 1993); Anonymous, *Memorials of Brooks's, 1764–1900* (London: Brooks's, 1907); Henry S. Eeles and Earl Spencer, *Brooks's, 1764–1964* (London: Country Life, 1964); Ziegler and Seward (eds), *Brooks's*, J. Mordaunt Crook and Charles Sebag-Montefiore, *Brooks's, 1764–2014: The Story of a Whig Club* (London: Paul Holberton, 2013); Crockford's, the social club whose building later became the Liberal-aligned Devonshire, has a chapter in Henry Turner Waddy, *The Devonshire Club and "Crockford's"* (London: Eveleigh Nash, 1919), pp. 116–52, and the Junior Carlton has a short chapter in Phelps, *Power and the Party*, pp. 35–9, the latter stressing how the Junior Carlton affected the Carlton.
80. A. L. Humphreys, *Crockford's* (London: Hutchinson, 1953), pp. 199–204.
81. Guy Boas, *The Garrick Club, 1831–1964* (London: Garrick Club, 1948 [rev. 1964 edition]), pp. 41–54; Richard Hough, *The Ace of Clubs: A History of the Garrick* (London: Andre Deutsch, 1986), p. 72; Lejeune, *Clubs* (1979), pp. 122–3; Phelps, *Power and the Party*, p. ix.
82. Compare Fagan, *Reform*, pp. 1–34; Crook, *Reform*, pp. 1–5; Woodbridge, *Reform*, pp. 1–38; and Burlingham and Billis, *Reformed* pp. 12–20.
83. Compare Petrie and Cooke, *Carlton*, pp. 15–37; Phelps, *Power and the Party*, pp. 1–13; and Jolles, *Jews*, pp. 3–8.
84. Timbs, *Club Life*, passim.
85. See Arthur Griffiths, *Clubs and Clubmen* (London: Hutchinson, 1907); Henry C. Shelley, *Inns and Taverns of Old London: Setting Forth the Historical and Literary Associations of Those Ancient Hostelries, Together with an Account of the Most Notable Coffee-Houses, Clubs, and Pleasure Gardens of the British Metropolis* (Boston: L. C. Page, 1909); Ralph Nevill, *London Clubs* (London: Chatto and Windus, 1912).
86. Henry Sweet Escott, *Club Makers and Club Members* (London: T. F. Unwin, 1914), particularly pp. 100–18, 147–70, 212–36.

87. Ibid., pp. 190–3, 198–201; Fagan, *Reform*, p. 69.
88. Taddei, 'Clubs' (1999), pp. 18–19.
89. Sampson, *Anatomy*, pp. 191–223. This chapter was retained in the second edition, Anthony Sampson, *The Anatomy of Britain Today* (London: Hodder and Stoughton, 1965), but omitted from all editions from the third, Anthony Sampson, *The New Anatomy of Britain* (London: Hodder and Stoughton, 1971), onwards.
90. See Lejeune, *Clubs* (1979) and Anthony Lejeune, *The Gentlemen's Clubs of London* (London: Stacey International, 2012), *passim*. Although the latter book is technically just an updated edition of the original, it contains sufficient new material – much of it by other authors – to be considered to be a different book.
91. Lejeune, *White's*, flyleaf; the publishers in question are A&C Black, better known for printing *Who's Who* than for forays into history. The book's inaccuracies are unsurprising – much of the book is sourced from conversations with club members, presenting unsourced third-hand information as fact. Lejeune's *modus operandi* was to secure invitations as a guest to all the surviving London clubs between 1969 and 1979, and to then write up a short chapter on each club based on anecdotes told over lunch or dinner, and seldom (if ever) substantiated. The book is utterly charming, but completely unreliable. The revised and updated 2012 edition is far, far worse, with multiple major errors on most pages; as is acknowledged by the revised edition's byline 'Anthony Lejeune and his friends' and several implicit references in its introduction, much of it was ghostwritten by others. Several chapters of the new edition reproduce inaccurate content from Wikipedia articles, verbatim.
92. Lejeune interviewed in Brian Wheeler, 'If anybody wants me, I'll be at my club', *BBC News*, 23 November 2003, http://news.bbc.co.uk/1/hi/magazine/3227664.stm (accessed 10 June 2010); Ephraim Hardcastle, 'Ferry blackballed by White's', *Daily Mail*, 5 February 2007, http://www.dailymail.co.uk/debate/columnists/article-434145/Ferry-blackballed-Whites.html (accessed 4 September 2010).
93. Enquiries with White's have revealed that the appendices of the 1892 history of the club in fact reproduced all archival holdings from before 1892, and that subsequent bomb damage in the Blitz resulted in the loss of many of the original papers, so that the privately-printed 1892 club history is now the only record of some of this material. Personal correspondence with Christopher Palmer-Tomkinson, former Chairman of White's, 16 September 2010, who was kind enough to pursue this; Rome, *Union Club*, especially pp. 10–35, extensively quotes from the papers of the Union Club, but these are believed to be lost since the club's dissolution in 1949.
94. Anonymous, *White's*, Vol. II, pp. 1–259.
95. George Macaulay Trevelyan, *Lord Grey of the Reform Bill: Being the Life of Charles, Second Earl of Grey* (London: Longmans, 1920), pp. 66, 106, 146n.
96. Le Marchant diary, 13 May 1832, quoted in Arthur Aspinall (ed.), *Three Early Nineteenth Century Diaries* (London: Williams & Norgate, 1952), p. 252;

John Vincent (ed.), *Disraeli, Derby and the Conservative Party: Journals and Memoirs of Edward Henry, Lord Stanley, 1849–1869* (Sussex: Harvester Press, 1978), p. 56.

97. Examples include Benjamin Disraeli, *Sybil, or the Two Nations* (reprint, London: Folio Society, 1983, of orig. edn, London, 1845); Anthony Trollope, *Phineas Finn* (reprint, London: Folio Society, 1997, of orig. edn, London, 1869); William Makepeace Thackeray, *The History of Pendennis* (reprint, London: Fontana, 1986, of orig. edn, London, 1849–50).

Chapter 1   The Development of Political Clubs

1. Gash, *Politics*, pp. 393–430.
2. See Timbs, *Clubs and Club Life*; Escott, *Club Makers*; Charles Graves, *Leather Armchairs: The Chivas Regal Book of London Clubs* (London: Cassell, 1963). Less recommended is the more usually cited Lejeune, *Clubs* (1979), and Lejeune, *Clubs* (2012), for reasons set out in the Introduction.
3. As noted in the Introduction, an obvious example can be found in both Shannon, *Gladstone* (1982), p. 43 and Ramsden, *Appetite for Power*, p. 47, each of which claims that the Carlton Club was founded in response to the Reform Club, rather than vice-versa. Richard Shannon, *Gladstone: God and Politics* (London: Hambledon Continuum, 2007), p. 20, repeats the mistake when noting that Gladstone joined the Carlton Club in the 1830s, the Carlton being described as a response to the Reform Club.
4. Notable exceptions to the neglect of these two clubs are John Wolffe's drawing upon the National Club archive throughout Wolffe, *Crusade*, *passim* and the editorial notes on the Free Trade Club in the recently published Anthony Howe (ed.), *The Letters of Richard Cobden: Volume One, 1815–1847* (Oxford: Oxford University Press, 2007); Anthony Howe (ed.), *The Letters of Richard Cobden: Volume Two, 1848–1853* (Oxford: Oxford University Press, 2009); Anthony Howe and Simon Morgan (eds), *The Letters of Richard Cobden: Volume Three, 1854–1859* (Oxford: Oxford University Press, 2012), *passim*.
5. See Clark, *Clubs*, especially pp. 71, 89, 181, 224, 228, 271; Capdeville, *L'Âge d'Or des Clubs* (2008), *passim*. Valérie Capdeville, '"Clubbability": A Revolution in London Sociability?', *Lumen*, 35 (2016), pp. 63–80.
6. Kellow Chesney, *The Victorian Underworld* (London: Temple Smith, 1970), pp. 288–9. For a fuller contextualisation on Victorian gambling, see Adrian Harvey, *The Beginnings of a Commercial Sporting Culture in Britain, 1793–1850* (Aldershot: Ashgate, 2004), *passim*, and Mike Aherne, 'A Dangerous Obsession? Gambling and Social Stability', Judith Rowbotham and Kim Stevenson (eds), *Behaving Badly: Social Panic and Moral Outrage – Victorian and Modern Parallels* (Aldershot: Ashgate, 2003), pp. 127–41, while a further perspective is offered by Carolyn Downs, 'Two Fat Ladies: The Hidden History of Women and Gambling', *History Today*, 57 (2007), vol. 7, pp. 27–9.

NOTES TO PAGES 24–27   233

7. See the timeline of 'Some important dates in the history of White's', Percy Colson, *White's, 1693–1950* (London: Heinemann, 1951), pp. 137–8.
8. Ibid., p. 137, and the 1755 move by White's was corroborated in Timbs, *Clubs*, p. 95. Lejeune, *Clubs* (2012), p. 225 dates this move by White's to 1753 but, as noted in the Introduction, almost every page of the latest edition of Lejeune is littered with multiple errors on basic matters of fact and chronology, and the book reproduces as fact unsubstantiated third-hand accounts, unchecked from the gossip of long liquid lunches, as well as lifting (incorrect) material verbatim from Wikipedia. It is, in short, about as trustworthy as a copy of Raspe's *The Surprising Adventures of Baron Münchhausen* with its well-known flights of fantasy, and so whenever discrepancies with Lejeune's account have occurred in this book, they have been routinely ignored; although Lejeune remains invaluable as a polemic. For an example of where Lejeune's embellishments and generalisations directly affect the remit of this book, see footnote 9 of this chapter.
9. Lejeune, *Clubs* (2012), pp. 225–31, including Lejeune's assertion on p. 228 that the term 'all Tories' equates with 'most members of White's'. This assertion is disproved by the data presented in Chapter 2.
10. Richard Ollard, 'The Brooks's of Charles James Fox', Ziegler and Seward (eds), *Brooks's*, pp. 36–7.
11. Timbs, *Clubs*, p. 104.
12. Anonymous, *Whites*, vol. 1, p. 150.
13. Colson, *White's*, p. 55.
14. Anonymous, *Whites*, vol. 1, p. 151.
15. *News and Sunday Herald*, 10 December 1835, quoted in Anonymous, *Whites*, vol. 1, p. 213.
16. Stewart, *Conservative*, p. 73.
17. *News and Sunday Herald*, 10 December 1835, quoted in Anonymous, *Whites*, vol. 1, p. 217.
18. George Otto Trevelyan, *The Early History of Charles James Fox* (London: Longmans, 1880), p. 81.
19. Wegg-Prosser (ed.), *Memorials of Brooks's*, p. x.
20. Timbs, *Clubs*, pp. 76–91, with pp. 79–87 on Charles James Fox and Brooks's; Richard Ollard, 'Fox', Ziegler and Seward (eds), *Brooks's*, pp. 33–44; Charles Sebag-Montefiore (ed.), *Charles James Fox | Brooks's and Whiggery | The Fox Club* (London: Brooks's, 2006), pp. 3–7.
21. Philip Ziegler, 'Brooks's of the Reform Bill', Ziegler and Seward (eds), *Brooks's*, p. 45.
22. Eeles and Spencer, *Brooks's*, pp. 82–3.
23. See Waddy, *Devonshire Club*, pp. 128–50; Humphries, *Crockford's*, especially pp. 1–104.
24. Quoted in O'Brien and Miles, *Peep into Clubland*, p. 7.
25. Rome, *Union Club*, p. 4n. The club had generally claimed a foundation date of 1805, but the discovery of a commemorative coin marking the club's foundation in 1799 prompted a re-evaluation of its origins.

26. Ibid., pp. 9–13.
27. Eeles and Spencer, *Brooks's*, p. 121; Colson, *White's*, p. 121; Fulford, *Boodle's*, pp. 37, 41.
28. Bernard Darwin, *British Clubs* (London: Collins, 1943), p. 11.
29. On 22 August 1863, Disraeli wrote to Lord Malmesbury suggesting that he join him among the trustees of the new Junior Carlton Club 'if no liability is incurred by the Trustees'. Malmesbury replied on the 27 August agreeing to the proposal, 'on the condition that I incur no liability. The fate of the Trustees of the Picadilly [sic] & Young Crockford's is a warning.' M. G. Wiebe, Mary S. Millar, Ann P. Robson and Ellen L. Hawman (eds), *Benjamin Disraeli Letters: Volume Eight, 1860–1864* (Toronto: University of Toronto Press, 2009), pp. 296–7. Another element of this share ownership has accounted for the closure of many of the nineteenth century clubs in the twentieth century, since diminishing membership and rising land values meant that each member's share of a club was worth more, and so several clubs have voted themselves out of existence to cash in their assets – as with the Constitutional Club. However, this phenomenon was only truly pronounced when club membership began declining after World War I. As long as clubs were expanding, as was the case throughout the nineteenth century, it was not a significant pressure.
30. Reform Club archive, Reform Club, London, MS 'Minutes of the Westminster Reform Club, 1834–8', 26 March 1834, ff. 16–9.
31. Compare, for instance, the text of Athenaeum Club, *An Alphabetical List of the Members, with the Rules and Regulations, of the Athenaeum* (London: William Clowes, 1826), with the rules in Carlton Club, *A List of the Members of the Carlton Club, April 1836, with a List of the Trustees and Committee* (London: Roake and Varty, 1836); Club rules listed in Reform Club, *Reform Club List of Members, August 1st 1836* (London: Reform Club, 1836); and Reform Club, *Reform Club Bye-Laws* (London: Reform Club, 1862).
32. Cohen, *In the Club* (2015), p. 27.
33. Anonymous, *White's*, vol. 1, p. 206.
34. Penelope J. Corfield, *Power and the Professions in Britain, 1700–1850* (London: Routledge, 1995), pp. 181–3.
35. *Illustrated London News*, 10 February 1844, p. 85.
36. *News and Sunday Herald*, 10 December 1835, quoted in Anonymous, *Whites*, vol. 1, p. 213.
37. F. H. W. Sheppard (ed.), *Survey of London, Vol. 29: St. James's, Westminster* (London: Athlone Press, 1960), p. 348.
38. J. Mordaunt Crook, 'Metropolitan Improvements: John Nash and the Picturesque', Celina Fox (ed.), *London: World City, 1800–1840* (New Haven, Connecticut: Yale University Press, 1992), p. 93.
39. Ibid., p. 77. See also Ralph B. Pugh, *The Crown Estate* (London: HMSO, 1960).
40. The only conspicuous survivor of Carlton House existed in the War Office on Pall Mall, which incorporated one room of the demolished house, and dominated a large central part of the street, between the Carlton Club and the

Oxford and Cambridge Club. This building, too, was eventually demolished and replaced in 1911 by the Royal Automobile Club, the largest clubhouse ever built; but the remaining room from Carlton House still stands today, integrated into the RAC as its White Drawing Room.

41. Alistair Cooke [subsequently Lord Lexden], 'Club and Party, 1832–2007', Charles Petrie and Alistair Cooke, *The Carlton Club, 1832–2007* (London: Carlton Club, 2007), pp. 226–7.
42. Michael Sharpe, *The Political Committee of the Reform Club* (London: Reform Club, 1996), p. 3.
43. Petrie and Cooke, *Carlton Club*, (2007), pp. 4, 249. Almost all of the thirty committee members in 1832 were parliamentarians: the Marquesses of Salisbury, Chandos and Graham, the Earls of Clanwilliam, De La Warr, Falmouth, Rosslyn and Wicklow, Lord Viscounts Maitland and Stormont, Lord Ellenborough, Lord Saltoun and Abernethy, Lord Stuart de Rothesay, Lord Eliot, Lord Granville Somerset, Sir Robert Bateson Bt MP, Hon. William S. Best MP, Sir George Clerk Bt MP, Rt Hon Henry Goulburn MP, Sir Alexander Gray Grant MP, Rt Hon Sir Henry Hardinge Bt, Hon Lloyd Kenyon MP, Winthrop M. Praed MP, Philip Pusey MP, Charles Ross MP, W.E. Tomline, Sir Richard Vyvyan Bt MP, Charles Baring Wall MP, and Sir John Walsh Bt MP.
44. Gash, *Politics*, p. 395.
45. See *The Times*, 2 June 1832, p. 5 for Berkshire, *The Times*, 4 May 1831, p. 3 for Beverley and *The Times*, 27 October 1831, p. 3 for Cambridge. Subsequently, *The Times*, 1 November 1831, p. 3 was more specific in implying bribery, referring to the Gang's 'needy dependents' amidst the Cambridge electorate.
46. *Sheffield Independent, and Yorkshire and Derbyshire Advertiser*, 3 March 1832, p. 3.
47. Norman Gash, *Sir Robert Peel: The Life of Sir Robert Peel after 1830* (rev. edn, London: Longman, 1986, of orig. edn, London: Longman, 1972), p. 25. This is corroborated by *Figaro in London*, 7 January 1832, p. 17, which refers to Charles Street Gang discussions on reorganisation, on 'the twelfth day of Christmas' in January 1832.
48. Gash, *Politics*, p. 395.
49. *Figaro in London*, 7 January 1832, p. 18.
50. *Sheffield Independent, and Yorkshire and Derbyshire Advertiser*, 3 March 1832, p. 7. This report also contains a list of derogatory punning cognomens for all of the Charles Street Gang members named, apparently leaked by a disgruntled staff member.
51. Timbs, *Clubs*, p. 233.
52. Cited in ibid.
53. 'The History of the Club', Carlton Club, 2009, http://www.carltonclub.co.uk/theclub.asp (accessed 27 January 2010).
54. *The Times*, 18 May 1832, p. 3. Revealingly, this is the last instance in which the national or local press referred to the 'Charles Street Gang'; it is fair to surmise that, by the summer of 1832, it had come to be identified with the successor organisation it had merged into.

55. CREST St. James's planning records, National Archives, Kew, London, CREST/35/2203, Carlton Club correspondence relating to architecture and planning of clubhouse, 1830–4.
56. Carlton Club archive, Carlton Club, London, MS 'Carlton Club Committee Minutes, Volume 2, 1835–9', 8 and 15 December 1835. Petrie only notes that the club was hosted by the Carlton hotel for a short time, and so subsequent accounts have tended to assume that the Carlton opened its purpose-built clubhouse in 1836; but the surviving minute book for the period makes it clear that this did not happen until several months into 1837.
57. This building was bombed in October 1940, when it was abandoned by the Carlton Club; and was finally demolished in 1955. Alistair Cooke, 'Post-war trials and tribulations', Petrie and Cooke, *Carlton*, p. 179.
58. Carlton Club, *List of Members* (1836), p. 3.
59. Mordaunt Crook, *Rise of the Nouveaux Riches*, pp. 244–5, 250. See also pp. 244–59 more generally for Mordaunt Crook's extensive lists of examples of the men who fit into these archetypes.
60. Fagan, *Reform Club*, p. 64.
61. Mordaunt Crook, *Reform Club*, p. 4; Lejeune, *Clubs* (1979), p. 205; and the ever-misleading Lejeune, *Clubs* (2012), p. 183.
62. Woodbridge, *Reform Club*, p. 1.
63. Stuart J. Reid, *Life and Letters of the First Earl of Durham, 1792–1840* (London: Longmans, 1906), vol. 2, pp. 74–80. For more extensive material on this, see Lambton MSS, Lambton Castle, County Durham, 'Mem'dum by Molesworth on formation of Reform Club (fwded by Parkes)', 7 February 1836, quoted in P. J. Salmon (ed.), *Letters of Joseph Parkes* (Oxford: privately printed, 1993). (Book is chronologically ordered, but pages are unnumbered.)
64. Reform Club archive, Reform Club, London, MS 'Reform Club Founding Resolution, 1836'.
65. See, for instance, Philip Ziegler, 'Brooks's of the Reform Bill', Ziegler and Seward (eds), *Brooks's*, pp. 45–58; W. Fraser Rae, 'Political Clubs and Party Organisation', *Nineteenth Century*, 3:15 (May, 1878), p. 912.
66. Parry, *Liberal Government*, p. 130.
67. David A. Haury, *The Origins of the Liberal Party and Liberal Imperialism: The Career of Charles Buller, 1806–1848* (New York: Garland Publishing, 1987), p. 91.
68. Reform Club archive, Reform Club, London, MS 'Reform Club Founding Resolution, 1836', Appendix: Minutes of meeting, 18 February 1836 at 3 Cleveland Row.
69. Gash, *Politics*, p. 403. This has been a remarkably resilient misapprehension, most recently echoed in the otherwise outstanding Joseph Coohill, *Ideas of the Liberal Party: Perceptions, Agendas and Liberal Politics in the House of Commons, 1832–1852* (Oxford: Wiley-Blackwell, 2011), p. 96; in the very same section Coohill very graciously cited this (then forthcoming) book in its original thesis form as hopefully clarifying our understanding of the political role of clubs. I can only hope it meets expectations, and apologise for the somewhat

churlish naming and shaming of this one detail which has been a recurring misunderstanding among historians for over a century!
70. There is no complete membership list for the Westminster Reform Club, but its membership can be calculated from the complete financial records of the Club's debts on its closure in 1836, when each member had to contribute 11 guineas to pay off the Club's debts. Reform Club archive, Reform Club, London, MS 'Minutes of the Westminster Reform Club 1834–8', ff. 183–91. Note that the Reform Club was limited to 1,200 members at its launch, but this figure excluded MPs and, if one includes them, the club's membership by the late 1830s was almost 1,500 – see Chapter 2.
71. *Morning Post*, 2 May 1835, p. 5.
72. Reform Club archive, Reform Club, London, MS 'Minutes of the Westminster Reform Club 1834–8', ff. 1–7, 10; Fraser Rae, 'Organisation', p. 912.
73. Reform Club archive, Reform Club, London, MS 'Minutes of the Westminster Reform Club 1834–8', undated letter (c.1870s?) from W. R. Sydney to C. De La Pryme, with reminiscences of the club, pasted into the inside front cover of the minute book.
74. *Age*, 14 April 1833, p. 118, which predicted that 'whatever [d'Eyncourt] patronises must fail – wherefore the days of the Westminster are numbered'. See also Seth Alexander Thévoz, 'Database of London Club Memberships of MPs, 1832–68.'
75. *Morning Chronicle*, 8 April 1833, p. 3.
76. *Satirist, and the Censor of the Time*, 6 April 1834, p. 112, which also taunted the club over the length of time taken to launch.
77. Reform Club archive, Reform Club, London, MS 'Minutes of the Westminster Reform Club 1834–8', f. 11. Note that this building was on the site of what has since the late 1830s been the Institute of Civil Engineers, mentioned earlier in this chapter.
78. Reform Club archive, Reform Club, London, MS 'Minutes of the Westminster Reform Club 1834–8', ff. 35, 65.
79. Reform Club archive, Reform Club, London, MS 'Minutes of the Westminster Reform Club 1834–8', 26 March 1834, f. 16.
80. Total membership figure calculated from the club's debts (which were divided per member at the time of closure in 1836, making 105 members), and a list of parliamentary members (69 of whom are mentioned by name in the club minute book – it is also conceivable that more than sixty-nine members were MPs).
81. The club also seemed light on aristocratic members. Its only titled member was Lord Dunboyne, an Irish peer who was not a representative peer, and so did not sit in the Lords. Reform Club archive, Reform Club, London, MS 'Minutes of the Westminster Reform Club 1834–8', f. 31.
82. Reform Club archive, Reform Club, London, MS 'Minutes of the Westminster Reform Club 1834–8', f. 125. The largest part of this debt was due to wine purchases, which amounted to £459 3s 8d.

83. Reform Club archive, Reform Club, London, MS 'Minutes of the Westminster Reform Club 1834–8', 26 June 1835, f. 156.
84. Reform Club archive, Reform Club, London, MS 'Minutes of the Westminster Reform Club 1834–8', ff. 195, 220.
85. It is worth noting that the Reform Club archive also contains minute books from another defunct club, the apolitical Parthenon Club. No-one has ever suggested that this club played any political role, and scrutiny of the minute book confirms this. In both cases, it is overwhelmingly likely that the individuals who held on to the minute books of the Westminster Reform and Parthenon Clubs later joined the Reform Club, and donated the minute books to the new club's archives. See Reform Club archive, Reform Club, London, 'Parthenon Club Minutes of the Committee, 1859–61'.
86. Fraser Rae, 'Organisation', pp. 908–32; Fagan, *Reform Club*, pp. 28–9.
87. Reform Club archive, Reform Club, London, MS 'Minutes of the Westminster Reform Club 1834–8', ff. 51, 99–100. Members who had an overdue subscription were asked to pay two years' subscription, so it can be assumed that this would have applied to Disraeli. The book does not record Disraeli's proposer and seconder, but these were disclosed by members of the club in *Liverpool Mercury etc.*, 8 May 1835, p. 4.
88. Gash, *Politics*, p. 396.
89. Taddei, *Clubs* (1999), p. 20.
90. Timbs, *Clubs* p. 235.
91. Greville diary 21 January 1859, quoted in Lytton Strachey and Roger Fulford (eds), *The Greville Memoirs, 1814–1860: Volume VII, January 1854 to November 1860* (London: Macmillan, 1938), p. 7.
92. While much of the interior was devastated by bomb damage in World War II, the facade of the building survives today.
93. Carlton Club archive, Carlton Club, London, MS 'Carlton Club Minute Book, Volume 3, 1839–1843', 25 February and 29 February 1840. (Note that the pages are unnumbered in the minute book, but that entries are dated.)
94. The Conservative Club, which merged with the Bath Club in 1959, during which time it became the Bath and Conservative Club (more jocularly known as the 'Lava-Tory Club'), finally closed in 1979, and only a small fraction of its papers survive in the London Metropolitan Archives today, meaning that much of the summary here has had to be based on secondary sources – what has survived by way of bills is scarcely useful.
95. Minute from 16 February 1864, quoted in Petrie and Cooke, *Carlton*, p. 54. A thorough search of every inch of the Carlton Club archive shows that this minute book is no longer held by the Club; yet it did apparently exist when Petrie wrote the book's first edition in 1955.
96. *John Bull*, 20 February 1864, p. 122.
97. Ibid.
98. The building no longer exists. In one of the most bizarre decisions taken by a London club, it was decided in 1963 to demolish the clubhouse (which was not

listed) and build on its site a modern, state-of-the-art concrete block decorated in a contemporary style, in which most floors were rented out as office space, save for the top two floors, which would promise to be 'the club of the future'. It was hoped that the existing building's ruinously expensive maintenance costs could be replaced by a profitable investment in leasing out office space which would serve to subsidise the new Club rooms upstairs. When the new building opened in 1968, much of the membership fled, and the remainder of the Junior Carlton finally merged into the Carlton in 1977, taking their archival holdings with them. Phelps, *Power and the Party*, pp. 35–9; Petrie and Cooke, *Carlton*, pp. 194–8, 210, 221, 255–6; *Nottinghamshire Guardian*, 11 March 1864, p. 4.

99. Wolffe, *Crusade*, pp. 210–20, 291–3.
100. Little has made it into print on the Free Trade Club, yet there is a realisation among historians that its parliamentary membership was significant, with Anthony Howe citing its membership as a good indicator of Cobdenite sympathy. History of Parliament Trust colloquium on 1832–68, London, 6 May 2011.
101. Alec Corio and Seth Alexander Thévoz, '"Defending the Protestant Principles of the Constitution": The National Club, c.1845–1855', paper presented to the Institute of Historical Research, 31 March 2011; Seth Alexander Thévoz, '"A Protestant Parliament for a Protestant England": the Politics of the National Club, 1845–1868', paper presented to the Oxford Modern British History seminar, 12 May 2011.
102. Address No.V, 6 April 1852, National Club, *Addresses of the National Club, Fourth Series* (London: Macintosh, 1852), p. 1.
103. Charles R. Dod (ed.), *The Parliamentary Companion: Twenty-Fifth Year, Second Edition, New Parliament* (London: Whittaker & Co., 1857), p. 163.
104. National Club MSS, Bodleian Library, Oxford, National Club, Dep.d.754, 20, National Club, *Addresses to the Protestants of the Empire Issued by the Committee of the National Club: Third Series*, No.VIII.
105. Charles Newdegate, *Hansard's Parliamentary Debates*, House of Commons Debates, 7 May 1849, vol. 104 cols 1396–446. By 'Christian', Newdegate invariably meant 'Protestant'.
106. Arthur Irwin Dassent, *The History of St. James's Square and the Foundation of the West End of London, with a Glimpse of Whitehall in the Reign of Charles the Second* (Macmillan, London, 1895), p. 124. Lord Clanricarde had leased the house to the Prince of Wales Club until 1846, and from 1 January 1850, the club-house hosted the East India United Service Club; Jacoby, *East India Club*, p. 17.
107. 'Peace and War Agitators', *Blackwood's Magazine*, Vol. 66 (1849), p. 582; Forrest, *Foursome in St. James's*, pp. 7–8.
108. *Illustrated London News*, 29 September 1849, p. 219. The National Reform Club, founded as the Free Trade Club's successor in September 1849, vanished without a trace and, by 1 January 1850, its building had been leased to the new East India United Service Club.

109. Taddei, *Clubs* (1998), p. 21.
110. Tom Clarke, *The Devonshire Club* (London: Devonshire Club, 1943), p. 11. The original name proposed for the long-mooted Devonshire Club was the 'Junior Reform Club'.
111. Quoted in Timbs, *Clubs*, pp. 216–17.
112. *The Times*, 15 March 1832, p. 2.
113. See Chapter 2.
114. The Travellers' clubhouse opened in 1827 and, like its later neighbour the Reform Club, shares an architect with the Houses of Parliament, Charles Barry. The Athenaeum's clubhouse opened in 1830, built by one of George IV's preferred architects, Decimus Burton. Although the United Service Club opposite the Athenaeum was built by John Nash, it was subsequently refaced by Burton, so that two of the four corners of Pall Mall with Waterloo Place are built in a broadly uniform style (although the Athenaeum takes its design inspiration from Greek elements, and the United Service Club from Roman elements).
115. As well as there being much anecdotal evidence of oversubscription for the Athenaeum in this period, scrutiny of the membership lists bears this out. As will be elaborated upon in Chapter 2, membership numbers were capped, and so new members could only join when existing members died or resigned. The annual membership lists of the Athenaeum were remarkably static by club standards. Numerous reflections on the Athenaeum's waiting list can be found in the insightful J. Mordaunt Crook, 'Locked Out of Paradise: Blackballing at the Athenaeum 1824–1935', Felipe Fernández-Armesto (ed.), *Armchair Athenians: Essays from the Athenaeum* (London: The Athenaeum, 2001), pp. 19–30.
116. Caroline Shenton, *The Day Parliament Burned Down* (Oxford: Oxford University Press, 2012), p. 37.
117. Timbs, *Clubs*, p. 199.
118. Again, see Chapter 2 for membership numbers per club.
119. Graves, *Armchairs*, p. 38. The Club itself gives a foundation date of 1821 at 'History', Oxford and Cambridge Club, http://oxfordandcambridgeclub.co.uk/club/about-the-club/history/ (accessed 27 February 2010), but this corresponds to a meeting at the Thatched House Tavern in June 1821 at which it was decided that such a club should be set up in future, and the club held its first meeting in April 1822.
120. See, for instance, Catherine Gladstone papers, Glynne-Gladstone MSS, Gladstone's Library, Hawarden, Flintshire, GG 774/14, GG 774/39, GG 774/47, GG 774/96, and GG777/89 W. E. Gladstone to Catherine Gladstone, 21 July 1858, 30 March 1858, 2 April 1858, 21 July 1859, and 22 April 1868 respectively.
121. Graves, *Armchairs*, p. 49. The clubs eventually merged in 1971.
122. As noted in the introduction, Marcus Binney recently completed the first full-length history of Boodle's, work on which had been started by the late David Mann, Binney and Mann (eds), *Boodle's*. Arthur's, which closed down in 1939,

had its building taken over by the Carlton Club since the latter was bombed in 1940. A visit to today's Carlton is thus very instructive in appreciating the architectural dimensions of an apolitical gambling club, but less helpful in reconstructing the rather more ambitious architectural intentions of the Victorian-era Carlton – a key theme of Chapter 4.
123. Alexander F. Baillie, *The Oriental Club and Hanover Square* (London: Longmans, 1901), p. 179; Boas, *Garrick Club*, p. 21 (the Marquess of Hartington indicated here was later the seventh Duke of Devonshire, and sat for Cambridge University); David Kynaston, *The City of London, Volume I: A World of its Own, 1815–1890* (London: Chatto & Windus, 1994), p. 152.
124. The proprietary club of Pratt's consists of two small basement rooms: a bar and a dining room that can seat just fourteen people around the dining table. Today, Pratt's is run by Nicholas Soames and enjoys a heavily aristocratic reputation, yet this seems to only date from the 1950s, when the then Duke of Devonshire took over the Club. For much of the nineteenth century, it was considered a disreputable and somewhat marginalised club. Sampson, *Anatomy of Britain*, p. 290.
125. Algernon West, *Recollections, 1832–1886* (New York: Harper, 1900), p. 49.
126. J. A. W. Gunn, John Matthews, Donald M. Schurman and M. G. Wiebe (eds), *Benjamin Disraeli Letters: Volume One, 1815–1834* (Toronto: University of Toronto Press, 1982), p. 364n.
127. Comparison of *Dod's Parliamentary Companion* for selected 'New Parliament Edition' years from 1836–68.

Chapter 2 Clubs and the MPs' World I: A Quantitative Analysis

1. Still enormously innovative in its approach (though modest in its conclusions) is W. O. Aydelotte, 'The House of Commons in the 1840s', *History*, XXXIX (1954), pp. 249–62, while his subsequent articles W. O. Aydelotte, 'Voting Patterns in the British House of Commons in the 1840s', *Comparative Studies in Society and History*, vol. V (1962–3), pp. 134–63 and W. O. Aydelotte, 'Parties and Issues in Early Victorian England', *Journal of British Studies*, V (1966), pp. 95–114 contain much more detailed analysis.
2. John R. Bylsma, 'Political Issues and Party Unity in the House of Commons, 182–1857: A Scalogram Analysis' (PhD thesis, University of Iowa, 1968); John R. Bylsma, 'Party Structure in the 1852–1857 House of Commons: a Scalogram Analysis', *Journal of Interdisciplinary History*, 7 (1977), pp. 375–93; R. G. Watt, 'Parties and Politics in Mid-Victorian Britain, 1857 to 1859: A Study in Quantification' (PhD thesis, University of Minnesota, 1975).
3. J. M. Kousser, 'Quantitative Social-Scientific History', Michael G. Kammen (ed.), *The Past Before Us* (reprint, Ithaca, New York: Cornell University Press, 1982, of orig. edn, Ithaca, New York: Cornell University Press, 1980), pp. 433–56.

4. John A. Phillips, 'QUASSHing M.P.s and Electors: New Perspectives on Parliamentary History', John A. Phillips (ed.), *Computing Parliamentary History: George III to Victoria* (Edinburgh: Edinburgh University Press, 1994), p. 2.
5. See Cox, *Efficient Secret*.
6. Taddei, *Clubs* (1999).
7. For a complete list of sources used on the database, please see Appendix. I am particularly grateful to Kathryn Rix for cross-checking the History of Parliament's list of MPs with my own, and for also conscientiously sending me various updates and disambiguations regarding nineteenth-century MPs over the course of the PhD.
8. Confusingly, Charles Dod's surname was spelt 'Dodd' for most of his lifetime. For the sake of consistency, he is referred to as 'Dod' throughout this chapter.
9. See Table 2, Coohill, 'Parliamentary Guides', p. 276.
10. The clubs picked out are the same as those set out in the Introduction and Chapter 1, which this book focuses on; White's, the Carlton, Conservative and Junior Carlton Clubs from the Conservative side; and Brooks's, the Westminster Reform, the Reform, and the Free Trade Clubs from the Liberal side, plus the Athenaeum and the Travellers' Clubs as the preferred apolitical clubs for MPs. Unfortunately, of these, the short-lived Free Trade Club has no known surviving papers, and the Conservative Club has only some small partial records. However, archives for the remaining seven clubs popular with MPs have yielded far more data.
11. The Reform Club, for instance, has a sizable gap in its annual membership lists, with no surviving lists between 1841 and 1847, making it impossible to tell whether an MP joined for a year or two and then resigned during that period. Gaps of 1–3 years are not uncommon among pre-1868 club membership lists. Only the Athenaeum retains complete membership lists from 1832; and, even then, it has gaps in the preceding eight years' membership lists.
12. Reform Club archive, Reform Club, London, MS 'Reform Club Minute Book 1836–41', f. 9. Browne was directly elected by the club's committee, bypassing the usual election process.
13. Five of the twenty-one MPs served in the Commons *after* 1868, making it probable that they were elected to the Athenaeum thereafter. Accordingly, it would be more accurate to put the tally of suspect claims to Athenaeum membership at 16 (5 per cent). It is also conceivable that some of these MPs belonged to the Athenaeum for a short time before 1832, and indeed the Athenaeum's pre-1832 membership records are incomplete; but given the notoriously long waiting list for the Athenaeum and the social prestige of being elected to it, this seems unlikely when compared to the likelihood that several of these MPs were simply lying.
14. Amy Milne-Smith argues that class distinctions, social advancement and snobbery were all powerful motives when joining a club. See Amy Milne-Smith, 'Clubland' (2006), pp. 39–60.

15. Charles R. Dodd [later Dod] (ed.) (1842), *Autobiography of Five Hundred Members of Parliament; Being a Collection of Letters and Returned Schedules Received by Charles R. Dodd During the First Four Reformed Parliament, viz., from 1832 to December 1842, and Constituting Materials for Compiling the Successive Editions of the Parliamentary Pocket Companion* [microfilm] (New Haven, Connecticut: Yale University, James Marshall and Marie-Louise Osborn Collection [copy held at London: History of Parliament Trust]), MS 'Walter F. Campbell'.
16. See, for example, letters from the Reform Club Secretary chasing up unpaid subscriptions from George Moffatt MP and R. Maxwell Fox MP on 24 February 1853 and 20 June 1853. See also his letter to the Rt. Hon. Edward Ellice MP on 28 May 1850 about a substantial debt to the club, plus interest. On 26 January 1849 and 23 February 1849 he wrote to William Collins MP and Cecil Lawless MP about their unpaid room bills. The aptly-named Lawless was in further trouble on 17 August 1850, when a twenty pound cheque of his bounced in the Coffee Room. Reform Club archive, Reform Club, London, MS 'Reform Club: Letters from the Club Secretary to Members, 1848–57', ff. 3, 4, 10, 12, 28.
17. Coohill, 'Parliamentary Guides', pp. 282–3. Coohill provides an inverse example of MPs Thomas Frewen Turner and Richard Edensor Heathcote only co-operating with Dod because their existing entries in the *Parliamentary Companion* were so inaccurate.
18. Charles R. Dodd [later Dod] (ed.) (1842), *Autobiography of Five Hundred Members of Parliament; Being a Collection of Letters and Returned Schedules Received by Charles R. Dodd During the First Four Reformed Parliament, viz., from 1832 to December 1842, and Constituting Materials for Compiling the Successive Editions of the Parliamentary Pocket Companion* [microfilm] (New Haven, Connecticut: Yale University, James Marshall and Marie-Louise Osborn Collection [copy held at London: History of Parliament Trust]), MS 'William Baird'; Carlton Club, London, Carlton Club candidates' books, candidate no. 957, vol. 4.
19. Charles R. Dodd [later Dod] (ed.) (1842), *Autobiography of Five Hundred Members of Parliament; Being a Collection of Letters and Returned Schedules Received by Charles R. Dodd During the First Four Reformed Parliament, viz., from 1832 to December 1842, and Constituting Materials for Compiling the Successive Editions of the Parliamentary Pocket Companion* [microfilm] (New Haven, Connecticut: Yale University, James Marshall and Marie-Louise Osborn Collection [copy held at London: History of Parliament Trust]), MS 'Benjamin Disraeli'.
20. Blake, *Disraeli*, pp. 81–2, 435; Humphreys, *Crockford's*, p. 105.
21. Quotation from Petrie and Cooke, *Carlton Club*, p. 1. Across the 1832–68 period, at one time or another the data drawn from *Dod's* New Parliament Editions labels some 972 MPs as having been 'Conservative' at one time or another, with another 73 having been 'Liberal Conservatives' (not including Liberal Conservatives who had been listed as Conservatives at some other time); a total of 1,045. This figure does not include MPs who were never included in a *Dod's* New Parliament Edition, so it excludes a number of MPs who sat relatively briefly, usually

by-election victors or those who lost their seats on petition. Additionally, it should be clarified that it is not contended that 1,024 of the 1,045 Conservatives MPs referred to were Carlton members for, as we shall see, the 1,024 Carlton Club MPs included a number who were categorised by *Dod's* as Liberals of various denominations.
22. The trend of declining MP membership at the Reform Club was already noted by J. Mordaunt Crook, who observed that in 1841 the club had 'nearly 200' MPs, and 'By 1855 the number of MPs had dropped to 145.' Mordaunt Crook, *Reform Club*, p. 16. These figures are slightly at odds with the data gathered here, due to the larger number of sources consulted here, but the fundamental pattern observed is the same.
23. For this graph, and the corresponding graphs in Graphs 2.7–2.9 for White's, the Reform Club and Brooks's, the proportions cited refer only to MPs who were members of that club by the end of the sample year. They do not take into account sitting MPs who did not join the club concerned until later in the Parliament. As such, they offer conservative estimates which *underestimate* the full extent of club membership among the various factions concerned, offering a snapshot rather than an aggregate. However, it should be noted that an earlier draft version of these graphs was prepared which *did* take into account MPs sitting in the sample years, and the final results were not significantly different. As we shall see later in this chapter, most MPs who joined a club did so within a year of being elected to Parliament, and so the rate at which MPs would join a club for the first time later in a Parliament appreciably slowed. Having had the choice between using these figures, and the figures giving slightly higher proportions taking into account MPs who joined later in a Parliament, I opted to use the former, as a sample offered a 'truer' picture than an inflated figure based on MPs who had not yet joined these clubs.
24. The Carlton candidates' books only begin in 1834. Members who joined before that have been compiled from numerous other sources, none of them comprehensive.
25. Quotation from Colson, *White's*, p. 115.
26. The Club's patrons were Benjamin Disraeli MP, Lord Malmesbury, Lord Colville, and Lieut.-Colonel Thomas Edward Taylor MP, but there is no evidence that they ever used the Club (unlike the Carlton). Benjamin Disraeli to the Earl of Derby, Friday 14 August 1863, Wiebe, Millar, Robson and Hawman (eds), *Disraeli Letters VIII*, pp. 293–4.
27. The five MPs were Col. Sir James Bourne, Sir Henry Edwards, William Ferrand, John Fleming and William Vansittart.
28. For the causes of the club's decline, see Alec Corio and Seth Alexander Thévoz, 'Defending the Protestant Principles of the Constitution: The National Club 1845–55' (forthcoming article).
29. For the fullest and most accurate existing previously published account of this, see Fraser Rae, 'Organisation', p. 913, and compare to the account in Chapter 1 of this book.

30. Lejeune, *Clubs* (1979), p. 205; Mordaunt Crook, *Rise of the Nouveaux Riches*, p. 259.
31. For the purposes of comparison, MPs listed in *Dod's* as Whigs, Radicals, Repealers and Reformers are all counted as 'Liberals', even though many would doubtless have repudiated such a label. For a strong argument in favour of conceptualising the post-Reform Whigs and Radicals as different wings of an early Liberal Party, see Parry, *Liberal Government*, especially pp. 128–32.
32. Newbould, *Whiggery*, p. 33.
33. Elements of this argument on the surprisingly diverse political composition of Brooks's have previously appeared in my chapter on the subject, Seth Alexander Thévoz, 'The MPs of Brooks's, 1832–68', Mordaunt Crook and Sebag-Montefiore (eds), *Brooks's*, pp. 38–49, which was based on a different data set, using the Stenton and Lees party labels rather than the *Dod's* ones used here.
34. See Athenaeum Club, *An Alphabetical List of the Members, with the Rules and Regulations, of the Athenaeum* (London: William Clowes, 1837).
35. Blake, *Disraeli*, p. 81.
36. Athenaeum, *List*, pp. 7–8. The cases were Benjamin Disraeli, Edward Cardwell and Sir Edward Bulwer-Lytton.
37. Reform Club archive, Reform Club, London, MS '1836 Reform Club Founding Resolution'. Appendix pages are unnumbered, but see appendix, entry for meetings held at 3 Cleveland Row, 18 and 25 February 1836.
38. Donald Southgate, *The Passing of the Whigs, 1832–1886* (London: Macmillan, 1962). See particularly the tables on 'The Whig Nobility and Electoral Contests 1832–85', pp. 438–46, and 'Other Families Which had an MP on the Liberal Side' pp. 447–55.
39. Amongst the Russells, these were Viscount Amberley, Lord Arthur Russell, Sir Charles Russell, Lord Charles James Fox Russell, Hon. Edward Southwell Russell, Francis Charles Hastings Russell, Lord John Russell, Lord William Russell. Amongst the Cavendishes, these were Hon Charles Compton Cavendish, Lord Cavendish of Keighley, Marquess Hartington, Lord Edward Cavendish, Lord Frederick Charles Cavendish, Lord George Henry Cavendish, Hon. Col. Henry Frederick Compton Cavendish, and Hon. William George Cavendish.
40. For the Russell family members listed in note 39 (barring Sir Charles), these ages were 24, 25, 19, 20, 23, 22 and 21 respectively.
41. Francis Sitwell. 'The Fox Club', Ziegler and Seward (eds), *Brooks's*, pp. 149–51.
42. For the Cavendish members listed above (barring Hon. Col. Henry Frederick), these ages were 23, 25, 21, 18, 30, 23 and 25 respectively.
43. These were Hon. Charles Compton Cavendish, Hon. Col. Henry Frederick Compton Cavendish, Hon. William George Cavendish, Marquess Hartington, Lord Frederick Charles Cavendish, and Lord George Henry

Cavendish. Of these, only Hon. Col. Henry Frederick Compton was not a member of Brooks's, and only Lord George Henry joined Brooks's at an appreciably different time from White's, joining the former in 1835 and the latter in 1846.

44. See Mandler, *Aristocratic Government*, especially pp. 33–43.
45. Summary of the tables included in Southgate, *Whigs*, pp. 438–46, 447–55.
46. Ian Bradley, *The Optimists: Themes and Personalities in Victorian Liberalism* (London: Faber and Faber, London, 1980), pp. 38–40. Bradley estimates total cumulative Whig representation in the Commons at just 27 between 1859 and 1874.
47. Brian Wheeler, 'If anybody wants me, I'll be at my club', *BBC News*, 23 November 2003, http://news.bbc.co.uk/1/hi/magazine/3227664.stm (accessed 10 June 2010).
48. Wegg-Prosser (ed.), *Memorials of Brooks's*, pp. 100, 102, 104.
49. See Parry, *Liberal Government*, especially pp. 128–49.
50. All that survives of the Westminster Reform Club's records is its committee's minute book, which makes no mention of any formal policy declaration by candidates for membership. As none of the Free Trade Club's papers are known to have survived, and none of the surviving correspondence regarding the club mentions this, it is impossible to say one way or the other what its arrangements were.
51. Wolffe, *Crusade*, pp. 211–19.
52. Even as a Peelite, Gladstone frequently wrote to his wife at Hawarden from either the Carlton Club, or from his house at Carlton Gardens, using purloined Carlton Club stationery. See, for instance, Glynne-Gladstone MSS, Catherine Gladstone papers, Gladstone's Library, Hawarden, Flintshire, GG 771/184-9, 194-5, 207-8, 221-4, 229-46, 259-79; GG 772/80-175, 191-5, 203, covering the years 1847–52. The last time Gladstone wrote to his wife on Carlton stationery was on 23 March 1858 (GG 774/27).
53. Derek Hansen, Ben Schneiderman and Marc A. Smith, *Analysing Social Media Networks with NodeXL* (Maryland, 2009) E-Book, pp. 31–9; Maksim Tsetovat and Alexander Kouznetsov, *Social Network Analysis for Startups* (Sebastopol, California [E-Book], 2011) E-Book, pp. 39–92. Note that every day, the Twitter website generates more social networking data than the totality of all data that social network analysts had to work with between 1970 and 2000, demonstrating how the scope for such analysis has come to the fore in the last decade.
54. Jennifer Regan-Lefebvre, 'London Clubs and Social Networking, 1870–1900', Cambridge Modern History seminar, 21 November 2011, Pembroke College, Cambridge; Arthur Downing, 'The Friendly Planet: Friendly Societies in the English-Speaking World and Australia in the Long Nineteenth Century' (MPhil thesis, University of Oxford, 2012); Arthur Downing, *Social Capital in Decline: Friendly Societies in Australia, 1850–1914*, University of Oxford discussion papers in economic and social history, No. 105 (October 2012).

55. This diagram has been generated in NodeXL, a specialist social network analysis plug-in developed for Microsoft Excel 2007/10.
56. An explanation which can be dismissed is the more superficial one of the Reform and Travellers' Clubs being next-door to each other, and the limited appeal of belonging to both: the Carlton Club was the next door along (with a narrow alley between the Reform and Carlton), yet had twice as many shared MP members with the Travellers'.
57. Milne-Smith, 'Clubland' (2006), pp. 49–60 has an overview of blackballing in the late Victorian period.
58. Darwin, *British Clubs*, p. 11; James Pickford, 'Gentlemen's Clubs Raise a Glass to Quiet Success: Relics of Nineteenth Century London See Membership Grow', *Financial Times*, 22 December 2012, p. 2. (Sidebar headed 'Black Balls, Bucks and Bets', found only in the print edition, not the online edition.)
59. Milne-Smith, 'Clubland' (2006), p. 56.
60. Athenaeum Club, *List* (1826), p. 2. There is a record of White's changing its rules in 1781 to one blackball being enough to exclude any candidate; however, there is no indication as to whether this was still the case in the mid-nineteenth century. Anonymous, *White's*, vol. 1, p. 148.
61. Knatchbull MSS, Kent History and Library Centre, Maidstone, Kent, U951/529, MS Rt. Hon. G.H. Knatchbull-Hugessen, First Lord Brabourne, 'Political Anecdotes, 1858–81' (Unpublished manuscript), f. 68 (20 February 1864).
62. *The Times*, 9 August 1848, p. 3. Ironically, the first ballot box ever used in a British parliamentary election, at the 1872 Pontefract by-election, is now kept in the library of Brooks's, the club most frequented by Russell.
63. Wegg-Prosser (ed.), *Memorials of Brooks's*, p. 155.
64. I have not subjected the Junior Carlton Club's Candidate Books to the same level of scrutiny as the Carlton Club's Candidate Books and the Reform Club's Ballot Book, because the Junior Carlton's records only start in 1864, meaning that the data derived would only cover the last four years of the pre-1868 period, and so would not give the same degree of long-term insight.
65. Carlton Club archive, Carlton Club, London, MS 'Carlton Club Candidates' Book', vol. 3, candidate no. 600.
66. Burlingham and Billis (eds), *Reformed Characters*, pp. 200–4.
67. Carlton Club archive, Carlton Club, London, MS 'Carlton Club Candidates' Book', vol. 1, candidate no. 116.
68. Figures have been adjusted to exclude duplicate entries by applicants, of which there were between one and 17 per volume, usually from applicants who had been on the waiting list for a long time and were eager to press their case, however hopelessly. The data runs to 1866, not 1868, because volume thirteen of the candidates' book covers 1866–9, and so inclusion of the data from volume thirteen could be misleading in covering both the pre- and post-Second Reform Act environment.

69. The Reform Club's first two blackballed candidates, proposed 4 July 1846, were a solicitor named Richard Pine, and someone named 'Alfred Th ...' who was sufficiently unpopular to have had his name crossed out in ink blots. There appeared to be no real pattern in the type of candidates blackballed – while many of them were lawyers, this was equally true of successful candidates. Reform Club archive, Reform Club, London, MS 'Reform Club Ballot Book, Vol. I, 1836–52'.
70. *New York Times*, 11 April 1860, p. 5.
71. *John Bull*, 20 February 1864, p. 122.
72. The Carlton Club's only two surviving pre-1868 minute books cover 1835–43. Extracts from an 1832–5 minute book were cited in the first edition of Petrie and Cooke, *Carlton Club*, published in 1955; but a thorough search of every inch of the Carlton Club archives showed that it must have disappeared at some point in the last 55 years.
73. For example, Roger Sinclair Aytoun MP was first elected to Brooks's in 1852, and later rejoined in 1866. It is unclear when he resigned. Wegg-Prosser (ed.), *Memorials of Brooks's*, p. 169.
74. J. B. Conacher, *The Peelites and the Party System, 1846–52* (Newton Abbot: David and Charles, 1972), p. 20.
75. The only previous use made of the Carlton Club candidates' books for any study is Jolles, *Jews and the Carlton*, a self-published monograph by an independent researcher, analysing Jewish Carlton members in the late nineteenth century, and non-Jewish members who had Jewish ancestry.
76. If MPs ceased to sit in Parliament, they still remained a member of the Club, but as a supernumerary member, which meant that once they ceased to be a member, there would be no ballot to replace them.
77. Carlton Club archive, Carlton Club, London, MS 'Carlton Club Candidates' Book', vol. 2, candidate no. 478.
78. Carlton Club archive, Carlton Club, London, MS 'Carlton Club Candidates' Book', vol. 6, candidate no. 1583.
79. Reform Club archive, Reform Club, London, MS 'Reform Club minute book 1836–41', 17 May 1837, f. 51.
80. 8 March 1839, ibid., f. 150.
81. Carlton Club archive, Carlton Club, London, MS 'Carlton Club minute book, Vol. 2: 1835–1839', 26 January 1836 and 5 April 1836. Alsager and Balfour were proposed and elected by the committee at the very same meeting, yet there are no references to them in the corresponding candidates' book for the period.
82. *John Bull*, 20 February 1864, p. 122.
83. Carlton Club archive, Carlton Club, London, MS 'Carlton Club Candidates' Book', vol. 3, candidate no. 746.
84. Athenaeum archive, The Athenaeum, London, MS 'List of original members of the Athenaeum', Mem 3/1/1, 1824.
85. Carlton Club archive, Carlton Club, London, MS 'Carlton Club Candidates' Book', vol. 3, candidate no. 762. The proposer's name on the unsuccessful

Notes to Pages 92–101

application is, sadly, illegible. His successful second application was put down on 22 February 1853.

86. Carlton Club archive, Carlton Club, London, MS 'Carlton Club Candidates' Book', vol. 9, candidate no. 2611.
87. Carlton Club archive, Carlton Club, London, MS 'Carlton Club Candidates' Book', vol. 4, candidate no. 990.
88. Charles Stuart Parker, *Life and Letters of Sir James Graham, Second Baronet of Netherby, P.C., G.C.B., 1792–1861* (London: John Murray, 1907), vol. 1, p. 18.
89. Carlton Club archive, Carlton Club, London, MS 'Carlton Club Candidates' Book', vol. 10, candidate no. 2701. Note that he was not blackballed, but simply did not come up for ballot.
90. See, for example, the case of George Dodd in Carlton Club archive, Carlton Club, London, MS 'Carlton Club Candidates' Book', vol. 3, candidate no. 772, where the letters 'MP' have been belatedly added in a different colour of ink.
91. Seth Alexander Thévoz, 'Database of MPs' Club Memberships, 1832–68'. For the Carlton Club, I noted every instance of an MP who was fast-tracked for membership, using the first 13 volumes of candidates' books held in the Carlton archives, which cover this period.
92. Charles R. Dodd [later Dod] (ed.) (1842), *Autobiography of Five Hundred Members of Parliament; Being a Collection of Letters and Returned Schedules Received by Charles R. Dodd During the First Four Reformed Parliament, viz., from 1832 to December 1842, and Constituting Materials for Compiling the Successive Editions of the Parliamentary Pocket Companion* [microfilm] (New Haven, Connecticut: Yale University, James Marshall and Marie-Louise Osborn Collection [copy held at London: History of Parliament Trust]), MS 'Henry Mitcalfe'.
93. Charles R. Dodd [later Dod] (ed.) (1842), *Autobiography of Five Hundred Members of Parliament; Being a Collection of Letters and Returned Schedules Received by Charles R. Dodd During the First Four Reformed Parliament, viz., from 1832 to December 1842, and Constituting Materials for Compiling the Successive Editions of the Parliamentary Pocket Companion* [microfilm] (New Haven, Connecticut: Yale University, James Marshall and Marie-Louise Osborn Collection [copy held at London: History of Parliament Trust]), MS 'John Collier'.
94. Seth Alexander Thévoz, 'Database of MPs' Club Memberships, 1832–68'.

Chapter 3 Clubs and the MPs' World II: Experiences in Clubland Space

1. *Saturday Review*, Vol. 41 (1876), p. 769.
2. *New York Times*, 12 June 1856, p. 4.
3. Regarding this party system – which it recognisably was by 1868 – the role of 'party' organisation is covered insofar as it impacted on political life within

Westminster, but 'party' activity with regards to constituency organisation and intervention is set out in Chapter 5.
4. Tristram Hunt, *Building Jerusalem: The Rise and Fall of the Victorian City* (London: Weidenfeld and Nicholson, 2004), p. 83.
5. M. H. Port, *The Houses of Parliament* (New Haven, Connecticut: Yale University Press, 1976), pp. 142–9.
6. Ibid., pp. 173–94 has details of the extensive construction work which was still underway throughout 1860–70.
7. Ibid., and M. H. Port, 'The Best Club in the World? The House of Commons, c.1860–1915', Clyve Jones and Sean Kelsey (eds), *Housing Parliament: Dublin, Edinburgh and Westminster* (Edinburgh: Edinburgh University Press, 2002), p. 170. In this respect, the new Houses of Parliament differed little from the 'cramped conditions and poor ventilation' of their predecessor – see Clare Wilkinson, 'Politics and Topography in the Old House of Commons, 1783–1834', Jones and Kelsey (eds), *Parliament*, pp. 141–65, especially pp. 162–3.
8. See, for instance, the case of Holland House, which is best captured in its final days of influence by Abraham D. Kriegel (ed.), *The Holland House Diaries 1831–1840: The Diary of Henry Richard Vassall Fox, Third Lord Holland, with Extracts from the Diary of Dr John Allen* (London: Routledge and Kegan Paul, 1977). Both White's and Brooks's remained proprietor-owned clubs throughout this period.
9. Gash, *Politics*, pp. 395–6.
10. See Hanham, *Elections*, pp. 99–105 for an overview of Clubland political developments in 1868–80.
11. See Jürgen Habarmas, *The Structural Transformation of the Public Sphere: An Inquiry into a Category of Bourgeois Society* (Cambridge: Polity Press, 1962 [trans. 1989]), *passim*.
12. Beat Kümin, 'Introduction', Beat Kümin (ed.), *Political Space in Pre-Industrial Europe* (Surrey: Ashgate, 2009), p. 9.
13. W. A. Munford, *William Ewart M.P., 1798–1869: Portrait of a Radical* (London: Grafton and Co., 1960), p. 72.
14. Mike Crang, 'Spaces in Theory, Spaces in History and Spatial Historiographies', Kümin (ed.), *Political Space*, p. 249.
15. Christina Parolin, *Radical Spaces: Venues of Popular Politics in London, 1790-c.1845* (Canberra, Australia: Australian National University E Press, 2012), pp. 147–79.
16. See, for instance, Stephen Parkinson, *Arena of Ambition: A History of the Cambridge Union* (London: Icon Books, 2009), especially Chapter 1 on 1815–1914, which approaches the Union private members' club as a space through which generations of future politicians passed; Rosemary Ashton, *142 Strand: A Radical Address in Victorian London* (London, Chatto and Windus, 2006), focussing on the address of radical publisher John Chapman, and its interaction with surrounding London society, and her almost deterministic recent book, Rosemary Ashton, *Victorian Bloomsbury*

(New Haven, Connecticut: Yale University Press, 2012), with its central thesis that the district moulded its intellectuals rather than vice-versa.
17. Henri Lefebvre, 'Reflections on the Politics of Space' (1970), Henri Lefebvre [trans. Gerald Moore, Neil Brenner and Stuart Elden, ed. Neil Brenner and Stuart Elden], *State, Space, World: Selected Essays* (Minneapolis, Minnesota: University of Minnesota Press, 2009), p. 171.
18. Ibid., p. 172.
19. Henri Lefebvre, 'The Worldwide and the Planetary' (1973), Henri Lefebvre, *Space*, p. 201.
20. Nirmal Puwar, *Space Invaders: Race, Gender and Bodies Out of Place* (Oxford: Berg, 2005), pp. 13–28, 77–117.
21. For more on temporality and space, see Parolin, *Radical Spaces*, pp. 213–42.
22. Pamela Horn, *Pleasures and Pastimes in Victorian Britain* (Stroud: Sutton Publishing, 1999), especially Chapter 1, pp. 1–19, which carries no less than ten references to Peter Bailey, *Leisure and Class in Victorian England: Rational Recreation and the Contest for Control, 1830–1885* (London: Methuen, 1978 [rev. 1987 ed.]).
23. Bailey, *Leisure*, pp. 116–32; see also Peter Bailey, *Music Hall: The Business of Pleasure* (Milton Keynes: Open University Press, 1986), pp. 60–3, 132–3, for its overview of how club spaces were flexible enough to accommodate different kinds of performances.
24. Bernard Capp, 'Comment from a Historical Perspective', Beat Kümin (ed.), *Space*, p. 236.
25. Ibid., p. 237.
26. Hawkins, *British*, p. 14. Hawkins stresses that such a world was closely bound up with the large parties of hostesses such as Lady Palmerston and Lady Waldegrave, as well as the dinner parties given during the parliamentary recess, an argument reiterated in the more recent Angus Hawkins, *Victorian Political Culture: 'Habits of Heart and Mind'* (Oxford: Oxford University Press, 2015), *passim*.
27. See Chapter 1.
28. Rome, *Union Club*, pp. 9–16.
29. Wegg-Prosser (ed.), *Memorials of Brooks's*, pp. 259–60.
30. Timbs, *Clubs*, p. 233.
31. Peter Marsh, 'The Reform Club: Architecture and the Birth of Popular Government', Gresham College lecture, 25 September 2007.
32. Vernon, *Politics*, pp. 217–25.
33. Jon Lawrence, *Electing Our Masters: The Hustings in British Politics from Hogarth to Blair* (Oxford: Oxford University Press, 2009), p. 15. See also pp. 14–42.
34. *Hansard*, House of Commons Debates, 18 March 1845, vol. 78, col. 1077. Hume was arguing for a repeal of the window tax, on the grounds that it made little sense when applied 'to the Reform Club, the Carlton Club, and other public buildings'. In the debate, the use of clubs as examples against the window tax was repeated by several parliamentarians before and after Hume's speech.

35. 23 September 1863, Angus Hawkins and John Powell (eds), *The Journal of John Wodehouse, First Earl of Kimberley for 1862–1902* (London: Royal Historical Society, 1997), p. 107.
36. Junior Carlton Club archive, Carlton Club, London, MS 'Junior Carlton Club General Meeting Minutes, Volume 1, 1865–1967', Minutes of the Second Annual General Meeting, 14 May 1866.
37. Asa Briggs, *Victorian People: A Reassessment of Persons and Themes, 1851–67* (Chicago: University of Chicago Press, 1955 [rev. 1972 ed.]), p. 287.
38. Hawkins, *British*, pp. 9–46, especially p. 14.
39. Fremantle MSS, Buckinghamshire County Record Office, Aylebury, Bucks., D-FR/80/15, where a range of these cards can be found.
40. K. D. Reynolds, *Aristocratic Women and Political Society in Victorian Britain* (Oxford: Clarendon Press, 1998), p. 168.
41. Eleanor Gordon and Gwyneth Nair, *Public Lives: Women, Family and Society in Victorian Britain* (New Haven, Connecticut: Yale University Press, 2003), p. 120. Gordon and Nair give the example of William Houldsworth in the 1860s, citing his house in Claremont Terrace, Glasgow as a fairly typical example of mid-Victorian middle-class sociability.
42. Charles Dickens, *Our Mutual Friend* (London: Chapman and Hall, 1864) Book II, Chapter 3, p. 5; M. H. Port, 'The Best Club in the World? The House of Commons, c.1860–1915', Jones and Kelsey (eds), *Parliament*, pp. 166–99.
43. Port, *Parliament*, p. 150.
44. While the National Liberal Club has tiled pillars throughout the building, the Club's original smoking room designed by Alfred Waterhouse was on the Club's lower ground floor, and had its walls entirely covered in tiles. See Peter Harris, 'A Meeting Place for Liberals: The National Liberal Club', *Journal of Liberal History*, 51 (Summer 2006), pp. 18–23 and R. W. Edis, 'The Constitutional Club', *The British Architect* (London: British Library, 1884).
45. Mordaunt Crook, *Rise of the Nouveaux Riches*, p. 258. Such a figure for subscribing membership does not necessarily indicate that overall membership had fallen this sharply, since the figure would not include either Honorary Members (who paid no subscription) or Life Members (who had paid a lump sum), and may or may not have included Supernumerary Members.
46. Port, *Parliament*, pp. 59–64. Port goes so far as to identify the Birmingham Grammar School corridor designs as 'critical' in inspiring the House of Commons' distinctive cloister motif on p. 63, providing convincing architectural plans.
47. Ibid., p. 70.
48. *Roland Quinault*, 'Westminster and the Victorian Constitution', *Transactions of the Royal Historical Society, Sixth Series*, 2 (Cambridge: Cambridge University Press, 1992), p. 89.
49. Hunt, *Jerusalem*, p. 177.
50. Distances have been calculated using 'Google Maps', http://maps.google.com (accessed 20 December 2011), and reflect the Reform Club as a starting point.

The Carlton Club was next door to the Reform Club. Some clubs, such as the Athenaeum and the United Service Club, would have been even closer to Parliament, while Brooks's and White's were much further away, being one point two miles by road. The roads used have been cross-checked with the facsimile *Piccadilly 1869: London Large Scale 07.72 (Old Ordnance Survey Maps of London – Yard to the Mile)* (London: Alan Godfrey, 1986), and have not appreciably changed in the last 160 years.

51. 'Landscape History: St. James's Park – From Pigs to Processions', Royal Parks, 2012, http://www.royalparks.org.uk/parks/st-jamess-park/about-st-jamess-park/landscape-history (accessed 12 February 2012). The bridge was demolished a century later and replaced by the present one.
52. Peter Marsh, 'Reform Club' lecture.
53. T. M. Parssinen, 'Association, Convention and Anti-Parliament in British Radical Politics, 1771–1848', *English Historical Review* (1973), LXXXVIII, p. 509.
54. *The Times*, 12 August 1836, p. 5. The eight MPs were Colonel Thomas Perronet Thompson, William Williams, Richard Potter, Alexander Dennistoun, Charles Augustus Tulk, Dr. John Bowring, Cornthwaite Hector, and Sharman Crawford.
55. *Hansard*, House of Commons Debate, 13 March 1854, vol. 131, col. 674.
56. Cobden to Sir Joshua Walmsley, 18 September 1852, Howe (ed.), *Letters: Volume Two*, p. 428.
57. Buckingham's complaint referred to the room as the Reading Room. Redesdale's reply called it the Morning Room. It appears that this was the kind of room which would later be described as a 'smoking room' from the 1850s.
58. Redesdale also facetiously added that the chimney place was reserved at the time for the notice of an appeal for a Duke of Wellington statue in Edinburgh.
59. Carlton Club archive, Carlton Club, London, MS 'Carlton Club Minute Book, Volume 3, 1839–1843', 7 April 1840.
60. Carlton Club archive, Carlton Club, London, MS 'Carlton Club Minute Book, Volume 3, 1839–1843', 21 April 1840.
61. Gash, *Sir Robert Peel*, p. 217.
62. The construction of the first Irish railway, covering the modest distance from Dublin to Kingstown, had been a long, drawn-out process, with construction beginning in 1831 but not concluding until three years later, and was marred by cost over-runs. Despite this inauspicious start, Joseph Lee draws parallels between the railway 'mania' found in England at the time, and its spread to Ireland; and the railways soon assumed paramount importance in the Irish economy, accounting for 80 per cent of capital investment in Ireland between 1825 and 1850. By 1844, the first railway in Ulster opened. John J. Dunne, 'The First Irish Railway by Shriek and Smoke to Kingstown', *Dublin Historical Record*, 43 (1990), pp. 44–6; Joseph Lee, 'The Provision of Capital for Early Irish Railways, 1830–1853', *Irish Historical Studies*, 16 (1968), pp. 33–63.

63. *Morning Post*, 18 June 1844, p. 5; *The Times*, 18 June 1844, p. 6.
64. *The Times*, 8 July 1844, p. 5.
65. *The Times*, 25 June 1844, p. 5. The threat was an empty one, and the club did not dissolve – see *The Times*, 8 July 1844, p. 5.
66. Benjamin Disraeli to the Editor of *The Times*, 2 July 1844, cited in M. G. Wiebe, J. B. Conacher, John Matthews and Mary S. Millar (eds), *Benjamin Disraeli Letters: Volume Four, 1842–1847* (Toronto: University of Toronto Press, 1989), p. 131.
67. *Hansard*, House of Commons Debates, 14 February 1834, vol. 21 cols 407–11. Hardinge had been quoting the anti-coercion views which Sheil had expressed after what one might euphemistically term a heavy dinner.
68. *Hansard*, House of Commons Debates, 12 May 1853, vol. 127 col. 223.
69. This distinction about proximity to club spaces denoting importance would continue into the early twentieth century, with press sometimes being camped outside the clubs waiting for news during major meetings. During the 1922 Carlton Club meeting which brought down the Lloyd George coalition, Pathé news cameras recorded the stream of Conservative MPs and peers leaving the meeting. See 'Fateful Meeting at the Carlton Club Aka The ... 1922', 2012, http://www.britishpathe.com/video/fateful-meeting-at-the-carlton-club-aka-the-fateful-1/.
70. For those interested in 'official' meetings, much detail can be found in Michael Sharpe's revealing pamphlet on the Reform Club's Political Committee – a considerably expanded version of his University of York MA thesis, which offers detailed analysis of the club's political actions after 1868, when the committee was formed. Sharpe, *Political Committee*.
71. Ibid., p. 18. Instances of MPs' meetings at the Reform Club include the critical 1842 meeting at which the Whigs' opposition to Peel's reintroduced income tax was settled. See Hansard, House of Commons Debates, 18 April 1842, vol. 62, col. 673.
72. Sharpe, *Political Committee*, pp. 19–21.
73. For Disraeli's querying the Carlton's authority to challenge the government, see *The Times*, 17 June 1844, p. 5. For the Carlton's supportive resolutions at that meeting, see *Dundee Courier*, 25 June 1844, p. 2.
74. Kriegel (ed.), *Holland House*, pp. 375–6.
75. Gash, *Sir Robert Peel*, p. 209.
76. *Hansard, House of Commons Debates, 3 March 1842, vol. 60, col. 1408*. Thomas Bermingham, Chairman of the General Irish Railway Committee, was recounting the outcome of the meeting to MPs.
77. Carlton Club archive, Carlton Club, London, MS 'Carlton Club Minute Book, Volume 3, 1839–1843', 7 April 1840.
78. *Hansard*, House of Commons Debates, 18 April 1842, vol. 62, col. 673; see also 17 March 1842, Howe (ed.), *Letters: Volume One*, p. 265.
79. *New York Times*, 19 April 1859, p. 1.

80. See J. A. W. Gunn, M. G. Wiebe et al, *Benjamin Disraeli Letters*, 8 vols (Toronto: University of Toronto Press, 1982–2009), *passim*, for countless examples of letters sent from the Carlton. At the time of writing, the published letters only go as far as 1864, but as Hughenden MSS, Bodleian Library, Oxford, MS Dep Hughenden 40/1/6, f. 250 makes clear, Disraeli also used the Junior Carlton as a mailing address after its foundation in 1864.
81. Gash, *Sir Robert Peel*, p. 197. Gash made his remarks with reference to 14 November 1837.
82. *News and Sunday Herald*, 10 December 1835, quoted in Anonymous, *White's*, vol. 1, p. 217.
83. The comment was reportedly a jibe about the number of careerist politicians 'on the make' he encountered at the Carlton. Tom Girtin, *The Abominable Clubman* (London: Hutchinson, 1964), p. 136.
84. Wilbur Devereux Jones, *Lord Derby and Victorian Conservatism* (Oxford: Basil Blackwell, 1956), p. 123.
85. Kriegel (ed.), *Holland House*, p. 351. Kriegel was unable to ascertain whether the 'Bulwer' referred to was William Henry Lytton Bulwer, Edward Lytton Bulwer, or Earl L. Bulwer, all of whom were members – see p. 483n.
86. Richard Shannon, *Gladstone: Heroic Minister, 1865–1898* (London: Allen Lane, 1999), p. 157.
87. Michael and Eleanor Brock (eds), *H. H. Asquith: Letters to Venetia Stanley* (Oxford: Oxford University Press, 1982), pp. 179, 206, 247, 250, 301, 353, 364.
88. Political clubs continued to be terrorist targets well into the twentieth century, with the last instances of terrorist acts against such clubs being IRA bombs at the Carlton Club in 1990 and the National Liberal Club in 1992.
89. Hawkins, *Forgotten Prime Minister*, vol. 2, p. 313.
90. 2 July 1866, Vincent (ed.), *Disraeli, Derby and the Conservative Party*, p. 256.
91. *Head Quarters*, 15 August 1866, p. 2.
92. *Penny Illustrated Paper*, 8 December 1866, p. 2.
93. 11 February 1867, Hawkins and Powell (eds), *Journal of John Wodehouse*, p. 196.
94. It is worth noting that Trafalgar Square, completed in 1845 to the designs of Reform Club and Travellers' Club architect Sir Charles Barry, had its large fountains designed to minimise the floor space for crowds to gather in, in the event of protests – but that this did not ultimately deter the square from becoming a focus for demonstrators in central London by the last third of the nineteenth century.
95. Peter Mandler, 'From Almack's to Willis's: Aristocratic Women and Politics, 1815–1867', Amanda Vickery (ed.), *Women, Privilege and Power: British Politics, 1750 to the Present* (Stanford, California: Stanford University Press, 2001), p. 159.
96. K. D. Reynolds, *Aristocratic Women*, p. 230.
97. Ibid., pp. 160–2.

98. National Club MSS, Bodleian Library, Oxford, Dep.D.754, MS 'Meeting of the Members and Friends of the National Club, held at Willis' Rooms, King-Street, St James's, on Saturday, May 2, 1846', f. 13.
99. John Vincent, *The Formation of the Liberal Party 1857–1868* (London: Constable, 1966), p. 19 presents the meeting as a mere ratification; see also Hawkins, *Parliament, Party and the Art of Politics*, pp. 251–3.
100. John Tosh, 'Gentlemanly Politeness and Manly Simplicity in Victorian England', *Manliness and Masculinities in Nineteenth-Century Britain: Essays on Gender, Family and Empire* (London: Longman, 2005), p. 90.
101. The first explicit reference to female club servants at the Carlton Club is in Carlton Club archive, Carlton Club, London, MS 'Carlton Club Minute Book, Volume 3, 1839–1843', 25 February 1840, when there was a complaint against the club's billiard marker for insulting a female servant.
102. *Report from the Select Committee on Norwich Election Petitions Withdrawal; With the Proceedings of Committee and Minutes of Evidence* (House of Commons Parliamentary Papers, 17 March 1853), pp. 67, 74.
103. *Age*, 13 June 1864, p. 4.
104. Carlton Club archive, Carlton Club, London, MS 'Carlton Club Minute Book, Volume 3, 1839–1843', 24 May 1842. This appears to have been the first documented instance of a woman setting foot inside the Carlton Club in a non-servant capacity. Borthwick seems to have given other creditors his club address, including to a Mrs. Lutton of Bath.
105. Crawford, *Women's Suffrage Movement*, pp. 123–4.
106. Petrie and Cooke, *Carlton Club*, p. 210n.
107. K. D. Reynolds, *Aristocratic Women*, p. 154. Reynolds goes on to argue that one need not *prove* that women exercised influence, but that they *believed* they did, and that the political system reflected this belief – something Reynolds does with admirable clarity – see p. 173.
108. Ibid., pp. 153–87.
109. Mandler, 'Almack's', Vickery (ed.), *Women*, p. 155.
110. Cited in Reynolds, *Women*, p. 170.
111. Mandler, 'Almack's', Vickery (ed.), *Women*, pp. 152, 153 and see pp. 152–67.
112. Kathryn Gleadle, *Borderline Citizens: Women, Gender and Political Culture in Britain, 1815–1867* (Oxford: Oxford University Press, 2009), pp. 100, 108.
113. Reynolds, *Aristocratic Women*, p. 171.
114. See Chapters 3 and 5.
115. Reynolds, *Aristocratic Women*, p. 174.
116. Ibid., p. 162.
117. Mandler, *Aristocratic Government*, especially pp. 44, 46.
118. See Chapter 2.
119. Disraeli to Lady Londonderry, 7 August 1848, J. A. W. Gunn, M. G. Wiebe et al. (eds), *Benjamin Disraeli Letters, Volume Five: 1848–1851* (Toronto: University of Toronto Press, 1993), p. 54.
120. Ibid.

121. Mandler, *Aristocratic Government*, p. 66.
122. See Chapter 1.
123. The most prominent example of a politically active Club Secretary postdates the period of this book: William Digby was founding Secretary of the National Liberal Club (1882–7) and sought to use the Club as an instrument of political activism. See Mira Matikkala, 'William Digby and the Indian Question', *Journal of Liberal History*, 58 (2008), pp. 12–21, and Mira Matikkala, 'Anti-Imperialism, Englishness, and Empire in Late-Victorian Britain' (PhD thesis, University of Cambridge, 2006).
124. See Amy Milne-Smith, *Clubland* (2011), pp. 9, 11, 111, 154, 163, and particularly pp. 87–108. Milne Smith describes the Clubland atmosphere as 'homosocial' because of its overwhelmingly single-sex nature, whilst emphasising that this word does not imply any homosexual dimension; with Milne-Smith extending this point to observe that there were no documented instances of Clubland homosexuality in the 1880–1910 period. My own search of Clubland archives in the 1832–68 period has, unsurprisingly, found no such *documented* examples, although that does not mean it did not exist.
125. Amanda Vickery, *Behind Closed Doors: At Home in Georgian England* (New Haven, Connecticut: Yale University Press, 2009), p. 52.
126. Vic Gatrell, *City of Laughter: Sex and Satire in Eighteenth Century London* (New York: Walker and Company, 2006), pp. 60–1, 110, 114, 144–5.
127. Marjorie Morgan, *Manners, Morals and Class in England, 1774–1858* (New York: St. Martin's Press, 1994), especially pp. 87–118, including the example of Radical MP Thomas Duncombe on pp. 103–4, who was adept at 'appearances' and 'packaging' in the rule-bound world outlined by Morgan.
128. The first *political* club to offer membership to women on an equal basis was the National Liberal Club, which was not founded until 1882, and did not admit women on equal terms until 1976. The next was the Reform Club in 1981. The Carlton did not admit women on an equal basis until 2008. White's, Brooks's and the National Club still do not admit women at all, while many extinct political clubs – such as the Devonshire Club which was merged in 1976 and the Junior Carlton which was dissolved in 1977 – never admitted women at any point in their history. Thus a legacy of largely-male political Clubland was to set in motion an exclusively male set of spaces which would continue long after such spaces had been challenged elsewhere.
129. *Hansard*, House of Commons Debates, 16 June 1853, vol. 128, col. 260.
130. James Howard Harris, [Third] Earl of Malmesbury, *Memoirs of an Ex-Minister* (London: Longmans, 1885), vol. 1, p. 24.
131. 22–30 January 1855, Vincent (ed.), *Disraeli, Derby and the Conservative Party*, p. 127.
132. See, for instance, Wright and Smith, *Parliament*, pp. 71–2, with its description of the 'gossiping association' of Bellamy's restaurant in the old Houses of Parliament, 1773–1834.

133. Charles Villiers to John Bright, 25 January 1859, quoted in Hawkins, *British*, p. 173.
134. Cited in Antony Taylor, 'Palmerston and Radicalism, 1847–1865', *Journal of British Studies*, 33 (1994), p. 161.
135. 1 March 1829, Wilson (ed.), *Greville Diary*, vol. 1, pp. 533–4.
136. 10 August 1866, Vincent (ed.), *Disraeli, Derby and the Conservative Party*, p. 265.
137. *Hansard*, House of Commons Debates, 2 April 1852, vol. 120, col. 584.
138. *New York Times*, 13 October 1855, p. 4. Note that the discussion took place on 27 September and was recorded the next day, but was not printed until a fortnight later. *New York Times*, 16 October 1855, p. 2 also reproduced some remarks made by 'a Russellite' at the Reform Club (possibly the same person) on 25 September 1855. The so-called Chatham House Rule, not defined until 1927, allows one to reproduce the substance of discussions without directly attributing the source.
139. See Anonymous, *The History of White's, with the Betting Book from 1743 to 1878, and a List of Members from 1736 to 1892: Volume II* (London: Algernon Bourke, 1892); Brooks's Club archive, London Metropolitan Archives, London, GB 0074 ACC/2371/GC/08, MS 'Brooks's Betting Book'.
140. Jules Verne [trans. Henry Frith], *Around the World in Eighty Days* (London: George Routledge, 1875). This popular novel's plot revolves around a wager made in the Reform Club, that Phileas Fogg cannot circumnavigate the globe in under eighty days. As the above section demonstrates, although wagers were commonplace in political clubs, *political* wagers were the most common of all.
141. See Amy Milne-Smith, *Clubland* (2011), and her preceding Milne-Smith, 'Clubland' (2006); Anonymous, *White's*, vol. 2.
142. Anonymous, *White's*, vol. 2, p. 226.
143. Ibid., p. 212.
144. Ibid., p. 223.
145. Ibid., p. 234.
146. Ibid., p. 241.
147. Cited in Fulford, *Boodle's*, p. 29.
148. Anonymous, *White's*, vol. 2, p. 210. The bet was only dated '1832', but was placed in the betting book between one wager from 6 June 1832, and another dated 26 June 1832.
149. Ibid., p. 222.
150. Ibid., p. 224. It is ambiguous as to whether the 'his' referred to Forrester, Sturt or Stanley.
151. Ibid., p. 237.
152. Ibid., p. 220 'May 19th, 1841. Lord Belfast bets Col. G. Damer £5 that if the present ministers dissolve Parliament now, they will have a majority in the next Parliament.'
153. Ibid., p. 217.

NOTES TO PAGES 138–143 259

154. Ibid., p. 217, F. W. S. Craig, *British Parliamentary Election Results, 1832–1885* (London: Macmillan, 1977), pp. 20–1.
155. Anonymous, *White's*, vol. 2, p. 233.
156. Ibid., p. 216, Craig, *Election Results*, pp. 424–5.
157. Anonymous, *White's*, vol. 2, p. 217.
158. Ibid., p. 216.
159. Ibid., p. 217.
160. Cited in Fulford, *Boodle's*, p. 29.
161. Anonymous, *White's*, vol. 2, p. 224.
162. Ibid., p. 228.
163. Ibid., p. 229.
164. Ibid., p. 240.
165. Milne-Smith, *Clubland* (2011), pp. 92–3.

Chapter 4 Clubs as an MP's Base: Accommodation, Dining, Information and Organisational Support

1. In March 1840, 67 MPs gave their club as their London address. Among these 67 MPs, the clubs in order of number of MPs resident were the Carlton (20 MPs), Reform (nine), United University (eight), Wyndham (five), Junior United Service (five), Brooks's (four), United Service (three), Oxford and Cambridge (two), Traveller's (two), and the Union (two). It should be noted that, at the time, the Reform Club was temporarily occupying Gwydir House on Whitehall until its larger, purpose-built clubhouse with more bedrooms was opened the following year.
2. Jenkins, *Parliament, Party and Politics*, p. 64.
3. See the preceding chapter for an explanation of club whipping arrangements.
4. Feargus O'Connell, 'We are Two Millions and Something More', *Northern Star and Leeds General Advertiser*, 5 June 1841, p. 2.
5. National Club MSS, Bodleian Library, Oxford, Dep.b.235, MS 'Minute-book of the General Committee, 1847–1854', ff. 2–3.
6. Carlton Club archive, Carlton Club, London, MS 'Carlton Club Candidates' Book', vol. 8, candidate no. 2246. The Army and Navy Club was on the opposite (north) side of Pall Mall, a few dozen metres from the Carlton.
7. Carlton Club archive, Carlton Club, London, MS 'Carlton Club Candidates' Book', vol. 4, candidate no. 958. It is striking that the St. James's area was increasingly filled with hotels in this period – Jermyn Street alone had at least four, the British, the Brunswick, the Cavendish and the Waterloo. Yet there is no evidence that these were regularly frequented by any sizeable number of MPs. See *Piccadilly 1869: London Large Scale 07.72 (Old Ordnance Survey Maps of London – Yard to the Mile)* (London: Alan Godfrey, 1986).
8. Seth Alexander Thévoz, 'Database of MPs' Club Memberships, 1832–68'.
9. For an account of the original Bellamy's before the destruction of the old House of Commons, see Arnold Wright and Philip Smith, *Parliament, Past and*

Present: A Popular and Picturesque Account of a Thousand Years in the Palace of Westminster, the Home of the Mother of Parliaments (London: Hutchinson, 1902), pp. 70–6. See also Shenton, *Parliament Burned Down*, pp. 71, 87, 121–4, 178, 263.

10. Wilkinson, 'Topography', in Jones and Kelsey (eds), *Parliament*, pp. 148, 163.
11. Wright and Smith, *Parliament, Past and Present*, p. 75.
12. For existing work on political dinners in the constituencies, see Marc Baer, 'Political Dinners in Whig, Radical and Tory Westminster, 1780–1880', Clyve Jones, Philip Salmon and Richard W. Davis (eds), *Partisan Politics, Principle and Reform in Parliament and Constituencies, 1689–1880: Essays in Memory of John A. Phillips* (Edinburgh: Edinburgh University Press, 2005), pp. 183–206; Peter Brett, 'Political Dinners in Early Nineteenth-Century Britain: Platform, Meeting Place and Battleground', *History*, LXXXI (1996), pp. 527–52; Matthew Cragoe, 'The Great Reform Act and the Modernization of British Politics: The Impact of Conservative Associations, 1835–1841', *Journal of British Studies*, 47 (2008), pp. 581–603; Gleadle, *Borderline*, pp. 68, 78, 79, 178.
13. To this day, the Reform Club still privately prints and sells this forty-page pamphlet. See Ann Arnold, *The Adventurous Chef: Alexis Soyer* (London: Reform Club, 2002); See also Timbs, *Clubs*, p. 234.
14. See Matthew Sweet, *Inventing the Victorians* (London: Faber and Faber, London, 2001), p. 106, which cites Soyer in the context of other Victorian French 'celebrity chefs' such as Louis Eustache Ude and Charles Elmé Francatelli.
15. *Hansard*, House of Commons Debates, 13 March 1854, vol. 131, col. 676.
16. The time the House of Commons met could vary by Parliament and by day of the week, but from the 1830s onwards it most commonly met at 4pm (although sometimes at noon or 2pm), with daily sittings averaging around seven to eight hours (not including breaks, such as those taken from 3pm to 5pm during early sittings, or dinner breaks from 7pm to 9pm during late sittings), meaning that sitting until at least 1am was quite normal. Naturally, these are *average* figures, and do not fully reflect the more extreme late-night sittings. See House of Commons hours of sitting and average times of daily sitting for the parliamentary sessions 1830–1868, Chris Cook and Brendan Keith, *British Historical Facts, 1830–1900* (rev. edn, London: Macmillan, 1984, of orig. edn, London: Macmillan, 1975), pp. 100–2.
17. Note that a 7pm serving time at Brooks's coincided precisely with the evening dinner break in the House of Commons.
18. Quoted in Arthur Aspinall, *Lord Brougham and the Whig Party* (Manchester: Manchester University Press, 1939), pp. 272–3n. Although this information was relegated to the footnotes, it should be noted that Aspinall realised the political significance of accumulating such information from Clubland, as early as the 1930s.
19. Cited in Lejeune, *White's*, p. 135.
20. Reform Club archive, Reform Club, London, MS 'Minutes of the Westminster Reform Club 1834–8' f. 18, 26 March 1834.

NOTES TO PAGES 144–146

21. Reform Club archive, Reform Club, London, MS 'Reform Club Minute Book 1836–41', f. 13, 2 August 1836.
22. See, for example, *The Times*, 23 November 1837, p. 2, describing Daniel O'Connell leading a group of MPs to the Reform Club.
23. This detail, from a February 1837 letter from Lord Marcus Hill to John Fielden in the Fielden papers at the University of Manchester, is cited in Coohill, *Liberal*, p. 97.
24. This was stated implicitly rather than explicitly – the Reform Club's committee decreed 'That during the Parliamentary recess members of the club shall be allowed to avail themselves of the privilege of introducing strangers.' Reform Club archive, Reform Club, London, MS 'Reform Club Minute Book 1836–41', f. 13, 2 August 1836.
25. *Hansard*, House of Commons Debates, 14 May 1860, vol. 158, col. 1226.
26. At the Carlton Club, the sitting MPs were Sir Robert Bateson Bt, the Hon. William S. Best, Sir George Clerk Bt., Sir Thomas Fremantle Bt., the Rt. Hon. Henry Goulburn, Sir Alexander Cray Grant Bt., the Rt. Hon Sir Henry Hardinge Bt.,the Hon. William Kenyon, Winthrop M. Praed, Philip Pusey, Charles Ross, Sir Richard R. Vyvyan Bt., Charles Baring Wall and Sir John Walsh Bt, Note that the figure of thirteen MPs does not include committee members like Lord Granville Somerset, who was not an MP at the time. Petrie and Cooke, *Carlton Club*, p. 249. The Westminster Club MPs are not all named, but included John Wilks, Matthew Wood, Rigby Wason, Morgan O'Connell, Daniel Whittle Harvey, Tennyson, Kennedy, Captain Fitzgerald, John O'Connell and Wallace – see Fraser Rae, 'Party Organisation', p. 912. At the National Club, the MPs were J. Heald, W. Long, J. Masterman, W. Copeland, and C. H. Frewin. See National Club MSS, Bodleian Library, Oxford, Dep.b.325, MS 'Minute-book of the General Committee, 1847–1854', f. 123, 29 July 1850.
27. *Illustrated London News*, 25 July 1846, p. 54; Timbs, *Clubs*, p. 230.
28. Greville diary 28 July 1850, quoted in Strachey and Fulford (eds), *Greville Memoirs*, vol. 6, p. 246.
29. Brown, *Palmerston*, p. 324.
30. *New York Times*, 4 May 1864, p. 3; *Age*, 13 June 1864, p. 4.
31. *Illustrated London News*, 25 July 1846 p. 54; Timbs, *Clubs*, p. 229.
32. Reynolds, *Aristocratic Women*, p. 167. Reynolds cites the example of Viscount Palmerston, whose heavy workload meant that organising dinners usually fell to his wife, with his two daughters helping to write invitations.
33. 20 December 1852, Vincent (ed.), *Disraeli, Derby and the Conservative Party*, p. 92; Greville diary 23 December 1852, quoted in Strachey and Fulford (eds), *Greville Memoirs*, vol. 6, p. 383. Beresford was acquitted of the central bribery charge in the inquiry. As Beresford was a Conservative Whip with a desk at the Carlton, dispensing Carlton Club funds, it is entirely plausible that had there been any money dispensed in bribes, its provenance could have been the Carlton, as this is consistent with the activities set out in Chapters 5 and 6. However, no

proof of this survives, and this remains speculation. The aftermath of the Carlton dinner itself provided the well-known occasion on which outraged Conservative MPs threatened to eject Gladstone – now a minister in the Aberdeen coalition – out of the window in the direction of the Reform Club.

34. A summary of the key speeches of this banquet, and the aftermath, can be found in Philip Guedalla, *Palmerston* (London: Hodder and Stoughton, 1926 [1937 ed.]), pp. 313–5.
35. *Hansard*, House of Commons Debates, 16 February 1855, vol. 136, col. 1469.
36. Algernon West, *Recollections 1832 to 1886* (New York: Harper 1900), p. 70; *New York Times*, 24 March 1854, p. 7.
37. *Lyttelton Times*, 17 June 1854, p. 9.
38. Greville diary 13 March 1854, quoted in Strachey and Fulford (eds), *Greville Memoirs*, vol. 7, p. 24.
39. *Hansard*, House of Commons Debates, 13 March 1854, vol. 131, cols 674–5.
40. *Hansard*, House of Commons Debates, 13 March 1854, vol. 131, col. 680.
41. *Hansard*, House of Commons Debates, 13 March 1854, vol. 131, col. 681.
42. Greville diary, 19 March 1854, quoted in Strachey and Fulford (eds), *Greville Memoirs*, vol. 7, p. 27.
43. *Hansard*, House of Commons Debates, 13 March 1854, vol. 131, col. 682.
44. *Hansard*, House of Commons Debates, 13 March 1854, vol. 131, cols 683–5. The charge of political bias in Napier's appointment was not as baseless as it may seem. Shortly after the banquet, Graham became enraged when he overheard one Reform Club member telling another, 'At last it is all out. We have long known that promotion in the navy was only given to Whigs and Radicals, but Sir James Graham has at last fairly confessed it.' See speech by the Liberal MP Michael Bass, *Hansard*, House of Commons Debates, 7 February 1856, vol. 140, cols 440–1.
45. *Hansard*, House of Commons Debates, 13 March 1854, vol. 131, cols 681–3.
46. *Hansard*, House of Commons Debates, 16 February 1855, vol. 136, col. 1470. See also *Hansard*, House of Commons Debates, 8 March 1855, vol. 137, cols 261–90, when Graham was again taunted over the incident, telling the House that his speech was 'an error which I was not prepared to repeat'.
47. See, for instance, the 16 November 1882 banquet at the Westminster Palace Hotel, which set up the new National Liberal Club, at which half a table (out of three tables of dinner guests) was set aside for press correspondents. National Liberal Club archive, National Liberal Club, London, MS 'Seating plan for 16 November 1882 banquet'.
48. Carlton Club archive, Carlton Club, London, MS 'Carlton Club Minute Book, Volume 2, 1835–9', Entries for 28 April 1835, 8 March 1836, 3 May 1836, 21 February 1837, 16 May 1837, 23 May 1837, 28 November 1837, 12 March 1839, and 28 May 1839; Carlton Club archive, Carlton Club, London, MS 'Carlton Club Minute Book, Volume 3, 1839–1843', 9 March 1841. That the London papers were being scrutinised can be deduced from a

reference to the Court Circular in the second volume of minutes, on 28 April 1835.
49. Fraser Rae, 'Party Organisation', p. 913.
50. Stephen Koss, *The Rise and Fall of the Political Press in Britain: Volume 1 – The Nineteenth Century* (London: Hamish Hamilton, 1981), p. 159.
51. Eeles and Spencer, *Brooks's*, p. 175.
52. Koss, *Press*, pp. 159–60.
53. Carlton Club archive, Carlton Club, London, MS 'Carlton Club Minute Book, Volume 2, 1835–9', 18 March 1835.
54. Ibid., 2 June 1838.
55. *The Times*, 28 June 1838, p. 3. Polhill was writing to correct the omission of his name from the third division the previous day.
56. *Hansard*, House of Commons Debates, 21 February 1833, vol. 15, col. 1082.
57. Carlton Club archive, Carlton Club, London, MS 'Carlton Club Minute Book, Volume 2, 1835–9', 16 August 1836. Trevor vigorously denied the charge.
58. *News and Sunday Herald*, 10 December 1835, quoted in Anonymous, *White's*, vol. 1, p. 218; also quoted in Lejeune, *White's*, p. 108.
59. William Henry Bellamy (ed.), *The National Club* (London: National Club, 1848), p. 6.
60. *Hansard*, House of Commons Debates, 17 May 1837, vol. 38, col. 857; *Caledonian Mercury*, 20 May 1837, p. 3. Buller was introducing his annual motion on the observance of the Sabbath, and he added that if Conservatives were serious about the issue, they would close the Carlton Club on Sundays.
61. West, *Recollections*, p. 48 West's description of standing by the telegraph wire of Brooks's is undated, but is included in a chapter spanning 1848–61. In the course of her research for a forthcoming University of London PhD on 'Space and Power in the New Palace of Westminster', Rebekah Moore has found a source which explicitly dates the installation of a telegraph at Brooks's to 1853 – personal information from Rebekah Moore. I eagerly await seeing the light this thesis will shed on this aspect of Clubland communication.
62. William White (ed. Justin McCarthy), *The Inner Life of the House of Commons* (rev. edn, London: T. Fisher Unwin, 1897, of orig. edn, 1856–71), vol. 1, pp. 90–5; the use of club telegraph messages was also cited in Jenkins, *Parliament*, p. 75.
63. *Hansard*, House of Commons Debates, 13 March 1865, vol. 177, col. 1619. Bright made the point to illustrate the contrast between the volume of Lords and Commons business, using the Reform Club notice board as his source.
64. For more on contemporary changes in postage, see M. J. Daunton, *Royal Mail: The Post Office since 1840* (London: Athlone Press, 1985), Chapter 1.
65. Colson, *White's*, p. 55.
66. Robert Steven, *The National Liberal Club: Politics and Persons* (London: Robert Houghton, 1925), p. 57.
67. Duncan Campbell-Smith, *Masters of the Post: The Authorized History of the Royal Mail* (London: Allen Lane, 2011), p. 82.

68. See Sir Robert Peel papers, Peel MSS, British Library, London, Add. MS 40615, 40616 and 40617.
69. Daunton, *Royal Mail*, p. 6.
70. See Pearson Hill, *The Post Office Fifty Years Ago* (London: Cassell, 1888), which reproduces Hill's influential pamphlet in full, and see Royal Mail archive, British Postal Museum and Archive, London, POST 19/27-31 for assorted statistics on postage gathered in answer to parliamentary inquiries on the topic.
71. *Hansard*, House of Commons Debates, 6 February 1840, vol. 51, col. 1312.
72. Royal Mail archive, British Postal Museum and Archive, London, POST 19/28, MS 'Accounts Showing the Time at which the Deliveries in London were Complete in the Month ending 25th November 1837 with the Corresponding Month in 1835', which shows that these were the times by which all central London mail had been delivered on a range of sample days in November 1835 and November 1837. There were two 'rogue' days on which the mail was delivered late (13 November 1837 and 20 November 1837) but, even then, all mail had been delivered by 12:30pm.
73. Sir John Mowbray, *Seventy Years at Westminster* (London: Blackwood, 1900), p. 136.
74. M. G. Wiebe, J. B. Conacher, John Matthews and Mary S. Millar (eds), *Benjamin Disraeli Letters: Volume Three, 1838–1841* (Toronto: University of Toronto Press, 1987), p. 248n. This appears to have happened throughout 1840.
75. Fremantle MSS, Buckinghamshire County Record Office, Aylebury, Bucks., D-FR/80/14, John Young to Sir Thomas Fremantle, 28 May 1840.
76. Carlton Club archive, Carlton Club, London, MS 'Carlton Club Minute Book, Volume 3, 1839–1843', 28 May 1842.
77. *The Times*, 7 March 1836, p. 5.
78. Ibid.
79. Such division lists were a staple of the Annual Reports published by the National Club from 1846 onwards, and continued until the latter part of the century, see National Club MSS, Bodleian Library, Oxford, Dep.c.683, 'Annual Reports'; see also Seth Alexander Thévoz, 'The National Club in Politics, 1845–1868', Oxford University Modern History Seminar paper, 12 May 2011.
80. Alec Corio and Seth Alexander Thévoz, 'Defending the Protestant Principles of the Constitution: the National Club, 1845–1855' (forthcoming journal article).
81. Hawkins, *Parliament, Party and the Art of Politics*, pp. 148–9.
82. Peter Marsh, 'Reform Club' lecture.
83. See Milne Smith, *Clubland* (2011), p. 109, for its portrait of a member in the 1880s who 'breakfasts, lunches, dines and sups at the club ... writes innumerable letters, shakes hands a dozen times a day, drinks coffee by the gallon,and has a nod for everybody. He lives, moves, and has his being within his club.'

Chapter 5 Clubs and Whips in the House of Commons

1. Since this chapter contains discussion of 'Whips' in the sense of parliamentarians ensuring the attendance of their colleagues, and 'whips' in the sense of written notes requesting the presence of a parliamentarian, 'Whips' with a capitalised 'W' is used to denote the person, while 'whips' in lower case denotes the written ephemera.
2. Required reading on the topic of whipping in this period includes J. M. Bourne, *Patronage and Society in Nineteenth-Century England* (London: Edward Arnold, 1986)); Coohill, *Liberal*, especially pp. 77–98; P. M. Gurowich, 'Party and Independence in the Early and Mid-Victorian House of Commons: Aspects of Political Theory and Practice 1832–68, Considered with Special Reference to the Period 1852–68' (PhD thesis, University of Cambridge, 1986); Angus Hawkins, '"Parliamentary Government" and Victorian Political Parties, c.1830 Clubs and Whips in the House of Commons c.1880', *English Historical Review* (1989) CIV (CCCCXII), pp. 638–669; T. A. Jenkins, *Parliament, Party and Politics in Victorian Britain* (Manchester: Manchester University Press, 1996); John C. Sainty, 'The Evolution of the Parliamentary and Financial Secretaryships of the Treasury', *English Historical Review*, XCI (1976), pp. 566–85; John Sainty and Gary W. Cox, 'The Identification of Government Whips in the House of Commons, 1830–1905', *Parliamentary History*, 16 (1997), pp. 339–58. It should be pointed out that a major obstacle to greater understanding of whipping has been the paucity of firsthand accounts made publicly available – indeed, it was not until the publication of Gyles Brandreth, *Breaking the Code – Westminster Diaries, 1992–97* (London: Weidenfeld & Nicholson, 1999) that any whip published a full-length account of their time in office, and then only covering the 1990s. As Brandreth pointed out in his introduction when justifying his title, he was ostracised by his former Whip's Office colleagues and was told that in serialising extracts of his diary, he had 'broken the code' of the Whips. This taboo was later repeated in Tim Renton, *Chief Whip: People, Power and Patronage in Westminster* (London: Politicos, 2004), which includes a brief overview of the history of whipping before going on to detail Renton's own tenure as Chief Whip under Margaret Thatcher, and which remains only the second in-depth account by a former Westminster Whip. Fortunately, our understanding of Victorian Whipping may soon be further enhanced by Stephen Ball's forthcoming publication of the diaries of mid-nineteenth century Liberal Whip Edward Knatchbull-Hugessen, whose rich archival holdings have been consulted in writing this chapter.
3. Sainty and Cox, 'Identification', *Parliamentary History*, pp. 339–58, particularly their graph demonstrating that 1832 coincided with a dramatic – and sustained – increase in the use of Whips as tellers for the government in divisions.

4. See Sainty, 'Secretaryships', pp. 566–85.
5. See Angus Hawkins, *British Party Politics, 1852–1886* (London: Macmillan, 1998), pp. 11–23.
6. Peter Fraser, 'The Growth of Ministerial Control in the Nineteenth-Century House of Commons', *English Historical Review*, 75 (1960), p. 462.
7. Coohill, *Liberal*, p. 77.
8. *Hansard*, House of Commons Debates, 8 April 1842, vol. 62, cols 76–83.
9. Sainty and Cox were able to identify government Whips with relative ease, usually by identifying Treasury officeholders. The identification of opposition Whips was more problematic, as it involved noting particularly frequent tellers in divisions, since telling was a major responsibility of the Whips. Throughout the 1832–5 period, it appears that telling duties were divided evenly among Conservative MPs, making it difficult to identify the Conservative Whip(s). This does not signify that there was no Whip, merely that they did not necessarily serve as tellers.
10. Not included in the list of Liberal Whips is Sir Denis Le Marchant, who according to Joseph Coohill was Liberal Whip for several months in 1841. Coohill bases this on extensive work in the Le Marchant papers demonstrating a much-neglected role in Liberal organisation throughout the early 1840s, not just in 1841. However, from Coohill's text it seems clear that Le Marchant was heavily involved in an election management role (of the kind which later party Whips would be involved in as well), but no evidence is presented that Le Marchant directly whipped parliamentarians in any divisions – crucially, he was not even an MP at the time, and would only briefly serve in the Commons between an 1846 by-election and the 1847 general election. Instead, Le Marchant's role is characterised by Coohill as having 'largely taken over central electoral administration', certainly in the handling of funds. Coohill, *Liberal*, p. 86. Certainly, Le Marchant can be seen as a counterpart to F. R. Bonham as election manager, but not as a Commons Whip, and as Coohill notes, there were sometimes parallel whipping operations among the Liberals. The responsibilities of a Whip in this period were loosely defined, and the identification of individuals necessitates a certain amount of retrospective projection, so that through using different definitions Coohill and Sainty and Cox reached separate conclusions on the identity of whips. Here, the Sainty and Cox list has been used, as it more directly mirrors the kind of activities described in this chapter, and is also more detailed in listing assistant Whips as well as Chief Whips – a dimension which is crucial to several points developed in this chapter. See Coohill, *Liberal*, pp. 78, 83–9. Note that if Le Marchant were listed in Figure 4.1a, it would show that he was elected to Brooks's in 1832. Seth Alexander Thévoz, 'Database of MPs' Club Memberships, 1832–68'. Note also that while F. T. Baring was included in the Sainty and Cox list, he was excluded from the Coohill list (with Charles Wood listed as having had a longer tenure, from 1832–5 rather than 1832–4), therefore Baring's status as a Whip is open to question. Whether or not one

accepts Baring as having been the Liberal Whip, he is included as the rest of the list is sourced from Sainty and Cox; and the fundamental patterns observed in this chapter about Liberal Whips holding membership at Brooks's and the Reform Club are not altered in any way by the inclusion or exclusion of Baring from the list.
11. Bourne, *Patronage*, p. 153.
12. Carlton Club archive, Carlton Club, London, MS 'Carlton Club Candidates' Book', vols 1–12.
13. Hylton MSS, Somerset Heritage Centre, Taunton, DD/HY 18/9/10, Lord Carrington to Sir William Jolliffe, 23 March 1861; Hylton MSS, Somerset Heritage Centre, Taunton, DD/HY 24/11/11 George Dundas to Sir William Jolliffe. This latter correspondence is undated, but can be identified as being from 1857 due to Hopwood's date of election to the Carlton, as a fast-tracked MP member.
14. See, for instance, Hylton MSS, Somerset Heritage Centre, Taunton, DD/HY 24/11/2 and DD/HY 24/11/21.
15. See Chapter 6 for a discussion of the role of election agents Rose and Spofforth at the Carlton and Junior Carlton Clubs, and Coppock at the Reform Club.
16. Hylton MSS, Somerset Heritage Centre, Taunton, DD/HY 18/8/62, Philip Rose to Sir William Jolliffe, 10 April 1857.
17. Hylton MSS, Somerset Heritage Centre, Taunton, DD/HY 24/19/21, Carlton Club Committee of Management appointment card, 21 June 1859, and Hylton MSS, Somerset Heritage Centre, Taunton, DD/HY 24/19/24, William Laiyers Scott to Sir William Jolliffe, 17 March 1859. The Committee of Management could appoint such members under Rule Five of the Carlton Club.
18. Reform Club archive, Reform Club, London, MS 'Reform Club Ballot Books', vols. 1–2 (1836–78); List of all Brooks's members and their proposers, in Wegg-Prosser (ed.), *Memorials of Brooks's*; Carlton Club archive, Carlton Club, London, MS 'Carlton Club Candidates' Book', vols. 1–12 (1834–69); Junior Carlton Club archive, Carlton Club, London, MS 'Junior Carlton Club Candidates' Book', vols. 1–4 (1864–9).
19. *Hansard*, House of Commons Debates, 19 April 1839, vol. 47, col. 359.
20. Carlton Club, *List* (1836), p. 4.
21. Reform Club archive, Reform Club, London, MS 'Reform Club Ballot Book', vol. 1 (1836–52); Reform Club, *List* (1836), p. 3.
22. Junior Carlton Club archive, Carlton Club, London, MS 'New Political Club', f. 1, Circular (marked 'CONFIDENTIAL').
23. Beresford was a founder member of the club's committee in 1845, while Newdegate was first proposed to the club on 10 May 1848, joined both the club and its committee shortly thereafter, and by 1852 he was chairing meetings of the committee. National Club MSS, Bodleian Library, Oxford,

Dep.b.235, MS 'Minute-Book of the General Committee, 1847–1854', ff. 1–32, 201.
24. "Anonymous" [James Grant], *Random Recollections of the House of Commons from the Year 1830 to the Close of 1835, Including Personal Sketches of the Leading Members of All Parties – by One of no Party* (London: Saunders and Otley, 1837), p. 45.
25. Benjamin Disraeli to Sarah Disraeli, 16 April 1836, J. A. W. Gunn, John Matthews, Donald M. Schurman and M. G. Wiebe (eds), *Benjamin Disraeli Letters, Volume Two, 1835–1837* (Toronto: Toronto University Press, 1985), p. 163.
26. Benjamin Disraeli to Sarah Disraeli, 14 November 1837, ibid., p. 312.
27. Benjamin Disraeli to Lord Stanley, 21 January 1851, M. G. Wiebe, J. B. Conacher, John Matthews and Mary S. Millar (eds), *Benjamin Disraeli Letters, Volume Five, 1848–1851* (Toronto: Toronto University Press, 1993), p. 403.
28. Benjamin Disraeli to the Earl of Derby, 14 August 1863, Wiebe, Millar, Robson and Hawman (eds), *Disraeli Letters VIII*, p. 293.
29. Knatchbull MSS, Kent History and Library Centre, Maidstone, U951/527/2, MS 'Political Journal of Edward Knatchbull-Hugessen', vol. 2, ff. 40, 42, 12 January 1866, 19 January 1866 (this entry referred to a dinner the previous night) and 24 January 1866.
30. *New York Times*, 12 June 1856, p. 4.
31. *Hansard*, House of Commons Debates, 19 August 1839, vol. 50 col. 390.
32. See Jenkins, *Parliament*, pp. 59–88; T. A. Jenkins, 'The Whips in the Early-Victorian House of Commons', *Parliamentary History*, 19 (2000), pp. 259–86.
33. T. A. Jenkins, 'Whips', p. 260. The capitalisation of the word 'Whip' in the quotation is mine, so as to avoid confusion between Whips and whips, as per the formatting of this chapter explained in footnote 1. Even the subsequent work of Joseph Coohill, drawing on largely neglected archives and shedding further light on whipping operations, still underlines the point that much detailed information about the mechanics of whipping among Liberals has not survived. Coohill, *Liberal*, p. 77.
34. Fremantle MSS, Buckinghamshire County Record Office, Aylesbury, Bucks., D-FR/80/5, Circular from Lord Redesdale to Conservative peers, 18 April 1837.
35. Fremantle MSS, Buckinghamshire County Record Office, Aylesbury, Bucks., D-FR/80/7/10-21, Bank receipts for multiple payments into the subscription fund.
36. Fremantle MSS, Buckinghamshire County Record Office, Aylesbury, Bucks., D-FR/80/5, Undated circular (c. March/April 1837), letter is a loose sheet inside the item, which is a book of subscribers.
37. Sainty and Cox, 'Whips', pp. 339–58.
38. Fremantle MSS, Buckinghamshire County Record Office, Aylesbury, Bucks., D-FR/80/7/3, W. S. S. Lascelles to Sir Thomas Fremantle, 30 May 1840.
39. Ibid.

40. Fremantle MSS, Buckinghamshire County Record Office, Aylesbury, Bucks., D-FR/80/5, Circular from Lord Redesdale to Conservative peers, 18 April 1837.
41. Fremantle MSS, Buckinghamshire County Record Office, Aylesbury, Bucks., D-FR/80/7/3, Matthias Attwood to Sir Thomas Fremantle (undated).
42. Fremantle MSS, Buckinghamshire County Record Office, Aylesbury, Bucks., D-FR/80/7, Lord Redesdale to Sir Thomas Fremantle, 2 September 1840.
43. Fremantle MSS, Buckinghamshire County Record Office, Aylesbury, Bucks., D-FR/80/7, Lord Redesdale to Sir Thomas Fremantle, 22 April 1840.
44. *Hansard*, House of Commons Debates, 26 February 1838, vol. 41, col. 108.
45. Assorted whips can be found in Fremantle MSS, Buckinghamshire County Record Office, Aylesbury, Bucks, D-FR/80/8.
46. Bourne, *Patronage*, p. 75.
47. Fremantle MSS, Buckinghamshire County Record Office, Aylesbury, Bucks., D-FR/80/11/2, Earl of Lincoln to Sir Thomas Fremantle. Lincoln had chaired the Carlton Club meeting and enclosed the full text of the resolution.
48. Newcastle Trust papers, Glynne-Gladstone MSS, Gladstone's Library, Hawarden, Flintshire, GG 2960/1, Earl of Lincoln to F. R. Bonham (copy), 2 December 1839. Lincoln wrote: 'I have not yet written to Campbell because Fremantle promised to let me know if Grieve would take Walker off his hands, but I will ascertain what are his feelings as to breaking the pair if he can.'
49. Peel MSS, British Library, London, Add. Ms. 40616/308, Sir James Graham to F. R. Bonham, 22 January 1845, f. 3.
50. Fremantle MSS, Buckinghamshire County Record Office, Aylesbury, Bucks, D-FR/80/7/22. There were six letters to Sandwich, two for Yarmouth, and two parcels to Leicester, all in early 1839. The Sandwich correspondence is most likely related to that year's by-election, Bonham's role in which is described in more detail in Chapter 6.
51. T. A. Jenkins, 'Whips in the Early-Victorian House of Commons', p. 266.
52. Ibid. As well as the original March/April subscription circular, copies repeating the subscription for the new parliamentary sessions can be found in Fremantle MSS, Buckinghamshire County Record Office, Aylesbury, Bucks., D-FR/80/6/3, 6 July 1838, later in D-FR/80/7/7 (1838), D-FR/80/6/4 (1839) and D-FR/80/7/9 and D-FR/80/12/2 (both 1840). These examples only cover the Conservatives' years in opposition.
53. For the role of John Newman, 'the Whip distributor' operating from Barton Street, see Jenkins, 'Whips', *Parliamentary History*, p. 275. For the Victoria Street office, see Hylton MSS, Somerset Heritage Centre, Taunton, DD/HY 18/8/1, circular from Sir William Jolliffe, 10 March 1859.
54. Fremantle MSS, Buckinghamshire County Record Office, Aylesbury, Bucks., D-FR/80/19.
55. Hylton MSS, Somerset Heritage Centre, Taunton, DD/HY 18/6/165, Votes of Members in office, and DD/HY 18/6/235, Votes of Members in office.

56. See Coohill, *Liberal*, pp. 80–2, 85–6, 90–1, particularly the whips cited from the papers of Edward J. Stanley in the Lincolnshire Record Office.
57. Bourne, *Patronage*, pp. 137–51.
58. Knatchbull MSS, Kent History and Library Centre, Maidstone, U951/527/2, MS 'Political Journal of Edward Knatchbull-Hugessen', vol. 2, f. 10, conversation recorded between Benjamin Disraeli and Liberal Whip Edward Knatchbull-Hugessen, 5 February 1865.
59. Parkes MSS, University College London, London, Parkes 25, Edward J. Stanley to Joseph Parkes, 30 December 1837. See Chapter 5 for further discussion of this fund. The letter names Stanley, Parkes and James Coppock as the prime movers behind this fund, and suggests its administration should be limited to 'no more than half a dozen people'.
60. Fremantle MSS, Buckinghamshire County Record Office, Aylesbury, Bucks., D-FR/80/9.
61. See Parry, *Liberal Government, passim*.
62. See Frank O'Gorman, *The Emergence of the British Two-Party System, 1760–1832* (London: Edward Arnold, 1982), and O'Gorman, *Voters, Patrons, and Parties, passim*.
63. See Derek Beales, 'Parliamentary Parties and the "Independent" Member, 1810–1860', Robert Robson (ed.), *Ideas and Institutions of Victorian Britain: Essays in Honour of George Kitson Clark* (London: G. Bell, 1967), pp. 1–19, in which Beales concludes that party alignments were strong in the 1835–45 period, but much weaker before and after, with 'independence' holding sway.
64. Hawkins, *British*, p. 21. See also Angus Hawkins, *Parliament, Party and the Art of Politics in Britain, 1855–59* (Stanford, California: Stanford University Press, 1987), especially pp. 266–89.
65. Sainty and Cox, 'Whips', *Parliamentary History*, p. 351.
66. J. B. Conacher, *The Aberdeen Coalition, 1852–1855* (Cambridge: Cambridge University Press, 1968), p. 29.
67. As described in Chapter 1, even when a club admitted guests in the middle of the century, it was usually only to a segregated guests' room, which would have been of little help to a Whip seeking to round up MPs in a club's members-only rooms, unless they belonged to the same club.
68. Gash, *Sir Robert Peel*, p. 619.
69. Angus Hawkins has argued that the Conservative parliamentary strategy during this period, far from being one of indecision and muddle, was led by Derby's strategy of 'masterly inactivity', an argument first published in Angus Hawkins, 'Lord Derby and Victorian Conservatism: A Reappraisal', *Parliamentary History*, 6 (1987), pp. 280–301, and most recently developed at length as a key theme of Angus Hawkins, *The Forgotten Prime Minister: The 14th Earl of Derby*, 2 vols (Oxford: Oxford University Press, 2007–8).
70. 6 March 1863, Vincent (ed.), *Disraeli, Derby and the Conservative Party*, p. 197.

NOTES TO PAGES 172–176   271

71. David Brown, *Palmerston: A Biography* (New Haven, Connecticut: Yale University Press, 2010), p. 341.
72. Peel MSS, British Library, London, Add. Ms. 40616/185, Sir James Graham to F. R. Bonham, 27 December 1840. For the background of this, see also Arvel B. Erickson, *The Public Career of Sir James Graham* (Oxford: Basil Blackwell, 1952), p. 152.
73. 22 November 1835, Richard A. Gaunt (ed.), *Unrepentant Tory: Political Selections from the Diaries of the Fourth Duke of Newcastle-under-Lyne, 1827–38* (Woodbridge: Boydell Press, 2006), p. 287; see also 22 November 1835, Philip Whitwell Wilson (ed.), *The Greville Diary, Including Passages Hitherto Withheld from Publication* (London: Heinemann, 1927), vol. 1, p. 442.
74. Gash, *Sir Robert Peel*, p. 330.
75. Jonathan Parry, presentation to the History of Parliament Trust's 1832–68 colloquium, Westminster Hall, London, 6 May 2011.
76. Anthony Howe, presentation to the History of Parliament Trust's 1832–68 colloquium, Westminster Hall, London, 6 May 2011. Note that the Cobden Club was not, by the definition set out in this book, a 'club', in that it had no physical premises; but it is included here because contemporary sources such as almanacs used to list it alongside the clubs which had a building.
77. See National Club MSS, Bodleian Library, Oxford, Dep.c.683, *Annual Reports of the National Club*, with a complete run of pre-1868 reports.
78. National Club, *Eighteenth Annual Report of the National Club* (London: National Club, 1863), pp. 4–5 has a detailed account of Newdegate's speech, and its reception. The club was incensed by the bill, believing it to be 'obviously a Popish measure'.
79. For instance, see National Club, *Eleventh Annual Report of the National Club* (London: National Club, 1857), p. 7.

Chapter 6 Clubs and Electoral Interventions

1. Charles Morris, *'All the Shallows.': A Letter to John Bull, Esquire, About Administrations in General, and the Earl of Derby's Administration in Particular* (1852), p. 6, *Bristol Selected Pamphlets*, University of Bristol Library [consulted at http://www.jstor.org/stable/60248526, 8 April 2011]; Henry Ralph Smythe, *Parliamentary Reform, Considered, under the Views Suggested by Evidence Given Before the Election Committees of 1853* (1854), p. 35, Knowsley Pamphlet Collection, University of Liverpool [consulted at http://www.jstor.org/stable/60100657, 8 April 2011].
2. See Benjamin Disraeli, *Coningsby* (reprint, London: Heron Books, 1967, of orig. edn, London, 1844) and Disraeli, *Sybil*. Taper was also briefly alluded to in Benjamin Disraeli, *Tancred* (reprint, London: Walter Dunne, 1904, of orig. edn, London, 1847).
3. Owen Dudley Edwards, 'Anthony Trollope, the Irish Writer', *Nineteenth-Century Fiction*, 38 (1983), p. 23.

4. Anthony Trollope, *The Prime Minister* (reprint, London: Folio Society, 1991, of orig. edn, London, 1876), p. 56.
5. O'Gorman, *Emergence of Two-Party System*, p. 120.
6. Arbuthnot to Wellington, 10 November 1833, John Brooke and Julia Gandy (eds), *The Prime Ministers' papers: Wellington, Political Correspondence I: 1833 – November 1834* (London: HMSO, 1975), p. 350.
7. *The Times*, 21 December 1832, p. 3. The Carlton is described here as 'the Conservative Club', as it was informally known at the time, since the rival 'Conservative Club' was not founded until 1840.
8. See Norman Gash, 'F. R. Bonham: Conservative "Political Secretary", 1832 – 47', *English Historical Review*, LXIII (1948), pp. 502 – 22; Gash, *Politics*, esp. pp. 393 – 430; Gash, 'Organisation of the Conservative Party, Part I', pp. 137 – 59; Gash, 'Organisation of the Conservative Party, Part II', pp. 131 – 52; Gash (ed.), *Pillars of Government*; Southgate, *Passing of the Whigs*; Stewart, *Conservative Party*; Bruce Coleman, *Conservatism and the Conservative Party in Nineteenth-Century Britain* (London: Edward Arnold, 1988).
9. Nancy D. LoPatin [subsequently LoPatin-Lummis], *Political Unions, Popular Politics and the Great Reform Act of 1832* (London: Macmillan, 1999), pp. 38 – 50; Salmon, *Electoral Reform*, pp. 43 – 58; Cragoe, 'Great Reform Act and Modernisation'.
10. Salmon, *Electoral Reform*, p. 58.
11. Phillips, *Great Reform Bill*, p. 26.
12. *Hansard*, House of Commons Debates, 24 March 1859, vol. 153, col. 781.
13. *Report from the Select Committee on Norwich Election Petitions Withdrawal; with the Proceedings of Committee and Minutes of Evidence* (House of Commons Parliamentary Papers, 17 March 1853), pp. 102 – 3.
14. Coleman, *Conservatism*, p. 107.
15. Gash, 'Bonham'; Gash, *Politics*; Gash, 'Organisation of the Conservative Party, Part I', pp. 137 – 59; Gash, 'Organisation of the Conservative Party, Part II', pp. 131 – 52; Salmon, *Electoral Reform*, pp. 48 – 52.
16. Gash, *Politics*, pp. 413 – 8, especially 'The disruption of 1846 put an inevitable termination to his political career ... Peel's death in 1850 was the irretrievable stroke' p. 417, and in 1863 'he died ... a forgotten and unnoticed figure.' p. 418.
17. Newcastle Trust papers, Glynne-Gladstone MSS, Gladstone's Library, Hawarden, Flintshire, GG 2960/5, F. R. Bonham to the Earl of Lincoln, 19 October 1849.
18. 10 January, 17 January 1853, M. R. D. Foot and H. C. G. Matthew (eds), *The Gladstone Diaries, Volume IV: 1848 – 1854* (Oxford: Clarendon Press, 1974), pp. 487, 489.
19. Catherine Gladstone papers, Glynne-Gladstone MSS, Gladstone's Library, Hawarden, Flintshire, GG 773/183, W. E. Gladstone to Catherine Gladstone, 26 March 1857.
20. Jessie Buckley, *Joseph Parkes of Birmingham; and the Part Which he Played in Radical Reform Movements from 1825 to 1845* (London: Methuen, 1926),

remains the only full-scale study of Parkes's career; see also G. B. A. M. Finlayson, 'Joseph Parkes of Birmingham, 1796–1865: a study in philosophic radicalism', *Bulletin of the Institute of Historical Research*, XLVI (1973), pp. 186–201, and Salmon (ed.), *Letters of Joseph Parkes*.
21. Richard Cobden to Joseph Parkes, 8 July 1846, Howe (ed.), *Letters: Volume One*, p. 446. Cobden was recalling how he had seen Parkes over the years.
22. William Durrant Cooper (1812–75) was a solicitor and antiquary who belonged to the Reform Club and held the position of member of its Library Committee.
23. James Coppock (1798–1857), solicitor and Whig agent.
24. Richard Cobden to Sir Charles Pelham Villiers, 11 Dec 1843, Howe (ed.), *Letters: Volume One*, pp. 346–7.
25. Lincoln R.O. 4 TdE H/53/5, cited in Salmon (ed.), *Letters of Joseph Parkes*, Parkes to Charles Tennyson, 4 August 1830.
26. Nancy LoPatin-Lummis, '"With All My Oldest and Native Friends". Joseph Parkes: Warwickshire Solicitor and Electoral Agent in the Age of Reform', Nancy LoPatin-Lummis (ed.), *Public Life and Public Lives – Politics and Religion in Modern British History: Essays in Honour of Richard W. Davis* (Oxford: Wiley-Blackwell/History of Parliament Trust Yearbook, 2008), p. 108.
27. Albert Nicholson, 'Coppock, James (1798–1857)', rev. H. C. G. Matthew, *Oxford Dictionary of National Biography*, Oxford University Press, 2004, http://www.oxforddnb.com/view/article/6279 (accessed 4 September 2012).
28. Coohill, *Liberal*, p. 96. Coohill speculates that this was due to Coppock's social status, but it should be noted that the radical flavour of the Westminster Reform Club's membership was far from aristocratic, and that its minute book makes clear that the club was desperate for members in its short-lived existence, suggesting some more deep-seated reason for Coppock's rejection.
29. Woodbridge, *Reform Club*, p. 116.
30. Anonymous letter-writer under the pseudonym, 'Philodemus', *The Times*, 9 December 1836, p. 7.
31. Salmon, *Electoral Reform*, pp. 54–7.
32. *Lyttelton Times*, 7 August 1852, p. 4.
33. Ibid. It is unclear at which election Coppock intervened on Roebuck's behalf, since Roebuck stood at Bath in 1837, 1841 and 1847, only being victorious the second time.
34. *Hansard*, House of Commons Debates, 16 March 1869, vol. 194, cols 1504–5.
35. Brown's neglect is underlined not only by the degree to which he is excluded from almost all historical accounts of Carlton electoral activity in the 1840s and 1850s, but also by his being the only national party agent of the period to have *not* been the subject of a *Dictionary of National Biography* profile – Bonham, Coppock, Parkes, Rose and Spofforth have all received such attention. See Norman Gash, 'Bonham, Francis Robert (1785–1863)', *Oxford Dictionary of National Biography*, Oxford University Press, 2004 http://www.oxforddnb.com/view/article/37207 (accessed 4 September 2012); Albert

Nicholson, 'Coppock, James (1798–1857)', rev. H. C. G. Matthew, *Oxford Dictionary of National Biography*, Oxford University Press, 2004, http://www.oxforddnb.com/view/article/6279 (accessed 4 September 2012); Philip J. Salmon, 'Parkes, Joseph (1796–1865)', *Oxford Dictionary of National Biography*, Oxford University Press, 2009, http://www.oxforddnb.com/view/article/21356 (accessed 4 September 2012); Mary S. Millar, 'Rose, Sir Philip, first baronet (1816–1883)', *Oxford Dictionary of National Biography*, Oxford University Press, 2004, http://www.oxforddnb.com/view/article/41059 (accessed 4 September 2012); E. J. Feuchtwanger, 'Spofforth, Markham (1825–1907)', *Oxford Dictionary of National Biography*, Oxford University Press, 2004, http://www.oxforddnb.com/view/article/52754 (accessed 4 September 2012).

36. 15 March 1851, Vincent (ed.), *Disraeli, Derby and the Conservative Party*, p. 56.
37. *The Times*, 3 August 1853, p. 2; *Report from the Select Committee on Norwich election Petitions Withdrawal; with the Proceedings of Committee and Minutes of Evidence* (House of Commons Parliamentary Papers, 17 March 1853), p. 16; Robert Blake, *The Conservative Party from Peel to Churchill* (reprint, London: Fontana, 1979, of orig. edn, London, 1970), p. 146.
38. *Report from the Select Committee on Norwich Election Petitions Withdrawal; with the Proceedings of Committee and Minutes of Evidence* (House of Commons Parliamentary Papers, 17 March 1853), p. 51 Testimony of Lt. Colonel L. S. Dickson MP, recounting a conversation with Brown.
39. *The Times*, 3 August 1853, p. 2; *Report from the Select Committee on Norwich Election Petitions Withdrawal; with the Proceedings of Committee and Minutes of Evidence* (House of Commons Parliamentary Papers, 17 March 1853), p. 16; Blake, *Conservative Party*, p. 146.
40. *Hansard*, House of Commons Debates, 28 April 1862, vol. 166, cols 1020–1; *Hansard*, House of Commons Debates, 23 April 1861, vol. 162, col. 991; Alistair Cooke, 'Club and Party, 1832–2007', Petrie and Cooke, *Carlton Club*, p. 229.
41. Caption of caricature of Markham Spofforth by 'Ape'[Carlo Pellegrini], *Vanity Fair*, 20 March 1880 [unnumbered plate].
42. Mary S. Millar, 'Rose, Sir Philip, first baronet (1816–1883)', *Oxford Dictionary of National Biography*, Oxford University Press, 2004 http://www.oxforddnb.com/view/article/41059 (accessed 4 September 2012).
43. Stewart, *Conservative*, p. 329.
44. Disraeli to Spofforth, 21 November 1863, Wiebe, Millar, Robson and Hawman (eds), *Disraeli Letters VIII*, pp. 329–30. Disraeli's dismissal of Carlton members as 'town loungers' is somewhat ironic, given his own daily use of the Carlton.
45. E. J. Feuchtwanger, *Disraeli, Democracy and the Tory Party: Conservative Leadership and Organisation after the Reform Bill* (Oxford: Clarendon Press, 1968), p. 112.
46. Millar, 'Rose'.
47. Stewart, *Conservative*, p. 280.

48. Gash, *Politics*, pp. 434–7; Stewart, *Conservative*, pp. 139–41; Coleman, *Conservatism*, p. 108; Salmon, *Electoral*, p. 101.
49. *Hansard*, House of Commons Debates, 2 February 1844, vol. 72, col. 157.
50. *The Times*, 2 March 1848, p. 7.
51. Junior Carlton Club archive, Carlton Club, London, MS 'Junior Carlton Club General Meeting Minutes, Volume 1, 1865–1967', Fifth Annual General Meeting, 24 May 1869.
52. Ibid.
53. Ibid.
54. Ibid.
55. Ibid.
56. Ibid.
57. *The Times*, 2 March 1853, p. 7.
58. Quoted in *The Times*, 7 July 1848, p. 8.
59. Reproduced in 'Appendix 11: Payments from the Central Fund to the Constituencies, 1859 Elections', Stewart, *Conservative*, p. 391. The list should be regarded as incomplete, because many entries refer to a surname (presumably the agent responsible) rather than a clearly identifiable constituency, and some entries in the archives were illegible, both to Stewart and myself.
60. Hylton MSS, Somerset Hertage Centre, Taunton, DD/HY 24/11/39. Note that the list is externally titled on the outer leaf 'List of Reports sent to Sir Wm. Jolliffe; & Political Correspondence during the Winter of 1856–57', written in another hand, but it is clear from Jolliffe's own hand that the list part of the document dates from 21 June 1855. Unlike the 1859 list reproduced by Stewart, this list is complete and fully legible.
61. Stewart, *Conservative*, p. 329.
62. Ibid., p. 391
63. Ibid. Note that due to some sums being illegible, £47,100 represents the sum of the legible amounts, and £52,500 Stewart's estimate based on the illegible amounts all being for the average payment of £300.
64. Petrie and Cooke, *Carlton*, p. 230.
65. *The Times*, 19 May 1853, p. 3.
66. *The Times*, 18 November 1853; p. 9.
67. *The Times*, 3 July 1858, p. 11. Cross described himself as an agent 'Not for the Carlton Club', acting for the unsuccessful Liberal candidate Colonel H. R. Addison.
68. Hylton MSS, Somerset Heritage Centre, Taunton, DD/HY 18/5/44, Philip Rose to Sir William Jolliffe, 19 December 1857. Later parts of the letter are illegible, but it appears to continue discussing the fortunes of fund-supported candidates.
69. *The Times*, 2 June 1832, p. 5.
70. Speech by Palmer to the electors of Berkshire, *The Times*, 4 June 1832, p. 3.
71. *The Times*, 2 May 1835, p. 3.

72. Henry Miller, 'Popular Petitioning and the Corn Laws, 1833–46', *English Historical Review*, 127 (2012), pp. 882–919.
73. Herries MSS, British Library, London, Vol. IV, General Correspondence, Add. MSS 57420, W. Forbes Mackenzie to J. C. Herries, 28 February 1833, f. 140.
74. *Oxford Mail*, 18 December 1837, p. 3; see also *The Times*, 20 December 1837, p. 6, which only counted fourteen petitions. The petitions included such disparate constituencies as Blackburn, Bolton, Frome and Preston.
75. *The Times*, 20 December 1837, p. 6.
76. *Report from the Select Committee on Norwich Election Petitions Withdrawal; with the Proceedings of Committee and Minutes of Evidence* (House of Commons Parliamentary Papers, 17 March 1853), pp. iv, 10. The committee named seven constituencies: Kidderminster (three Conservative petitions), Gloucester (four Conservative petitions), Middlesex (two Conservative petitions), and Youghal (one Liberal petition), and the two-member constituencies of Norwich (two Conservative petitions), County Down (two Liberal petitions) and West Norfolk (three Liberal petitions).
77. Ibid., pp. 4, 8. Testimony of Kitton before the committee. Norwich Conservative candidate Lt. Colonel L.S. Dickson disagreed, however, believing Norwich's petitions to have been traded for Youghal rather than West Norfolk, but this was a rumour 'On my word of honour as an officer, I say that I heard it from a gentleman, a member of the Carlton Club,' pp. 65–6.
78. Ibid., pp. 5, 16, 85. The introductory meeting with Brown in his Carlton office was dated 8 November 1852.
79. Ibid., p. 7. One was found: Lord Ranelagh.
80. *The Times*, 27 May 1835, p. 6.
81. See Anonymous, *Addresses of the National Club, August 1846 to September 1847 – First Series* (London: Macintosh, 1848); Anonymous, *Addresses of the National Club, November 1847 to February 1848 – Second Series* (London: Macintosh, 1849); Anonymous, *Addresses of the National Club, Third Series* (London: Macintosh, 1851); Anonymous, *Addresses of the National Club, Fourth Series* (London: Macintosh, 1852).
82. Address No. 1, 14 August 1846, Anonymous, *Addresses of the National Club (I)*, pp. 3–5.
83. National Club MSS, Bodleian Library, Oxford, Dep.b.235, MS 'Minute-book of the General Committee, 1847–1854', 9 and 16 November 1847.
84. National Club MSS, Bodleian Library, Oxford, Dep.b.235, MS 'Minute-book of the General Committee, 1847–1854'; National Club MSS, Bodleian Library, Oxford, Dep.b.236, MS 'Minute-book of the General Committee, 1861–1870'. The minute book for the intervening years 1854–61 no longer survives.
85. See Wolffe, *Crusade*.
86. I am grateful to Angus Hawkins for first having made this point, in feedback to my seminar paper, Seth Alexander Thévoz, '"A Protestant Parliament for a Protestant England": The Politics of the National Club, 1845–1868', Oxford Modern British History seminar paper, 12 May 2011.

87. See G. H. Jackson, *The Cobden Club* (London: Cobden-Sanderson, 1938).
88. Reform Association, *The County Electors' Manual; or, Practical Instructions for the Annual Registration of Voters in Counties* (London: James Ridgeway, 1835); Reform Association, *The Borough Electors' Manual; or, Practical Instructions for the Annual Registration of Voters in Cities and Boroughs* (London: James Ridgeway, 1835).
89. Hayes Lyon papers, Cheshire and Chester Local Studies Centre, Chester, Cheshire, DHL/78/5 and DHL/78/6.
90. Reform Association, *County*, pp. 5, 17–8, with the same passages also appearing in Reform Association, *Borough*, pp. 5, 17–8.
91. Ibid., pp. 21–2.
92. John Hayes Lyon papers, Cheshire and Chester Local Studies Centre, Chester, Cheshire, DHL/57a/53, Circular from Coppock to Lyon (Undated, but DHL/57a/54 makes it clear that it was sent 'a few days ago' before 15 August 1838).
93. William Wilshere MSS, Hertfordshire Record Office, Hertford, Hertfordshire, DE.X.14.32, Coppock to Wilshere, 9 October 1838.
94. John Hayes Lyon papers, Cheshire and Chester Local Studies Centre, Chester, Cheshire, DHL/57a/54, Copy of letter from Lyon's brother to Coppock, 15 August 1838.
95. Coohill, *Liberal*, p. 82.
96. Michael Markus, 'A Pocket Borough? Reformed Politics in Ripon, 1832–67', *Parliamentary History*, 27 (2008), pp. 330–60 queries Gash's central supposition that Ripon was a pocket borough of Elizabeth Lawrence's, and so casts doubt on Gash's comment that Conservative candidates 'owed their nominations to decisions taken at Studley [Royal, the home of the Lawrences], the Carlton and Westminster.' p. 340.
97. See, for instance, *Hansard*, House of Commons Debates, 4 June 1841, vol. 58, col. 1151, in which Liberal MP Sir Harry Verney alleged that the Conservative candidate in Nottingham at the previous general election had been 'sent down by the Conservative Club'. (As the Conservative Club was not launched until later in the year, this was a reference to the Carlton, which was confusingly often dubbed 'the Conservative Club' until the creation of a separate club of that name.) The phrase 'sent down by the Carlton' had been popularised in Disraeli's novel *Sybil*.
98. Hughenden MSS, Bodleian Library, Oxford, Dep. Hughenden 28/4 f. 99, John Monckton, 'Account of the General Election of August 1837'.
99. *The Times*, 3 August 1853, p. 2. After being defeated, they attempted to petition the result. The petition was abandoned after Lord Douro inherited the Dukedom of Wellington and accepted a post in the Aberdeen coalition.
100. Hylton MSS, Somerset Heritage Centre, Taunton, DD/HY 18/8/6, Marquess of Bath to Sir William Jolliffe, undated, but c. 1855–7.
101. Helen W. Swartz and Marvin Swartz (eds), *Disraeli's Reminiscences* (London: Hamish Hamilton, 1975), p. 38. *Tancred* merely uses a detailed description of

the setting, the less salubrious end of Mayfair, for its first chapter, rather than documenting the circumstances of the by-election. See Disraeli, *Tancred*, pp. 1–10.
102. Gash, *Politics*, p. 462.
103. *Dorset County Chronicle*, April 1835, p. 3.
104. The most detailed account remains R. E. Foster, 'Peel, Disraeli and the 1835 Taunton By-Election', *Transactions of the Somerset Archaeological and Natural History Society*, CXXVI (1982), pp. 111–18.
105. Benjamin Disraeli to Sarah Israeli, 26 April 1835, J.A.W. Gunn, John Matthews, Donald M. Schurman and M. G. Wiebe (eds), *Disraeli Letters, Volume Two, 1835–1837* (Toronto: Toronto University Press, 1985), p. 31.
106. Ian Machin, *Disraeli* (London: Longman, 1995), p. 28. A closer reading of Bonham's letter in Gash, *Politics*, pp. 462–3 reveals this may be an exaggeration. In a letter dated 24 April 1835 to Mr. Beaden, the Taunton Conservative solicitor, Bonham simply pledged to pay 'the greater part if not the whole Three Hundred Pounds he wants – however I cannot guarantee it.'
107. *Morning Chronicle*, 25 April 1835, p. 3; *Bury and Norwich Post, and East Anglian*, 29 April 1835, p. 1.
108. Sir Thomas Gladstone (Second Baronet) papers, Glynne-Gladstone MSS, Gladstone's Library, Hawarden, Flintshire, GG 519, F. R. Bonham to Sir Thomas Gladstone, 10 December 1834. The letter is simply dated 'Dec 10th', and an archivist has erroneously dated it to December 1835. In fact, Sir John Walsh, referenced in the letter as the incumbent, had already retired at the general election earlier that year, so the letter can be dated to December 1834. As Philip Salmon has noted, very little of Bonham's correspondence was believed to have survived beyond two small collections in the Peel papers, and so the Bonham letters found in the Gladstone papers and never before quoted elsewhere offer a fresh insight into Bonham's practices as an agent.
109. Sir Thomas Gladstone (Second Baronet) papers, Glynne-Gladstone MSS, Gladstone's Library, Hawarden, Flintshire, GG 519, Sir Thomas Gladstone to F. R. Bonham (copy), 22 December 1838.
110. Sir Thomas Gladstone (Second Baronet) papers, Glynne-Gladstone MSS, Gladstone's Library, Hawarden, Flintshire, GG 528/1, MS Sir Thomas Gladstone, 'To the Gentlemen who did me the honour to constitute a Committee at *Sandwich* (or *Deal & Walmer*) for promoting my return to Parliament' (copy), 11 February 1839.
111. Sir Thomas Gladstone (Second Baronet) papers, Glynne-Gladstone MSS, Gladstone's Library, Hawarden, Flintshire, GG 528/39, F. R. Bonham to Sir Thomas Gladstone, 3 February 1839.
112. Ibid.
113. Sir Thomas Gladstone (Second Baronet) papers, Glynne-Gladstone MSS, Gladstone's Library, Hawarden, Flintshire, GG 528/25, F. R. Bonham to Sir Thomas Gladstone, 4 February 1839.

114. Sir Thomas Gladstone (Second Baronet) papers, Glynne-Gladstone MSS, Gladstone's Library, Hawarden, Flintshire, GG 528/12, F. R. Bonham to Sir Thomas Gladstone, 14 February 1839.
115. Catherine Gladstone papers, Glynne-Gladstone MSS, Gladstone's Library, Hawarden, Flintshire, GG 769/57-8, William Ewart Gladstone to Catherine Gladstone, 16 June 1841.
116. Catherine Gladstone papers, Glynne-Gladstone MSS, Gladstone's Library, Hawarden, Flintshire, GG 769/59-60, William Ewart Gladstone to Catherine Gladstone, 17 June 1841; Catherine Gladstone papers, Glynne-Gladstone MSS, Gladstone's Library, Hawarden, Flintshire, GG 769/61-2, William Ewart Gladstone to Catherine Gladstone, 19 June 1841; Catherine Gladstone papers, Glynne-Gladstone MSS, Gladstone's Library, Hawarden, Flintshire, GG 769/67-8, William Ewart Gladstone to Catherine Gladstone, 22 June 1841.
117. See, in particular, Shannon, *Gladstone* (1982), and the even clearer argument laid out in Shannon, *Gladstone* (2007). The historiography of Gladstone and religion is far too broad to be adequately summarised in one footnote, but the work of David Bebbington is particularly important – see, for instance, David Bebbington, *The Mind of Gladstone: Religion, Homer and Politics* (Oxford: Oxford University Press, 2004), esp. pp. 43–141 and 232–56.
118. Anonymous, *Addresses of the National Club: National Club, August 1846 to September 1847 – First Series* (London: Macintosh, 1848). Unnumbered, undated address (from *c*. late 1846).
119. F.D. Maurice, *Thoughts on the Duty of a Protestant in the Present Oxford Election: A Letter to a London Clergyman* (London: John W. Parker, 1847), pp. 3, 7–8. Pamphlet was published after the 1847 dissolution of Parliament.
120. See, for instance, the contemporaneous National Club addresses contained in *Addresses of the National Club, August 1846 to September 1847 – First Series* (London: Macintosh, 1848) and *Addresses of the National Club, November 1847 to February 1848 – Second Series* (London: Macintosh, 1849). It is, however, worth recognising that this was not the only pamphlet distributed in the constituency for the election, and there is no suggestion of any club's involvement in other publications, for instance, the pro-Gladstonian Anonymous [Mackarness John Fielder], *A Few Words to the Country Parsons Touching the Election for the University of Oxford, by One of Themselves* (London: W. H. Dalton, 1847).
121. Sir Thomas Gladstone (Second Baronet) papers, Glynne-Gladstone MSS, Gladstone's Library, Hawarden, Flintshire, GG 1396/4, Undated three-page printed statement by W. E. Gladstone.
122. Entry for Wednesday 5 January 1853, Foot and Matthew (eds), *Gladstone Diaries IV*, p. 485.
123. *The Times*, 14 January 1853, p. 4.
124. M. R. D. Foot and H. C. G. Matthew (eds), *The Gladstone Diaries, Volume III: 1840–1847* (Oxford: Clarendon Press, 1974), p. 444n.

125. Northcote, *Re-Elections in 1852 and 1853*, p. 10.
126. Ibid., p. 17.
127. Ibid., p. 10.
128. Quoted in ibid., p. 21.
129. *Morning Herald*, 3 January 1853, p. 3.
130. Northcote, *Re-Elections in 1852 and 1853*, pp. 16, 22.
131. Ibid., p. 19.
132. The Provost of Oriel, *A Letter to the Principal of Magdalen Hall upon the Future Representation of the University of Oxford* (Oxford: John Henry Parker, 1853), p. 4.
133. Seth Alexander Thévoz, 'Database of Club Memberships of MPs, 1832–68'.
134. Hylton MSS, Somerset Heritage Centre, Taunton, DD/HY 24/9/53, Charles Hay Frewen to Sir William Jolliffe, 31 March 1855.
135. Northcote, *Re-Elections in 1852 and 1853*, p. 19.
136. Stewart, *Conservative*, p. 140.
137. Ostrogorski, *Democracy and Organisation*, vol. 1, p. 149.
138. See Michael Sharpe, 'The Political Committee of the Reform Club' (MA thesis, University of York, 1996).

Conclusion

1. For a Carlton-centred appraisal, see Gash, 'Political Secretary'; Gash, *Politics*, esp. pp. 393–427; Gash, 'Organisation of the Conservative Party, Part I'; Gash, 'Organisation of the Conservative Party, Part II'; Stewart, *Conservative*, esp. pp. 130–42, 261–9; Coleman, *Conservatism*, esp. pp. 107–9; Petrie and Cooke, *Carlton Club*. For a more Reform Club-orientated view, see LoPatin [subsequently LoPatin-Lummis], *Political Unions*, pp. 38–50, Salmon, *Electoral Reform*, pp. 43–58; Cragoe, 'Great Reform Act and Modernisation', pp. 581–603.
2. O'Gorman, *Emergence of Two-Party System*, p. 120.
3. See, for instance, Stewart, *Conservative*, pp. 136–42, 268–9, 281, 337, and Foster, *'Taunton'*, pp. 111–18.
4. See Hawkins, 'Parliamentary Government', pp. 638–69; Hawkins, *Parliament, Party and the Art of Politics*, esp. pp. 266–79.
5. Davis, 'Radical Clubs', Feldman and Stedman Jones (eds), *Metropolis: London*, pp. 1–29. See also my forthcoming article with Luke Blaxill on elections and politically-affiliated working men's clubs in the 1885–1910 period.
6. As with the 1832–68 period, no study of MPs' club memberships has been conducted beyond 1868; however, even a brief flick through the biographies of MPs in the first volume of *Who Was Who* (covering everyone with a *Who's Who* entry who died between 1897 and 1915) clearly shows an overwhelming majority of MPs continuing to belong to the major political clubs until at least World War I. *Who Was Who, Vol. I: 1897–1915* (London: A&C Black, 1920).

7. Hanham, *Elections*, p. 101.
8. See Chapter 2.
9. Ibid.
10. Jenkins, 'Edwardian Brooks's', Ziegler and Seward (eds), *Brooks's*, pp. 69–80, provides evidence of the continued relevance of Brooks's until at least the 1880s, citing the tallies of cabinet ministers belonging to the Club in successive Liberal administrations throughout the nineteenth (and early twentieth) century.
11. The National Club continued to have its own premises until 1913, when it took up a room in the Junior Carlton Club, and continues to exist as a dining society within the present-day Carlton Club, but by the mid-1850s its political impact had sharply faded. The Conservative Club continued until 1979 (re-named the Bath Club after the two merged in 1959), but as noted, its parliamentary impact remained peripheral.
12. See Chapter 1.
13. See Chapter 4 for a further contextualisation of the nature of club spaces.
14. Ibid.
15. Ibid.
16. See Chapter 5.
17. Ibid.
18. See Chapters 2 and 5.
19. See Chapter 6.
20. See Chapter 2.
21. See Chapter 6.
22. Ibid.

BIBLIOGRAPHY

PRIMARY SOURCES

Manuscript collections
Athenaeum Club, London
Athenaeum Club archive.

Bodleian Library, Oxford, Oxon
Hughenden MSS.
National Club MSS.

British Library, London
Gladstone MSS.
Herries MSS.
Holland MSS.
Peel MSS.
Perceval MSS.

British Postal Museum and Archive, London
Royal Mail archive.

Carlton Club, London
Carlton Club archive.
Junior Carlton Club archive.
(*Please note that at the time of viewing, the Carlton and Junior Carlton archives were still physically held in the Carlton Club. They have subsequently been transferred to the London Metropolitan Archive, London, so as to make them open to researchers.*)

Bibliography

Buckinghamshire County Record Office, Aylesbury, Bucks
Fremantle MSS.

Cheshire and Chester Local Studies Centre, Chester, Cheshire
Hayes Lyon MSS.

Gladstone's Library, Hawarden, Flintshire
Glynne-Gladstone MSS.

Hertfordshire Record Office, Hertford, Hertfordshire
Wilshere MSS.

History of Parliament Trust, London
Charles R. Dodd [later Dod] (ed.) (1842), *Autobiography of Five Hundred Members of Parliament; Being a Collection of Letters and Returned Schedules Received by Charles R. Dodd During the First Four Reformed Parliament, viz., from 1832 to December 1842, and Constituting Materials for Compiling the Successive Editions of the Parliamentary Pocket Companion* [microfilm] (New Haven, Connecticut: Yale University, James Marshall and Marie-Louise Osborn Collection [copy held at London: History of Parliament Trust]).

Kent History and Library Centre, Maidstone, Kent
Knatchbull MSS.
Stanhope MSS.

London Metropolitan Archive
Brooks's archive.

National Archives, Kew, London
CREST St. James's planning records.
Russell MSS.

National Liberal Club, London
National Liberal Club archive.

Reform Club, London
Parthenon Club minute book.
Reform Club archive.
Westminster Reform Club minute book.

Somerset Heritage Centre, Taunton
Hylton MSS.

University College London

Brougham MSS.
Joseph Parkes MSS.

Books

Dod, Charles R (ed.), *Dod's Parliamentary Companion 1833* (London, 1833).
——, *Dod's Parliamentary Companion 1835 (New Parliament Edition)* (London, 1835).
——, *Dod's Parliamentary Companion 1836* (London, 1836).
——, *Dod's Parliamentary Companion 1838 (New Parliament Edition)* (London, 1838).
——, *Dod's Parliamentary Companion 1841 (New Parliament Edition)* (London, 1841).
——, *Dod's Parliamentary Companion 1842* (London, 1842).
——, *Dod's Parliamentary Companion 1847 (II) (New Parliament Edition)* (London, 1847).
——, *Dod's Parliamentary Companion 1848* (London, 1848).
——, *Dod's Parliamentary Companion 1852 (II) (New Parliament Edition)* (London, 1852).
——, *Dod's Parliamentary Companion 1857 (II) (New Parliament Edition)* (London, 1857).
——, *Dod's Parliamentary Companion 1858* (London, 1858).
——, *Dod's Parliamentary Companion 1860 (New Parliament Edition)* (London, 1860).
——, *Dod's Parliamentary Companion 1861* (London, 1861).
——, *Dods's Parliamentary Companion 1864* (London, 1864).
——, *Dod's Parliamentary Companion 1865 (New Parliament Edition)* (London, 1865).
Grant, James [as "Anonymous"], *Random Recollections of the House of Commons from the Year 1830 to the Close of 1835, Including Personal Sketches of the Leading Members of All Parties – by One of No Party* (London: Saunders and Otley, 1837).
Harris, James Howard, [Third] Earl of Malmesbury, *Memoirs of an Ex-Minister*, 2 vols (London: Longmans, 1885).
Mowbray, Sir John, *Seventy Years at Westminster* (London: Blackwood, 1900).
Report of Her Majesty's Commissioners Appointed to Inquire into the State, Discipline, Studies, and Revenues of the University and Colleges of Oxford; Together with the Evidence, and an Appendix (London: HMSO, 1852).
White, William White (ed. McCarthy, Justin), *The Inner Life of the House of Commons*, 2 vols (rev. edn, London: T. Fisher Unwin, 1897, of orig. edn, 1856–71).
West, Algernon, *Recollections, 1832–1886* (New York: Harper, 1900).

Works of fiction – novels and plays

Dickens, Charles, *Our Mutual Friend* (London: Chapman and Hall, 1864).
Disraeli, Benjamin, *Coningsby* (reprint, London: Heron Books, 1967, of orig. edn, London, 1844).
——, Sybil, or the Two Nations (reprint, London: Folio Society, 1983, of orig. edn, London, 1845).
——, Tancred (reprint, London: Walter Dunne, 1904, of orig. edn, London, 1847).
'Mrs. Gore' [Frances, Catherine Grace], *Cecil, a Peer: A Sequel to Cecil, or, The Adventures of a Coxcomb, Volume II* (London: T. and W. Boone, 1841).
Thackeray, William Makepeace, *The History of Pendennis* (reprint, London: Fontana, 1986, of orig. edn, London, 1849–50).

Trollope, Anthony, *Phineas Finn* (reprint, London: Folio Society, 1997, of orig. edn, London, 1869).
——, *The Prime Minister* (reprint, London: Folio Society, 1991, of orig. edn, London, 1876), p. 56.
Verne, Jules [trans. Frith, Henry], *Around the World in Eighty Days* (London: George Routledge, 1875).

Pamphlets

A Letter to the Principal of Magdalen Hall upon the Future Representation of the University of Oxford (Oxford: John Henry Parker, 1853).
A List of the Members of the Carlton Club, April 1836, with List of the Trustees and Committee (London: Roake and Varty, 1836).
A Statement of Facts Connected with the Election of the Right Hon. W.E. Gladstone as Member for the University of Oxford in 1847, and with his Re Elections in 1852 and 1853 (Oxford: John Henry Parker, 1853).
Addresses of the National Club, August 1846 to September 1847 – First Series (London: Macintosh, 1848).
Addresses of the National Club, Fourth Series (London: Macintosh, 1852).
Addresses of the National Club, November 1847 to February 1848 – Second Series (London: Macintosh, 1849).
Addresses of the National Club, Third Series (London: Macintosh, 1851).
An Alphabetical List of the Members, with the Rules and Regulations, of the Athenaeum (London: William Clowes, 1837).
An Authentic Copy of the Poll for a Burgess to Serve in Parliament for the University of Oxford, taken on the 4th, 5th, 6th, 7th, 8th, 10th, 11th, 12th, 13th, 14th, 15th, 17th, 18th, 19th, and 20th of January, 1853. Candidates: The Rt. Hon. William Ewart Gladstone, D.C.L. of Ch.Ch., Dudley Montagu Perceval, Esq., B.A. of Ch.Ch. / by authority of the Vice-Chancellor (Oxford, 1853).
Maynooth and the Jew Bill: Further Illustrations of the Speech of the Rt. Hon. Spencer Perceval on the Roman Catholic Question in May, 1805; with Four Letters to the Editor of the 'Morning Herald' and a Petition Against the 'Jewish Disabilities Removal' Bill (London: William Blackwood, 1845).
The Borough Electors' Manual; or, Practical Instructions for the Annual Registration of Voters in Cities and Boroughs (London: James Ridgeway, 1835).
The Coalition of December 1852, and the Contest of January 1853: A Letter Addressed to the Members of the Bristol Church Union (London: Joseph Masters, 1853).
The County Electors' Manual; or, Practical Instructions for the Annual Registration of Voters in Counties (London: James Ridgeway, 1835).
The Irish Church: The Reform Association to the Reformers of England, Scotland and Wales (London: T. Brettell, 1835).
The National Club (London: National Club, 1848).
The Post Office Fifty Years Ago (London: Cassell, 1888).
Thoughts on the Duty of a Protestant in the Present Oxford Election: A Letter to a London Clergyman (London: John W. Parker, 1847).
Athenaeum Club, *An Alphabetical List of the Members, with the Rules and Regulations, of the Athenaeum* (London: Athenaeum Club, 1826).
Edis, R.W., 'The Constitutional Club', *The British Architect* (London: British Library, 1884).

Hook, W.F., *The Coalition: A Letter to a Member of the Convocation* (Oxford: I. Shrimpton, 1853).
Woodgate, Henry Arthur, *A Question Respectfully Suggested to the Members of the Convocation* (Oxford: John Henry Parker, 1852).

Newspapers and journals

Age
Blackwood's Magazine
Bury and Norwich Post
Dorset County Chronicle
Figaro in London
Hansard, House of Commons debates
Hansard, House of Lords debates
Head Quarters
John Bull
Liverpool Mercury
Illustrated London News
Lyttelton Times
Morning Chronicle
Morning Post
Nelson Examiner and New Zealand Chronicle
New York Times
News and Sunday Herald
North British Review
Northern Star and Leeds General Advertiser
Nottinghamshire Guardian
Oxford Mail
Penny Illustrated Paper
Satirist, and the Censor of the Time
Saturday Review
Sheffield Independent, and Yorkshire and Derbyshire Advertiser
The Times
Vanity Fair

SECONDARY SOURCES

Books – club histories

Anonymous, *The History of White's, with the Betting Book from 1743 to 1878 and a List of Members from 1736 to 1892*, 2 vols (London: Algernon Bourke, 1892).
Anonymous, *The Savile Club, 1868 to 1923* (London: Savile Club, 1923).
Black, Barbara, *A Room of His Own: A Literary–Cultural Study of Victorian Clubland* (Athens, Ohio: Ohio University Press, 2012).
Boas, Guy, *The Garrick Club, 1831–1964* (London: Garrick Club, 1948 [rev. edn, 1964]).
Burlingham, Russell and Billis, Roger (eds), *Reformed Characters: The Reform Club in History and Literature, an Anthology with Commentary* (London: Reform Club, 2005).

Bibliography

Clarke, Tom, *The Devonshire Club* (London: Devonshire Club, 1943).
Colson, Percy, *White's: 1693–1950* (London: Heinemann, 1951).
Cohen, Benjamin B., *In the Club: Associational Life in Colonial South Asia* (Hyderabad, Orient Blackswan, 2015).
Cowell, Frank Richard, *The Athenaeum: Club and Social Life in London 1824–1974* (London: Heinemann, 1975).
Darwin, Bernard, *British Clubs* (London: Collins, 1943).
Eeles, Henry S. and Earl Spencer, *Brooks's, 1764–1964* (London: Country Life, 1964).
Escott, T.H.S., *Club Makers and Club Members* (London: T.F. Unwin, 1914).
Fagan, Louis, *The Reform Club: Its Founders and Architect* (London: B. Quaritch, 1887).
Fitzgerald, Percy, *The Garrick Club* (London: Elliot Stock, 1904).
Forrest, Denys, *Foursome in St. James's* (London: East India Club, 1982).
Fulford, Roger, *Boodle's, 1762–1962: A Short History* (London: Boodle's, 1962).
Girtin, Tom, *The Abominable Clubman* (London: Hutchinson, 1962).
Graves, Charles, *Leather Armchairs: The Chivas Regal Book of London Clubs* (London: Cassell, 1963).
Griffiths, Arthur, *Clubs and Clubmen* (London: Hutchinson, 1907).
Hough, Richard, *The Ace of Clubs: A History of the Garrick* (London: Andre Deutsch, 1986).
Humphreys, A.L., *Crockford's* (London: Hutchinson, 1953).
Jackson, G.H., *The Cobden Club* (London: Cobden-Sanderson, 1938).
Jackson, Louis C., *History of the United Service Club* (London, United Service Club, 1937).
Jacoby, Charlie, *The East India Club: A History* (London: East India Club, 2009).
Lejeune, Anthony, *The Gentlemen's Clubs of London* (London: Macdonald and Jane's, 1979).
———, *White's: The First Three Hundred Years* (London: A&C Black, 1993).
———, *The Gentlemen's Clubs of London* (London: Stacey International, 2012) {heavily revised and rewritten version of the above}.
Milne-Smith, Amy, *London Clubland: A Cultural History of Gender and Class in Late Victorian Britain* (London: Palgrave Macmillan, 2011).
Nevill, Ralph, *London Clubs* (London: Chatto and Windus, 1912).
O'Brien, Anita and Miles, Chris, *A Peep into Clubland: Cartoons from Private London Clubs* (London: Cartoon Museum, 2009).
Petrie, Sir Charles and Cooke, Alistair [Lord Lexden], *The Carlton Club* (rev. edn, London: Carlton Club, 2007, of orig. edn, London: Eyre and Spottiswoode, 1955).
Phelps, Barry, *Power and the Party: A History of the Carlton Club, 1832–1982* (London: Macmillan, 1983).
Shelley, Henry C., *Inns and Taverns of Old London: Setting Forth the Historical and Literary Associations of Those Ancient Hostelries, Together with an Account of the Most Notable Coffee-Houses, Clubs, and Pleasure Gardens of the British Metropolis* (Boston: L.C. Page, 1908 [1909 ed.]).
Steven, Robert, *The National Liberal Club: Politics and Persons* (London: Robert Houghton, 1925).
Timbs, John, *Clubs and Club Life in London, with Anecdotes of its Famous Coffee Houses, Hostelries, and Taverns from the Seventeenth Century to the Present Time* (reprint, London: Chatto and Windus, 1908, of orig. edn, London, 1866).
Waddy, Henry Turner, *The Devonshire Club and "Crockford's"* (London: Eveleigh Nash, 1919).

Wegg-Prosser, J.F (ed.), *Memorials of Brooks's, from the Foundation of the Club, 1764, to the Close of the Nineteenth Century, Compiled from the Records of the Club* (London: Ballantyne, 1907).

Woodbridge, George, *The Reform Club, 1836–1978: A History from the Club's Records* (New York: Clearwater, 1978).

Ziegler, Philip and Seward, Desmond (eds), *Brooks's: A Social History* (London: Constable, 1991).

Books – edited collections of documents

Aspinall, Arthur (ed.), *Three Early Nineteenth Century Diaries* (London: Williams and Norgate, 1952).

Brock, Michael and Eleanor (eds), *H. H. Asquith: Letters to Venetia Stanley* (Oxford: Oxford University Press, 1982).

Brooke, John and Gandy, Julia (eds), *The Prime Ministers' Papers: Wellington, Political Correspondence I: 1833-November 1834* (London: HMSO, 1975).

Brooke, John and Sorenson, Mary (eds), *The Prime Ministers' Papers: W.E. Gladstone III: Autobiographical Memoranda 1845–1866* (London: HMSO, 1978).

Foot, M.R.D. and Matthew, H.C.G. (eds), *The Gladstone Diaries, Volume III: 1840–1847* (Oxford: Clarendon Press, 1974).

——, *The Gladstone Diaries, Volume IV: 1848–1854* (Oxford: Clarendon Press, 1974).

Gaunt, Richard A (ed.), *Unrepentant Tory: Political Selections from the Diaries of the Fourth Duke of Newcastle-under-Lyne, 1827–38* (Woodbridge: Boydell, 2006).

Gunn, J.A.W., Matthews, John, Schurman, Donald M. and Wiebe, M.G (eds), *Benjamin Disraeli Letters: Volume One, 1815–1834* (Toronto: University of Toronto Press, 1982).

——, *Benjamin Disraeli Letters, Volume Two, 1835–1837* (Toronto: Toronto University Press, 1985).

Hawkins, Angus and Powell, John (eds), *The Journal of John Wodehouse, first Earl of Kimberley for 1862–1902* (London: Royal Historical Society, 1997).

Howe, Anthony (ed.), *The Letters of Richard Cobden: Volume One, 1815–1847* (Oxford: Oxford University Press, 2007).

——, *The Letters of Richard Cobden: Volume Two, 1848–1853* (Oxford: Oxford University Press, 2009).

Howe, Anthony and Morgan, Simon (eds), *The Letters of Richard Cobden: Volume Three, 1854–1859* (Oxford: Oxford University Press, 2012).

Kriegel, Abraham D (ed.), *The Holland House Diaries 1831–1840: The Diary of Henry Richard Vassall Fox, Third Lord Holland, with Extracts from the Diary of Dr John Allen* (London: Routledge and Kegan Paul, 1977).

Salmon, Philip (ed.), *Letters of Joseph Parkes* (Oxford: Privately published, 1993).

Stenton, Michael and Vincent, John (eds), McCalmont, Frederick Haynes, *McCalmont's Parliamentary Poll Book: British Election Results 1832–1918* (rev. edn, Sussex: Harvester Press, 1971 of orig. edn, London, 1853).

Strachey, Lytton and Fulford, Roger (eds), *The Greville Memoirs*, 8 vols (London: Macmillan, 1938).

Swartz, Helen W. and Swartz, Marvin (eds), *Disraeli's Reminiscences* (London: Hamish Hamilton, 1975).

BIBLIOGRAPHY

Vincent, John (ed.), *Disraeli, Derby and the Conservative Party: Journals and Memoirs of Edward Henry, Lord Stanley, 1849–1869* (Sussex: Harvester Press, 1978).
Wiebe, M.G., Conacher, J.B., Matthews, John and Millar, Mary S (eds), *Benjamin Disraeli Letters: Volume Three, 1838–1841* (Toronto: University of Toronto Press, 1987).
——, *Benjamin Disraeli Letters: Volume Four, 1842–1847* (Toronto: University of Toronto Press, 1989).
——, *Benjamin Disraeli Letters, Volume Five, 1848–1851* (Toronto: Toronto University Press, 1993).
Wiebe, M.G., Millar, Mary S., Robson, Ann P. and Hawman, Ellen L (eds), *Benjamin Disraeli Letters: Volume Eight, 1860–1864* (Toronto: University of Toronto Press, 2009).

Books – historical works

Abbott, Evelyn and Campbell, Lewis, *The Life and Letters of Benjamin Jowett, Master of Balliol College, Oxford*, 2 vols (London: John Murray, 1897).
Ashton, Rosemary, *142 Strand: A Radical Address in Victorian London* (London: Chatto and Windus, 2006).
——, *Victorian Bloomsbury* (New Haven, Connecticut: Yale University Press, 2012).
Aspinall, Arthur, *Lord Brougham and the Whig Party* (Manchester: Manchester University Press, 1939).
Bailey, Peter, *Leisure and Class in Victorian England: Rational Recreation and the Contest for Control, 1830–1885* (London: Methuen, 1978 {rev. 1987 ed.}).
——, *Music Hall: The Business of Pleasure* (Milton Keynes: Open University Press, 1986).
Beales, Derek, *From Castlereagh to Gladstone, 1815–1885* (London: Nelson, 1969).
Bebbington, David, *The Mind of Gladstone: Religion, Homer and Politics* (Oxford: Oxford University Press, 2004).
Bentley, Michael, *Politics Without Democracy, 1815–1914: Perception and Preoccupation in British Government* (Oxford: Blackwell, 1986 {rev. 1999 ed.}).
Bill, E.G.W., *University Reform in Nineteenth-Century Oxford: A Study of Henry Halford Vaughan, 1811–1885* (Oxford: Clarendon Press, 1973).
Blake, Robert, *Disraeli* (London: Eyre and Spottiswoode, 1966).
——, *The Conservative Party from Peel to Churchill* (reprint, London: Fontana, 1979, of orig. edn, London, 1970).
Bourne, J.M., *Patronage and Society in Nineteenth-Century England* (London: Edward Arnold, 1986).
Bradley, Ian, *The Optimists: Themes and Personalities in Victorian Liberalism* (London: Faber and Faber, 1980).
Brandreth, Gyles, *Breaking the Code – Westminster Diaries, 1992–97* (London: Weidenfeld & Nicholson, 1999).
Brent, Richard, *Liberal Anglican Politics: Whiggery, Religion, and Reform 1830–1841* (Oxford: Clarendon Press, 1987).
Briggs, Asa, *Victorian People: A Reassessment of Persons and Themes, 1851–67* (Chicago, Illinois: University of Chicago Press, 1955 {rev. edn, 1972}).
——, *The Age of Improvement, 1783–1867* (London: Longman, 1959).
Brown, David, *Palmerston: A Biography* (New Haven, Connecticut: Yale University Press, 2010).

Buckley, Jessie, *Joseph Parkes of Birmingham; and the Part Which he Played in Radical Reform Movements from 1825 to 1845* (London: Methuen, 1926).
Burns, Arthur and Innes, Joanna (eds), *Rethinking the Age of Reform: Britain 1780–1850* (Cambridge: Cambridge University Press, 2003).
Butler, R.A. (ed.), *The Conservatives: A History from their Origins to 1965* (London: Allen and Unwin, 1977).
Cannadine, David, *The Decline and Fall of the British Aristocracy* (New Haven, Connecticut: Yale University Press, 1990).
Capdeville, Valérie, L'Âge d'Or des Clubs Londoniens (1730–1784) (Paris: Editions Champion, 2008).
Chesney, Kellow, *The Victorian Underworld* (London: Temple Smith, 1970).
Clark, Peter, *British Clubs and Societies, 1580–1800: The Origins of an Associational World* (Oxford: Oxford University Press, 2000).
Coleman, Bruce, *Conservatism and the Conservative Party in Nineteenth-Century Britain* (London: Edward Arnold, 1988).
Conacher, J.B., *The Aberdeen Coalition, 1852–1855* (Cambridge: Cambridge University Press, 1968).
——, *The Peelites and the Party System, 1846–52* (Newton Abbot: David and Charles, 1972).
Coohill, Joseph, *Ideas of the Liberal Party: Perceptions, Agendas and Liberal Politics in the House of Commons, 1832–1852* (Oxford: Wiley-Blackwell, 2011).
Corfield, Penelope J., *Power and the Professions in Britain, 1700–1850* (London: Routledge, 1995).
Cox, Gary W., *The Efficient Secret: The Cabinet and the Development of Political Parties in Victorian England* (Cambridge: Cambridge University Press, 1987).
Dasent, Arthur Irwin, *The History of St. James's Square and the Foundation of the West End of London, with a Glimpse of Whitehall in the Reign of Charles the Second* (London: Macmillan, 1895).
Daunton, M.J., *Royal Mail: The Post Office Since 1840* (London: Athlone Press, 1985).
Davis, Richard W., *Political Change and Continuity, 1760–1885: A Buckinghamshire Study* (Newton Abbot: David and Charles, 1972).
——, (ed.), *Lords of Parliament: Studies, 1714–1914* (Stanford, California: Stanford University Press, California, 1995).
Erickson, Arvel B., *The Public Career of Sir James Graham* (Oxford: Basil Blackwell, 1952).
Feinstein, Charles H. and Thomas Mark, *Making History Count: A Primer in Quantitative Methods for Historians* (Cambridge: Cambridge University Press, 2002).
Feldman, David and Stedman Jones, Gareth (eds), *Disraeli, Democracy and the Tory Party: Conservative Leadership and Organisation After the Reform Bill* (Oxford: Clarendon Press, 1968).
——, *Metropolis: London* (London: Macmillan, 1989).
Feuchtwanger, E.J., *Gladstone* (London: Allen Lane, 1975).
Fisher, D.R (ed.), *History of Parliament: The Commons, 1820–1832*, 6 vols (Cambridge: Cambridge University Press, 2009).
Fox, Celina (ed.), *London – World City, 1800–1840* (New Haven, Connecticut: Yale University Press, 1992).
Gash, Norman, *Politics in the Age of Peel: A Study in the Technique of Parliamentary Representation, 1830–1850* (London: Longman, 1953).

——, *Sir Robert Peel: The Life of Sir Robert Peel after 1830* (rev. edn, London: Longman, 1986, of orig. edn, London: Longman, 1972).
——, *Aristocracy and People: Britain 1815–1865* (London: Edward Arnold, 1979).
Gatrell, Vic, *City of Laughter: Sex and Satire in Eighteenth Century London* (New York: Walker and Company, 2006).
Gaunt, Richard, *Sir Robert Peel: The Life and Legacy* (London: I.B.Tauris, 2010).
Ginter, Donald E (ed.), *Voting Records of the British House of Commons, 1761–1820*, 6 vols (London: Hambledon Press, 1994).
Gleadle, Kathryn, *Borderline Citizens: Women, Gender, and Political Culture in Britain, 1815–1867* (Oxford: Oxford University Press, 2009).
Gordon, Eleanor and Nair, Gwyneth, *Public Lives: Women, Family and Society in Victorian Britain* (New Haven, Connecticut: Yale University Press, 2003).
Guedalla, Philip, *Palmerston* (London: Hodder and Stoughton, 1926 [1937 ed.]).
Habermass, Jürgen, *The Structural Transformation of the Public Sphere: An Inquiry into a Category of Bourgeois Society* (Cambridge: Polity Press, Cambridge, 1962 [trans. 1989]).
Hall, Catherine, McClelland, Keith, and Rendell, Jane (eds), *Defining the Victorian Nation: Class, Race, Gender and the British Reform Act of 1867* (Cambridge: Cambridge University Press, 2000).
Hanham, H.J., *Elections and Party Management: Politics in the time of Disraeli and Gladstone* (London: Longmans, 1959).
Harvey, Adrian, *The Beginnings of a Commercial Sporting Culture in Britain, 1793–1850* (Aldershot: Ashgate, 2004).
Harvie, Christopher, *The Lights of Liberalism: University Liberals and the Challenge of Democracy, 1860–86* (London: Allen Lane, 1976).
Haury, David A., *The Origins of the Liberal Party and Liberal Imperialism: The Career of Charles Buller, 1806–1848* (New York: Garland Publishing, 1987).
Hawkins, Angus, *Parliament, Party and the Art of Politics in Britain, 1855–59* (Stanford, California: Stanford University Press, 1987).
——, *British Party Politics, 1852–1886* (London: Macmillan, 1998).
——, *The Forgotten Prime Minister: The 14th Earl of Derby, Volume I – Ascent, 1799–1851* (Oxford: Oxford University Press, 2007).
——, *The Forgotten Prime Minister: The 14th Earl of Derby, Volume II – Achievement, 1851–1869* (Oxford: University Press, 2008).
——, *Victorian Political Culture: 'Habits of Heart and Mind'* (Oxford: Oxford University Press, 2015).
Hewitt, Rachel, *Map of a Nation: A Biography of the Ordnance Survey* (London: Granta, 2010).
Hill, R.L., *Toryism and the People, 1832–1845* (London: Constable, 1929).
Hilton, Boyd, *The Age of Atonement: The Influence of Evangelicalism on Social and Economic Thought, 1795–1865* (Oxford: Oxford University Press, 1988).
——, *A Mad, Bad, and Dangerous People? England 1783–1846* (Oxford: Oxford University Press, 2006).
Hinchcliffe, Peter, *Benjamin Jowett and the Christian Religion* (Oxford: Clarendon Press, 1987).
Horn, Pamela, *Pleasures and Pastimes in Victorian Britain* (Stroud: Sutton Publishing, 1999).
Huch, Ronald K. and Ziegler, Paul R., *Joseph Hume: The People's M.P* (Philadelphia, Pennsylvania: Diane Publishing, 1985).

Hunt, Tristram, *Building Jerusalem: The Rise and Fall of the Victorian City* (London: Weidenfeld and Nicholson, 2004).
Hurd, Douglas, *Robert Peel: A Biography* (London: Weidenfeld and Nicholson, 2007).
Jaggard, Edwin, *Cornwall Politics in the Age of Reform, 1790–1885* (Woodbridge: Boydell, 1999).
Jenkins, Roy, *Gladstone* (London: Macmillan, 1995).
Jenkins, T.A., *The Liberal Ascendancy, 1830–1886* (London: Macmillan, 1994).
——, *Parliament, Party and Politics in Victorian Britain* (Manchester: Manchester University Press, 1996).
Jones, Wilbur Devereux, *Lord Derby and Victorian Conservatism* (Oxford: Basil Blackwell, 1956).
Koss, Stephen, *The Rise and Fall of the Political Press in Britain: Volume 1 – The Nineteenth Century* (London: Hamish Hamilton, 1981).
Kümin, Beat (ed.), *Political Space in Pre-Industrial Europe* (Surrey: Ashgate, 2009).
Kynaston, David, *The City of London, Volume I: A World of its Own, 1815–1890* (London: Chatto and Windus, 1994).
Lawrence, Jon, *Electing Our Masters: The Hustings in British Politics from Hogarth to Blair* (Oxford: Oxford University Press, 2009).
Lefebvre, Henri [trans. Moore, Gerald, Brenner, Neil and Elden, Stuart, ed. Brenner, Neil and Elden, Stuart], *State, Space, World: Selected Essays* (Minneapolis, Minnesota: University of Minnesota Press, 2009).
Llewelyn, Alexander, *The Decade of Reform: The 1830s* (Newton Abbot: David and Charles, 1972).
LoPatin, Nancy D. [subsequently LoPatin-Lummis, Nancy D.], *Political Unions, Popular Politics and the Great Reform Act of 1832* (London: Macmillan, 1999).
LoPatin-Lummis, Nancy D (ed.), *Public Life and Public Lives – Politics and Religion in Modern British History: Essays in Honour of Richard W. Davis* (Oxford: Wiley-Blackwell/History of Parliament Trust Yearbook, 2008).
Lubenow, William C., *Liberal Intellectuals and Public Culture in Modern Britain, 1815–1914: Making Words Flesh* (Woodbridge: Boydell and Brewer, 2010).
McCallum, R.B. and Readman, Alison, *The British General Election of 1945* (Oxford: Oxford University Press, 1947).
Machin, Ian, *Disraeli* (London: Longman, 1995).
Mandler, Peter, *Aristocratic Government in the Age of Reform: Whigs and Liberals, 1830–1852* (Oxford: Clarendon Press, 1990).
Monypenny, William Flavelle and Buckle, G.E., *The Life of Benjamin Disraeli, Earl of Beaconsfield*, 6 vols (London: John Murray, 1910–1920).
Moore, D.C., *The Politics of Deference: A Study of the Mid-Nineteenth Century English Political System* (Sussex: Harvester Press, 1976).
Mordaunt Crook, J., *The Rise of the Nouveaux Riches: Style and Status in Victorian and Edwardian Architecture* (London: John Murray, 1999).
Morgan, Marjorie, *Manners, Morals and Class in England, 1774–1858* (New York: St. Martin's Press, 1994).
Munford, W.A., *William Ewart M.P., 1798–1869: Portrait of a Radical* (London: Grafton and Co., 1960).
Newbould, Ian, *Whiggery and Reform, 1830–41: The Politics of Government* (Stanford, California: Stanford University Press, 1990).

O'Gorman, Frank, *The Emergence of the British Two-Party System, 1760–1832* (London: Edward Arnold, 1982).

———, *Voters, Patrons, and Parties: The Unreformed Electoral System of Hanoverian England, 1734–1832* (Oxford: Clarendon Press, 1989).

Ostrogorski, Moisei, *Democracy and the Organisation of Political Parties*, 2 vols (reprint, New York: Macmillan, 1970, of orig. edn, London: Macmillan, 1902).

Parker, Charles Stuart, *Life and Letters of Sir James Graham, Second Baronet of Netherby, P.C., G.C.B., 1792–1861*, 2 vols (London: John Murray, 1907).

Parkinson, Stephen, *Arena of Ambition: A History of the Cambridge Union* (London: Icon Books, 2009).

Parolin, Christina, *Radical Spaces: Venues of Popular Politics in London, 1790–c.1845* (Canberra, Australia: Australian National University E Press, 2012).

Parry, Jonathan, *The Rise and Fall of Liberal Government in Britain* (New Haven, Connecticut: Yale University Press, 1993).

Phillips, John A., *The Great Reform Bill in the Boroughs: English Electoral Behaviour, 1818–1841* (Oxford: Clarendon Press, 1992).

Port, M.H., *The Houses of Parliament* (New Haven, Connecticut: Yale University Press, 1976).

Pugh, Ralph B., *The Crown Estate* (London: HMSO, 1960).

Puwar, Nirmal, *Space Invaders: Race, Gender and Bodies Out of Place* (Oxford: Berg, 1985).

Ramsden, John, *An Appetite for Power: A History of the Conservative Party Since 1830* (London: HarperCollins, 1998).

Reid, Stuart J., *Life and Letters of the First Earl of Durham, 1792–1840*, 2 vols (London: Longmans, 1906).

Renton, Tim, *Chief Whip: People, Power and Patronage in Westminster* (London: Politicos, 2004).

Reynolds, K.D., *Aristocratic Women and Political Society in Victorian Britain* (Oxford: Clarendon Press, 1998).

Rush, Michael, *The Role of the Member of Parliament since 1868: From Gentlemen to Players* (Oxford: Oxford University Press, 2001).

Salmon, Philip, *Electoral Reform at Work: Local Politics and National Parties, 1832–1841* (Woodbridge: Boydell, 2002).

Sampson, Anthony, *The Anatomy of Britain* (London: Hodder and Stoughton, 1962).

———, *The Anatomy of Britain Today* (London: Hodder and Stoughton, 1965).

———, *The New Anatomy of Britain* (London: Hodder and Stoughton, 1971).

Shannon, Richard, *Gladstone: Peel's Inheritor, 1809–1865* (reprint, London: Penguin, 1999, of orig. edn, London: Hamish Hamilton, 1982).

———, *Gladstone: Heroic Minister, 1865–1898* (London: Allen Lane, 1999).

———, *Gladstone: God and Politics* (London: Hambledon Continuum, 2007).

Shenton, Caroline, *The Day Parliament Burned Down* (Oxford: Oxford University Press, 2012).

Shields, Andrew, *The Irish Conservative Party, 1852–1868: Land, Politics and Religion* (Dublin: Irish Academic Press, 2007).

Smith, E.A., *The House of Lords in British Politics and Society, 1815–1911* (London: Longman, 1992).

Southgate, Donald, *The Passing of the Whigs, 1832–1886* (London: Macmillan, 1962).
Stewart, Robert, *The Politics of Protection* (Cambridge: Cambridge University Press, 1971).
——, *The Foundation of the Conservative Party, 1830–1867* (London: Longman, 1978).
Sweet, Matthew, *Inventing the Victorians* (London: Faber and Faber, 2001).
Tosh, John, *Manliness and Masculinities in Nineteenth-Century Britain: Essays on Gender, Family and Empire* (London: Longman, 2005).
Trevelyan, George Macaulay, *Lord Grey of the Reform Bill: Being the Life of Charles, Second Earl Grey* (London: Longmans, 1920).
Trevelyan, George Otto, *The Early History of Charles James Fox* (London: Longmans, 1880).
Vernon, James, *Politics and the People: A Study in English Political Culture, c.1815–1867* (Cambridge: Cambridge University Press, 1993).
Vickery, Amanda, *Behind Closed Doors: At Home in Georgian England* (New Haven, Connecticut: Yale University Press, 2009).
Vincent, John, *The Formation of the Liberal Party 1857–1868* (London: Constable, 1966).
West, Algernon, *Recollections 1832–1866* (London: Smith, Elder & Co, 1899).
Wolffe, John, *The Protestant Crusade in Great Britain, 1829–1860* (Oxford: Clarendon Press, 1991).
Woodward, Llewelyn, *The Age of Reform, 1815–1870* (Oxford: Oxford University Press, 1962).
Wright, Arnold and Smith, Philip, *Parliament, Past and Present: A Popular and Picturesque Account of a Thousand Years in the Palace of Westminster, the Home of the Mother of Parliaments* (London: Hutchinson, 1902).
Ziegler, Philip, *Melbourne* (London: Collins, 1976).

Books – reference works

Ashton, David and Reid, Paul W., *Ashton & Reid on Clubs and Associations*, 2nd edn (London: Lexis Nexis, 2011), pp. 3–4.
Cook, Chris and Keith, Brendan, *British Historical Facts, 1830–1900* (rev. ed., London: Macmillan, 1984, of orig. edn, London: Macmillan, 1975).
Craig, F.W.S., *British Parliamentary Election Results, 1832–1885* (London: Macmillan, 1977).
Crawford, Elizabeth, *The Women's Suffrage Movement: A Reference Guide, 1866–1928* (London: Routledge, 2000).
Rallings, Colin and Thrasher, Michael, *British electoral facts, 1832–2012* (London: Biteback, 2012).
Sheppard, F.H.W (ed.), *Survey of London, Vols. 29–30: St. James's, Westminster* (London: Athlone Press, 1960).
Stenton, Michael (ed.), *Who's Who of British Members of Parliament, Volume I, 1832–1885: A Biographical Dictionary of the House of Commons* (Sussex: Harvester Press, 1976).
Stenton, Michael and Lees, Stephen (eds), *Who's Who of British Members of Parliament, Volume II, 1886–1918: A Biographical Dictionary of the House of Commons* (Sussex: Harvester Press, 1978).
Who Was Who, Vol. I: 1897–1915 (London: A&C Black, 1920).

Pamphlets

Arnold, Ann, *The Adventurous Chef: Alexis Soyer* (London: Reform Club, 2002).
Jolles, Michael, *Jews and the Carlton Club – With Notes on Benjamin Disraeli, Henri Louis Bischoffsheim, and Saul Isaacs MP* (London: Privately published, 2002).
Mordaunt Crook, J., *The Reform Club* (London: Reform Club, 1973).
Sebag-Montefiore, Charles (ed.) *Charles James Fox | Brooks's and Whiggery | The Fox Club* (London: Brooks's, 2006).
Sharpe, Michael, *The Political Committee of the Reform Club* (London: Reform Club, 1996).
Shipley, Stan, *Club Life and Socialism in Mid-Victorian London* (London: Journeyman/London History Workshop Centre, 1971).

Essays and articles

Aherne, Mike, 'A Dangerous Obsession? Gambling and Social Stability', Rowbotham, Judith and Stevenson, Kim (eds), *Behaving Badly: Social Panic and Moral Outrage – Victorian and Modern Parallels* (Aldershot: Ashgate, 2003), pp. 127–41.
Aydelotte, W.O., 'The House of Commons in the 1840s', *History*, XXXIX (1954), pp. 249–62.
———, 'Voting Patterns in the British House of Commons in the 1840s' *Comparative Studies in Society and History*, V (1962–3), pp. 134–63.
———, 'Parties and Issues in Early Victorian England', *Journal of British Studies*, V (1966), pp. 95–114.
Baer, Marc, 'Political Dinners in Whig, Radical and Tory Westminster, 1780–1880', Jones, Clyve, Salmon, Philip and Davis, Richard W (eds), *Partisan Politics, Principle and Reform in Parliament and Constituencies, 1689–1880: Essays in Memory of John A. Phillips* (Edinburgh: Edinburgh University Press, 2005), pp. 183–206.
Beales, Derek, 'Parliamentary Parties and the "Independent" Member, 1810–1860', Robson, Robert (ed.), *Ideas and Institutions of Victorian Britain: Essays in Honour of George Kitson Clark* (London: G. Bell, 1967).
Berry, Helen, 'Rethinking Politeness in Eighteenth-Century England: Moll King's Coffee House and the Significance of "Flash Talk"', *Transactions of the Royal Historical Society*, sixth series, XI (Cambridge: Cambridge University Press, 2001), pp. 65–82.
Brady, David W. and Bullock III, Charles S., 'Party and Factional Organisation in Legislatures', *Legislative Studies Quarterly*, 8 (1983), pp. 599–654.
Brett, Peter, 'Political Dinners in Early Nineteenth-Century Britain: Platform, Meeting Place and Battleground', *History*, LXXXI (1996), pp. 527–52.
Bylsma, John R., 'Party Structure in the 1852–1857 House of Commons: A Scalogram Analysis', *Journal of Interdisciplinary History*, 7 (1977), pp. 375–93.
Capdeville, Valérie, '"Clubbability": A Revolution in London Sociability?', *Lumen*, 35 (2016), pp. 63–80.
Coohill, Joseph, 'Parliamentary Guides, Political Identity and the Presentation of Modern Politics, 1832–1846', *Parliamentary History*, 22 (2005), pp. 272–88.
Corio, Alec and Thévoz, Seth Alexander, 'Defending the Protestant Principles of the Constitution: The National Club 1845–55' (forthcoming journal article).

Cragoe, Matthew, 'The Great Reform Act and the Modernisation of British Politics: The Impact of Conservative Associations, 1835–1841,' *Journal of British Studies*, 47 (July 2008), pp. 581–603.

Cromwell, Valerie, 'Mapping the Political World of 1861: A Multidimensional Analysis of House of Commons Division Lists', *Legislative Studies Quarterly*, 7 (1982), pp. 281–97.

Davidoff, Leonore, 'The Legacy of the Nineteenth-Century Bourgeois Family and the Wool Merchant's Son', *Transactions of the Royal Historical Society, Sixth Series*, XIV (Cambridge: Cambridge University Press, 2004), pp. 25–46.

Downs, Carolyn, 'Two Fat Ladies: The Hidden History of Women and Gambling', *History Today*, 57 (2007), vol. 7, pp. 27–9.

Dunne, John J., 'The First Irish Railway by Shriek and Smoke to Kingstown', *Dublin Historical Record*, 43 (1990), pp. 44–6.

Edwards, Owen Dudley, 'Anthony Trollope, the Irish Writer', Nineteenth-Century Fiction, 38 (1983), pp. 20–6.

Finlayson, G.B.A.M., 'Joseph Parkes of Birmingham, 1796–1865: A Study in Philosophic Radicalism', *Bulletin of the Institute of Historical Research*, XLVI (1973), pp. 186–201.

Fisher, D.R., 'Peel and the Conservative Party: The Sugar Crisis of 1844 Reconsidered', *Historical Journal*, 18 (1975), pp. 279–302.

Fogel, Robert Williams, 'The Limits of Quantitative Methods in History', *American Historical Review*, 80 (1975), pp. 329–35.

Foster, R. E., 'Peel, Disraeli and the 1835 Taunton by-election', *Transactions of the Somerset Archaeological and Natural History Society*, CXXVI (1982), pp. 111–18.

Fraser, Peter, 'The Growth of Ministerial Control in the Nineteenth-Century House of Commons', *English Historical Review*, 75 (1960), pp. 444–63.

Fraser Rae, W., 'Political Clubs and Party Organisation', *Nineteenth Century*, 3 (1878), pp. 908–32.

Gash, Norman, 'F. R. Bonham: Conservative "Political Secretary", 1832–47', *English Historical Review*, LXIII (1948), pp. 502–22.

———, 'The Organisation of the Conservative Party, 1832–1846, Part I: The Parliamentary Organisation', *Parliamentary History*, 1 (1982), pp. 137–59.

———, 'The Organisation of the Conservative Party, 1832–1846, Part II: The Electoral Organisation', *Parliamentary History*, 2 (1983), pp. 131–52.

Grice, Andrew, 'The Westminster Gentlemen's Club is Dead', *The Independent*, 19 May 2009.

Harris, Peter, 'A Meeting Place for Liberals: The National Liberal Club', *Journal of Liberal History*, 51 (Summer 2006), pp. 18–23.

Hawkins, Angus, 'Lord Derby and Victorian Conservatism: A Reappraisal', *Parliamentary History*, 6 (1987), pp. 280–301.

———, '"Parliamentary Government" and Victorian Political Parties, c.1830–c.1880', *English Historical Review* (1989) CIV (CCCXII), pp. 638–669.

Jenkins, T.A., 'The Whips in the Early-Victorian House of Commons', *Parliamentary History*, 19 (2000), pp. 259–86.

Kousser, J.M., 'Quantitative Social-Scientific History', Kammen, Michael G (ed.), *The Past Before Us* (reprint, Ithaca, New York: Cornell University Press, 1982, of orig. edn, Ithaca, New York: Cornell University Press, 1980), pp. 433–56.

Lee, Joseph, 'The Provision of Capital for Early Irish Railways, 1830–1853', *Irish Historical Studies*, 16 (1968), pp. 33–63.

Mandler, Peter, 'From Almack's to Willis's: Aristocratic Women and Politics, 1815–1867', Vickery, Amanda (ed.), *Women, Privilege and Power: British Politics, 1750 to the Present* (Stanford, California: Stanford University Press, 2001), pp. 152–67.

Markus, Michael, 'A Pocket Borough? Reformed Politics in Ripon, 1832–67', *Parliamentary History*, 27 (2008), pp. 330–60.

Matikkala, Mira, 'William Digby and the Indian Question', *Journal of Liberal History*, 58 (2008), pp. 12–21.

Miller, Henry, 'Popular Petitioning and the Corn Laws, 1833–46?', *English Historical Review*, 127 (2012), pp. 882–919

Milne-Smith, Amy, 'A Flight to Domesticity? Making a Home in the Gentlemen's Clubs of London, 1880–1914', *Journal of British Studies*, 45 (2006), pp. 796–818.

——, 'Club Talk: Gossip, Masculinity, and the Importance of Oral Communities in Late Nineteenth-Century London', *Gender and History*, 21 (2009), pp. 86–109.

Moore, D.C., 'Concession or Cure: The Sociological Premises of the First Reform Act', *Historical Journal*, 9 (1966), pp. 39–59.

Mordaunt Crook, J., 'Locked Out of Paradise: Blackballing at the Athenaeum 1824–1935', Fernández-Armesto, Felipe (ed.), *Armchair Athenians: Essays from the Athenaeum* (London: The Athenaeum, 2001), pp. 19–30.

Newbould, Ian, 'Whiggery and the Growth of Party 1830–1841: Organisation and the Challenge of Reform', *Parliamentary History*, 4 (1985), pp. 137–56.

Parssinen, T.M., 'Association, Convention and Anti-Parliament in British Radical Politics, 1771–1848', *English Historical Review*, LXXXVIII (1973), pp. 504–33.

Phillips, John A., 'QUASSHing M.P.s and Electors: New Perspectives on Parliamentary History', Phillips, John A (ed.), *Computing Parliamentary History: George III to Victoria* (Edinburgh: Edinburgh University Press, 1994), pp. 1–10.

Pickford, James, 'Gentlemen's Clubs Raise a Glass to Quiet Success: Relics of 19th Century London See Membership Grow', *Financial Times*, 22 December 2012, p. 2.

Port, M.H., 'The Best Club in the World? The House of Commons, c.1860–1915', Jones, Clyve and Kelsey, Sean (eds), *Housing Parliament: Dublin, Edinburgh and Westminster* (Edinburgh: Edinburgh University Press, 2002), pp. 166–99.

Price, Richard, 'The Working Men's Club Movement and Victorian Social Reform Ideology', *Victorian Studies*, XV (1971), pp. 117–47.

Quinault, Roland, 'Westminster and the Victorian Constitution', Transactions *of the Royal Historical Society, Sixth Series*, 2 (Cambridge: Cambridge University Press, 1992), pp. 79–104.

Rendell, Jane, 'The Clubs of St. James's: Places of Public Patriarchy – Exclusivity, Domesticity and Secrecy', *Journal of Architecture*, 4 (1999), pp. 167–89.

Richardson, Sarah, 'The Role of Women in Electoral Politics in Yorkshire During the 1830s', *Northern History*, 32 (1996), pp. 133–51.

Sainty, John C., 'The Evolution of the Parliamentary and Financial Secretaryships of the Treasury', *English Historical Review*, XCI (1976), pp. 566–85.

Sainty, John and Cox, Gary W., 'The Identification of Government Whips in the House of Commons, 1830–1905', *Parliamentary History*, 16 (1997), pp. 339–58.

Stewart, Robert, 'The Ten Hours and Sugar Crises of 1844: Government and the House of Commons in the Age of Reform', *Historical Journal*, XII (1969), pp. 35–57.
Sweringa, Robert P., 'Computers and Comparative History', *Journal of Interdisciplinary History*, 5 (1974), pp. 267–286.
Taylor, Antony, 'Palmerston and Radicalism, 1847–1865', *Journal of British Studies*, 33 (1994), pp. 157–79.
Thévoz, Seth Alexander, 'Club Government', *History Today*, 63, February 2013, pp. 52–3.
——, 'Cambridge University Liberal Club, 1886–1916: A Study in Early Student Political Organisation', *Journal of Liberal History*, 91, Summer 2016, pp. 10–22.
Wheeler, Michael, 'Gladstone and Ruskin', Jagger, Peter J (ed.), *Gladstone* (London: Hambledon Press, 1998), pp. 177–95.
Wilkinson, Clare, 'Politics and Topography in the Old House of Commons, 1783–1834', Jones, Clyve and Kelsey, Sean (eds), *Housing Parliament: Dublin, Edinburgh and Westminster* (Edinburgh: Edinburgh University Press, 2002), pp. 141–65.

Seminar papers and presentations

Corio, Alec and Thévoz, Seth Alexander, '"Defending the Protestant Principles of the Constitution": The National Club, c.1845–1855', Institute of Historical Research paper, 31 March 2011.
Downing, Arthur, *Social Capital in Decline: Friendly Societies in Australia, 1850–1914*, University of Oxford discussion papers in economic and social history, No. 105 (October 2012).
Howe, Anthony, presentation to the History of Parliament Trust's 1832–68 colloquium, Westminster Hall, London, 6 May 2011.
Marsh, Peter and Vonberg, Paul, 'The Reform Club: Architecture and the Birth of Popular Government', Gresham College, 25 September 2007.
Parry, Jonathan, presentation to the History of Parliament Trust's 1832–68 colloquium, Westminster Hall, London, 6 May 2011.
Regan-Lefebvre, Jennifer, 'London Clubs and Social Networking, 1870–1900', Cambridge Modern History seminar, Pembroke College, Cambridge, 21 November 2011.
Taddei, Antonia, *London Clubs in the Late Nineteenth Century*, University of Oxford discussion papers in economic and social history, No. 98 (April 1999).
Thévoz, Seth Alexander, '"A Protestant Parliament for a Protestant England": The Politics of the National Club, 1845–1868', Oxford Modern British History seminar paper, 12 May 2011.

Maps

Piccadilly 1869: London Large Scale 07.72 (Old Ordnance Survey Maps of London – Yard to the Mile) (London: Alan Godfrey, 1986).

Theses

Bylsma, John R., 'Political Issues and Party Unity in the House of Commons, 1852–1857: A Scalogram analysis' (PhD thesis, University of Iowa, 1968).

Downing, Arthur, 'The Friendly Planet: Friendly Societies in the English-Speaking World and Australia in the Long Nineteenth Century' (MPhil thesis, University of Oxford, 2012).

Gurowich, P.M., 'Party and Independence in the Early and Mid-Victorian House of Commons: Aspects of Political Theory and Practice 1832–68, Considered with Special Reference to the Period 1852–68' (PhD thesis, University of Cambridge, 1986).

Marlow, Laurence, 'The Working Men's Club Movement, 1862–1912: A Study of the Evolution of a Working Class Institution' (PhD thesis, University of Warwick, 1980).

Matikkala, Mira, 'Anti-Imperialism, Englishness, and Empire in Late-Victorian Britain' (PhD thesis, University of Cambridge, 2006).

Milne-Smith, Amy, 'Clubland: Masculinity, Status and Community in the Gentlemen's Clubs of London, c.1880–1914' (PhD thesis, University of Toronto, 2006).

Raymond, Harold Bradford, 'English Political Parties and Electoral Organisation 1832–1867' (PhD thesis, Harvard University, 1952).

Richardson, Sarah, 'Independence and Deference: A Study of the West Riding Electorate, 1832–1841' (PhD thesis, University of Leeds, 1995).

Sharpe, Michael, 'The Political Committee of the Reform Club' (MA thesis, University of York, 1993).

Taddei, Antonia, 'London Clubs in the Late Nineteenth Century' (MSci thesis, University of Oxford, 1998).

Walsh, David, 'Working Class Political Integration and the Conservative Party: A Study of Class Relations and Party Political Development in the North-West, 1800–1870' (PhD thesis, University of Salford, 1991).

Watt, R.G., 'Parties and Politics in Mid-Victorian Britain, 1857 to 1859: A Study in Quantification' (PhD, University of Minnesota, 1975).

Oxford Dictionary of National Biography entries

Feuchtwanger, E.J., 'Spofforth, Markham (1825–1907)', *Oxford Dictionary of National Biography*, Oxford University Press, 2004, http://www.oxforddnb.com/view/article/52754 (accessed on 4 September 2012).

Gash, Norman, 'Bonham, Francis Robert (1785–1863)', *Oxford Dictionary of National Biography*, Oxford University Press, 2004 http://www.oxforddnb.com/view/article/37207 (accessed on 4 September 2012).

Millar, Mary S., 'Rose, Sir Philip, first baronet (1816–1883)', *Oxford Dictionary of National Biography*, Oxford University Press, 2004, http://www.oxforddnb.com/view/article/41059 (accessed on 4 September 2012).

Nicholson, Albert, 'Coppock, James (1798–1857)', rev. H.C.G. Matthew, *Oxford Dictionary of National Biography*, Oxford University Press, 2004, http://www.oxforddnb.com/view/article/6279 (accessed on 4 September 2012).

Salmon, Philip J., 'Parkes, Joseph (1796–1865)', *Oxford Dictionary of National Biography*, Oxford University Press, 2009, http://www.oxforddnb.com/view/article/21356 (accessed on 4 September 2012).

Online sources

'Club', *Oxford English Dictionary*, 2013, http://0-www.oed.com.pugwash.lib.warwick.ac.uk/view/Entry/34789 (accessed on 10 November 2013).

'Clubbable|Clubable', *Oxford English Dictionary*, 2013, http://0-www.oed.com.pugwash.lib.warwick.ac.uk/view/Entry/34790 (accessed on 10 November 2013).

'Clubland', *Oxford English Dictionary*, 2013, http://0-www.oed.com.pugwash.lib.warwick.ac.uk/view/Entry/34788 (accessed on 10 November 2013).

'Fateful Meeting at the Carlton Club Aka The... 1922', 2012, http://www.britishpathe.com/video/fateful-meeting-at-the-carlton-club-aka-the-fateful-1/ (accessed on 4 December 2012).

'Google Maps', 2011 http://maps.google.com [used to calculate distances between roads which have not changed since the period covered here] (accessed on 20 December 2011).

Hardcastle, Ephraim, 'Ferry blackballed by White's', *Daily Mail*, 5 February 2007, http://www.dailymail.co.uk/debate/columnists/article-434145/Ferry-blackballed-Whites.html (accessed on 4 September 2010).

'History', Oxford and Cambridge Club, 2009, http://oxfordandcambridgeclub.co.uk/club/about-the-club/history/ (accessed on 4 February 2010).

'The History of the Club', Carlton Club, 2009, http://www.carltonclub.co.uk/theclub.asp (accessed on 27 January 2010).

'Landscape History: St. James's Park – From Pigs to Processions', Royal Parks, 2012, http://www.royalparks.org.uk/parks/st-jamess-park/about-st-jamess-park/landscape-history (accessed on 12 February 2012).

Morris, Charles, *"All the Shallows.": A Letter to John Bull, Esquire, About Administrations in General, and the Earl of Derby's Administration in Particular* (1852), Bristol Selected Pamphlets, University of Bristol Library (consulted at http://www.jstor.org/stable/60248526, 8 April 2011).

Sheppard, F.H.W (ed.), Floor plans of the Athenaeum, White's, Carlton and Reform Clubs, *London Metropolitan Archive* online, 2011, http://www.british-history.ac.uk (accessed on 14 May 2011).

Smythe, Henry Ralph, *Parliamentary Reform, Considered, under the Views Suggested by Evidence Given Before the Election Committees of 1853* (1854), Knowsley Pamphlet Collection, University of Liverpool (accessed at http://www.jstor.org/stable/60100657, 8 April 2011).

Wheeler, Brian, 'If anybody wants me, I'll be at my club', *BBC News*, 23 November 2003, http://news.bbc.co.uk/1/hi/magazine/3227664.stm (accessed on 10 June 2010).

E-Books

Hansen, Derek, Schneiderman, Ben and Smith, Marc A., *Analysing Social Media Networks with NodeXL: Insights from a Connected World* (Maryland, 2009) E-Book.

Tsetovat, Maksim and Kouznetsov, Alexander, *Social Network Analysis for Startups* (Sebastopol, California, 2011) E-Book.

INDEX

INDEX OF CLUBS
Albemarle Club, 127
Almack's, 124–5, 225, 255–6
Army and Navy Club, 23, 46, 142, 159, 259
Arthur's, 23, 25, 29, 46–7, 160, 240
Athenaeum Club, 23, 242, 247
  archives, 8, 72, 226, 248
  building, 46, 106, 108, 240
  foundation of, 67
  library, 150
  membership, 46, 67, 69, 74
  rules, 67, 69, 83, 234

Bath Club, 238, 281
Bath and Conservative Club, 238
Beaconsfield Club, 211
Boodle's, 7, 9, 23–5, 47, 234
  apolitical, 24, 26
  aristocratic nature of, 7, 212
  betting books, 136
  building, 25, 27, 29, 105
  histories of, 230, 240, 258–9
  membership, 39, 46, 98, 212–13
  Whips in, 160
Brooks'
  aristocratic nature of, 7, 13
  betting book, 19, 136
  histories of, 16
  location of, 23, 29
  membership, 53, 65–7, 70–2, 77, 80, 82–3, 89, 94, 97, 102, 122, 209, 211–12, 216
  non-existent political fund, 193
  newspapers, 149
  origins of, 25
  political affiliation and influence, 24, 26, 35–6, 62, 73, 75–6, 130, 172
  Reform Bill, involvement in, 25
  rules, 144
  size, 105–6, 113
  telegraph, 150
  variant spellings of, 24, 122, 162, 193
  Whips in, 158–60, 162, 170–1, 173, 214

Carlton Club
  accommodation, 142, 274
  address, club members', 126, 256, 259
  admission rates, 86
  archives, 226, 248
  blackballing, 82, 86
  bribery, allegations of, 189, 191, 261
  building, 27, 41, 106, 109–11, 132–5, 213, 236, 241
  Conservative Club, relation to, 40
  Conservative Party headquarters, 11–12, 209

dining, 143, 145, 281
electoral candidate selection, role in, 199–202, 204–5, 216
electoral interventions, 176–95
facilities, 29, 46
in fiction, 175–6, 277
foundation of, 30–5, 44, 144, 232, 235
gossip at, 134–5
historiography of, 9–11, 16–17, 19, 230, 235
Junior Carlton, relation to, 41, 239
location of, 23, 123, 247, 253
mail service, 152, 246, 255
meetings at, 117, 254
membership, 7–8, 48, 54–75, 70, 80–99, 122, 209, 211, 216, 226, 243–4, 259
newspapers, 148–50
political affiliation and influence, 11, 22, 31, 34, 100–2, 112, 118–121, 129, 141, 153, 158, 165, 168, 171, 211, 217, 254
political fund, 201, 207, 215, 261–2
Reform Act, relation to, 31, 34
Reform Club, relation to, 35–7
resignations from, 13
rules, 14, 34, 67, 126, 234, 256
terrorist incident at, 255
waiting list, 87, 89, 90
whipping, role in, 157–174, 214
women, admission of, 257
City Carlton Club, 211
City Constitutional Club, 211
City of London Club, 47
Cobden Club, 44, 172, 196, 271, 277
Cocoa Tree Club, 23, 48, 210
Colonial Club, 23, 210
Conservative Club, 23, 29, 40–1, 44, 63, 73, 126, 158, 173, 238, 242, 272, 277, 281
Constitutional Club, 44, 114, 234, 252
Crockford's, 16, 23, 25, 27–9, 54, 210, 230, 233

Devonshire Club, 44, 230, 233, 240, 257

East India United Service Club, 23, 47, 56, 229, 239
Eldon Club, 4
Erectheum Club, 23, 210

Fox Club, 25, 70, 233, 245
Free Trade Club, 21–3, 27, 40, 73, 96, 102, 106, 145, 196, 232, 242, 246
  MP memberships, 81, 239
  political affiliation, 42–4, 129, 172

Garrick Club, 17, 47, 70, 160, 230, 241
Grillions, 54
Guards' Club, 16, 23, 28, 30, 46

Junior Carlton Club
  archives, 8, 247, 252
  building, 106–7, 132, 187, 238
  Carlton Club, relation to, 41, 239
  electoral activities, 183–90, 208, 215
  foundation of, 27, 41, 44, 234
  guests, 112
  historiography of, 8, 16, 226, 230
  library, 150
  location, 23
  membership, 62–3, 78, 80, 82, 87, 91, 211
  National Club host, 281
  political affiliation and influence, 22, 41, 72–4, 98, 122, 129, 187, 255
  Political Committee, 188–9
  private printing, 195
  terrorist incident, 123
  Whips in, 158–62, 164, 170
  women, exclusion of, 257
Junior Constitutional Club, 211
Junior United Service Club, 23, 46, 259

INDEX

Ladies' Boodle's, 225
Ladies' Institute, 127, 224
Land Surveyors' Club, 29
Law Club, 29

Marlborough Club, 23

National Club
 building, 27, 125, 142, 225
 decline of, 40, 212, 244, 281
 dining club, 281
 facilities, 150
 foundation of, 42
 historiography of, 16, 21, 232, 239, 244, 276
 involvement in elections, 203–6
 membership, 63, 144, 158, 162, 205, 257, 261
 political affiliation and influence, 22, 43–4, 48, 102, 153
 Protestant affiliation and importance of, 42–3, 63, 73–4, 80, 173, 206
 textual influence, 196–7, 207, 264, 279
National Liberal Club, 114, 211, 252, 255, 257, 262–3
National Reform Club, 44, 239
Naval and Military Club, 47

Oriental Club, 47, 56, 241
Oxford and Cambridge Club, 30, 46, 77, 98, 160, 235, 240, 259

Parthenon Club, 23, 210, 238
Pratt's, 23, 47, 56, 241
Prince of Wales Club, 239

Reform Club
 accommodation, 46
 archives, 238, 242
 bets, 136
 blackballing and acceptance rates, 82, 86–8, 248

Brooks', alleged political supercession of, 35–6, 212
Carlton Club, relation to, 4, 9, 36
dining, 18, 143, 145, 260
electoral candidate selection, role in, 199, 202–4, 216
electoral interventions, 176–7, 179–82, 188–9, 193–9, 203, 207, 215–17
in fiction, 258
foundation of, 2, 4, 13, 17, 28, 33–7, 44, 180, 232, 236
Garibaldi's breakfast visit, 126, 145
gossip in, 258, 262
guests, 261
historiography of, 8, 209–11, 227, 230, 280
Liberal Party headquarters, 11–12, 31, 153, 209
location, 23, 253
membership, 10, 34, 42, 53, 56–7, 62–77, 80–3, 93–8, 105, 122–3, 209, 211, 216, 237, 244
Napier dinner, 116, 146–7
newspapers, 149
political affiliation and influence, 14, 22, 31, 36, 39, 80, 100, 102–3, 121, 129, 141, 158, 251
Political Committee, 119–20, 208, 254
political meetings at, 120–1
premises, 34, 101, 106–10, 113–15, 132–3, 213, 259
rules, 28, 144, 234
telegraph, 150
Westminster Reform Club, relation to, 36–8, 237
Whips' activities and influence in, 158, 162–4, 169–70, 172, 174, 214, 267
women, admission of, 257
Rota Club, 2
Royal Automobile Club, 114, 235

St Stephen's Club, 211

Thatched House Club, 41
Travellers Club, 16, 22–3, 25, 28, 30, 39, 45–6, 52–4, 77–80, 95, 98, 101, 112, 114, 134, 150, 159, 160, 171, 229–30, 240, 242, 247, 255, 259

Union Club, 45, 49, 130–1, 229, 231, 233, 251, 259
  building, 106, 225
  impact, 27–8, 189
  structure and rules, 98, 189
United Service Club, 16, 23, 28, 46–7, 98, 229, 239–40, 253, 259
United University Club, 23, 46, 98, 142, 198, 225, 259

Welsh Club for MPs, 12
Westminster Reform Club
  failure of, 27, 36, 210
  finances, 38–9, 105, 106
  foundation of, 37–8
  location and size, 48, 225, 237
  newspapers at, 148–9
  political affiliation and influence, 22, 98, 212
  political membership, 39, 43, 54, 64–5, 73, 78, 81, 95, 172–3, 181, 201, 237–8, 273
  records, 246
  Reform Club, precursor to, 17, 37
White's
  aristocratic nature of, 7, 71–2, 212
  betting book, 19, 136, 138
  blackballing, 28, 247
  Brooks', rivalry with, 25
  building, 25, 27, 102, 105–7, 213
  declining political influence, 71, 97
  depictions of, 26
  dining, 144, 149
  elections to, 91–2
  facilities, 29, 122, 149, 151
  foundation, 24, 223
  histories of, 16, 19, 28, 230–1, 233, 258
  location, 23, 29, 253
  membership, 28, 39, 57, 61–2, 70, 78, 92, 244, 257
  political affiliation and connections, 22, 24, 74, 76, 79–81
  proprietor-owned, 250
  rules, 72, 92, 114
  Whips in, 158–61
Willis's Rooms (Almack's), 124–5, 255–6
Wyndham Club, 23, 28, 259

Young Crockford's, 234

INDEX OF TERMS

Aberdeen, Earl of, 32, 123, 203
Aberdeen coalition, 132, 170, 262, 277
Adam, William MP, 158
Aherne, Mike, 232
Ailsa, Lord, 138
Albemarle Street, 6
Alexander, John MP, 92
Allen, Dr John, 120, 250
Alsager, Richard MP, 91, 248
Althorp, Viscount, 73
Anglicans, 42–3
Anson, Colonel, 138
Arbuthnot, Charles MP, 32, 176, 272
  aristocracy, 2, 7, 29, 34, 36, 102, 255–6, 261
  membership of clubs, 46–7, 62, 66, 70–2, 92, 95, 150, 183, 212, 237, 241, 273
  salons, at, 125–31
Arnold, Ann, 260
Arundel, Earl of, 90
Ashley, Lord, 172
Ashton and Reid, *Clubs and Associations*, 2
Ashton, Rosemary, 250
Aspinall, Arthur, 231, 260
Asquith, H. H., 123, 255
assembly rooms, 125
Attwood, John MP, 92
Attwood, Matthias MP, 166, 269
Attwood, Thomas MP, 65, 176
Aydelotte, W. O., 50, 241

Baer, Marc, 143, 260
Bailey, Peter, 104, 251
Baillie, Henry James MP, 89
Baird, William MP, 54, 243
Balfour, Thomas MP, 91, 248
Ballie, Alexander F., 241
Ballot Act of 1872, 83
Baring, Alexander MP, 32
Baring, Sir Francis Thornhill MP, 72, 159, 266–7
Baring, William Bingham MP, 73
Baring, Francis MP, 73
Baring, Henry MP, 118, 138, 160, 167, 171
Barneby, John MP, 84
Barry, Sir Charles, 101, 103, 107, 114, 240, 255
Barton Street, 168, 269
Barry, Edward, 113
Bateson, Sir Robert Bt, 235, 261
Bateson, Sir Thomas MP, 112, 139, 160
Bath, 181, 273
Bath, Marquess of, 137–8, 200, 277
Baude, Baron, 134
Beales, Derek, 170, 226, 270
Beaumont, W. B. MP, 77
Bebbington, David, 279
Bedford, Duke of, 70, 83
Belfast, Lord, 137–8, 258
Bellamy's, 143, 257, 259
Bentinck, George W. F., 136, 137
Bentley, Michael, 226
Beresford, William MP, 145–6, 158, 160, 162, 171, 173, 182, 191, 261, 267
Beresford-Hope, Alexander MP, 92
Berkeley, F. W. F. MP, 139
Berkeley, Grenville MP, 159, 170
Berkeley, Henry MP, 183
Bessborough, Lord, 136
Betting, 19, 136–9, 258
Birmingham Political Union, 176, 180
Black, Barbara, 5, 15, 224
blackballing, 28, 83–4, 86–7, 98, 216
Blake, Robert, 9, 11, 13, 20, 227–8, 243, 245, 274
Blandford, Marquess of, 13, 228
Boas, Guy, 230, 241
Bonham, Francis Robert MP, 11, 17, 33, 90, 151, 160–2, 167, 171–2, 177–82, 191, 198, 201–2, 217, 227, 266, 269, 271–3, 278–9

Borthwick, Peter MP, 126, 152, 256
Boswell, James, 5
Bourne, J. M., 156, 158, 166, 169, 265, 267, 269, 270
Boyle, the Hon. Major W. G., 138
Brackley, Viscount, 83
Bradley, Ian, 16, 246
Brand, Henry MP, 159, 163–4
Brandon, David, 107
Brandreth, Gyles, 265
Brett, Peter, 143, 260
Briggs, Asa, 112, 226, 252
Bright, John MP, 43, 121, 133, 143, 146–7, 150, 177, 258, 263
British Hotel, 204, 259
Brock, Michael and Eleanor, *H. H. Asquith: Letters to Venetia Stanley*, 255
Brooke, John, 272
Brown, David, 145, 261, 271
Brown, Gordon MP, 1
Brown, Henry Edwards, 126, 177–8, 180–6, 195, 273–4, 276
Browne, Robert Dillon MP, 53
Browne, the Hon. William MP, 72
Brunswick Hotel, 259
Buccleuch, Duke of, 165
Buckingham, Duke of, 117, 253
Buckley, Jessie, 272
Buller, Charles MP, 150, 236, 263
Bulwer, Henry Lytton MP, 39, 255
Bunbury, Thomas MP, 142
Burdett, Sir Francis, 138, 172, 200
Burghley, Lord MP, 184
Burlingham, R. and Billis, R., *Reformed Characters*, 230, 247
Burns, A. and Innes, J., *Rethinking the Age of Reform*, 228
Butler, R. A., 228
Butler, Sir E., 138
Bylsma, John R., 50, 241
Byng, the Hon. George Charles Henry MP, 73, 138

Cadogan, Frederick, 137
Campbell, John Henry MP, 90
Campbell, Walter MP, 53, 243
Campbell-Smith, Duncan, 151, 263
Canada House, 106
Capdeville, Valerie, 2, 23, 223, 232
Carden, Sir Robert W. MP, 92
Carlton Hotel, 23, 33, 236
Carlton House, 6, 29, 234–5
Carlton House Terrace, 29, 33
Carlton Terrace, 35
Castlerosse, Viscount, 72
Catholic emancipation, 7, 43, 137, 173, 196
Cavendish family, 70–1, 245
Cavendish Hotel, 259
Cavendish, Lord Edward, 71
    see also Hartington, Marquis of
Cavendish, Lord Frederick, 83
Cavendish, the Hon. Charles Compton MP, 70
Cavendish, the Hon. Colonel Henry Frederic Compton MP, 70
Cawdor, Lord, 92
Chandos, Marquis of, 165, 178, 201, 205–6, 235
Charles Street, 32, 39, 102, 176
Charles Street Gang, 31–3, 45, 193, 235
Charlton, Edmund Lechmere MP, 86
Chatham House Rule, 136, 258
Chesney, Kellow, 232
chocolate houses, 23
City of London, 47
Clanricarde, Lord, 43, 239
Clark, Peter, 2, 3, 15, 23, 223–4, 229, 232
Clarke, Tom, 240
Clerk, Sir George MP, 118, 166, 235, 261
Cleveland Square Group, 198
'club government', 2, 7–8, 10, 21, 52, 114, 193, 209–11, 214, 216–7, 225

INDEX

Clubland
  culture and influence, 101, 109, 114, 116, 121, 123, 127, 131–9, 154, 173, 175, 193, 209, 217, 224, 229, 257, 263–4
  decline of, 155
  definition, 5, 6, 22, 48, 225
  development of, 28–9, 44, 47, 49, 51, 71, 94, 213
  distance from Parliament, 102, 115, 142, 155, 214
  literature on, 10–19, 27
  myths about, 216
  salons, relation to, 125–6
clubs
  apolitical clubs, 9, 22, 26–7, 45, 82
  architecture of, 105–14, 155
  archives of, 8, 17, 28, 48, 52, 54, 101, 120, 226, 238, 242, 248–9, 257, 268, 275
  candidates for, 10, 46, 69, 73, 83–92, 98–9, 161–2, 184–5, 276
  clubhouses, 27, 29, 39, 105–10
  definition and origins of, 2–3, 15, 18, 23–5, 33, 44, 225
  development and expansion of, 28–9, 30
  economics of, 14, 27, 38–9, 167
  effects on constituency elections, 10, 12, 44, 154, 175–7, 183, 189, 197–204, 215
  false stories about, 17, 229
  guests at, 27, 105, 111–12, 126, 144, 177, 213, 231, 270
  historiography of, 10, 15–19, 21, 23, 48
  'histories' of, 9, 15–16
  libraries, 147–50
  meetings at, 116–18, 119, 121, 124
  members-owned clubs, 28, 49, 213
  mixed-sex clubs, 127
  myths about, 216
  organisation of, 144, 153, 189
  political affiliations of, 11, 12, 73–5

political clubs, 21, 42, 48, 59, 113
prestige of, 45, 47, 139
printing, 195–6
proprietary clubs, 27, 213
resignation from, 82, 86, 88
rules of, 28, 69, 72, 189
second homes, use as, 52, 126, 141–2, 151–3, 255–6, 259
services at, 151–2, 154
single-issue clubs, 42
size of, 25, 38, 105
survival rate, 16
spatial theory of, 101–11, 209, 213
terrorist action targeting, 123
waiting lists, 87–8, 90
Cobden, Richard, 43, 116, 134, 172, 179, 232, 253, 273
Cobdenites, 81, 172, 196, 212, 239
Codrington, Sir Edward, 133
coffee room, 23, 105, 214, 243
Cohen, Benjamin B., 15, 28, 229, 234
Colchester, G. M., 161
Cole, Lord, 165
Coleman, Bruce, 176, 178, 184, 209, 272, 275
Collett, John MP, 88
Collier, John MP, 93, 249
Colquhoun, J. C., 43, 204
Colson, Percy, 62, 151, 230, 233–4, 244, 263
Commons, House of *see also* Bellamy's; Parliament; Westminster, Palace of 7, 112–13, 119, 121, 145, 210, 241
  exclusion of women, 128
  facilities, 101–2, 113, 259, 260
  London, best club in, 1, 250, 252
  overlap with club memberships, 47, 63, 65, 82, 94, 242
  political composition of, 57, 59, 70–2, 246, 251
  relation to clubs, 6, 22, 54, 114, 122, 142, 144, 146–7, 150
  sittings, 260

subject of a bet, 137
Whips in clubs, 156–74, 214, 265–9
Conacher, J. B., 170, 248, 270
Conservative Associations, 191–2
Conservative Operative Societies, 11
Conservatives
  groupings of, 57, 62
  club membership, 9–12, 57, 58, 61, 94
Coohill, Joseph, 52, 54, 156, 169, 174, 176, 198, 236, 243, 261, 265–8, 270, 273
Cook, C. and Keith, B., *British Historical Facts*, 178, 260
constituencies, 2–4, 12, 31, 42, 109, 117, 137–9, 143, 153–4, 167–8, 180, 182, 187, 190–209, 215–17, 250, 260, 275–6, 279
  Bath, 181, 273
  Berwick-upon-Tweed, 12, 183, 191
  Beverley, 31, 235
  Blackburn, 276
  Bolton, 276
  Cambridge, 31, 189, 235
  Canterbury, 191–2
  Cheltenham, 139
  Denbighshire, 139
  Frome, 183, 200, 276
  Great Yarmouth, 167, 198
  Leicester, 167, 191, 269
  Liverpool, 12, 138
  Maidstone, 191, 199
  Middlesex, 138
  Newark, 202, 208, 216
  Norwich, 126, 182, 195, 199, 256, 272, 274, 276
  Oxford University, 139, 179, 203–6
  Oxfordshire, 139
  Preston, 276
  Sandwich, 167, 192, 202, 269, 278
  South Cheshire, 197
  Sudbury, 201
  Taunton by-election, 39, 201, 278
  West Norfolk, 195, 276
  Westminster, 200

Constituency Conservative Associations in receipt of payments from Carlton Club, list of, 190–2
Copley, Sir Joseph, 136, 138
Coppock, James, 162, 177–82, 194–5, 198, 217, 270, 273, 274
Corfield, Penelope J., 234
Corio, A. and Thevoz, S. A., *Defending the Protestant Principles of the Constitution*, 239, 244, 264
Corn Laws, 42, 117, 145, 194, 276
corruption, 41, 123, 176, 182, 184, 207–8
Cox, Gary W. 13, 51, 156, 160
Cragoe, Matthew, 260
Craig, F. W. S., 259
Crang, Mike, 103, 250
Crawford, Elizabeth, 224, 256
Croker, John Wilson MP, 32, 46
Cruikshank, George, 131
Cruikshank, Isaac, 130
Cumberland, Duke of, 32

Dalrymple-Horn-Elphinstone, Sir James, 93
Damer, George MP, 137, 258
Damer, L. Dawson, 139
Darwin, Bernard, 27, 82, 234, 247
Dasent, Arthur Irwin, 229
Daunton, M. J., 263–4
Davis, John, 9, 280
de Horsey, Mr, 136
de Lisle, Lord, 137
de Wilde, Samuel, 131
Derby, Earl of *see also* Stanley, Lord, 19, 41, 121–2, 152, 168, 171–2, 189, 226, 244, 268, 270
Derbyites, 162, 171, 179, 181–2, 204, 206, 217
Devonshire House, 106
D'Eyncourt, Charles Tennyson MP, 37, 237
Dickens, Charles, 1, 17, 113, 223, 7252

Index

Dickson, Colonel T. S., 126, 199, 274, 276
dining, 12, 15, 18, 42, 101, 103–5, 113, 122, 126–31, 143–7, 153, 214, 231, 251, 254, 260–2, 264
  dining societies, 12, 15, 25, 70, 281
  scale of in clubs, 145–6, 262
  speeches given, 146–7, 154
Disraeli, Benjamin, 19, 169, 232, 244, 254–8, 268, 270
  activity in clubs, 121–2
  Athenaeum, membership of, 69, 245
  Carlton, at the, 111, 120, 122, 152, 163, 199–201, 254–5, 274
  clubs blackballed from, 54
  complaining about gossip, 133
  constituency elections of, 199–201
  Crockford's, involvement in, 27, 54
  informant on club meetings, 119
  Junior Carlton, at, 41, 122, 189, 234
  novels, 17, 175, 215, 271, 277–8
  salons, at, 129
  solicitors and agents, 180, 183
  speeches given, 111, 147
  unpaid subscriptions, 39
  Westminster Reform Club, membership of, 39, 65, 238
  Young England movement, 89
Disraeli Letters, ed. Gunn, Wiebe et al., 234, 241, 244, 254–6, 264, 268, 274, 278
Dod (Dodd), Charles, 52–8, 242–3
Dod's Parliamentary Companion, 43, 48, 52–8, 69, 74–5, 79, 93, 96, 142, 241, 245
Douro, Marquess of, 199, 277
Dover Street, 6
Downing, Arthur, 79, 246
Downs, Carolyn, 232
Dunbar, Sir William MP, 159
Duncan, George MP, 142
Duncombe, the Hon. Arthur MP, 146
Duncombe, Thomas MP, 157, 164, 257
Dundas, George MP, 161, 267

Dundas, Sir James Deans, 147
Dunne, John J., 253
Durham, Earl of, 35–6, 38

East India Company, 47, 56
Eden, Lord, 32
Edis, R. W., 252
Edwards, Lt. Colonel MP, 184
Edwards, Owen Dudley, 176, 271
Eeles, Henry S. and Earl Spencer, *Brooks's*, 230, 233–4, 263
Eldon, Lord, 32
election agents, 11, 126, 151, 161–2, 175–82, 182–6, 192–5, 198, 200, 207, 217, 267, 273, 275, 278
election funding, 184–8, 190, 193, 206
election petitions, 194–5, 276–7
Ellenborough, Lord, 32, 235
Ellice, Edward MP, 2, 10, 17, 35–6, 159, 162, 180, 193, 209, 217, 243
Ellmore, Dr J., 39
Enniskellen, Lord, 152
Erickson, Arvel B., 271
Erskine May, Sir Thomas, 7
Escott, Margaret, 12, 228
Escott, T. H. S., 18, 21, 230, 232
Evans, Sir George de Lacy, 47

Fagan, Louis, 18, 35, 39, 230–1, 236, 238
fast-tracking, 67, 72, 82, 90–3, 161, 216
Feldman, D. and Stedman Jones, G. *Metropolis: London*, 226, 280
Feuchtwanger, E. J., 186, 274
Finlayson, G. B. A. M., 273
Fisher, D. R., 13, 228
Fitzroy, A., 16, 229, 230
Fitzroy Square, 93
Fitzwilliam family, 71
Foley, Lord, 136
Foot, M. R. D. and Matthew, H. C. G. *The Gladstone Diaries*, 204, 272, 279
Forester, Colonel G. C. W. MP, 177–8, 195

Forester, Lord, 137
Forrest, Denys, 229, 239
Forrester, H. W., 137
Foster, R. E. 278, 280
Fox, Celina, 234
Fox, Charles James, 24–6, 131, 233
　Foxites, 24–5, 62, 70
Fraser, Peter, 266
Fraser Rae, W., 10, 18, 39, 227, 236–8, 244, 261, 263
Freemasons, 15, 216
Fremantle, Sir Thomas MP, 113, 118, 160–1, 164–9, 202, 261
French, Fitzstephen MP, 116, 146
Fulford, Roger, 230, 234, 238, 258–9, 261–2

gambling, 2, 23, 25, 47–8, 113, 131, 232, 241
Gaming Act of 1845, 23
Garibaldi, Giuseppe, 126, 145
Gasford, Lord, 91
Gash, Norman, 2, 8–14, 20–1, 31–2, 36, 39, 102, 118, 176, 178, 186, 197, 199, 201, 209, 210, 217, 223, 227, 228, 232–238, 253–5, 270–5, 277–80
Gaskell, James More MP, 160
Gaunt, Richard, 271
Gillray, James, 26
Gladstone, Sir John, 202
Gladstone, Thomas MP
　connection with Carlton and F. R. Bonham, 201
　election, 201–2
　papers, 278
Gladstone, William Ewart MP
　benefactor of clubs, 46
　Carlton, resignation from, 13
　elections of, 202–6
　political positions relative to clubs, 43, 76, 88, 123, 179, 232, 246, 262, 279

Reform Club membership, 123
　subject of a bet, 136, 139
Glasgow, Lord, 136–7
Gleadle, Kathryn, 128, 143, 224, 256, 260
Glyn, George, G. MP, 159
Gooch, Sir Thomas MP, 137
Gordon, E. and Nair, G., *Public Lives*, 252
Gore, J. R. Ormsby MP, 185
gossip, 14, 18, 25–6, 101, 130–4, 136–40, 147, 154–5, 214, 229, 233, 257
Goulburn, Henry MP, 32–3, 235, 261
Goulburn, Sir W., 202
Graham, Sir James MP, 13, 269, 271
　Brooks', election to, 92
　Carlton, membership of, 13, 172, 235
　Carlton, withdrawal from, 88
　Napier dinner, 146–7, 262
　subject of a bet, 138
　Whips, opinions on, 167
Grant, James, 162
Graves, Charles, 21, 232, 240
Great Fire of 1834, 7, 49, 101, 139, 143
Great George Street, 29, 37, 142, 225
Greville, Charles, 40, 133, 145–6, 172, 238, 258, 261–2, 271
Grey, Earl, 19, 25, 122, 137, 228
Griffiths, Arthur, 18
Grote, George MP, 69, 117, 121
Guedalla, Philip, 262
guests, 27, 105, 111–12, 126, 144, 177, 213, 231, 270
Gurowich, P. M., 156, 265

Habermas, Jurgen, 103–4, 115, 250
Hadfield, George MP, 182
Hall, C., McClelland, K. and Rendell, J. *Defining the Victorian Nation*, 224
Hamilton, Duke of, 182, 206
Hanham, H. J., 4, 7, 224, 226, 250, 281

Index

Hansen, D., Schneiderman, B. & Smith, M. A., *Analysing Social Media Networks*, 246
Hardcastle, Ephraim, 231
Hardinge, Sir Henry MP, 32, 119, 235, 254, 261
Hardy, John MP, 121
Harris, James, 257
Harris, Peter, 252
Harrowby, Earl of, 32
Hartington, Marquis of, 47, 71, 163, 241, 245
Harvey, Adrian, 232
Harvey, Daniel MP, 121, 149
Haury, David A., 36, 236
Hawkins, Angus, 6, 105, 112, 153, 156, 170, 210, 226, 251, 255–6, 258, 264–6, 270, 276, 280
Hawkins, A. and Powell, J., *Journal of John Wodehouse*, 252, 255
Haymarket, 6, 225
Herbert, Sir Thomas MP, 147
Herries, J. C. MP, 32, 194, 276
Herries, Sir Henry, 33
Hill, Lord Marcus, 158–9, 261
Hill, R. L., 9, 11, 227
Hilton, Boyd, 226
Hobhouse, Thomas, 203
Hodgson, William Nicholson, 187
Holland, Baron, 122, 130
Holland House, 102, 129, 130, 250
Holmes, William MP, 32–3
homosociality, 257
Hopwood, John Thomas, 161, 267
Horn, Pamela, 104, 251
Hotham, Lord, 165
Hough, Richard, 230
Howe, Anthony, 172, 232, 239, 271
Howe, A. and Morgan, S., *The Letters of Richard Cobden*, 232
Huch, R. K. and Ziegler, P. R., *Joseph Hume*, 9, 227
Hume, Joseph MP, 36–7, 110, 251
Hunt, Tristram, 114

Ingestre, Lord, 138
Inglis, Sir Robert MP, 32
Innes, Joanna, 14, 228
Institute of Civil Engineers, 28–9, 237
Ireland, 153, 253
Irish MPs and club members, 12, 37, 121, 128, 228, 237, 271
Irish Municipal Corporations Bill, 121
Irish railways, 118, 253

Jackson, Major-General Sir Louis, 16, 229
Jacoby, Charlie, 229, 239
Jaggard, Edwin, 224
Jenkins, T. A., 141, 156, 164, 167–8, 259, 263, 265, 268–9, 281
Jermyn Street, 26, 142, 259
Jersey, Earl of, 33
Jersey, Lady, 127
Jewish emancipation, 43, 137, 173, 204, 206
Jews' admission to Parliament, 153, 196
John Bull, 149, 150, 238, 248, 271
Jolles, Michael, 230, 248
Jolliffe, William MP, 160, 161, 168, 183, 184, 186, 190, 191, 200, 206, 267, 269, 275, 277, 280
Jones, Wilbur Devereux, 255

Keith-Falconer, C. K., 186
Kelly, Sir Fitzroy, 168
Kemble, Henry, MP, 157
Kensington, Lord, 33
Keogh, William MP, 132
Kimberley, Earl of, 112, 252
King George IV, 29
King Street, 124
Kitton, W. M., 195, 276
Knatchbull-Hugessen, Edward H. MP, 83, 159, 163, 247, 265, 268, 270
Knightley, Rainald MP, 136
Knox, Robert, 132
Koss, Stephen, 149, 263

Kousser, J. M., 50–1, 241
Kriegel, Abraham D., 250, 254–5
Kumin, Beat, 103, 250–1
Kynaston, David, 241

Labouchere, Henry, 201
Lascelles, William MP, 165, 268
Law Society, 29
Lawrence, Jon, 109, 251
Lee, Joseph, 253
Lefebvre, Henri, 104, 115, 251
Lefroy, Thomas Langlois MP, 121
Lejeune, Anthony, 17, 35, 66, 224, 230–3, 260, 263
  details in research of, 17, 19, 233, 236
Le Marchant, Sir Denis, 19, 231, 266
Lempriere, Dr C., 204–5
Lennox, Lord Henry, 137
Lewis, Wyndham, 199
Liberal Conservatives, 57–62, 74, 76, 94–7, 243
Liberal Registration Association, 120
Liberal Party, emergence of, 13, 66, 73, 120, 125, 153, 170–1, 236, 245, 256
Liberals
  electoral activity in clubs, 176–8, 181–4, 193, 195, 198, 208, 217
  groupings of, 57, 64, 66, 95, 245
  memberships, 25, 31–7, 43–4, 56–7, 63–9, 72–7, 80, 82, 94–8, 141, 144, 146, 212, 216
  salons, at, 125, 129
  Whips, 158–174
Lichfield House, 106
Lincoln, Earl of MP, 165, 179, 269, 272
Liverpool, 12, 138
Llewelyn, Alexander, 13, 228
London Library, 150
Londonderry, Marquis of, 32
Lonsdale, Earl of, 71
LoPatin/LoPatin-Lummis, Nancy D., 176, 180, 272–3, 280

Lords, House of, 6–7, 72, 101, 137, 145, 226
Lubenow, William C., 3, 223, 292
Lyndhurst, Lord, 32
Lyon, John Hayes, 197–8, 277
Lytton, Sir Bulwer, 168

Machin, Ian, 278
Mackenzie, W. Forbes MP, 160, 194, 276
Maidstone, 199
Maidstone, Lord, 191
Malmesbury, Lord, 41, 132, 234, 244, 257
Manchester money men, 115
Mandler, Peter, 71, 124–5, 127–30, 246, 255–7
Markus, Michael, 199, 277
Marsh, Peter, 108, 115, 153, 251, 253, 264
Martin, John, 195
masculinity, 5, 14, 101, 124, 126, 128, 130–1, 140, 213, 229
Masterman, John, 47, 261
Matikkala, Mira, 257
Maurice, F. D., 203, 279
Maxwell, Somerset Richard MP, 152
Maynooth Grant, 42, 44, 63, 153, 173, 203, 206
Melbourne, Lord, 44, 122, 137
Meller, Captain MP, 112
membership of clubs
  caps on, 27, 88
  changing, 171
  clubless MPs, 93–7
  deception about, 48, 53
  elections to, 82, 84, 86
  fast-tracking, 67, 72, 82, 90–3, 161, 216
  MPs, 22–47, 50, 53, 55–99
  multiple clubs, 77–82, 98
  proposers, 72–3, 82–7, 92, 161, 165, 183–6, 238, 248, 267
  reasons for, 47, 70–72, 242

Index

regional representation, 73
resignation from, 13, 82, 86, 88
statistical analysis of, 13, 40, 50–2, 67, 79–80, 89, 211, 249
supernumerary, 89, 91, 92, 98
Millar, Mary S., 186, 234, 254, 264, 268, 274
Miller, Henry, 194, 276
Milne-Smith, Amy, 5, 14, 15, 136, 139, 224, 229, 242, 247, 257–9
Milton, John, 5, 225
ministers, 13, 31, 120, 123, 146–7, 151, 168, 258
Mitcalfe, Henry MP, 93
Molesworth, Sir William, 35, 120–1, 146–7, 236,
Monckton, John, 199, 277
Moore, D. C., 224
Moore, Rebekah, 263
Mordaunt Crook, J., 14, 29, 34–5, 66, 229–30, 234, 236, 240, 244–5, 252
Morgan, Marjorie, 131, 257
Morning Room, 165, 214, 253
Morpeth, Lord, 93
Morris, Charles, 271
Mostyn, Sir Thomas, 12
Mowbray, John MP, 152
Mulgrave, Earl of, 158
Munford, W. A., 103, 250
Munster, Lord, 137

Napier, Admiral Sir Charles, 116, 146–8, 262
Nevill, Ralph, 18, 230
Nevill, Viscount, 184, 186
New Palace Yard, 42, 225
New Square, 106, 225
Newbould, Ian, 11, 67, 227, 245
Newcastle, Duke of, 172
Newcastle-under-Lyme, 204
Newdegate, Charles MP, 43, 63, 153, 160, 162, 173, 196, 239, 267, 271
newspapers, 148–9

Nicholl, Sir John, 12
Nicholson, Albert, 180, 273
Noel, Gerard MP, 160, 184–6
Norreys, Lord, 139
Northcote, Sir Stafford, 205, 280
nouveaux riches, 14, 34, 229, 236, 245, 252

Old Palace Yard, 142, 173
Onslow, Guildford MP, 138
Ord, William MP, 69
Oriel College, Oxford, 205, 280
Ormsby Gord, J. R. MP, 184
Ostrogorski, Moisei, 10, 20, 207–8, 227, 280
Oxford University
    1847 general election, 203–5
    1853 by-election, 179, 203–6
O'Brien, A. and Miles, C., *A Peep into Clubland*, 227, 233
O'Connell, Daniel MP, 36, 65, 138, 145, 166, 172, 261
O'Connell, Maurice MP, 119
O'Connor, Feargus MP, 141, 259
O'Ferall, Richard MP, 159, 162
O'Gorman, Frank, 7, 12, 170, 176, 209, 226, 228, 270, 272, 280, 293

Pall Mall, 6, 20, 22, 29, 30, 34, 38, 41–2, 45, 106, 113, 123–4, 149, 175, 187, 210, 225, 234, 240, 259
Palmer, Robert MP, 193, 275
Palmer, Roundell, 203
Palmer-Tomkinson, Christopher, 231
Palmerston, Viscount, 122, 133, 145–7, 149, 170–1, 261
Palmerston, Viscountess, 125, 127–30, 251
Parker, Charles Stuart, 249
Parker, John MP, 159
Parkes, Joseph, 2, 35, 177–81, 196–7, 217, 270, 272–4
Parkinson, Stephen, 250
Parliament, Houses of *see also* Commons, House of; Lords,

House of; Westminster, Palace of, 7, 240
  facilities, 101, 113–15, 257
  noise, 250
parliamentary agents, 177–83, 185–6
Parolin, Christina, 103–4, 250–1
Parry, Jonathan, 13, 36, 73, 170, 172, 228, 236, 245–6, 270–1
Parssinen, T. M., 116, 253
Peel, Sir Robert, 11, 13, 45, 113, 121, 137, 151–2, 168, 171, 213–4, 217
  activity in clubs, 122
  Carlton Club, role in foundation, 33
  Conservative Club, role in foundation, 40
  ministries, 17, 32, 118, 169, 172
Peelites, 81, 88, 170–1, 179, 217, 248
peers, 7, 38, 42, 62, 89, 91, 101–2, 137, 144, 164, 167, 190, 211, 237, 268
Pelham-Clinton, Lord Robert, 43
Perceval, Alexander MP, 32
Perceval, Dudley M., 204, 206
Perceval, Spencer, 204
Petrie, Sir Charles and Cooke, Alistair, *The Carlton Club*, 17, 230, 235, 238–9, 243, 248, 256, 261, 274–5, 280
Phelps, Barry, 17, 32, 230, 239
Phillips, John A., 51, 176, 224, 242, 260, 272
Piccadilly, 6, 22, 29, 102, 113, 253, 259
Pickford, James, 247
Pigot, Sir Robert, 200
Pitt the Younger, 24, 26
Pittites, 24, 62
Planta, Joseph MP, 32–3
  house of, 23
Plymley, Katherine, 128
Plymouth, 93
Polhill, Frederick MP, 149, 263

Political Unions, 36, 176, 180, 193, 207, 272, 280
Port, M. H., 113, 250, 252
porters, 105, 108, 127, 152, 165, 213
Praed, William Mackworth MP, 26, 32
Praed, Winthrop M. MP, 235, 261
Price, Richard, 9, 226
Protestantism (political influence of), 22, 42–3, 63, 73–4, 80, 173, 179, 196, 203–4, 206, 239, 244, 264, 276
protests, 123–4
Pugh, Ralph B., 234
Puwar, Nirmal, 104, 251

Quinault, Roland, 114, 252

Radicals, 14, 22, 35–7, 43–5, 57, 62–7, 69, 73, 76, 95–6, 103, 110, 124–5, 129, 150, 170, 181, 193, 196, 201, 212, 216
Raikes, Thomas, 24
Ramsden, John, 4, 224, 232
Ranelagh, Lord, 276
Redesdale, Lord, 117–18, 161–2, 164–6, 253, 268–9
Reform Act of 1832
  beginning of political era, 2, 6, 12–3, 20, 24–5, 46, 106, 163, 176, 193
  effect on political groupings and electoral landscape, 7, 9, 15, 38, 31, 66, 71, 73, 95, 173, 212, 218, 224, 260, 272
  effects on Clubland, 24–5, 31–2, 34, 36–7, 48, 105, 114, 153–4, 209–10
Reform Act, Second, 7, 20, 47, 63, 102, 187, 208, 211, 217, 247
Reform Association, 13, 17, 176, 181, 194, 196–8, 277
Reformers, 14, 35–6, 57, 64, 66, 69, 76, 94–5, 121, 131, 147, 245
Regan-Lefebvre, Jennifer, 79, 246

INDEX

Regent Street, 22, 42–3
Reid, Stuart J., 236
Rendell, Jane, 14, 228
Renton, Tim, 265
Repealers, 57, 64–5, 76, 95, 245
reporters (press), 116, 123, 134, 144–7, 176, 201, 254
Reynolds, Kim, 113, 127–9, 252, 255–6, 261
Richardson, Sarah, 224
Robinson, George MP, 162
Rokeby, Lord, 138
Rope, Charles, 166
Rose, Philip, 161, 177–81, 183–6, 190, 191, 200, 217, 267, 273–5
Ross, Charles MP, 138, 160, 235, 261
Rowlandson, Thomas, 131
Royston, Lord, 137
Rush, Michael, 11–12, 228
Russell, Lord John, 45, 83, 114, 122, 146, 163, 212, 245, 247
Russell, Sir Charles, 70, 245
Russell family, 70–1, 73, 245

Sainty, John C., 157, 265–6
Sainty and Cox, *The Identification of Government Whips*, 160, 165, 170, 265–6, 268, 270
Salisbury, Marquess of, 33, 90, 165, 235
Salmon, Philip, 9, 176, 178, 186, 209, 227, 236, 260, 272–5, 278, 280
salons, 29, 113, 121, 125–7, 129–130, 139, 140, 145, 151, 213
Sampson, Anthony, 10, 18, 227, 231, 241
Scarlett, Sir James MP, 32
Sebag-Montefiore, Charles, 230, 233, 245
Shannon, Richard, 4, 123, 224, 232, 255, 279
Sharpe, Michael, 119, 120, 235, 254, 280
Sheil, Richard MP, 119, 254
Shelley, Henry, 18, 230, 287

Shelley, Sir John, 83, 144
Shenton, Caroline, 46, 240, 260
Sheppard, F. H. W., 234
Sherwood, Robert, 5, 245
Shields, Andrew, 12, 13, 228
Shipley, Stan, 9, 227
Shotter Boys, Thomas, 30
Sibthorpe, Colonel, 88
Simpson, General James, 136
Sinclair, Sir George MP, 162
Smirke, Sidney, 30, 106, 109
Smirke, Sir Robert, 101, 106, 110
Smith, E. A., 7
Smith, J. Travers, 178
Smith, James, 45
smoking rooms, 105, 113–14, 165, 214, 252–3
Smythe, Henry Ralph, 271
Soames, Nicholas MP, 241
Southgate, Donald, 13, 70, 72, 176, 228, 245, 272, 294
Soyer, Alexis, 18, 103, 143, 145, 260
Spencer, Earl, 83
Spofforth, Markham, 161, 177–81, 183–6, 217, 267, 273–4
Spooner, Richard MP, 43, 153, 173, 206
St James's, 5, 6, 14, 22, 23, 29, 30, 48, 102, 103, 113, 115, 122, 124, 131, 142, 163, 210, 229, 234, 236, 239, 259
St James's Hotel, 142
St James's Park, 115, 253
St James's Square, 43, 44
St James's Street, 24, 25, 26, 29, 30, 40, 102, 125
St James's Theatre, 42
Stanley, Edward J., MP, 37, 69, 159, 162, 169, 270
Stanley, Lord, 13, 35, 122–3, 132, 134, 137, 145, 171–2, 182, 232, 258, 268
Stenton, M. and Lees, S., *Who's Who of British Members of Parliament*, 245

Steuart, Robert MP, 159
Steven, Robert, 263
Stewart, Robert, 9, 11, 12, 20, 24, 176, 186, 190, 192, 207, 209, 227–8, 233, 272, 274–5, 280
Strachey, Lytton and Fulford, Roger, *The Greville Memoirs*, 238, 261–2
Sturt, Gerald, 137, 139
Sturt, Henry Charles MP, 72
Sturt, Henry Gerard MP, 72
subscriptions (fees), 1, 3, 51, 125, 148
 dependence of clubs upon, 39–40, 188
 election fundraising, used for, 187
 statistical analysis of, 51
 unpaid, 39, 243
sugar duties, 119, 120, 213
Swartz, H. W. and Swartz, M., *Disraeli's Reminiscences*, 277
Sweet, Matthew, 260

Taddei, Antonia, 13, 14, 40, 51, 228, 231, 238, 240, 242
Taunton by-election, 39, 201, 278
Taylor, Antony, 258
Taylor, Colonel Thomas Edward, 41, 158, 160–2, 173, 184, 244
telegraph, 150, 154
Thackeray, W. M., 17, 19, 232
Thatched House Tavern, 31, 240
Thevoz, Seth Alexander, 55–6, 60–1, 63, 65, 68, 77–8, 81, 97, 160, 225, 228–9, 237, 239, 244–5, 249, 259, 264, 266, 276, 280
Thynne, Lord Edward, 138, 200
Timbs, John, 17, 18, 21, 25, 32, 40, 108, 143, 224, 230, 232–3, 235, 238, 240, 251, 260–1
Tomline, George, 139
Tosh, John, 125, 256
Trafalgar Square, 106, 123–4, 225, 255
treating, 187

Trevelyan, George Macaulay, 13, 19, 228
Trevelyan, George Otto, 25, 233
Trevor, George MP, 166
Trevor, Lord A. E. Hill MP, 184
Trevor, the Hon. Arthur MP, 149
Trollope, Anthony, 19, 127, 175, 215, 232, 271–2, 285
Tufnell, Henry, 158–9
Turner, Thomas Frewen MP, 54, 243

Verne, Jules, 136, 258
Vernon, James, 8–9, 109, 226–7, 251
Vickery, Amanda, 130, 255–7
Victoria Street, 168, 191
Villiers, Sir Charles Pelham, 43, 133, 179, 258, 273
Vincent, John, 232, 256–8, 261, 270, 274

Waddy, Henry Turner, 230, 233
Waldegrave, Lady, 127, 251
Walmsley, Sir Joshua, 253
Walsh, Sir John, 235, 261, 278
Waterloo Hotel, 259
Waterloo Place, 6, 33, 240
Watt, R. G. 50, 241
Wedgwood, Josiah MP, 65
Wegg-Prosser, J. F., 233, 246–8, 251, 267
Wellington, Duke of, 45, 126, 133, 176, 199, 253, 272, 277
 Carlton, contempt for, 122
 false story concerning Wellington in East India United Service Club, 229
 involvement in club foundations, 17, 32, 47, 56
 ministries and effect on Clubland, 31–2, 34, 44
West, Algernon, 241, 262
Westminster, Palace of, 101, 114, 154–5, 213, 260, 263
Wetherell, Sir Charles MP, 32, 162
Wharncliffe, Lord, 32

Wheeler, Brian, 231, 246
Whigs, 2, 11, 13, 14, 22, 24–5, 35–7, 45, 57, 62, 64, 66–7, 70–2, 80, 83, 94–6, 103, 106, 114, 120–5, 129–30, 138, 164, 169–72, 180–1, 193, 197, 212, 216, 224, 227–8, 230, 245–6, 254, 262, 273
Whips, 7, 10, 13, 35, 156–7
  in clubs, 139, 144, 157–8, 161–4, 173
  Conservative Party, 41, 113, 117–8, 145, 158–9, 165–9, 265
  distinction between 'Whip' and 'whip', 268
  Liberal, 158, 160
  methods of, 168, 174
  role in candidate selection, 200
  role in clubs' foundations, 141, 162
  role in party identification, 169–71
whips, subscriptions to, 157, 164–8, 172, 184, 214
White, Luke, the Hon. MP, 159
White, William, 263
Whitehall, 29, 34, 42, 115, 151, 225, 229, 239, 259
Whitehall Gardens, 173, 225
Whitehaven, 193
Whitmore, Henry MP, 160, 184
Wilkinson, Clare, 250, 260
Williams, Hume, 187
Williams, William MP, 187, 253

Wilshere, William, 198, 277
Wolffe, John, 42, 74, 196, 232, 239, 246, 276
women
  all-women clubs, 5, 127, 224
  aristocratic women, 127–8, 252, 255–6, 261
  exclusion of women from clubs, 4, 15, 104, 127, 131, 140, 145, 257
  guests, 112, 126–7
  political activity of, 4–5, 104, 127–9, 224
  salons, at, 125–8, 213, 251
Wood, Charles MP, 37, 159, 266
Woodbridge, George, 181, 230, 236, 273
Woodward, Llewelyn, 11, 227
working men's clubs, 2, 8, 9, 104, 210, 226, 280
Working Men's Conservative Associations, 11
Wright, A. and Smith, P., *Parliament, Past and Present*, 257–60
Wynn, Sir Watkin Williams MP, 137

Yarmouth, 202, 269
Yates, Edmund, 17
Young, John MP, 152, 160, 264

Ziegler, Philip, 25, 233, 236
Ziegler, P. and Seward, D., *Brooks's: A Social History*, 230, 233, 245, 281